Rediscovering the
Islamic Classics

Rediscovering the Islamic Classics

HOW EDITORS AND PRINT CULTURE TRANSFORMED AN INTELLECTUAL TRADITION

Ahmed El Shamsy

PRINCETON UNIVERSITY PRESS
PRINCETON AND OXFORD

Published by Princeton University Press

41 William Street, Princeton, New Jersey 08540
6 Oxford Street, Woodstock, Oxfordshire OX20 1TR
press.princeton.edu

Library of Congress Cataloging-in-Publication Data

Names: El Shamsy, Ahmed, 1976– author.
Title: Rediscovering the Islamic classics : how editors and print culture transformed an intellectual tradition / Ahmed El Shamsy.
Description: Princeton, NJ : Princeton University Press, 2020. | Includes bibliographical references and index.
Identifiers: LCCN 2019028879 (print) | LCCN 2019028880 (ebook) |
ISBN 9780691174563 (hardback) | ISBN 9780691201245 (ebook)
Subjects: LCSH: Publishers and publishing—Egypt—Cairo—History. | Islamic literature—Publishing—Egypt—Cairo—History. | Editors—Egypt—Cairo—History. | Book collectors—Egypt—Cairo—History.
Classification: LCC Z466.E486 C354 2020 (print) | LCC Z466.E486 (ebook) |
DDC 070.50962/16—dc23
LC record available at https://lccn.loc.gov/2019028879
LC ebook record available at https://lccn.loc.gov/2019028880

British Library Cataloging-in-Publication Data is available

Editorial: Fred Appel and Jenny Tan
Production Editorial: Natalie Baan
Text Design: Leslie Flis
Jacket Design: Layla Mac Rory
Production: Erin Suydam
Publicity: Nathalie Levine and Kathryn Stevens
Copyeditor: Hank Southgate

Jacket Image: Folio from *Kitāb Tajrīd al-ʿināya* by Ibn al-Laḥḥām (d. 803/1400 or 1401), copied in 1447 (courtesy of Leipzig University Library); page from *Sharḥ al-Haytamī ʿalā Bāfaḍl al-Ḥaḍramī* by al-Haytamī (d. 974/1566), printed in 1892 (photo by author).

This book has been composed in Linux LibertineO

Printed on acid-free paper. ∞

Printed in the United States of America

10 9 8 7 6 5 4 3 2 1

For Hanna

فيا أيها القاريء له والناظر فيه هذه بضاعة صاحبها المزجاة مسوقة إليك وهذا فهمه وعقله معروض عليك لك غنمه وعلى مؤلفه غرمه ولك ثمرته وعليه عائدته فإن عدم منك حمداً وشكراً فلا يعدم منك مغفرة وعذراً وإن أبيت إلا الملام فبابه مفتوح

Dear reader, these are the deficient wares peddled to you by the author; this is his understanding and his mind, laid out before you. Yours is the benefit, while the toil is the author's; yours is the fruit, his the cost. So, even if he does not earn your praise or gratitude, do not deprive him of your forgiveness and excuses. And if you refuse even that and find only fault—so be it!

Ibn Qayyim al-Jawziyya (d. 751/1350), *Ṭarīq al-hijratayn*

Contents

Illustrations

Acknowledgments

My writing of this book was made possible by two yearlong sabbaticals, the first in 2014–15 at the Zentrum Moderner Orient (now Leibniz Zentrum Moderner Orient) in Berlin with funding from the Volkswagen Foundation, and the second in 2017–18 at Harvard Law School's Islamic Legal Studies Program: SHARIASource (now the Program in Islamic Law). I am grateful to the director of the ZMO, Ulrike Freitag, and the director of the Program in Islamic Law, Intisar Rabb, for their generous welcome and their support of my research.

Back home at the University of Chicago, I have benefited from the insights and friendship of my colleagues and students in the Department of Near Eastern Languages and Civilizations. I would especially like to thank the students in my "Islamic Classics and the Printing Press" and "Critical Arabic Philology" seminars for their close reading of several key texts with me. I have had the chance to present aspects of my research in numerous conferences, workshops, and lectures, and I am thankful for the comments and suggestions I have received on these occasions. In particular, the workshop on Islamic print culture that I organized at the ZMO in May 2015 and the conference on Islamicate book history organized by Maribel Fierro, Sabine Schmidtke, and Sarah Stroumsa in March 2015 provided opportunities for illuminating discussions on aspects of my project.

Over the years, countless exchanges with colleagues near and far have helped me refine the arguments and check the evidence presented in the following pages (even when said colleagues vehemently disagree with me), and I am immensely grateful for the generosity with which they have shared their time and knowledge. They include Rodrigo Adem, Murteza Bedir, Jonathan Brown, Michael Cooperson, Garrett Davidson, Mohammad Fadel, Frank Griffel, Bernard Haykel, Konrad Hirschler, Matthew Ingalls, Wadad Kadi, Ahmad Khan, Henri Lauzière, Jennifer London, Matthew Melvin-Koushki, Adam Mestyan, Roy Mottahedeh, Elias Muhanna, Najah Nadi, Avigail Noy, Bilal Orfali, Maurice Pomerantz, Jawad Qureshi, Umar (Amr) Ryad, Muhammad Yusri Salama, Walid Saleh, Saud al-Sarhan, Kathryn Schwartz, Fihr Shakir, Himmet Taskomur, Amir Toft, Josef van Ess, Paul Walker, Robert Wisnovsky, Jan Just Witkam, Kyle Wynter-Stoner, Muhammad Qasim Zaman, and Aron Zysow. As always, Hanna Siurua was the first audience for all ideas in this book, and I thank her for the endless patience with which she helped me improve them. Finally, I harbor the fond hope that our daughters, Maya and Minna, will deem the rewards of our travels for this book worth the accompanying upheaval.

Rediscovering the Islamic Classics

Introduction

It was the late summer of my second year in graduate school, and my train was speeding away from the urban moloch of Cairo toward Alexandria on the Mediterranean coast, cutting through the Nile delta, whose lush greenery was sprinkled with the white of the first cotton buds of the season. I was taking some time off from the neatly printed books of Harvard's Widener Library to explore Arabic manuscripts at the Egyptian National Library in Cairo. After it had closed for the day, I had spent a few hours book shopping around the Azhar mosque, one of the oldest still functioning institutions of learning in the world, and was now on my way back to my temporary home.

I was exhausted and had clearly gotten too much sun, but I was making an effort to review the notes I had taken that day. My haphazard stabs at the National Library's large manuscript collection, at the time housed in a dingy concrete block in Cairo's Bulaq district, had yielded a surprising find: a work on Islamic law, written 1,200 years earlier by an Egyptian named Abū Yaʿqūb al-Buwayṭī, which recent academic publications had declared extinct. Sitting at the microfilm reader that morning (the library did not allow access to the manuscript itself) and realizing what I was looking at, I had scrolled frantically through the text, scribbling notes as I went. The work appeared to be a complete treatment of the principal areas of Islamic law, and it included a methodological discussion on how to read and interpret scripture—one of the oldest such discussions to be found. I had immediately requested a copy of the manuscript, but this would not be ready until the following week, so for now all I had were my hastily jotted notes. The last thing I had written in my notebook was the name of the copyist—a certain ʿAbd al-Raʾūf from Kazan, the Tartar Muslim city on the Volga River—and the year in which the manuscript had been copied: 1325. That year fell in the Mamluk period, when Egypt and Syria were the intellectual centers of the Muslim world. But revisiting my notes, I frowned: why had I written only 1325, without its Hijri counterpart? The Islamic Hijri calendar is more than six centuries behind the Gregorian calendar, though the gap shrinks by about eleven days each year, as the Hijri calendar tracks lunar rather than solar years.[1] When I wrote down the date, I reasoned, I must have automatically converted it into its Gregorian

[1] In this book, I generally use only Common Era dates, but I provide both Hijri and CE death dates for Muslims who died before 1700 CE.

equivalent, but why had I not made a note of the original Hijri date also? I was too worn out to ruminate on the matter further that day, but when I awoke the following day with my headache gone, the answer struck me: 1325 was not the Common Era date; it was the Hijri date. This meant that the manuscript of al-Buwayṭī's book had been copied as recently as in 1907 CE. No wonder I had, in my groggy exhaustion after a long day of work, misread my own notes. Why would a hugely important work have been copied by hand in the twentieth century, even as it remained unknown in the published literature?

Puzzling though the manuscript's provenance was, I had to push it to the back of my mind. My dissertation research focused on the early period of Islam, and it was the content of al-Buwayṭī's book, not the textual history of this particular manuscript, that was immediately relevant to my investigation of the genesis of Islamic law. But the twentieth century reasserted itself a year later, when I found a second manuscript copy of the same book in Istanbul's magnificent Süleymaniye Library. This copy had been written in 1228 CE (AH 625), but a short note had later been added to the otherwise empty last page: "I, the poor servant of God ʿAbd al-Raʾūf from Kazan, have made a copy of this work on the seventh day of [the month of] Jumādā al-Ākhira, 1325 [July 18, 1907]."[2] The Cairo manuscript thus turned out to be a copy of the Istanbul one. Why had a work originally composed in Egypt ended up in Istanbul, and how had its copy found its way back to Cairo? Examining the two manuscripts for further clues, I noticed an ownership seal on the margin of the Cairo copy, carrying the name Aḥmad Bey al-Ḥusaynī. Some digging revealed that al-Ḥusaynī was an Egyptian lawyer who died in 1914; he possessed quite a collection of manuscripts and had evidently traveled to Istanbul in order to procure the text I had stumbled on in Cairo.

I was intrigued by this individual I had never heard of whose hunt for written treasure had yielded such a find in my own quest. Once I returned to Egypt for further archival work connected to my dissertation project, I looked for more information about al-Ḥusaynī and unexpectedly came across his name in the card catalog of the Egyptian National Library as the author of a twenty-four-volume manuscript book with the cryptic title *Murshid al-anām li-birr umm al-imām*, "The people's guide to respecting the imam's mother." Curious, I asked to see the work's first volume. I spent the rest of the day reading al-Ḥusaynī's extensive introduction, and by the evening I knew that I would one day write the book that you are holding now.

* * *

When we think of the classics of Islamic thought today, we think in the first instance of works written by the founders of the various schools of theology,

[2] Al-Buwayṭī, *Mukhtaṣar* (Süleymaniye MS), fol. 196b.

law, philosophy, linguistics, Sufism, and historiography and by subsequent scholars who shaped these fields through their seminal contributions. The aisles of the bookshops around al-Azhar that I browsed for hours during my visits to Cairo could be relied on to contain, for example, Sībawayh's eighth-century grammar, al-Ashʿarī's tenth-century survey of Islamic theology, al-Ṭabarī's voluminous ninth-century exegesis of the Quran, al-Makkī's tenth-century Sufi manual, al-Shāfiʿī's ninth-century legal treatise, and Ibn Khaldūn's fourteenth-century sociology of history, usually in multiple editions and copies. These same classics formed the basis of the foundational works of Orientalist scholarship that I pored over in preparation for my qualifying exams at Harvard, and they are the same works I now teach in my classes as the "great books" of the Muslim world.

But this landscape of relatively established classics was not what al-Ḥusaynī faced at the turn of the twentieth century. Far from ubiquitous, these works were scarce and difficult if not impossible to find; not only had most not yet been edited and printed, but there were few manuscript copies of them, and the whereabouts of those few that existed were often unknown. Instead, the literature that *was* available and abundant consisted of a very different pool of writings: dense, technical commentaries on earlier works, typically written centuries after the original works' composition. It was this state of affairs that drove al-Ḥusaynī to embark on the grand quest that he describes in the introduction to his massive book. Deeply dissatisfied with what he saw as the narrow horizons of Islamic scholarship in his time, he had set out to gather the largely forgotten foundational early works of the Shāfiʿī school of law, to which he adhered, laboriously hunting down manuscript fragments across the Middle East, and then sought to reintroduce them to his contemporaries in the form of an exhaustive synthetic commentary on al-Shāfiʿī's magnum opus, *al-Umm* (The mother[book]).[3] In addition to producing this commentary, which brought together and summarized countless key works of earlier Shāfiʿī scholarship, al-Ḥusaynī arranged and financed the publication of the *Umm* itself; the seven-volume book appeared in print between 1903 and 1908, much earlier, thanks to al-Ḥusaynī, than the foundational legal works of most other schools.[4] Given its rich information on contemporary juristic trends and debates, the *Umm* subsequently became the lens through which Western scholars of Islamic law, such as Joseph Schacht, perceived the early history of their subject.[5]

[3] A more accurate rendition of the title of the commentary is thus "The people's guide to respecting Imam al-Shāfiʿī's *Umm*."

[4] The *Muwaṭṭaʾ* of Mālik b. Anas (d. 179/795), the founder of the Mālikī legal school, had been printed in 1864, but Mālik's treatment provided little information on the historical development of the law. For a detailed discussion of al-Ḥusaynī and his work, see chapter 4.

[5] See Schacht, *Origins of Muhammadan Jurisprudence.*

Al-Ḥusaynī's account changed the way in which I viewed the "classics" on which my work—like that of other scholars of premodern Islam—was largely based. I realized that I had been wrong to assume that the printed classical literature, whose many known gaps were gradually being filled as new editions were completed and published, naturally reflected the essence of the Islamic intellectual tradition. To me as to Schacht, familiarity with al-Shāfiʿī's *Umm* had seemed indispensable to any serious study of Islamic law; but al-Ḥusaynī's description of scholarship in his time made it clear that just a century or two ago, even Shāfiʿī jurists saw absolutely no need to have read al-Shāfiʿī's own words in order to be considered leading experts in their field. The fact that books that had been so thoroughly marginalized and ignored had, in such a short time, attained the status of classics clearly owed much to their availability in printed form, but as al-Ḥusaynī's travails demonstrated, their printing was by no means inevitable: in the case of many of these long-forgotten works, the publication of a reasonably complete and accurate text constituted a major achievement that had required the marshaling of an array of philological, organizational, and financial resources, all underpinned by considerable time and commitment. But commitment by whom, and for what purpose?

These are the questions that this book seeks to answer.[6] My aim is to sketch the transformation of the Arabo-Islamic intellectual tradition that accompanied the adoption of printing in the Middle East, and to bring to light the stories of the hitherto mostly invisible individuals who effected this transformation. They collected books, resurrecting forgotten works, ideas, and aesthetics that they felt could contribute to the revival of Islamic and Arabic culture; they inaugurated institutions dedicated to the preservation and dissemination of their discoveries; and they developed practices and systems of editing and publication that led to a wave of printed editions of classical works from the late nineteenth century onward. Their motivations, goals, and approaches were diverse. Some sought to reinvigorate the established scholarly tradition, others to undermine it. Some emphasized the socially relevant messages conveyed in rediscovered older works, while others focused on their aesthetically superior form. Some consciously adapted the Orientalist tradition of editing and scholarship, whereas others sought to excavate an indigenous Arabic philology to counterbalance Orientalism and its claims to privileged expertise. All had to contend with the formidable challenges posed by centuries of cultural neglect of the classical literature: locating and obtaining manuscripts in the absence of catalogs, piecing together complete works out of scattered fragments, deciphering texts in spite of errors and damage, and understanding their meaning without recourse to adequate

[6]Similar questions were posed by Muhsin Mahdi in his programmatic 1995 article "From the Manuscript Age to the Age of Printed Books."

reference material. Their painstaking, frequently solitary, and often innovative efforts opened up the narrow postclassical manuscript tradition into a broad literature of printed, primarily classical works—the literature that we today consider the essential canon of Islamic texts.

This renaissance of classical literature by means of print was part of a broader constellation of sociocultural changes that has often been referred to as the *nahḍa*, "awakening." Although there is no agreed-on definition of this phenomenon, developments that are typically placed under its umbrella include the large-scale translation of European works into Arabic, the adoption of European genres of literature, and engagement with the modern natural and social sciences.[7] An interest in the classical past appears less often among the features of the *nahḍa*,[8] although Western observers contemporaneous to it pointed out the connection.[9] But as this book shows, the resurrection of the classical heritage, particularly in the form of published editions of classical texts, was an integral facet of the activities of many key *nahḍa* figures.[10] They were not, as is often assumed, rejecting the Arabo-Islamic intellectual tradition wholesale in favor of an imported modernity. Instead, they drew on the classical tradition in order to undermine the postclassical one, which they decried as restrictive and ossified, and in order to reconstruct a classical literature that could serve as the foundation of an indigeneous modernity.

My focus on the individual agents of this cultural transformation reflects my conviction that the technology of print was not a *cause* of the transformation as much as it was a *site* and a *means* of it. Influential studies of the history of print in the West, published between the 1960s and the 1980s, portrayed an inherent logic that connected the adoption of printing to subsequent sociocultural changes.[11] It is undeniably true that a manuscript culture differs in many respects from a written culture perpetuated through mechanical reproduction. But I reject the deterministic hypothesis that grants technology the power to override individual agency and to move societies along a fixed, inevitable trajectory—especially when the hypothesis rests on the blanket generalization of a particular (in this case Western) historical experience. Instead, this book tells the stories of the people who harnessed the multidirectional potential of print to further their diverse agendas, and it describes how the printing of rediscovered classical works,

[7]For definitions and descriptions of the *nahḍa*, see, for example, Patel, *Arab* Nahḍah; Di-Capua, "Arab Project of Enlightenment"; Sing, "Decline of Islam."

[8]Contrast Tomiche's flat denial of a connection between *nahḍa* and renaissance in "Nahḍa" with the title of El-Ariss's anthology *The Arab Renaissance: A Bilingual Anthology of the* Nahda.

[9]See Pedersen's insightful observation in *Arabic Book*, 138 (originally published in 1946).

[10]Important *nahḍa* intellectuals discussed in this book include ʿAlī Mubārak, Rifāʿa al-Ṭahṭāwī, Aḥmad Fāris al-Shidyāq, Muḥammad ʿAbduh, and Rashīd Riḍā.

[11]McLuhan, *Gutenberg Galaxy*; Ong, *Orality and Literacy*; Eisenstein, *Printing Press.*

together with a host of related phenomena, such as the reassertion of classical Arabic and the foundation of modern libraries, permanently transformed the landscape of Islamic thought in the nineteenth and early twentieth centuries.

* * *

The narrative of this book opens in the early nineteenth century, when Arabo-Islamic book culture was still carried overwhelmingly in manuscript form, its practices of teaching, copying, and transmission perpetuating a continuous written discourse that was, by then, well more than a millennium old. But the literature that was taught, transmitted, and circulated at this time represented only a fraction of the extant Arabic literary corpus: early and classical works had been marginalized and often forgotten, and many clung to existence in rare, dispersed copies or fragments. In chapter 1, I outline the key factors that constrained the availability of such books—namely, the dramatic decline of traditional libraries and the voracious appetites and deep pockets of European collectors of Arabic books. Meanwhile, chapter 2 examines the reasons for the dearth of indigenous interest in these works: the dominant scholasticism of postclassical academic discourse preferred late commentary works over their classical predecessors, and the growing influence of Sufi esotericism undermined the authority of book-based learning altogether.

The adoption of printing to reproduce Arabic and Islamic literature changed the literary landscape. Not only could copies of books now be made available in much larger quantities than when each had to be copied by hand; more importantly, access to the presses was open to anyone who wished to publish a particular text and could come up with the money to have it printed. Chapter 3 describes the birth of the Arabic printing industry and the new opportunities that it created for the propagation of established as well as novel ideas and works, and chapter 4 uncovers the emerging constituency of elite bibliophiles such as ʿAbd al-Ḥamīd Nāfiʿ and Aḥmad Taymūr whose enthusiasm for classical literature, supported by social capital and access to financial resources, drove the rediscovery of long-lost classical works. As the movement to publish classical texts gained momentum, the challenges of reconstituting fragmentary and corrupted texts gave rise to the new cultural function of the editor, inaugurated by Aḥmad Zakī and described in chapter 5.

The technology of printing appealed to reformers of various stripes, who recognized its potential for promoting social and religious change. Chapter 6 discusses the editing and publishing activities of Ṭāhir al-Jazāʾirī and Muḥammad ʿAbduh, both of whom believed in the power of eloquent language and the importance of ethical literature in the project of public edification. In chapter 7, I introduce other, less well-known reformist scholars, such as Jamāl al-Dīn al-Qāsimī and Maḥmūd Shukrī al-Ālūsī, who formed a transnational network of like-minded individuals dedicated to rescuing classical texts from oblivion. Their choice of works to publish reflected their goal of challenging the postclassical scholarly orthodoxy on both methodological and substantive grounds. Their emphasis on the objective representation and evaluation of positions on their own merits found an echo in the developing discourse of textual criticism, discussed in chapter 8, within which philologists such as Muḥammad Shākir and Aḥmad Shākir grappled with issues of truth and authenticity and confronted the complex legacy of Orientalist scholarship in the shadow of European political and economic dominance.

Finally, a word on terminology and the limitations of the book's scope. I have striven to minimize the use of labels, and the few labels that I do use should be considered descriptive rather than evaluative. Accordingly, a "reformist" is simply someone who seeks to reform something, not necessarily along progressive lines; "scholasticism" is not intended (as it is sometimes used) as a term of abuse but simply as a descriptor of a specific mode of scholarship; and "postclassical" thought is so called because its central feature was its sidelining of the classical textual corpus. Geographically, my investigation of the Arabo-Islamic scholarly tradition and the printing movement has dictated a focus on the heartlands of this tradition where, for many decades, the movement was concentrated—especially Egypt, the Levant, and Iraq—with only marginal attention to regions less influential in the early stages of this movement and almost total disregard for editions and writings in languages other than Arabic. I do not discuss lithography, a technique of reproducing manuscripts mechanically that dominated the Indian, Iranian, and North African printing industries in the nineteenth and early twentieth centuries, because it represented a continuation of the preprint scribal tradition and lacked the features of moveable-type printing—such as clear script, distinct editors, and substantial print runs—that made the latter so pregnant with possibility.[12] Lastly, the aim of this book is to trace the evolution of the discourses of Islamic scholarship, and I therefore consider non-scholarly religious practices and ideas only insofar they are reflected in the arena of scholarship.

[12] See Messick, "On the Question of Lithography." Lithographs were produced in limited print runs, and they generally carry next to no information on the scribe or the other circumstances of publication.

CHAPTER 1

The Disappearing Books

The Arabo-Islamic literary tradition is vast and diverse, in chronological and disciplinary terms as well as geographically. It represents a written conversation carried on since the seventh and eighth centuries of the Common Era, initially inscribed on materials such as parchment and papyrus and since the mid-eighth century overwhelmingly on paper. It contains genres that were considered religious in nature, such as Quranic exegesis, collections of the Prophet Muḥammad's sayings (hadith), Islamic law, and theology, but it also encompasses other subjects, such as philosophy, history, linguistics, grammar, lexicography, prose literature, and poetry.

What is remarkable about this tradition is, firstly, its size: it contained millions of books. Although the majority succumbed, over time, to the archenemies of the written word—humidity, fire, war, insects, and censorship—it is estimated that from the period between 700 and 1400, for example, around six hundred thousand manuscripts have survived to the present day.[1] The extant classical Arabic corpus dwarfs the surviving body of classical Greek and Latin texts combined by several orders of magnitude.[2] The second striking feature of the Arabo-Islamic tradition is its linguistic continuity and internal coherence. Whereas for most English-speakers Chaucer's fourteenth-century Middle English is difficult to comprehend and the Old English of the tenth-century *Beowulf* resembles a foreign language, literary Arabic has undergone only limited change since the recording of the Quran in the seventh century. As a result, an educated Arabic-speaker today can read and understand works written throughout this period. Finally, the tradition not only extends far back in time but also spans and connects an immense geographic area with countless local vernaculars, from the Volga region in the north to sub-Saharan Africa in the south and from Spain and Mauritania in the west to Central Asia and India in the east.

Given the breadth of this literary ocean, navigating it successfully—for example, finding out who wrote on a particular issue and then locating and

[1]Bloom, *Paper before Print*, 93.

[2]See Romanov, "Algorithmic Analysis," S245; Belinkov et al., "Shamela." Important databases of digitalized Arabic texts are al-Maktaba al-Shāmila (http://shamela.ws) and OpenITI (https://iti-corpus.github.io). A parallel database of Greek and Latin texts is the Perseus Collection, for which see http://www.perseus.tufts.edu/hopper/collection?collection=Perseus:collection:Greco-Roman.

procuring a copy of that writing—can be a daunting challenge even in the present age of modern research libraries, systematic cataloging, and the Internet. How, then, did scholarship operate in the centuries before the adoption of print in the early nineteenth century, when books still had to be written and copied by hand? Where would scholars go in order to find and consult books? What tools were available for maintaining, reproducing, and organizing the literary corpus?

It is tempting to divide the history of Arabo-Islamic book culture into two simple stages, manuscript and print, each stage marked by distinct, uniform characteristics. But a range of factors, including economic and institutional constraints, scholarly trends, and basic assumptions about the nature of knowledge, modulate book culture in decisive ways. To understand why printing caught on in the Arabic-speaking world precisely when it did, and why it took the forms and had the consequences that it did, we must appreciate the unique features of Islamic intellectual culture before the printing revolution, in the sixteenth to nineteenth centuries. The first and most basic feature of this culture relates to the availability, or lack thereof, of books.

A time-traveling visitor from, say, twelfth-century Baghdad or fifteenth-century Damascus would have found many familiar features in Islamic scholarship as practiced in the early nineteenth-century Arab Middle East. Circles of students still gathered around teachers in the courtyards and classrooms of endowed mosques and madrasas, studying and reproducing handwritten books using time-honored methods of face-to-face transmission. But one difference that would have struck the hypothetical visitor's eye was the significantly reduced availability of books. Whereas medieval Baghdad and Damascus—like medieval Cairo, Aleppo, and other Arab cities—had a wealth of thriving libraries housed in mosques, madrasas, and Sufi lodges and supported by perpetual endowments, by the nineteenth century most of these institutions in the Arab East were mere shadows of their former selves or had disappeared altogether, and their collections were mostly no longer accessible to scholars or the broader public. Only echoes of the past literary grandeur remained. The Egyptian historian al-Jabartī (1754–1822 or 1825) began his work *ʿAjāʾib al-āthār fī al-tarājim wa-l-akhbār* (The amazing records of lives and events) by listing the pearls of Arabic historiography, but then admitted,

> These are now merely titles; the works themselves do not exist anymore. We have seen only fragments of some of them remaining in the endowed libraries of madrasas, whose collections have been scattered by booksellers and sold by administrators, and carried to the Maghreb and across the Sahara. The last remains were lost in conflicts and wars or were taken away by the French to their lands.[3]

[3] Al-Jabartī, *ʿAjāʾib al-āthār*, 1:11.

The accounts of European visitors support al-Jabartī's doleful assessment. The French traveler Constantin François de Chassebœuf (1757–1820) reported on his travels in Egypt and Syria in the 1780s that "books of any kind are very rare. The reason of this is evident. In these countries every book is a manuscript; the writing of which is necessarily slow, difficult and expensive. The labour of many months produces but one copy."[4] Chassebœuf's assumption that Arabic books were naturally rare because of the constraints of manuscript production was misguided.[5] A fellow Frenchman, the Orientalist Étienne Marc Quatremère (1782–1857), also noted the scarcity of books in the early nineteenth-century Middle East, but unlike Chassebœuf he was familiar with historical accounts of rich libraries in the first Islamic millennium—libraries that had been filled with handwritten works. Quatremère explained the collapse of the literature with reference to a series of cataclysms of war and fire that destroyed the extensive libraries of the classical age, especially the devastation that the Mongols wrought on the libraries of Baghdad in 1258.[6] This narrative was and remains influential, but it overlooks additional factors, mentioned by al-Jabartī, that are subtler but equally or more powerful.

THE BOOK DRAIN TO EUROPE

In the nineteenth century, the reality of European political and economic dominance cast an omnipresent shadow on the traditional heartlands of Islamic learning and literary production. The Arab lands were of interest to Europeans for a variety of reasons, including their strategic position and their potential as a market for industrial products. But they also represented a storehouse of a still little-known intellectual tradition. Beginning with the Orientalists who accompanied Napoleon on his invasion of Egypt in 1798, book collectors, often in collaboration with or in the role of colonial administrators and consuls, made careers and fortunes out of the systematic, large-scale acquisition of Arabic manuscripts for the libraries of Europe and, later, North America.[7]

[4] Chassebœuf, *Travels through Syria and Egypt*, 2:450.

[5] For the economics of manuscript production, see Shatzmiller, "Early Knowledge Economy."

[6] Quatremère, "Mémoire sur le goût des livres chez les Orientaux." Konrad Hirschler, in *Written Word*, 130, deservedly problematizes Quatremère's account, pointing out that reports of total destruction were often exaggerated. But it is nonetheless true that a manuscript culture is much more vulnerable to the extinction of individual works, and destructive events such as the Mongol invasion of Baghdad and the subsequent breakdown of urban economies clearly depleted libraries to a significant degree.

[7] On earlier, seventeenth- and eighteenth-century European collectors of Arabic books, see Bevilacqua, *Republic of Arabic Letters*, and Hamilton, " 'To Divest the East.' " However,

When Ulrich Jasper Seetzen (1767–1811), a German physician, adventurer, and hobby Orientalist,[8] arrived in Cairo in 1807, he set out to do what he had previously done in Anatolia and Syria: buy up as many Arabic manuscripts as possible and send them back to his patron, Prince August of the German principality of Gotha, who established one of the great Arabic manuscript collections of Europe.[9] However, Seetzen was forced to observe that "my acquisition of manuscripts has encountered more difficulty than I expected. There are eleven booksellers in the Khalīlī market, more than in Aleppo, but they claim that the French have taken all the manuscripts and that those still available have become very expensive on account of their rarity."[10] Orientalists attached to the French expedition had indeed removed significant numbers of manuscripts from Cairo. The Arabist Jean-Joseph Marcel (1776–1856), who was responsible for the Arabic printed material produced by the French expedition, had carefully collected manuscripts found in the buildings destroyed by the French, including a part of the Azhar mosque shelled by French artillery. He also took priceless parchment fragments from the central mosque of old Cairo (Fustat), which count among the earliest extant copies of the Quran.[11] But although the French were said to have carried off thirty camel loads of manuscripts from buildings destroyed in fighting, Seetzen managed to obtain and send back 1,574 manuscripts less than two years later.[12] (For context, in the early twentieth century, after decades of systematic acquisitions, the Egyptian National Library still possessed fewer than 20,000 manuscripts.)[13] Nonetheless, he had to accept some constraints. The prominent Orientalist Joseph von Hammer-Purgstall (1774–1856) had asked him to look for a copy of the famous tenth-century *Kitāb al-Aghānī* (Book of songs), but Seetzen was told by an Egyptian scholar that not a single copy of the work survived in Egypt. The French had taken the last one.[14]

Seetzen was a dedicated collector with a discerning eye. When visiting the central mosque of Fustat, he found more fragments of the ancient Quranic codex of which Marcel had already taken a significant portion for his "little

compared to their later incarnations, these early collectors were mere dilettantes; see, for example, the description of the modus operandi of Paul Lucas (1664–1737) in Dyab, *D'Alep à Paris*.

[8] On Seetzen, see Stein, *Ulrich Jasper Seetzen*.

[9] Pertsch, *Die orientalischen Handschriften der herzoglichen Bibliothek zu Gotha*.

[10] Seetzen, *Reisen*, 3:165.

[11] These fragments, now in St. Petersburg, are part of the codex discussed in Déroche, *La transmission écrite du Coran*.

[12] Seetzen, *Reisen*, 3:386, 1:xli.

[13] Sayyid, *Dār al-Kutub al-Miṣriyya*, 31.

[14] Kilpatrick, *Making the Great Book of Songs*, 1; Hammer-Purgstall, *Erinnerungen und Briefe*, 2:826.

FIGURE 1.1. Ulrich Jasper Seetzen. Mezzotint by F. C. Bierweiler of a painting by E. C. Dunker; first published in 1818. Courtesy of the Rijksmuseum, Amsterdam.

Oriental museum."[15] Immediately recognizing their antiquity, he tried to bribe the female caretakers of the mosque to allow him to steal the fragments. When they refused, pointing out that the fragments were part of the mosque's endowment, he attributed their refusal to religious bigotry.[16] However, he does seem to have managed to acquire a dozen leaves of the ancient Quran, which he forwarded to Germany.[17] Subsequently, the French vice-consul Jean-Louis Asselin de Cherville (1772–1822), having been alerted to the existence of the valuable pages, used his political clout to acquire the fragments, and after his death they eventually ended up in what is now the Bibliothèque nationale de France in Paris.[18]

[15]Déroche, *La transmission écrite du Coran*, 11.

[16]Seetzen, *Reisen*, 3:389–90.

[17]Seidensticker, "How Arabic Manuscripts Moved," 80.

[18]Déroche, *La transmission écrite du Coran*, 14; Dehérain, "Asselin de Cherville."

Another significant contributor to the Bibliothèque nationale's Arabic manuscript holdings was Charles-Henri-Auguste Schefer (1820–98).[19] Schefer served in the French diplomatic service in various Middle Eastern countries between 1843 and 1857, accumulating along the way more than 800 manuscripts in Arabic, Persian, and Turkish. Of these, around 250 Arabic manuscripts ended up in the Bibliothèque nationale, among them some of the most spectacular illustrated Arabic manuscripts known, such as a copy of the twelfth-century *Maqāmāt* (Assemblies) of al-Ḥarīrī.[20] The large-scale requisition of Arabic manuscripts by French troops in Egypt was mirrored by the British looting of the imperial Mughal library in India in 1858. The more than 2,900 manuscripts of the library, including 200 unica, were added to the India Office Library (today part of the British Library).[21]

The European consuls who resided in the still formally independent Muslim countries not only played an important political and economic role but also used their enormous influence to buy up Arabic manuscripts, often out of personal interest, given that they were in many cases trained Orientalists themselves, and also because they could make a handsome profit when reselling these manuscripts to wealthy libraries in Europe. Johann Gottfried Wetzstein (1815–1905) is a good example. After training in Protestant theology and Semitic languages in Leipzig with Heinrich Leberecht Fleischer (1801–88), Wetzstein taught Arabic in Berlin and then served as the Prussian consul in Damascus from 1849 to 1861. During his tenure, he bought more than 2,500 manuscripts that he then sold on to the royal library in Berlin and the university library in Tübingen.[22] These manuscripts included many unique copies of otherwise lost works as well as Quranic fragments written within a generation after Muḥammad's death.[23] Wetzstein also arranged the sale to his alma mater in Leipzig of a complete library, that of the Damascene Rifāʿī family, which contained more than 450 manuscripts. In securing the purchase, he narrowly beat out another bidder, an agent of the Orientalist Theodore Preston, who taught as Lord Almoner's Professor of Arabic at Cambridge between 1855 and 1871.[24]

[19] See Nasiri-Moghaddam, "Schefer."

[20] Paris: Bibliothèque nationale de France, Arabe 5847.

[21] Sims-Williams, "Arabic and Persian Collections of the India Office Library," 50; Seyller, "Inspection and Valuation of Manuscripts"; Mufti, *Forget English!*, 41–51.

[22] Klemm, *Refaiya 1853*, 21.

[23] Such as the now-famous Quranic fragment at the Universitätsbibliothek Tübingen, Ma VI 165: http://corpuscoranicum.de/handschriften/index/sure/17/vers/40?handschrift=107 (accessed July 8, 2019). The discovery was reported in mainstream media; see, for example, "Sensations-Fund in Tübingen: Forscher entdecken uralten Koran aus Frühzeit des Islam," *Focus*, November 10, 2014, http://www.focus.de/wissen/mensch/geschichte/wissenschaft-koranhandschrift-aus-fruehzeit-des-islam-entdeckt_id_4263442.html.

[24] Klemm, *Refaiya 1853*, 24.

European consuls also supplied the British Library. One such supplier was Alfred von Kremer (1828–89), an Austrian Orientalist who served as the Austrian vice-consul and then consul in Cairo and Beirut between the 1850s and the early 1870s. In 1886, he sold 198 volumes to the British Library, including several rare works. Robert Taylor (1790–1852), consul and resident of the East India Company in Baghdad from 1828 to 1843, contributed 250 volumes, and his successor Henry Rawlinson (1810–95), British consul in Baghdad from 1843 to 1855, added another 75.[25]

As a final example, the Asiatic Museum in St. Petersburg began its famed collection of Islamic manuscripts with the acquisition of seven hundred manuscripts from Joseph Rousseau (1780–1831, a relative of Jean-Jacques Rousseau), who had been French consul in Syria and Baghdad. And after Jean-Joseph Marcel's death, his heirs sold his Quranic manuscripts to St. Petersburg in 1864.[26]

The tens of thousands of Arabic manuscripts that flowed out of the Islamic world in the nineteenth century made a significant difference to the Arabic written tradition. The Hungarian Orientalist Ignaz Goldziher (1850–1921) observed in 1874, after his return to Europe from a lengthy stay in the Middle East,

> Really valuable and useful manuscripts are increasingly rare in the Arab book markets because European bibliophiles have slowly migrated them to the huge collections of Europe. Thus we should look for the manuscripts of scholarly significance—at least the Arabic ones—in the British Museum or the Indian Office in London, in the Bodleian in Oxford, in the Refaiya in Leipzig, in the Legatum Warnerianum in Leiden, or in the Sprenger-Wetzstein- and Petermann-collections in Berlin rather than where they had originated from. The energy of the European lust for knowledge, coupled with financial sacrifice, wiped the most ancient and most important sources of Arabic philology and Muslim science of religion out from their original homeland to [Europe] where these studies have found a new home in the last decades.[27]

In a manuscript culture, book copies are produced on demand only, and the number of copies of any individual work, even a relatively popular one, is likely to be modest by print culture standards. The more obscure a work is, the more its availability and survival are affected by the removal of even a few copies. The European, and later American, hunt for Arabic manuscripts particularly prized the oldest available works—those of which only few copies had survived. Consequently, this hunt, and the financial and political

[25] Rieu, *Catalogue of the Persian Manuscripts in the British Museum*, 3:xiv; *Supplement to the Catalogue of the Arabic Manuscripts in the British Museum*, v–vii.

[26] Daftary, *Fifty Years in the East*, 81; Déroche, *La transmission écrite du Coran*, 171.

[27] Mestyan, "Ignác Goldziher's Report," 454.

clout that undergirded it, led to a dramatic drain overseas of the available classical literature.[28]

It is unlikely that many scholars in the central Arab lands recognized the full implications of this drain in the first half of the nineteenth century, since the core texts in active teaching use remained widely available. But they expressed both respect and puzzlement in the face of the dedicated European pursuit of Arabic manuscripts. When Seetzen resided in Cairo in the early 1800s, he met regularly with a certain ʿUthmān al-Mīqātī, with whom he discussed scholarly topics, particularly astronomy. At some point, Seetzen recalls, al-Mīqātī "inquired about what one does with the Arabic manuscripts in Europe. . . . I assured him that all works, especially geographical and historical texts but also theological ones, will be fully or partially translated and popularized through print. That seemed very peculiar to him. 'But,' he asked, 'for what purpose do you want excerpts from our theological works?' "[29] Orientalism, as the systematic attempt to capture the history and ideas of non-European literate societies, must have seemed both grand and strangely purposeless in the eyes of people such as al-Mīqātī. There were, of course, Christian missionaries of several denominations who sought to gain adherents among Muslims and thus had an instrumental interest in Islamic thought, but most Orientalist book collectors clearly did not belong to this category.

One of the most avid European collectors was the Austrian Aloys Sprenger (1813–93), whose significant collection of manuscripts is now part of the Staatsbibliothek in Berlin. In 1853, Sprenger laid out the rationale for collecting Arabic books thus:

> Certain it is that mankind would not lose much in arts and sciences, if all works in Eastern languages were destroyed. They contain few facts, if any, in Astronomy, Medicine, Mathematics, Natural History, or any other science, which are new to us. Even in poetry and philosophy, their works contain few sentiments or ideas which we can admire or would like to adopt.
>
> A century or two ago people thought if they could only understand the language of birds, these *disinterested* bipeds would reveal to them where treasures are hidden, they would teach them the mysteries of nature, and enlighten them on the most important questions connected with our existence. In like manner some persons thought that in those venerable looking old oriental manuscripts every science under the sun was locked up. Naturalists and orientalists have dug up their respective vineyards. Treasures they found none, but both parties have rendered the soil fertile. Naturalists, though they have

[28]The role of European libraries in draining the Arab world of manuscripts was also noted by Muḥammad Rāghib al-Ṭabbākh in 1937 in "Dūr al-kutub fī Ḥalab qadīman wa-ḥadīthan."

[29]Seetzen, *Reisen*, 3:386–87.

learned no mysteries from the speeches of birds, have founded a noble science by dissecting their bodies, studying and·comparing their physiology, observing their habits, and following up their geographical distribution. Man is a nobler object of study than birds, and the philosophy of history is a higher pursuit than the philosophy of nature. The acquaintance with the literature of the east shows us man reflected in his own creation under peculiar circumstances and through a longer period than the literatures of Europe exhibit him.[30]

Instead of repeating earlier notions of Eastern wisdom to be discovered and learned from, Sprenger announces an alternative project: although the works he has collected have no useful substance whatsoever, they allow the reconstruction of a civilization that for him is clearly inferior to that of Europe but that can be studied on a larger historical scale than is possible in the European case. His analogy to the dissection of animals is revealing and suggests a partial explanation for the uneasiness of Muslim scholars who encountered Orientalist book collecting. Although this activity aimed at a comprehensive reconstruction of the Islamic intellectual heritage, it did not perceive its object as a living and breathing intellectual tradition. Rather, the collectors sought Oriental books as the raw material for the construction of a taxidermic replica, a stuffed corpse of the Islamic cultural edifice to be placed in the mental museum of European thought.

A well-worn trope of Orientalist book hunters in the Islamic world was the academic equivalent of the white man's burden—namely, the claim that they were rescuing manuscripts that were on the verge of destruction. Here is Sprenger again, complaining that Muslims in his time

allow their books to rot, to be devoured by insects and destroyed by neglect, though a Moslim never wilfully tears up a book. . . . As a general rule they place no value on old books and generally on works containing facts, and take little pains to preserve them, their destruction therefore proceeds with great rapidity. In some oriental towns you find bags and bags of odd leaves of the most valuable volumes, which if complete would give occupation to a learned society of Europe for a quarter of a century. Under these circumstances the duty of taking care of the patrimony of our eastern brethren devolves upon the enlightened public of Europe, and every man who finds an opportunity ought to secure as many good books as he can.[31]

In addition to the neglect portrayed by Sprenger, Orientalists invoked diverse other threats faced by Arabic manuscripts in their native lands. Seetzen decried the problems of inadequate storage. Jean-Joseph Marcel recounted

[30] Sprenger, "Catalogues of Oriental Libraries," 535.

[31] Sprenger, *Catalogue of the Bibliotheca Orientalis Sprengeriana*, v.

heroically saving Arabic manuscripts from the fire ravaging the Azhar mosque after his fellow French soldiers had shelled it[32] and rescuing the Quranic parchment in Fustat from neglect and humidity—even though it had survived in the same location for probably more than a thousand years.[33] The rescue theme is, of course, not particular to the acquisition of Arabic manuscripts. It is also found, for example, in the spectacular tale that Constantin von Tischendorf told in 1844 about saving the Codex Sinaiticus—one of the oldest and most reliable copies of the New Testament—from monks in Egypt who were allegedly about to burn it after diligently preserving it for 1,500 years.[34] It is remarkable how willfully Western scholarship has overlooked the genesis of the textual corpora from other cultures that were assembled in the libraries of Europe during the great gold rush of the nineteenth century. I have already mentioned Seetzen's and Asselin de Cherville's willingness to steal manuscripts from endowed libraries (Seetzen also openly expressed readiness to buy stolen books in a letter to Hammer-Purgstall),[35] and the abundance of endowment stamps in works preserved in Western manuscript libraries suggests that their lack of scruples was by no means exceptional. Indeed, the Syrian historian Muḥammad Kurd ʿAlī (1876–1953) claimed that the Prussian consul Wetzstein employed a local agent who systematically stole books from private and endowed libraries in Damascus.[36]

Nevertheless, most of the manuscripts that flowed from the Middle East to Europe in this period were no doubt sold willingly (if not always legally) by their proprietors. An unusual case is that of the Egyptian scholar Amīn al-Madanī al-Hulwānī (d. 1898), who in 1883 traveled to the International Colonial and Export Exhibition in Amsterdam with the express aim of selling Arabic manuscripts to European collectors. Finding no buyers in Amsterdam, al-Madanī moved his wares to nearby Leiden, where the sixth International Orientalist Congress was just taking place. Through the mediation of the Swedish count Carlo Landberg (1848–1924), who was an experienced manuscript dealer, al-Madanī sold 664 of his manuscripts to the Brill publishing house.[37] Brill subsequently sold these manuscripts to the Leiden University Library and another 1,171 manuscripts it later acquired from al-Madanī to the American collector Robert Garrett (1875–1961), who eventually donated them to Princeton University.[38] Al-Madanī's decision to sell appears to have been prompted by personal financial woes, but it was probably also influenced

[32] Tājir, *Harakat al-tarjama*, 15.
[33] Tillier, review of Déroche, *La transmission écrite du Coran*, 112–13.
[34] Parker, *Codex Sinaiticus*, 130; Soskice, *Sisters of Sinai*, 119–22.
[35] Hammer-Purgstall, *Erinnerungen und Briefe*, 2:828.
[36] Kurd ʿAlī, *Khiṭaṭ al-Shām*, 6:193.
[37] The manuscripts are listed in Landberg, *Catalogue de manuscrits arabes*.
[38] Hitti, Faris, and ʿAbd al-Malik, *Descriptive Catalog of the Garrett Collection*, iii.

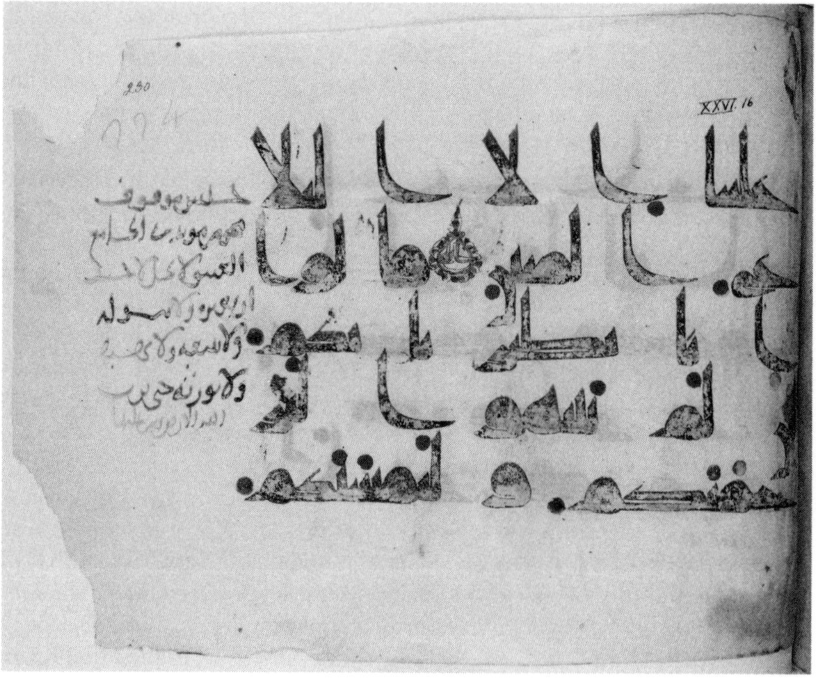

Figure 1.2. Endowment inscription in Paris Quran fragment (Bibliothèque nationale de France, MS Arabe 351, fol. 230r). The marginal text reads, "An endowment placed in the ancient mosque [of old Cairo] to be sacrosanct forever. No one may lend it, replace it with another copy, sell it, gift it, or inherit it until God inherits the earth and its people." Courtesy of the Bibliothèque nationale de France.

by an encounter with Landberg, who suggested to al-Madanī the potential monetary value of his collection.[39]

European libraries of the nineteenth century were willing to pay enormous sums of money to augment their collections of Arabic manuscripts, which in turn made many of the aforementioned Orientalists wealthy men and must have further fired their motivation. Perhaps the most dramatic example of these libraries' hunger for Arabic books was the Bavarian state library's 1858 quest to acquire the book collection of the French Orientalist Quatremère, which consisted of 1,250 manuscripts and around 30,000 printed works. To finance the purchase, the library sold off a significant part of its existing collection, including its copy of the Gutenberg Bible.[40] And in 1884,

[39] Schwartz, "Eastern Scholar's Engagement"; Roman, *Development of Islamic Library Collections*, 121, 174–75.

[40] Rebhan, *Die Wunder der Schöpfung*, 19–22; Roman, *Development of Islamic Library Collections*, 117.

the Königlich Preußische Staatsbibliothek in Berlin bought 1,052 volumes of Arabic manuscripts from Landberg (who may have originally acquired them from al-Madanī) for the breathtaking sum of 70,000 marks—the equivalent of a hundred years' wages for an ordinary German worker at the time.[41]

THE DECLINE OF TRADITIONAL LIBRARIES

The grave-robber mentality of some Orientalist book buyers, fueled both by the intellectual project of reconstructing the Islamic intellectual edifice and by the prospect of making a fortune as de facto agents of European libraries, was only one side of the process that depleted manuscript libraries in the Islamic world, particularly in the eastern Arab countries.[42] The other was the severely weakened state of indigenous institutions of book culture.

The typical publicly accessible library in the Arab world after the Mongol conquests and before the nineteenth-century establishment of modern libraries was a relatively small-scale affair, usually attached to an endowed madrasa, mosque, or Sufi lodge.[43] Such libraries did not aspire to comprehensiveness. There were palace libraries in the first centuries of Islamic book culture that did make it their mission to contain all available books, at least those written in Arabic, and that were said to house hundreds of thousands, if not millions, of books. However, access to these palace libraries was restricted, and they were generally closed to anyone outside the court.[44] A more typical library in the nineteenth century was that described by the British author and diplomat Andrew Archibald Paton (1811–74), who visited the library of the Aḥmadiyya madrasa in Aleppo in the 1840s:

> A formidable key was then produced, and we proceeded to the seminary. In the first court were the tombs of the founder and his family. The inner court was surrounded with an arcade laid with mats, where in good weather the lessons are given, and in winter in the rooms opening on it. A marble fountain occupied the centre of the court. Taking off our shoes we entered a small mosque, and passing through an inner apartment, found ourselves at the door and screen of the library. . . . This library is the best in Syria: but let not the gentle reader suppose a Bodleian, or a Bibliothèque du Roi; it might have passed for the dusky study of a bencher at Lincoln's Inn. Around the walls of an

[41] Ahlwardt, *Kurzes Verzeichniss der Landberg'schen Sammlung*, iii. For wages at the time, see Hoffmann, Grumbach, and Hesse, *Das Wachstum der deutschen Wirtschaft*, 468–71.

[42] The libraries of the Ottoman capital did not suffer the same fate, as I note later in this chapter.

[43] Behrens-Abouseif, *Book in Mamluk Egypt*, 19–28.

[44] Hirschler, *Written Word*, 129.

ordinary-sized room were placed substantial cases in which the books were contained, not standing upright but laying flat upon each other, the titles being written with ink on the leaf-edges in large characters. . . . On asking the attendant where the reading-room was, he pointed to the arcades of the quadrangle we had passed through. . . . I was promised a catalogue of the books in this library, on offering to remunerate the copyist liberally; but although I asked for it afterwards repeatedly, it never was forthcoming.[45]

When the Aḥmadiyya library was cataloged half a century later, it contained around 1,400 works, comprising about 3,000 volumes.[46] One suspects that the relatively high number of surviving books in the library was at least in part due to the successful withholding of information about them from men like Paton.

While the Aḥmadiyya library's holdings were successfully maintained into the nineteenth century by its overseers, who in Paton's time were still descendants of its founder, the holdings of other madrasas disappeared over time, often in conjunction with the institutions to which they belonged. The disappearance of the madrasa, the key repository of books in the premodern Middle East, was cataloged in detail by the Egyptian politician and historian ʿAlī Mubārak (1823 or 1824–93). In his monumental urban geography of Cairo, Mubārak surveyed the present situations of the Cairene institutions of learning described by the fifteenth-century historian al-Maqrīzī (d. 845/1442) and found that of the seventy madrasas listed by al-Maqrīzī, every single one, with the exception of al-Azhar, had ceased its teaching functions and remained in use as a mere place of prayer. Mubārak lamented the loss of dedicated teaching institutions that provided wages to instructors, and he attributed their collapse to the unchecked diversion of the endowments that supported them. Between the fifteenth and eighteenth centuries, he says, "the madrasas were neglected; greedy hands extended toward their endowments; their trustees used them in contravention of their charters, withholding funds from teachers, students, and services and beginning to disperse them [the endowments]; and this went on every year on account of the disturbances and unrest in the land, until teaching ceased altogether and their books were sold and looted."[47]

The disappearance of madrasas and other institutions that had contained quasi-public libraries in this time period coincided, not incidentally, with the consolidation of Ottoman rule over Syria and Egypt after the Ottoman conquest of these lands in 1517. The region's political and economic center moved to Istanbul, and the former twin hubs of Arab culture, Cairo and Damascus, were downgraded to mere provincial capitals. The move triggered a flow of

[45] Paton, *Modern Syrians*, 238–39.

[46] Maṣrī, "al-Maktaba al-waqfiyya fī Ḥalab," 7.

[47] Mubārak, *al-Khiṭaṭ*, 1:87–88; see also Paton, *History of the Egyptian Revolution*, 2:462.

talent and resources out of the provinces and severely diminished the opportunities for high-level patronage of scholarship in the old Arabic-speaking metropolises. With the shift in political power came a shift in the fortunes of the Arabic language, which was replaced as the primary language of administration by Turkish and Persian in the three great empires of the Ottomans, the Safavids, and the Mughals. The scribal classes, which had been a crucial engine of Arabic written culture ever since the famed literary courtiers ʿAbd al-Ḥamīd al-Kātib and Ibn al-Muqaffaʿ in the eighth century, began to favor Turkish and Persian in their literary output—a trend that continued until the nineteenth century. Even the religious scholars in non-Arabic-speaking areas wrote increasingly in languages other than Arabic.

These shifts resulted in plummeting institutional support for Arabo-Islamic scholarship. Few new institutions of learning were founded, and even already established endowed institutions were affected. Although in theory charitable endowments were to endure in perpetuity, in practice they tended to lapse when the designated source of income faltered (because of unfavorable agricultural prices or economic decline, for example)[48] or when major renovations to the endowed structure could not be paid out of its regular income. While built structures might survive without renovations, premodern paper was at constant risk of deterioration through oxidation and insects, so book collections had to be systematically monitored and periodically recopied.[49] Librarians were necessary for the functioning of libraries, but their incomes were precarious and often depended on later supplementation of the original endowment.[50] Books were also relatively easy to convert into money, which made them the first casualty of shortfalls in endowment income and of embezzlement in times of political instability and the attendant diminished legal supervision. In addition, since the original patrons often appointed their descendants as supervisors of the endowments, the descendants' ensuing sense of entitlement over the endowed properties frequently led them to substantially change the nature of the endowments by, for instance, exchanging the endowed object for another (a widely questioned but nonetheless legal procedure known as *istibdāl*). As an example, the abovementioned Rifāʿī family in mid-nineteenth-century Damascus decided to replace the library endowed by the family's ancestor a century earlier with an orchard. Given that the orchard was worth only half the sum for which the family subsequently sold the library to the German state of Saxony

[48] As a consequence of the devastating confluence of recurring outbreaks of the plague and economic crises, Egypt's population in 1800 was only half of what it had been in antiquity; McCarthy, "Nineteenth-Century Egyptian Population," 1.

[49] Bagnall, "Alexandria: Library of Dreams," 358–59.

[50] See, for example, the eighteenth-century re-endowment of a librarianship in one of al-Azhar's libraries established by the Ottoman Bashīr Āghā; Badr and Crecelius, "Awqaf of al-Hajj Bashir Agha," 294.

in 1853, the exchange was enormously profitable.[51] The process of decline was not linear: important libraries continued to have librarians and directors who maintained their holdings and renovated their facilities, such as Khalīl b. Muḥammad al-Maghribī (d. 1763), who energetically reorganized and safeguarded the Muʾayyad mosque library in Cairo. But the absence of effective oversight meant that a corrupt employee could loot the holdings of a library with relative ease, as happened also to the Muʾayyad library after al-Maghribī.[52]

An illustrative case of the decline of libraries in the Arab world is the library of the Maḥmūdiyya madrasa in Cairo, endowed in the late fourteenth century by a powerful Mamluk amir who had bought the private library of the famous Ibn Jamāʿa scholarly family. Containing around four thousand volumes, the library was relatively large, and it was celebrated for the quality of its holdings and the high proportion of early copies, including many autographs.[53] In order to prevent the loss of these precious books, the endowment deed specified that the works could not be removed from the library. But whereas al-Suyūṭī (d. 911/1505) encountered the library in its full splendor, by the time its holdings were transferred to the Egyptian National Library in the late nineteenth century, a mere fifty-eight of its books could still be found—less than 1.5 percent of the library's original holdings.[54] Amid the lawlessness following the Ottoman conquest of Cairo, a contemporary observer had described the plunder of "the precious books housed in the Maḥmūdiyya, the Muʾayyadiyya, the Ṣarghatmashiyya, and other madrasas."[55] Many of the missing works can today be located in the libraries of Istanbul, having been brought there as booty or acquisitions of the Ottoman conquest or through later sales.[56] For example, the thirteenth-century manuscript of al-Buwayṭī's *Mukhtaṣar* that I describe in the introduction to this book contains ownership notes that provide glimpses of its route to the Süleymaniye Library in Istanbul.[57] The manuscript appears to have been copied for a Syrian scholar called Abū Naṣr Futūḥ al-Khuwayyī al-Sāmānī (d. 634/1237), who studied in

[51] Liebrenz, "Die Rifāʿīya," 268.

[52] Al-Jabartī, *ʿAjāʾib al-āthār*, 1:328; Bint al-Shāṭiʾ, *Turāthunā*, 39.

[53] On Mamluk-era libraries generally, see al-Nashshār, *Tārīkh al-maktabāt fī Miṣr*; Behrens-Abouseif, *Book in Mamluk Egypt*, 46–50. On the Maḥmūdiyya library in particular, see al-Nashshār, *Tārīkh al-maktabāt fī Miṣr*, 283–87. Kyle Wynter-Stoner is currently preparing a study of the Maḥmūdiyya for his dissertation at the University of Chicago.

[54] Sayyid, "Naṣṣān qadīmān fī iʿārat al-kutub," 129.

[55] Ibn Īyās, *Badāʾiʿ al-zuhūr*, 5:179.

[56] Sayyid, *Dār al-Kutub al-Miṣriyya*, 16–17. Jan Just Witkam has observed the same trend; see Witkam, "Philologist's Stone," 36. An example of a work from the Maḥmūdiyya library that today resides outside Egypt is al-Ṭabarī's history, whose volumes ended up, inter alia, in the Topkapı Palace library in Istanbul (MS Ahmet III 2929) and in the Staatsbibliothek in Berlin (MS Sprenger 41). I am grateful to Kyle Wynter-Stoner for this information.

[57] Al-Buwayṭī, *Mukhtaṣar* (Süleymaniye MS), fol. 1a.

Egypt.[58] In the fifteenth century, it was in the possession of the Qāḍī ʿAjlūn scholarly family in Egypt,[59] but by the eighteenth century it had traveled to Istanbul, where it became part of the library of highest religious official of the Ottoman Empire, Shaykh al-Islām Dāmādzāde (1665–1742). Dāmādzāde's library was eventually incorporated into the Murad Molla Library, founded by and named after Dāmādzāde's grandson. Finally, after the Murad Molla Library was damaged in the great earthquake of 1999, its holdings were transferred to the Süleymaniye Library.[60]

The decay of established libraries in Egypt already struck the Ottoman traveler Evliya Çelebi (d. after 1095/1684), who visited Alexandria in 1672, a decade after having seen the library of St. Stephen's Cathedral in Vienna:

> [In Vienna] they have seventy or eighty servants who sweep the library and dust off the books once a week. In our Alexandria, on the other hand, there is a great mosque known as the Perfumers' mosque [Jāmiʿ al-ʿaṭṭārīn] supported by many pious foundations including hundreds of shops, *hans*, baths and storerooms; but the mosque itself lies in ruin, and its library that houses thousands of important volumes—including priceless Korans calligraphed by Yaqut Mustaʿsımi, Abdullah Kırımi, Şemsullah Gamravi and Sheikh Cuşi—is rotting because of the rain.[61]

While the formerly extensive holdings of existing libraries in the Arab lands shrunk through mismanagement, neglect, and theft, the few new libraries founded there in the Ottoman period—whether public or private—were modest to begin with. The private library established in Damascus in the 1780s by the book dealer Aḥmad al-Rabbāṭ (d. after 1820) held no more than a few hundred works in its prime.[62] The new library of Muḥammad Bey Abū al-Dhahab (d. 1775) in Cairo contained fewer than five hundred books, and it was forced to cease most of its functions within a few years because of the diversion of its revenues contrary to the endowment deed.[63] The shifting balance between the Arabic-speaking provinces and the Ottoman center is illustrated by the informal handlists of manuscripts in Egypt, Syria, Rhodes, and Istanbul that were compiled by the Royal Library in Vienna and

[58] On al-Sāmānī, see Ibn al-Ṣabūnī, *Takmilat Ikmāl al-Ikmāl*, 224–25.

[59] The Qāḍī ʿAjlūn family was an influential Syrian-Egyptian scholarly family in the fourteenth and fifteenth centuries. The owner of this work seems to have been Abū al-Faḍl Muḥammad b. ʿAbd Allāh b. Qāḍī ʿAjlūn (d. 876/1472); see Ḥājjī Khalīfa, *Sullam al-wuṣūl*, 3:158.

[60] Erünsal, "Murad Molla."

[61] Evliya Çelebi, *Ottoman Traveller*, 230.

[62] Liebrenz, "Library of Aḥmad al-Rabbāṭ," 21. Meanwhile, in Istanbul, the eighteenth century saw a wave of newly established manuscript libraries; see Erünsal, *Ottoman Libraries*, chap. 4.

[63] Crecelius, "Waqf of Muhammad Bey Abu al-Dhahab," 70, 74.

published by Gustav Flügel in 1858.[64] The volume of handlists contained fewer than forty pages on the manuscripts of Egypt and Syria while devoting more than five hundred to the holdings in Istanbul. (Today, the Süleymaniye Library houses roughly ninety thousand Arabic manuscripts, the Egyptian National Library about sixty thousand; the latter's collection is estimated to have tripled over the course of the twentieth century.)[65] The better organization of Istanbul's libraries and their greater accessibility to European visitors cannot explain this wide discrepancy. Beyond Istanbul, book collections fared better in the libraries of the relatively isolated Yemen.[66] However, few scholars from Egypt or the Levant had access to these collections.

THE EMERGENCE OF MODERN LIBRARIES

Around the middle of the nineteenth century, Arab scholars began to raise the alarm regarding the plunder of their homelands' literary heritage. The Levantine author and publisher Aḥmad Fāris al-Shidyāq (1804 or 1805–87) observed the effects of the buying frenzy of foreign book collectors in the 1850s, though he defiantly insisted that the material impoverishment of the Arab lands' book holdings had not undermined Arab knowledge.[67] By contrast, the Egyptian reformer Muḥammad ʿAbduh (1849–1905) bemoaned the intellectual stultification that he saw as the inevitable result of the loss of books:

> Not once did we ask ourselves whether we were preserving the books and the knowledge that we needed to preserve: we lost our books and with them our precious knowledge. If you are looking for a rare book, a fine collection, a valuable reference, or a useful item from our tradition of learning, you will find it in the libraries of European countries such as the one in Cambridge, in England.[68]

Such concerns eventually gave rise to concerted action to stem the drain of Arabic books abroad. An important role in this effort was played by the

[64] Ḥājjī Khalīfa, *Kashf al-ẓunūn* (Flügel ed.), vol. 7.

[65] For the Süleymaniye, see "Süleymaniye Yazma Eser Kütüphanesi"; for the Egyptian National Library, see Sayyid, *Dār al-Kutub al-Miṣriyya*, 30. According to Ayman Fuʾād Sayyid, the National Library's manuscript holdings at the beginning of the twentieth century amounted to fewer than 20,000 works. Today, he estimates that all Egyptian depositories together contain about 125,000 manuscripts, which is likely to be significantly less than the number of manuscripts in Istanbul's various libraries, not to mention the important Arabic manuscript collections in cities such as Bursa, Konya, Kayseri, and Ankara. In 2005, Osman Özgüdenli estimated that Turkish libraries outside Istanbul held about 104,000 manuscripts in Arabic, Persian, and Turkish, with Arabic texts predominating. See Özgüdenli, "Persian Manuscripts."

[66] See, for example, Hollenberg, Rauch, and Schmidtke, *Yemeni Manuscript Tradition*.

[67] Al-Shidyāq, *Leg over Leg*, 4:441.

[68] ʿAbduh, "Travels in Europe," 169 (English) and 176 (Arabic), replacing "archives" in El-Ariss's translation with "libraries."

establishment of modern libraries—institutions that were inspired by and often modeled directly on European research libraries. This technology of amassing and storing knowledge systematically and making it easily accessible caught the imagination of Middle Eastern visitors to Europe as much as did European feats of engineering.

The attractions of such institutions are vividly portrayed in ʿAlī Mubārak's four-volume fictional account, published in 1882, of the travels of an Egyptian scholar named ʿAlam al-Dīn.[69] In one of the chapters, Shaykh ʿAlam al-Dīn visits the house of an Orientalist in Paris and beholds his library, which Mubārak describes as follows:

> [It was] almost square, and on all sides, except where the door was, there were sturdy book cabinets of coconut wood, with skillful copper ornaments of different shapes and forms on their doors. The cabinets contained books, sturdy and well arranged in rows, every section by itself, with a splendor pleasing to the eye. The place was clean and the floor was furnished with a charcoal-colored carpet. The ceiling was painted with the most amazing and pleasing images. And in the middle of the library there was a table, of the same wood as the cabinets, and on it all that was needed for writing in addition to several books. The shaykh was amazed by this order and by what this library had to offer in both beauty and perfection, remarking how rare something like this was in the lands of the East, and how it resembled the libraries of kings.[70]

The shaykh's amazement grows upon observing the library's holdings. Its Eastern wing contains works from the Islamic world in Persian, Turkish, and especially Arabic. The works are ordered by subject, and within subjects alphabetically, and when ʿAlam al-Dīn examines the library's catalog, he finds an astonishing breadth of literature in Arabic, a richness "that one cannot find gathered in a single library in the lands of Islam."[71] Then ʿAlam al-Dīn is shown an ancient copy of the Quran, still written on gazelle skin.[72]

This is a fictional account, but Mubārak's description of the Orientalist's library as uniquely comprehensive is important. In fact, it seems that he copied the titles of the works that ʿAlam al-Dīn identifies in the Parisian library from the famous bibliography, *Kashf al-ẓunūn* (The removal of doubts), of the seventeenth-century Ottoman intellectual Kātip Çelebī, known in Arabic as Ḥājjī Khalīfa (d. 1067/1657).[73] Almost immediately after its completion, this

[69] Gubara, "Al-Azhar in the Bibliographic Imagination," 299–301.

[70] Mubārak, *ʿAlam al-Dīn*, 4:1264.

[71] Mubārak, *ʿAlam al-Dīn*, 4:1266.

[72] Mubārak, *ʿAlam al-Dīn*, 4:1267.

[73] Compare, for example, the entries on Quranic exegesis in Mubārak, *ʿAlam al-Dīn*, 4:1265; and in Ḥājjī Khalīfa, *Kashf al-ẓunūn* (al-Adkāwī ed.), 1:427–42.

work, which lists more than fourteen thousand titles, became the key reference on the Islamic intellectual tradition for Orientalists, and it also served as a shopping list for the purchase of manuscripts.[74] Mubārak's systematic use of titles from this bibliography in his description of the Orientalist library thus reflects a wider Western project of knowledge: the compilation of the ideal library containing the knowledge of the East and the West, its Arabic holdings representing a range of literature unmatched by any single collection in the Islamic world, as well as such rare artifacts as ancient Quranic copies written on parchment.[75]

Mubārak's story demonstrates an emerging awareness among nineteenth-century Muslim scholars of the powerful tool of a research library. Other Arab travelers to Europe, such as the Egyptian imam Rifāʿa al-Ṭahṭāwī (1801–73) and the abovementioned Aḥmad Fāris al-Shidyāq, experienced it, too, admiring European libraries and remembering the difficulties they had encountered in accessing texts in the dispersed and uncataloged libraries of their native lands.[76]

After his return from Europe, Mubārak took a series of elite positions in the Egyptian government, and he was instrumental in the establishment of modern libraries in Egypt and later elsewhere.[77] Initial attempts to place already established libraries under government supervision had ended in abject failure. In 1848, the ministry of endowments began to hire librarians to control access to manuscripts and protect them from plunder, thus effectively taking the first step toward the nationalization of hitherto private libraries. But the wages paid were so paltry and the candidates hired so unqualified that the librarians became agents of the further dispersal of the libraries that they were meant to preserve. For example, a certain Ibn al-Sulaymānī was put in charge of three libraries (those of the Sulṭān Ḥasan complex and of two defunct madrasas, Azbak b. Ṭaṭakh and Qaytbay al-Maḥmūdī), but to supplement his meager salary he sold sugarcane juice under the stairs of the Sulṭān Ḥasan mosque and combined this business with the sale of manuscripts from all three libraries, significantly depleting their holdings.[78]

After Ismāʿīl's accession to the khedival throne in 1863, Mubārak made a pitch for the foundation of an Egyptian national library on the model of the French national library. On March 23, 1870, the khedive issued an executive order to "collect the valuable manuscripts that have not yet been lost to dispersion and that were endowed by rulers, princes, scholars, and authors to

74 Irwin, *Dangerous Knowledge*, 114; Hammer-Purgstall, *Erinnerungen und Briefe*, 2:867.

75 Badrān, *Munādamat al-aṭlāl*, 119–20; Chartier, *Order of Books*, chap. 3.

76 Al-Ṭahṭāwī, *Imam in Paris*, 257–59; Roper, "Aḥmad Fāris al-Shidyāq," 234; Shidyāq, *Kashf al-mukhabbā*, 439–41, 289.

77 On Mubārak's career, see Kenny, "ʿAlī Mubārak."

78 De Tarrazi, *Khazāʾin al-kutub*, 1:190; Sayyid, *Dār al-Kutub al-Miṣriyya*, 22.

mosques, mausoleums, and centers of knowledge, so that out of the gathering of this scattered material the nucleus of a national library may emerge."[79] The new library was housed on the first floor of the Muṣṭafā Fāḍil Pasha Palace on Darb al-Gamāmīz Street in Cairo until 1904, when it moved to a custom-designed building in Bāb al-Khalq.[80] The Russian Orientalist Ignaty Krachkovsky (1883–1951) visited the new building shortly after its opening and later described it as follows:

> The Khedival Library has a particular style and order, completely different from other Oriental libraries. It occupies the second floor of a large building built in a mixed European and Oriental style. The first floor is occupied by the Arabic Museum, which is as famous as the library. From the large entrance hall a wide staircase leads up to an exhibition room with cases containing unique codices of old manuscripts of the Quran and illustrated manuscripts. The stairs lead also to a large reading room with long tables. The number of visitors to the library is consistently high, half of them young students and the other half professional copyists, who sit at two separate tables. The many users of the library are Arabs, but the director of the library always used to be German. This is how it was until World War I.[81]

The Khedival Library was later renamed the Sultanic Library (Dār al-Kutub al-Sulṭāniyya) and then, after Egypt's formal independence in 1922, the Egyptian National Library (Dār al-Kutub al-Miṣriyya). It eventually became one of the two most important manuscript collections in the Arabic world. However, it took decades of comprehensive cataloging and further collecting for this nucleus to become a fully operational modern library.

A few years after the founding of the Khedival Library, in 1879, the Ottoman governor of Syria, Midḥat Pasha, enacted a number of educational reforms with the help of local Muslim scholars, prominent among them Ṭāhir al-Jazā'irī (1852–1920), whose work is discussed in greater detail in chapter 6. The reforms included the opening of primary schools to eliminate illiteracy. As part of his educational program, Midḥat Pasha suggested to the Ottoman sultan the foundation of a public national library, with the following justification: "Even though the books were endowed under the condition of benefiting the public, they have been restricted by the hands of those in charge of them, and the people have been deprived of reading them; so they should be gathered and put in one place, so everyone can benefit from them."[82] The sultan approved the plan, and al-Jazā'irī organized the assembly of the hold-

[79] Sayyid, *Dār al-Kutub al-Miṣriyya*, 21.

[80] Spater Mag, "Egyptian Library."

[81] Krachkovsky, *Maʿ al-makhṭūṭāt*, 49–50. The German directors of the library included Ludwig Stern (1873–74), Karl Vollers (1886–96), and Bernhard Moritz (1896–1911).

[82] Badrān, *Munādamat al-aṭlāl*, 119–20.

FIGURE 1.3. The Khedival Library in Cairo, 1904 or 1905. Courtesy of Special Collections, Fine Arts Library, Harvard University.

ings of the ten most significant libraries of Damascus on the premises of the Ẓāhiriyya madrasa, creating what became the second of the two foremost Arabic manuscript libraries (alongside the Egyptian National Library). Al-Jazāʾirī then became something of a traveling advocate for the formation of such libraries throughout the Levant. He was involved in founding libraries in Hama, Homs, and Tripolis, as well as the famous Khālidī Library in Jerusalem.[83]

The establishment of these centralized libraries was not uncontroversial, since it involved the dissolution of endowed libraries. In both Egypt and Syria, people involved in the running of endowments decried the forced removal of books from their institutions as illegal breaches of the endowment deeds, and Ṭāhir al-Jazāʾirī even received death threats.[84] It is impossible to determine whether this resistance was motivated more by genuine outrage at governmental overreach or by a desire to perpetuate the lucrative under-the-table trade in endowed manuscripts.

[83]Raymond, "Khâlidiyya Library in Jerusalem"; al-Bānī, *Tanwīr al-baṣāʾir*, 25.
[84]De Tarrazi, *Khazāʾin al-kutub*, 1:191–92; Kurd ʿAlī, *Kunūz al-ajdād*, 7.

However, the establishment of these libraries did not end the outflow of manuscripts, since private individuals continued to amass significant personal collections that were subsequently liquidated by their heirs after their owners died. It would take until the very end of the nineteenth century for it to become customary for great book collectors or their descendants to donate their books to public libraries. In Egypt this movement in fact began not with the National Library, but with the founding of a unified library for al-Azhar. Until 1897, each portico (*riwāq*)—as the subsections of al-Azhar were called—had maintained its own, uncataloged library. But in that year, the rector of al-Azhar, Ḥassūna al-Nawawī (1839–1925), and Muḥammad ʿAbduh, then the grand mufti, convinced the Egyptian government to merge these collections into a single central library and to assign to it an annual budget for employing librarians and acquiring new books.[85] ʿAbduh was active in encouraging private book collectors and their descendants to donate their collections to al-Azhar, notably securing the 1898 donation to al-Azhar of the priceless collection of Sulaymān Pasha Abāẓa, who had served as the minister of education since 1882. The collection comprised two thousand books, of which one thousand were in manuscript form, including two hundred autographs and works by famous calligraphers such as the tenth-century Ibn Muqla.[86] The Azhar Library subsequently also became a repository for the private libraries of former rectors of al-Azhar and grand muftis.

* * *

At the time when Napoleon's Orientalists landed in Egypt and began to scour its libraries, markets, and mosques for Arabic manuscripts, the Arabo-Islamic manuscript tradition was already more than a millennium old, with established modes of reproducing texts that could satisfy the demands of the literate population. However, the inevitable ephemerality of manuscripts meant that any works not in active use—particularly older works—were vulnerable, as they were not recopied in sufficient numbers to ensure their viability and survival. It was precisely such early and rare works that Orientalists, seeking to discover the origins of Islam or the ancient wisdom of the East, targeted for collection, their efforts supported by the overwhelming financial and military resources that European societies could muster. At the same time, classical libraries, maintained by private endowments, had been critically weakened by economic decline and, in the case of Arab centers of learning, by the provincialization of the Arab lands. These trends facilitated the partial or total dispersal of many of these collections. As a result, Arab societies

[85]De Tarrazi, *Khazāʾin al-kutub*, 1:198–99.

[86]Riḍā, "Maʾthara jalīla," 483; Shawqī, *Shawqiyyāt*, 3:3–4. The footnote to Shawqī's poem claims that Abāẓa died in 1901, but that is not possible if it is true that his heirs donated his library after his death.

lost a significant part of their literary patrimony first to Istanbul, where the works were subsequently difficult to access, and then to Europe, where they became for all intents and purposes lost to Islamic scholarship.

The height of the book drain out of the Arab world coincided with the emergence of modern state institutions in the region. Modernizing administrations recognized the threat posed by the rapid loss of their countries' literary heritage, and they sought to combat it by establishing centralized modern libraries that eventually supplanted the privately controlled endowed manuscript libraries. But classical Islamic literature was threatened not only in a physical sense, by the removal, sale, and loss of books; it was also being marginalized intellectually by the nature of Islamic scholarship in the sixteenth to nineteenth centuries, which took a turn into scholasticism and esotericism, with dramatic consequences for the value of old books.

CHAPTER 2

Postclassical Book Culture

At the beginning of the nineteenth century, the continuing loss of manuscripts to Europe and the dire state of endowed libraries in the Arabic-speaking world meant that the full breadth of the Arabo-Islamic classical heritage was slipping progressively further out of reach of Muslim scholars. The weakening and dissolution of the traditional institutions dedicated to the systematic preservation of books left literary reproduction largely at the mercy of the market: copyists would reproduce books only if there was demand for them. But scholars in this period showed surprisingly little interest in older, classical works. The reason for this lack of interest lay in a scholarly culture that rested on the twin pillars of textual scholasticism and epistemological esotericism.

SCHOLASTICISM: ONLY POSTCLASSICAL BOOKS MATTER

In the nineteenth century, just as in the ninth or the fifteenth, Islamic religious literature was taught in circles of learning, which were held in madrasas, in mosques, or in private homes. Typically, a teacher or an assistant read out the text being taught, while students, each having either copied the text by hand before the class or bought a readymade copy produced by a professional scribe, compared their copies against the recitation, correcting any errors along the way and perhaps making marginal notes based on the teacher's elucidation of the text. Studying a text thus involved not only understanding the text, by mastering its arguments and comprehending its linguistic features, but also perpetuating the text, by producing an error-free copy of it and joining a chain of transmission that led from the present all the way back to the text's author.

Unsurprisingly, this method of teaching was laborious and time-consuming and could not accommodate the teaching of large corpora of texts. In the ideal case, students would gain a teacher-guided introduction into each field of study via a basic teaching text (*matn*, pl. *mutūn*) that would provide them with a firm foundation in the field's subject matter and terminology and then allow them to venture out and explore other works by themselves. But from the sixteenth century onward, education in the various corners of the

Muslim world was structured around an increasingly uniform curriculum of works, all rooted in such concise teaching texts.[1] The teaching texts were encased in multiple layers of subsequent commentary, consisting of primary commentaries (*shurūḥ*, sing. *sharḥ*) written by either the *matn* author or, more commonly, later scholars; glosses (*ḥawāshī*, sing. *ḥāshiya*), usually but not always based on commentaries; and sometimes tertiary commentaries (*taqārīr*, sing. *taqrīr*), that is, commentaries on glosses on commentaries. These works, and especially the commentary layers, were predominantly products of the sixteenth to nineteenth centuries; for convenience, I will refer to these centuries as the postclassical period, to contrast with the "classical" period of Muslim scholarship (the ninth to fifteenth centuries).[2]

The dominance of the postclassical textual clusters was not confined to teaching. The same relatively limited roster of late works also makes up the bulk of the contents of the private libraries of prominent postclassical Egyptian and Syrian scholars,[3] and it is mirrored in the holdings of public libraries as well as in the works cited in the writings of postclassical authors.[4] These sources indicate that at least in seventeenth- to nineteenth-century Egypt and Syria, Muslim scholars were familiar with a surprisingly narrow range of scholarly literature, most of it written within three centuries of their lifetimes. In the field of Sunni theology, for instance, the significant postclassical libraries whose contents can be reconstructed were overwhelmingly focused on a handful of short teaching texts with their accompanying commentaries, the most recent of which were often authored during the lifetime of the library's owner or founder. To give two examples, the library of Shams al-Dīn al-Anbābī (1824–96), who served as rector of al-Azhar, contained fifty-six works on theology, of which the thirty-six most extensive works were based on seven teaching texts;[5] and in the Cairene Abū al-Dhahab Library,

[1]Robinson, "Ottomans-Safavids-Mughals"; Filipovic and Ahmed, "Sultan's Syllabus"; Erünsal, *Ottoman Libraries*, 134–35. For the origins of many of these teaching texts in the fourteenth-century Timurid milieu, see van Ess, *Die Träume der Schulweisheit*.

[2]I am aware of the fierce debates regarding periodization and of the charge that the classical/postclassical dichotomy is used as a polemical tactic to discredit the latter; see Bauer, "In Search of 'Post-Classical' Literature." I contend, however, that the distinction serves a useful purpose here, since the nature and frame of reference of literary production in the sixteenth to nineteenth centuries differ meaningfully, as I show, from those in the preceding period. The adjective "postclassical" comes with baggage, but so does every other term that might be proposed as an alternative, such as "early modern."

[3]El Shamsy, "Islamic Book Culture"; de Jong and Witkam, "Library of al-Šayḵ Ḵālid al-Šahrazūrī al-Naqšbandī."

[4]See Crecelius, "*Waqfīyah* of Muḥammad Bey Abū al-Dhahab," II, 135–41; the handlists of manuscripts in Egypt and Syria in Ḥājjī Khalīfa, *Kashf al-ẓunūn* (Flügel ed.), vol. 7; and El Shamsy, "*Ḥāshiya* in Islamic Law," 295. A similar emphasis already marks the sixteenth-century palace library of Beyazıt II; see Atçıl, "*Kalām* (Rational Theology) Section."

[5]El Shamsy, "Islamic Book Culture," 70.

FIGURE 2.1. A manuscript page with a commentary and a gloss from a sixteenth-century work on grammar (Ibn ʿArabshāh, *Ḥāshiya ʿalā al-Ḍiyāʾiyya*, fol. 2r). Courtesy of Leipzig University Library.

mentioned in chapter 1, thirty-five of the forty-seven works on theology were writings and commentaries clustered around a mere three teaching texts.[6] A similar pattern is visible in the citations provided by the famous Egyptian scholar Ibrāhīm al-Laqqānī (d. 1041/1632) in his five-hundred-page commentary on his own base text on theology.[7] Al-Laqqānī cites only ten works by other authors, and of the eighty-nine individual citations, sixty-five refer to a single work.[8] Only three other works are cited more than once.[9]

In stark contrast, works that we today would consider the principal staples of the various disciplines—in Sunni theology, for example, works by al-Ashʿarī (d. ca. 324/935), al-Māturīdī (d. 333/944), al-Bāqillānī (d. 403/1013), al-Juwaynī (d. 478/1085), al-Ghazālī (d. 505/1111), and Ibn Taymiyya (d. 728/1328)—are largely absent from these libraries, as are texts representing sects beyond Sunnism.[10] Their absence does not, of course, mean that copies of these works were not found in the Arab lands at all, but the complaint made by Muḥammad ʿAbduh in 1902 suggests that these libraries were typical in their limited scope:

> Someone searching for the *Mudawwana* of Mālik [d. 179/796] or the *Umm* of al-Shāfiʿī [d. 204/820] or one of the early Ḥanafī tomes finds himself in the situation of someone looking for a Quran in the house of an atheist. . . . You will not find [the Muslims] today in possession of a single work of Abū al-Ḥasan al-Ashʿarī or Abū Manṣūr al-Māturīdī, and you will be hard-pressed to see a work by Abū Bakr al-Bāqillānī or Abū Isḥāq al-Isfarāyīnī [d. 418/1027]. And if you search for the works of these giants in Muslim libraries, the search will exhaust you and you will find almost no reliable copy.[11]

Therefore, there does not seem to have been any accepted body of literary "classics" beyond the teaching text clusters with which an educated scholar might have been expected to be familiar, and no expectation that a newly founded library should offer a wider spectrum of works. Accordingly, when the Russian Orientalist Wladimir Ivanow (1886–1970) sought a Muslim scholar in Bukhara with whom to study al-Ghazālī's seminal critique of philosophy, *Tahāfut al-falāsifa* (The incoherence of the philosophers), whose manuscript he had just acquired locally, he was directed to a man reputed to be particularly

[6] Crecelius, "*Waqfīyah* of Muḥammad Bey Abū al-Dhahab," II, 140–41.

[7] Al-Laqqānī, *Hidāyat al-murīd li-Jawharat al-tawḥīḍ.*

[8] That work is al-Taftazānī's (d. 792/1392) commentary on his own text, *Sharḥ al-Maqāṣid.*

[9] The three other texts cited more than once are al-Ījī's (d. 756/1355) *Mawāqif* (eight citations), al-Ghazālī's (d. 505/1111) *Ihyāʾ ʿulūm al-dīn* (six citations), and Zakariyyā al-Anṣārī's (d. 926/1520) *Sharḥ al-risāla al-Qushayriyya* (four citations). It is noteworthy that al-Ghazālī's work deals only marginally with theology, and al-Anṣārī's is a commentary on a work on Sufism.

[10] See also El-Rouayheb, "Rethinking the Canons."

[11] ʿAbduh, "al-Islām wa-l-Naṣrāniyya," in *al-Aʿmāl al-kāmila*, 3:338, 359. ʿAbduh's lament is quoted at greater length in chapter 6.

knowledgeable in the fields of theology and philosophy—but discovered that the man had never heard of al-Ghazālī's work. Instead, the "professor" pointed him in the direction of two elementary teaching texts on logic.[12]

The authoring of commentaries on basic teaching texts goes back at least to the third century of Islam (ninth century CE), but the emergence of glosses as a key medium of scholarship is characteristic of the postclassical age. The proliferation of glosses created a specific kind of literary momentum and produced a self-contained referential universe in which earlier works were progressively sidelined and forgotten. Eventually, the older literature came to survive only in secondhand citations of individual opinions attributed to particular scholars or intellectual currents, often in oversimplified or distorted form.[13] The resulting scholarly discourse can be usefully described as scholastic in nature.[14]

The scholasticism of the postclassical commentary literature is evident in its preoccupation with the lexical, rhetorical, and logical features of the commented-upon text.[15] A significant part of a typical commentary, particularly in the case of glosses, is dedicated to lexicographic treatment of individual words in the base text. This feature reflects a particular ideal of what it means to master a text—namely, complete comprehension of the meaning of every word and its grammatical place in the sentence. Furthermore, rhetorical analysis, in the sense of identifying the text's rhetorical figures,[16] was

[12] Daftary, *Fifty Years in the East*, 119–20.

[13] While this is true for both religious disciplines and the rational and natural sciences, my discussion here focuses on the former. On the postclassical commentary tradition in the rational and natural sciences, see Saliba, *Maʿālim al-aṣāla wa-l-ibdāʿ*; and Ahmed, "Post-Classical Philosophical Commentaries/Glosses." These studies discuss the issue of originality and stagnation in postclassical Islamic thought. My inquiry, by contrast, focuses on the literary horizons and textual practices of the era.

[14] The term "scholasticism" has its origins in European intellectual history. I do not mean to use it as a term of abuse (as it sometimes is used); rather, I wish to highlight the clear parallels between postclassical Muslim scholars and their late medieval European counterparts in their manner of reading texts, their reliance on rhetoric and Aristotelian logic to understand the texts, the culture of textual production in the form of layered commentaries, and the theoretical preoccupations evident in these commentaries. For European scholasticism, see the example of Peter Lombard and his *Sentences*, the central theological textbook of the Middle Ages, which formed the basis of hundreds of commentaries and glosses: Evans and Rosemann, *Mediaeval Commentaries on the Sentences of Peter Lombard.*

[15] For a detailed description of the genre of legal glosses, see El Shamsy, "*Ḥāshiya* in Islamic Law."

[16] As laid down by al-Qazwīnī (d. 739/1338) in his influential *Talkhīṣ al-Miftāḥ*. It is for this reason that the works of al-Zamakhsharī (d. 538/1144) and al-Bayḍāwī (d. 719/1319?), which emphasize rhetorical analysis, became the primary exegetical lenses for the Quran and the basis for further layers of commentary; see Saleh, "Gloss as Intellectual History," 231; Maden, "Tefsirde Şerh Hâşiye ve Ta'lîka Literatürü," 183–220; Zubir, "Balāgha as an Instrument of Qur'ān Interpretation."

the preferred mode of textual investigation, trumping and eventually marginalizing examination of the text's substantive content and historical context.

Besides lexicography and rhetoric, Aristotelian logic served as the third key tool to analyze texts. Statements were reformulated as syllogisms, and watertight definitions were sought for terms used in the text.[17] Like rhetoric, logic provided an allegedly objective auxiliary science to understand texts. However, its use had the effect of turning commentaries into highly technical discussions, and it ran the risk of forcing the analyzed text into a procrustean bed formed by predetermined rhetorical figures and rules governing formally correct definitions.[18] This way of approaching texts—through the formal analytical tools of lexicography, rhetoric, and logic—was memorably described by the eighteenth-century Ottoman scholar Sājaqlīzāde as deep reading (*al-muṭālaʿa al-ʿamīqa*).[19]

This definition of depth in reading displays a focus on a text's formal features that ignores the historical context in which the text was written and often overshadows its actual content.[20] An eloquent example of the formalistic nature of this approach to texts is provided by the account of the Syrian publisher Muḥammad Munīr Āghā (d. 1948) of textual analysis and teaching during his student days in the late nineteenth century:

> In the first year after my arrival in Egypt, I attended the teaching [circle] for al-Nasafī's creed at al-Azhar, with a professor who was greatly respected and famous at the time. He was more than seventy years old, and we thought that his age would have given him extensive experience in teaching and pedagogy, so that a student could complete his studies with him in a short time. But by Lord, how did the poor student fare? Reading the first sentence [of the work], "The people of truth say: The essences of things truly exist, and knowledge of them is—contra the Sophists—verifiable as real," consumed fifteen days of our youth. Once its explication was completed (an explication that often had no relation to theology, except for a few bits here and there), we exclaimed: "We have survived a great calamity and traversed a lifeless desert!" However, attendance was voluntary in those days, and we were subsequently joined by a group of fellow students who had tarried in their villages. They made their apologies, which the shaykh accepted, and they begged him not to withhold the benefits of his teaching from them, so in response to their entreaties he repeated the [same first] sentence and everything else he had covered, taking

[17] El-Rouayheb, "Rise of 'Deep Reading,'" 221.

[18] El Shamsy, "*Ḥāshiya* in Islamic Law," 297–98; al-Ramlī, *Nihāyat al-muḥtāj*, 1:360.

[19] Sājaqlīzāde, *Tartīb al-ʿulūm*, 204. See also El-Rouayheb, *Islamic Intellectual History*, chap. 3; al-ʿAẓm, *al-Ṣubābāt*, 95.

[20] On this point, my conclusions match those of Madkour, "Past, Present, and Future," 215.

> the same amount of time [as the first time around] or even expanding it a little. It continued like that until the end of the school year, and we did not even manage to cover the introduction of the work! Someone who hears this story may find it difficult to believe, but it is the truth. The shaykhs limit their ambitions to discussing the meaning of terms, reporting what the commentators have said and what the gloss writers have concluded, and explaining what they disagree on.[21]

Munīr Āghā's experience illustrates the scholasticism that characterized both the postclassical teaching of core texts (*mutūn*) such as al-Nasafī's creed and the authoring of written commentaries on these texts. The practice of postclassical commentary, whether written or oral, undoubtedly required a significant amount of erudition, but it was an erudition that could easily strike someone seeking to learn about the substantive positions in the base text as a "lifeless desert": the introduction that Munīr Āghā's teacher failed to cover in its entirety over the course of an academic year takes up only a few lines in the printed edition, and the whole text covers a mere half a dozen pages.

Aḥmad al-Shidyāq—who, like Munīr Āghā, would come to play an important role in the publication of classical works—ruthlessly mocked the solipsism of this type of scholarship in his celebrated parody *al-Sāq ʿalā al-sāq* (*Leg over Leg*). In one passage, a fictional shaykh explains the features of rhetoric that a student must master:

> Certain scholars have said that metaphors may be divided into the literal and the analogical, the literal into the categorical and the presumptive, and the categorical firstly into the make-believe and the factual, secondly into the primary and the subordinate, and thirdly into the abstracted and the presumed, with some claiming that this last may be sub-divided into the aeolian, the ornitho-sibilant, the feebly chirping, the tongue-smacking, the faintly tinkling, the bone-snapping, the emptily thunderous, and the phasmic, while the aeolian itself may be sub-divided into the stridulaceous, the crepitaceous, and the oropharyngeal, the crepitaceous may be sub-sub-divided into the absquiliferous, the vulgaritissimous, the exquipilifabulous, the seborrhaceous, the squapalidaceous, and the kalipaceous, the crepitaceous into the panthero-dyspneaceous, the skrowlaceous and the skraaaghhalaceous, as well as the transtextual and the intertextual, and the oropharyngeal into the enteric, the dipteric, the vermiculo-epigastric, the intestinal, the audio-zygo-amatory, the anal-resonatory, the oro-phleboevacuative, the capro-audio-lactative, the ovo- (or assino-) audio-lactative, and other "may-be-sub-divideds."[22]

[21] Munīr Āghā, *Namūdhaj*, 41–42.
[22] Al-Shidyāq, *Leg over Leg*, 1:167–69.

Given the immensity of this body of wisdom, concludes the shaykh complacently, "laying all that out in detail takes an age, and one could spend his whole life just on the science of figurative usages and then die and still know little about it, or forget by the end of the book or books what he'd learned at the beginning."[23]

Although the classification elucidated by al-Shidyāq's shaykh is fictional, the beginning of the passage is in fact taken from a core postclassical text on rhetoric.[24] And while most of the specific categories are fanciful inventions, the passage captures the scholastic preoccupation with classification and definition. Compare the above passage to a section from an actual nineteenth-century gloss on rhetoric, written by Muḥammad al-Disūqī (d. 1815) in Egypt:

> If you were to object and say that "figurative language" [in this case] is itself identical with predication and attribution, and that therefore [given my explanation of "figurative language of judgment"] what follows is that something will be codependent on itself or attributed to itself [which is absurd], I reply: What is intended by a judgment that is "related" and "dependent" is specifically the predicative attribution, while that which judgment is related to and dependent on is attribution in general, whether predicative [full sentence], ascriptive [construct form], or effective [direct object], so that the relation is one from a particular to a general or dependency of a particular upon a general.[25]

As Avigail Noy has suggested, the idea of "figurative language of judgment" discussed in this section may well prefigure the "conceptual metaphor" of modern linguistics.[26] The classificatory distinction between this and other types of figurative language is meaningful and indicative of sophisticated linguistic analysis, but it had already been developed in the eleventh century. The contribution of the late postclassical commentator in this section is to defend not the concept itself but merely the terms used to refer to it against every conceivable hypothetical objection, resulting in a scholastic performance *par excellence.*

Postclassical scholarly culture celebrated distinctive forms of creativity and originality. Nowhere are these more evident than in the varieties of formal playfulness that postclassical scholars integrated into their writings. For example, the Yemeni scholar Ibn al-Muqri' (d. 837/1433) composed a basic teaching text on law that—when read in columns rather than across lines—

[23] Al-Shidyāq, *Leg over Leg*, 1:165. The work was originally published in 1855.

[24] Al-Sakkākī, *Miftāḥ al-ʿulūm*, 373: "Al-istiʿāra tanqasimu ilā muṣarraḥ wa-mukannā . . ."

[25] Al-Disūqī, *Ḥāshiyat al-Disūqī*, 1:174. I am grateful to Avigail Noy for helping me grasp the meaning of this section.

[26] Noy, "Emergence of *ʿIlm al-Bayān*," 387.

contains four other discrete texts on poetic meter, poetic rhyme, history, and grammar.[27] Unsurprisingly, texts such as Ibn al-Muqri'"s were intended not as pedagogical tools but rather as performances of ingenuity, and subsequent scholars vied with each other to compose works that incorporated ever greater numbers of secondary texts.[28] Another, similar genre consisted of compositions that refrained from using certain letters; an example is Yūsuf al-Shirbīnī's (fl. 1098/1686) seventeenth-century poem and accompanying commentary that made use of only half of the Arabic alphabet.[29] A related form of artistic expression was the *badīʿiyya* poem, a poem in praise of Muḥammad that had to showcase all of the formal rhetorical figures of Arabic—a literary manifestation of the postclassical preoccupation with rhetoric.[30] A less ambitious but extremely common stylistic device was the expression of an important date in the form of a riddle. In a chronogram, the numerical values of the letters in a word or a line of poetry would, through various mathematical operations, reveal the date in question.[31] In another type of riddle, the date was concealed in layers of fractions: Ismāʿīl Ḥaqqī of Bursa (d. 1725) reported having completed one of his works on "the second tenth of the second third of the third sixth of the second half of the eighth tenth of the tenth tenth of the first century of the second millenium after the Prophet's exodus," which translates to Tuesday, 12 Ramaḍān 1098 (July 22, 1687).[32] Such displays of literary cleverness, especially by masters such as al-Shirbīnī or al-Barbīr (d. 1811),[33] were often impressively crafted and highly entertaining, but like Munīr Āghā's lessons, they tended to be preoccupied with formal features to the neglect of content.

The commentary, the stereotypical genre of postclassical scholarship, is characterized by a particular hierarchy of authority among its textual layers. On the one hand, a commentary attributes a privileged status to the work commented upon and presents itself primarily as serving and expounding the base text (notwithstanding occasional instances in which the commentary disagrees with either the base text or an earlier level of

[27] Ibn al-Muqriʾ, *ʿUnwān al-sharaf al-wāfī*. I am not aware of a treatment of this phenomenon in Arabic works, but for a study of it in Sanskrit writings, see Bronner, *Extreme Poetry*. I thank Na'ama Rokem for drawing my attention to this work.

[28] Al-Akwaʿ, *Hijar al-ʿilm*, 1:39.

[29] Al-Shirbīnī, *Ṭarḥ al-madar*. The work uses only letters that are undotted (*muhmal*). The opposite practice of using only dotted letters (*muʿjam*) also existed; see Bauer, "Die *Badīʿiyya*," 79.

[30] Bauer, "Die *Badīʿiyya*."

[31] An extreme example is a poem by Bahlūl (d. 1749) in which the numerical value of the letters in each of the 108 lines adds up to the year of the poem's composition; see al-Yousfi, "Poetic Creativity," 69. See also de Bruijn, "Chronograms"; Gacek, *Arabic Manuscripts*, 59.

[32] Quoted in Ritter, "Philologika xii: Datierung durch Brüche," 246.

[33] See al-Shirbīnī, *Ṭarḥ al-madar* and *Hazz al-quḥūf*; and al-Barbīr, "Mufākhara bayna al-māʾ wa-l-hawāʾ," in *al-Mufākharāt wa-l-munāẓarāt*, 11–49.

commentary).[34] But on the other hand, by superimposing itself textually on the base text, the commentary effectively determines the latter's meaning; and in quantitative terms, the commentary overwhelms the base text, whose reproduction usually represents only a small fraction of the commentary work. As successive layers of commentary are added over the first layer, the actual words of the base text sometimes disappear entirely.

The layered accumulation of commentaries constitutes a form of traditionalism, in that writings are justified and infused with authority by means of reference to the past, evoking a strong sense of continuity. The proponents of the postclassical commentary tradition defended the superiority of this tradition over direct, unmediated engagement with the classical works by appeal to the former's unbroken chain of transmission (*isnād*). This continuity, they argued, guaranteed both the textual accuracy of the transmitted text and the preservation of the correct understanding of its meaning. According to the Kurdish scholar Muḥammad b. Sulaymān al-Kurdī (d. 1780), who taught in Medina, a scholar may legitimately cite only those works that he or she has studied with a teacher who is connected to the original author of the work via an uninterrupted chain of transmission.[35] The only exceptions are so-called relied-upon (*muʿtamad*) works, which are so widespread that their accuracy can be taken for granted. An example of such a work for al-Kurdī is al-Ramlī's (d. 1004/1596) commentary *Nihāyat al-muḥtāj* (The end of the quest), which al-Ramlī had transmitted in Egypt to more than four hundred listeners in a single reading, thus establishing countless chains of transmission and making accurate copies of the work so ubiquitous as to ensure the work's authenticity. Al-Kurdī's rule, while demonstrating a strong commitment to textual accuracy, also removes the vast majority of existing works, and particularly older ones, from the pool of potentially citable sources.

This textual traditionalism, which had the effect of marginalizing earlier texts, was part and parcel of a larger structure of authority. This structure was most clearly articulated for Islamic law, which could be described as the central Islamic discipline both because it dominated Islamic literary output in terms of volume and because it was the core discipline taught in madrasas. The common position among postclassical Sunni jurists was that the great jurists of the twelfth and thirteenth centuries represented the last generation of legal scholars who possessed the expertise required to carry out some degree of independent legal reasoning (*ijtihād*) directly on the basis of the revealed texts.[36] For the next few centuries, then, the legitimate scope of

[34] See, for example, Ibrāhīm al-Bājūrī correcting the base text's grammar in *Ḥāshiyat al-Bājūrī*, 1:168.

[35] Al-Kurdī, *al-Fawāʾid al-madaniyya*, 39; see also El Shamsy, "*Ḥāshiya* in Islamic Law," 294.

[36] There were also scholars who went against the postclassical mainstream by calling for or practicing renewed *ijtihād*, but they represent a minority. For such scholars, see Dallal, *Islam without Europe*.

legal scholarship was by and large limited to evaluating the opinions of these earlier authorities against each other through commentaries. This stage came to an end around the sixteenth century, and after that the task of jurists consisted solely of mediating between the most authoritative commentaries by authoring successive glosses on them. Glosses thus represented the cutting edge of legal thought, but the temporal reach of this thought did not extend back beyond the sixteenth century. The position that independent reasoning was no longer an option (the so-called closing of the "gates of *ijtihād*") precluded substantive engagement with (as opposed to mere quoting of) earlier works as well as the texts of revelation.[37]

It is possible that this postclassical scholasticism was at least partly a result of the declining availability of books described in the preceding chapter—a coping mechanism of sorts at a time when older books were increasingly scarce and difficult to find. Through the "canonization" of a small core of works, known and read by all, the continuation of a scholarly discourse could be ensured, even in the face of diminishing resources. In the rational sciences, such as the field of logic, the fall into oblivion of earlier works was not necessarily a problem, but the literary, historical, and religious sciences were inevitably impoverished by the progressive forgetting of the disciplines' foundational literature. Conversely, scholasticism, by limiting the horizon of scholarly engagement to a modest corpus of recent origin, contributed to the disappearance of older works, since the lack of demand meant that they were no longer recopied. This trend was magnified by another factor that undermined not only classical literature but book culture altogether: the rise of esotericism, which postulated divine inspiration as the only way of achieving certain knowledge and elevated it over book learning, which was demoted to a counterfeit form of knowledge.

ESOTERICISM: THE FALLING PRESTIGE OF BOOK LEARNING

A crucial determinant of the position of books in society is their perceived relationship to truth. Can truth be set down in books? Can a reader access truth by reading? The explosion of Arabo-Islamic book culture into diverse genres in the ninth and tenth centuries was to a large part propelled by the optimism that the realm of writing, together with systematic methods of reasoning, could establish truth. The reality of Muḥammad's prophetic mission and of the Quran's divine nature could be definitively laid out, juristic and theological disputes settled, moral rules grounded, logical proofs constructed,

[37] El Shamsy, "*Ḥāshiya* in Islamic Law," 290–93.

the wisdom of Greek and Indian sages translated, historical reports verified, and rules of interpretation discovered and theorized, in order to render language clearer and texts open to systematic understanding.

It is true that Islamic written culture always maintained a distinctively oral component. This is particularly true of the memorization of the Quran and the transmission of hadith reports. The residual orality was, to an important extent, tied to the way in which the truth was to be extracted from texts. Beginning students were always meant to learn introductory texts in person from teachers and typically to memorize these texts before progressing to other works, and advice manuals targeted at aspiring students stress the pitfalls of trying to master such texts without a teacher's personal guidance.[38] People who did seek to tackle texts by themselves were labeled "book learners" (*ṣuḥufiyyūn*),[39] prone to misunderstanding the texts they read and deprived of the companionship of scholars and of the additional education such companionship provided. However, the critique of mere book learning should not be exoticized. Even in the allegedly thoroughly written culture of today, someone whose knowledge of a subject derives purely from personal reading without formal study is rarely considered a bona fide expert on that subject.

Despite these caveats, in the classical period a book was still, as the famous al-Jāḥiẓ (d. 255/868 or 869) put it with his characteristic playfulness, "a receptacle of knowledge, a container crammed with good sense, a vessel full of jesting and earnestness. . . . It will amuse you with anecdotes, inform you on all manner of astonishing marvels, entertain you with jokes or move you with homilies, just as you please. You are free to find in it an entertaining adviser, an encouraging critic, a villainous ascetic, a silent talker or hot coldness."[40] In other words, a book could be a self-standing repository of knowledge that could be read and enjoyed privately; it was by its very nature distinct from the person of its author and accessible in the author's absence, far from the time and place in which it was written. With books seen as independent storehouses of knowledge, the consumption of books and the affiliated bibliophilic impulses, such as the passion for reading, discovering, and collecting books, became identified with erudition and scholarly merit. The story that al-Jāḥiẓ was killed by a falling stack of books was part and parcel of his reputation as a uniquely learned individual.[41]

The image of the sage intoxicated by the company of his books and the insights he has gleaned from them gave way, in the postclassical period, to another image—that of the sage struggling to break free of the stranglehold

[38] Ibn Jamāʿa, *Tadhkirat al-sāmiʿ*, 97, 114.
[39] Al-Ḥarīrī, *Durrat al-ghawwāṣ*, 183.
[40] Al-Jāḥiẓ, *al-Ḥayawān*, quoted in Irwin, *Night and Horses and the Desert*, 90.
[41] Pellat, "Al-Jāḥiẓ," 81.

of books over his mind and striving to reach a plane of God-given, unquestionable truth beyond the contingency of scholarly discussions. This new image was driven by the diffusion of esoteric Sufi ideas into other fields of knowledge, and the consequent devaluation of books in the process of truth-finding established a new ideal of erudition with strongly bibliophobic elements.

Already Plato depicted book learning as a form of counterfeit knowledge,[42] and Neoplatonists such as Plotinus (d. 270) and Proclus (d. 485) elaborated this position, insisting that true knowledge could not be found in books.[43] As an alternative to book learning, the Neoplatonists developed nondiscursive methodologies, including visionary insight. This epistemological orientation did not lead Neoplatonists to abandon philosophical writing altogether, but it bore the strong conviction that the real stuff of philosophy was not and could not be found on the pages of books. A similar antibookish movement is visible in postclassical Islamic thought as it embraced a specific type of Sufism that had been fundamentally influenced by Neoplatonism.[44]

The most influential Neoplatonist Sufi with regard to attitudes toward books in the postclassical age was Ibn ʿArabī (d. 638/1240). Ibn ʿArabī's ideas on the relationship between books and knowledge were diametrically opposed to classical scholarly conventions, and the success of his views appears to have undermined core principles of Islamic written culture established in the classical age. His magnum opus, *al-Futuḥāt al-makkiyya* (The Meccan revelations), contains several statements about the manner of the work's composition. At one point he proclaims, "I swear by God, not a single letter of this book have I written that was not in accordance with a divine dictation, a spiritual inbreathing, and a casting by God in my heart!"[45] This statement entails a strong claim to authority: instead of being based on mastering the literature of a field of study and then weighing the various arguments to reach a conclusion, Ibn ʿArabī's book claims a direct connection to the divine that circumvents and makes irrelevant all earlier discussions on the topic.

Such claims to charismatic authority by esoteric Sufis had been regarded with alarm by scholars of other fields in the classical period. In the introduction to his creed, al-Nasafī (d. 537/1142) states categorically that "inspiration is not among the valid sources of knowledge."[46] Similarly, in their respective

[42] Plato, *Phaedrus* 274e–275b.

[43] Rappe, *Reading Neoplatonism*, ix, 3, 21.

[44] See, for example, Morewedge, "Neoplatonic Structure"; and Chittick, "Circle of Spiritual Ascent."

[45] Ibn ʿArabī, *al-Futuḥāt al-makkiyya*, 3:504 (chap. 373).

[46] Al-Nasafī, *al-ʿAqāʾid al-Nasafiyya*, 19.

handbooks on legal theory, al-Dabbūsī (d. 430/1038),[47] al-Samʿānī (d. 489/1096),[48] and al-Subkī (d. 771/1370) affirm that inspiration, in al-Subkī's words, "is not a valid argument, since fallible humans cannot fully trust their intuition; this contrasts with the position of some Sufis."[49] Earlier Sufis, such as ʿAbd al-Qādir al-Jīlānī (d. 561/1166), had also emphasized the fallibility of individual, subjective inspiration and stressed that it had to be measured against the norms of revelation.[50]

How Ibn ʿArabī envisioned the relationship between his inspiration and the scholarly and intellectual work of others is indicated by his account of his alleged meeting with the great Spanish philosopher Averroes (Ibn Rushd, d. 595/1198). When Averroes asked Ibn ʿArabī whether the latter's spiritual insights matched Averroes's own rational investigations, Ibn ʿArabī replied, "Yes! No! Between the yes and the no, the spirits take off from matter, and the necks separate themselves from their bodies."[51] In response, according to Ibn ʿArabī, Averroes turned pale and later "thanked God for having lived in this age to see someone who entered a spiritual retreat ignorant and then emerged from it in such a state, having neither attended classes nor read on his own or with a teacher," but who had clearly "opened the locks of His gates." No other source, including Averroes himself, reports this encounter, so we have no confirmation whether Averroes really found Ibn ʿArabī's reply such a profound revelation of the limits of linear, discursive exposition. But what is important in the anecdote is its portrayal of the philosopher's deferring to the Sufi's insights that were gained without books.

The claim that spiritual unveiling and inspiration could provide resolutions to difficult intellectual problems precedes Ibn ʿArabī and is already present, for example, in al-Ghazālī's autobiographical account.[52] What made Ibn ʿArabī's version of the theory so influential is that it integrated Sufi ideas into a developed Neoplatonic philosophical cosmology within which the active intellect (in Ibn ʿArabī's terminology called *al-ḥaqīqa al-muḥammadiyya*) could directly inspire the elect (*khāṣṣa*) with knowledge that is far superior to anything that can be obtained either through reason or through instruction by others.[53] Ibn ʿArabī's view of knowledge is nicely summarized in a letter that he wrote to the most eminent Sunni scholar of his time, Fakhr al-Dīn al-Rāzī (d. 606/1209). Al-Rāzī was an authority on theology, philosophy, exegesis, and legal theory, but Ibn ʿArabī nevertheless felt that al-Rāzī's

[47] Al-Dabbūsī, *Taqwīm al-adilla*, 392–99.

[48] Al-Samʿānī, *Qawāṭiʿ al-adilla*, 2:348–52.

[49] Al-Subkī, *Jamʿ al-jawāmiʿ*, 111. See also al-Subkī, *Sharḥ Mukhtaṣar Ibn Ḥājib*, 4:587–91.

[50] See, for example, al-Jīlānī, *Futūḥ al-ghayb*, 26.

[51] Ibn ʿArabī, *al-Futuḥāt al-makkiyya*, 2:372–73.

[52] Al-Ghazālī, *al-Munqidh min al-dalāl*, 36–37.

[53] On the idea of the active intellect among Arab philosophers, see Herbert Davidson, *Alfarabi, Avicenna, and Averroes on Intellect.*

knowledge was deficient and advised him to gain true knowledge through inspiration. He writes as follows:

> For me, a man is not complete in knowledge until his knowledge comes directly from God, without mediation by transmission or teacher; for whoever does the latter is still only learning from created things, and this is defective for the people of God. . . . But if you, my brother, were to set out under the guidance of a shaykh from the people of God, he would lead you to witness the truth, and you would receive knowledge about things through true inspiration, without effort or hardship, as [the Quranic sage] al-Khiḍr did. There is no true knowledge except through unveiling and direct witnessing; not through reflection, conscious thought, conjecture, or guesswork.[54]

This statement indicates that Ibn ʿArabī did not consider his approach to be limited to Sufism; rather, he saw it as an alternative methodology for the core disciplines of Islamic scholarship. Two centuries earlier, Ibn Ḥazm (d. 456/1064) had still affirmed that "mastery of the sciences can be achieved only through studying, and studying means hearing, reading, and writing; all three of these elements are necessary, and there is no way apart from these to master the sciences."[55] Now Ibn ʿArabī was promising not only a new avenue to mastery of the various disciplines but a way of avoiding doubt and reaching certainty in the process. This promise proved enticing to subsequent scholars, including al-Rāzī, whose later works show traces of this approach.[56] But it is with later adherents of Ibn ʿArabī that the claim of inspiration as privileged access to truth begins to affect and eventually transform fields of inquiry that had been founded on rational or textual scholarship.

The fortunes of Ibn ʿArabī's ideas in the Arab world changed in the sixteenth century, particularly in the wake of the Ottoman takeover of the Arab heartlands in 1517.[57] Having earlier been considered unacceptable and even heretical by influential Sunni scholars, his esoteric doctrines now came to be seen as a higher truth in harmony with the other Islamic disciplines. The most important figure in this process of rehabilitation was the Egyptian scholar ʿAbd al-Wahhāb al-Shaʿrānī (d. 973/1565).[58] Al-Shaʿrānī, a star scholar of his age and one of the most widely read authors of the postclassical period,[59] seems to have embraced Sufism for very similar reasons as did al-Ghazālī—namely,

54 Quoted in al-Shaʿrānī, *al-Ṭabaqāt al-kubrā* (al-Sāyiḥ and Wahba ed.), 1:14 (*naẓar, fikr wa-ẓann, wa-takhmīn*).

55 Ibn Ḥazm, *Rasāʾil Ibn Ḥazm*, 4:65.

56 Janos, "Intuition, Intellection, and Mystical Knowledge."

57 Knysh, *Ibn ʿArabi*, 81. On the increased institutional power of Sufi brotherhoods after the Ottoman conquest, see Sabra, "Household Sufism"; de Jong, Ṭuruq *and* Ṭuruq*-Linked Institutions*.

58 On al-Shaʿrānī, see Sabra, "Illiterate Sufis and Learned Artisans."

59 Hudson, "Reading al-Shaʿrānī."

as a way of transcending the spiritually barren landscape of academic careerism.[60] In a move reminiscent of Goethe's Faust, whose historical model was coincidentally a contemporary of al-Shaʿrānī, a thoroughly educated scholar turns to the esoteric in order to gain what he considers to be true knowledge. In the case of al-Shaʿrānī, an antiliterary tendency is evident in his Sufi education. In his autobiography, he first enumerates the books he memorized as a student, then the ones he read with teachers, and then those he read by himself.[61] After listing these achievements of learning rooted in written scholarship, he recounts his first meeting with his Sufi master, a certain ʿAlī (d. 939/1532 or 1533), who made his living as a palm plaiter and was consequently known as al-Khawwāṣ. ʿAlī al-Khawwāṣ was illiterate and immediately told al-Shaʿrānī to discard his prized books:

> The first time we met, he ordered me to sell all my books and to give the proceeds as charity, and that is what I did, yet my books were so precious to me! . . . Afterward I thought of them a lot, because of all the notes I had written in their margins and all the efforts I had invested in them, and it was as if my knowledge had been snatched from me.[62]

To break this attachment, al-Khawwāṣ advised his disciple to seclude himself and to engage in spiritual exercises to get his mind off his books. Finally, al-Shaʿrānī reports, he reached a state in which

> my heart's slate was wiped clean of transmitted knowledge . . . and refilled with divinely granted knowledge, and the beginning of this was at the shore of the Nile where the Berber houses and the water wheels supplying the citadel are. While I was standing there, the doors of otherworldly knowledge opened for me, each door wider than the distance between heaven and earth. I then began to talk about the meaning of the Quran and the sayings of Muḥammad and derived from them law and the rules of grammar and principles, and I was in no need of consulting the books authored by scholars on these topics. I filled about a hundred quires and presented them to my master, ʿAlī al-Khawwāṣ; but he ordered me to erase them, saying, "This knowledge is [still] tainted by conscious thought and acquired learning, and divinely granted knowledge is free of such things." So I erased them, and he ordered me to work on purifying my heart [further].[63]

The central concern in this narrative is the inferiority of book learning over esoteric, direct, and certain knowledge. The educated scholar subjugates himself unquestioningly to an illiterate master, who first seeks to wipe clean

[60] Al-Shaʿrānī, *Laṭāʾif al-minan*, 1:48.
[61] Al-Shaʿrānī, *Laṭāʾif al-minan*, 1:33–42.
[62] Al-Shaʿrānī, *Laṭāʾif al-minan*, 1:51.
[63] Al-Shaʿrānī, *Laṭāʾif al-minan*, 1:52.

the educational slate of his student, eliminating the latter's library, the emotions attached to the library, and any mental processes related to the rational formulation of scholarly exposition.[64] This symbolic subjugation of book learning to esoteric knowledge became a topos throughout the postclassical period.[65] The revered Sufi of the West, al-Dabbāgh (d. 1720), not only was illiterate but also had not memorized any part of the Quran.[66] The influential Egyptian scholar Ibrāhīm al-Bājūrī (1763 or 1764–1860) similarly boasted that his spiritual master was illiterate.[67] In the hagiographic accounts of their adherents, such Sufi masters were clearly portrayed as quasi-prophetic in their illiteracy. They did not need to participate in the written scholarly culture of the preceding millennium, because they received their knowledge as divine gifts rather than as achievements of learning and cognitive processes. Accordingly, their authority rested not on their expertise in a specific field of knowledge and its literature, but rather on a charismatic claim to insight and sainthood. The primary means for making this claim to spiritual insight among postclassical Sufis were miracles (again paralleling the model of prophets), and the recounting of such miracles became a key feature of later Sufi biographical writing, as well as a stereotypical narrative element in postclassical popular literature.[68]

Reaching saintly status required the abandonment of book-based learning. In addition, the relationship between master and disciple became so focused on the charismatic authority of the master that the disciple's acquisition of an education that might serve as the basis of independent judgment and action became superfluous, if not outright dangerous. Earlier Sufis, such as ʿAbd al-Qādir al-Jīlānī, had used the metaphor of a corpse in the hands of a washer to convey the necessary submission of an aspiring Sufi to his God-given fate;[69] al-Shaʿrānī transferred this metaphor to the relationship between the Sufi disciple and the master.[70] Classical handbooks for beginning students of the Islamic sciences had described the teacher as an advisor whose advice should be taken only when it is convincing,[71] but al-Shaʿrānī's vision barred the disciple from exercising any personal discernment or judgment,

[64] See also al-Shaʿrānī, *Laṭāʾif al-minan*, 1:38.

[65] Chodkiewicz, *Ocean without Shore*, 32.

[66] See al-Sijilmāsī al-Lamaṭī, *al-Ibrīz*, 13; see also O'Fahey, *Enigmatic Saint*, 43, on the importance of the *Ibrīz* for West African Sufism. I am grateful to Janan Delgado for alerting me to this text.

[67] Spevack, *Archetypal Sunnī Scholar*, 90.

[68] Kruk, *Warrior Women*, 168.

[69] Al-Jīlānī, *Futūḥ al-ghayb*, 9.

[70] Al-Shaʿrānī, *al-Anwār al-qudsiyya* (Surūr and al-Shāfiʿī ed.), 1:189. The trope became common; see, for example, Jamal, *Naṣīḥat al-murīd*, 351; Bashir, *Sufi Bodies*, chap. 7.

[71] The Arabic term is *mushāwir*; see Ibn Jamāʿa, *Tadhkirat al-sāmiʿ*, 97. On the significance of the term *mushāwara*, see El Shamsy, "Rethinking *Taqlīd*," 10.

indeed going so far as to undermine their very basis. Since, according to al-Shaʿrānī, the master is a mirror of the disciple's spiritual state, the latter's suspecting of the former of heresy is simply evidence of his or her own deplorable spiritual condition. Only when the disciple sees the master as a believer and a saint has the disciple reached that elevated status her- or himself.[72] This principle thus inverts the usual logic of evaluating another person on the basis of that person's behavior; instead, the master as a living saint has become the absolute standard against which the disciple must measure his or her own progress.[73]

In this mental world, books stand for superficial, even false knowledge, and using such knowledge to evaluate and challenge the position of the master constitutes an expression of arrogance and of the passions of the unrefined self. True knowledge originates in the heart. Beginners have access to true knowledge only through the heart of the master, but as they progress on the spiritual path, they can eventually access it directly.[74] Time becomes irrelevant, and books thus no longer serve the function of vessels carrying knowledge across the ocean of time.

This erasure of chronological distance in postclassical Sufism is most clearly evident in the reconstruction of chains of transmission (*asānīd*, sing. *isnād*). Originally used to verify the authenticity of hadith reports, chains of transmission, which listed the names of all the consecutive transmitters of a given report, allowed each link in the chain to be evaluated for reliability (the transmitter's truthfulness and the accuracy of her or his memory) and plausibility (the likelihood that the transmitter had in fact overlapped in time and place with the previous transmitter in the list).[75] The importance of the methods of critical hadith scholarship for the emergence and development of historical consciousness, philological standards, and literary culture in classical Islam is immense. The number of links in a chain of transmission also functioned as an indicator of the chronological distance to the prophetic age—like the growth rings on a tree. But in the esoteric epistemology of postclassical Sufism, the elaborate charts of the hadith scholars were meaningless: although the chains of hadith reports had, by al-Shaʿrānī's time, accumulated at least ten links between the Prophet and contemporary transmitters, al-Shaʿrānī claimed that only one or two links separated him from the Prophet, because the souls of his teacher and the teacher's teacher had met and been instructed by Muḥammad in person—not merely in a dream, but while fully awake.[76] This continuity of direct access to the Prophet, not just to reports

[72] Jamal, *Nasīḥat al-murīd*, 351; al-Kurdī, *Tanwīr al-qulūb*, 587.
[73] Meier, "Zum Vorrang des Glaubens," 31–36.
[74] Jamal, *Naṣīḥat al-murīd*, 212.
[75] Brown, *Hadith*, chap. 3.
[76] Al-Shaʿrānī, *Laṭāʾif al-minan*, 1:26–27.

about him, came to be extended to all pious deceased individuals, whom one could meet and even study with[77] and who continued to wield miraculous powers that enabled them to emerge from their graves and fulfill wishes.[78]

Al-Shaʿrānī also said that he was connected to the Prophet's handshake through a chain consisting of only three links—two humans and one supernatural being (*jinnī*), who was ancient and had shaken Muḥammad's hand in the latter's lifetime nine hundred years earlier.[79] Although the idea of nonhuman transmitters of prophetic knowledge was not entirely new, the scope of such transmissions had increased dramatically by al-Shaʿrānī's time,[80] and they fed into the wider disintegration of hadith scholarship as a critical textual and historical discipline.

This new, esoteric theory of knowledge thus claimed superiority over book learning. Within its logic, no history had to be bridged, because Muḥammad and the saints were constantly present and could be consulted. The way to reach this knowledge was by deconstructing and abandoning the methodology of classical book learning altogether, not just by freeing one's mind from what one had read and taking illiteracy as an ideal, but by undermining the intellectual tools underlying this literature—the critical approach to textual sources, the construction of rigorous and intelligible arguments, and the evaluation of observed reality by means of established principles. The sign of a true savant was the ability to dispense with such fallible efforts and to receive knowledge directly as a gift from God as the culmination of inner, spiritual struggle.

One might object that these claims originated in Sufi circles and had little impact beyond Sufism, but that is not the case. In fact, the postclassical period witnessed the spread of esotericism from Sufism to all other fields of Islamic learning. Al-Shaʿrānī began his highly influential work on Islamic law, *al-Mīzān* (The scales), with the startling claim that all of the formative Muslim jurists were objectively correct in their opinions despite their apparent differences, and that criticizing any of their opinions was similar to criticizing prophets for bringing differing divine laws.[81] Al-Shaʿrānī's claim contradicted the pragmatism that had underpinned the formal ethos of tolerance among the schools of law, encapsulated in the statement "I am correct but could be wrong, while you are wrong, though possibly correct." This statement recognized that given the inevitable hazards of interpretation and analogy, law was necessarily a realm of probability, and its rules could never

[77] Al-Ṣanʿānī, *al-Inṣāf*, 41; al-Shaʿrānī, *al-Ṭabaqāt al-kubrā* (al-Sāyiḥ and Wahba ed.), 1:326, 2:271.

[78] Al-Bājūrī, *Ḥāshiyat al-imām al-Bayjūrī*, 252. For the prominence of these ideas up to the twentieth century, see al-Kurdī, *Tanwīr al-qulūb*, 496.

[79] Al-Shaʿrānī, *Laṭāʾif al-minan*, 1:27.

[80] Garrett Davidson, "Carrying on the Tradition," 70–75.

[81] Al-Shaʿrānī, *al-Mīzān* (ʿUmayra ed.), 1:59–62, esp. 62.

claim to be absolutely certain. By contrast, al-Shaʿrānī's radically new conception of the law rejected the possibility of legitimate differences of opinion, and he provided a characteristically esoteric justification for his position: he had undergone spiritual exercises that had eventually yielded a vision of the divine law as a fountain from which all the opinions the great jurists sprang forth.[82] On the basis of this vision, he asserted that "all great Muslim jurists are guided by God in every instance, and whoever does not arrive at this conclusion through unveiling and vision is obliged to believe it on trust."[83] By applying his esoteric epistemology to law, al-Shaʿrānī both sanctified the opinions of the school founders and radically distorted the actual genesis of their doctrines, which emerged not out of divinely inspired visions but rather from fierce debates between jurists who clearly considered themselves to be right and their opponents wrong. Further, al-Shaʿrānī's stance represented a severe rebuke to anyone engaging in debates with rival legal schools—a practice that had been the engine of much intellectual activity in the past. The subordination of law to inspiration is also evident in the claim made by the Indian scholar Shāh Walī Allāh of Delhi (1703–62) that when he visited the holy shrine in Mecca, God revealed to him by divine vision that His saints were absolved of all legal obligations.[84]

The immense popularity of al-Shaʿrānī's *Mīzān* meant that his ideas enjoyed wide circulation, and it is consequently not a stretch to assume that they posed a significant challenge to the rigor of legal thought and the polemical tradition of legal scholarship. Their influence can still be seen in the writings of the famous Egyptian grand mufti Muḥammad al-ʿIlīsh (1802–82) in the late nineteenth century. Al-ʿIlīsh tried to counter calls for renewed legal reasoning unfettered by the precedent of the classical legal schools by citing al-Shaʿrānī's claim that according to his illiterate teacher al-Khawwāṣ, the school founders' teachings could not be challenged because the founders had encountered Muḥammad in their dreams and had presented him with their opinions, which he had personally approved.[85] Even later, Aḥmad al-Jazāʾirī (1833–1902), the brother of the Algerian leader Amir ʿAbd al-Qādir, argued that legal problems whose solutions had eluded earlier recipients of divine inspiration could not possibly be solved by their successors on the basis of mere reasoning.[86]

The idea that nonrational visions could constitute knowledge appeared even in the Islamic discipline that generally insisted on the highest eviden-

[82] Al-Shaʿrānī, *al-Mīzān* (ʿUmayra ed.), 1:125–26.

[83] Al-Shaʿrānī, *al-Mīzān* (ʿUmayra ed.), 1:62.

[84] Walī Allāh, *Fuyūḍ al-Ḥaramayn*, 23. The title is clearly a riff on Ibn ʿArabī's *al-Futūḥāt al-makkiyya* (The Meccan revelations), as the two titles are synonymous. I am grateful to Muhammad Qasim Zaman for this reference.

[85] Al-ʿIlīsh, *Fatḥ al-ʿalī al-mālik*, 1:92, quoting al-Shaʿrānī, *al-Mīzān* (ʿUmayra ed.), 1:182.

[86] Weismann, *Taste of Modernity*, 238.

tiary standards, namely, theology. For example, the Tunisian judge al-Bakkī (d. 916/1510), a contemporary of al-Shaʿrānī, argued in his influential commentary on Ibn Ḥājib's creed that there were three equally valid paths to knowledge: reason (addressed by the discipline of theology), transmission (the focus of the discipline of hadith), and spiritual encountering and inspiration (*al-wijdān wa-l-kashf*).[87] Al-Bakkī laid out the positions of all three approaches in his book, but he did not present them as equals; rather, they appear as a progression, beginning with the scripturalism of the hadith scholars, ascending to the rational discussions of the theologians, and finally culminating in the insights of the Sufis. The Sufis could affirm, on a more profound level, the positions of the first two groups, but they could also radically disagree with them.[88]

The nineteenth-century Egyptian scholar al-Bājūrī also granted divine inspiration an important role, describing it in his gloss on a seventeenth-century creed as a perfectly valid basis for belief and thus contradicting the classical view that reserved this position for reason alone.[89] As a consequence, he accepted as authentic otherwise unconfirmed reports attributed to Muḥammad, with the reasoning that these probably had their origins in inspired encounters.[90] Al-Bājūrī also made the highly significant and controversial claim that dead saints could fulfill the wishes of supplicants at their graves, giving al-Shaʿrānī's word as his sole evidence.[91]

The influential eighteenth-century scholar ʿAbd al-Ghanī al-Nābulsī (1641–1731) went even further, explicitly proclaiming the superiority of esoteric insight over classical theological arguments, dethroning the method of theological investigation, and acclaiming esoteric Sufism as the authoritative path to correct belief.[92] In his defense of Ibn ʿArabī's idea of the unity of being, he described the difference between those adhering to Ibn ʿArabī's doctrines and those opposing him as follows:

> The critic objects [to Ibn ʿArabī's ideas] on the basis of his limited understanding and limited exposure to their terminology and his ignorance, because their knowledge is based on inspiration and direct witnessing, whereas the knowledge of the others is based on conscious thoughts. The beginning of the former's path is spiritual exercises and good deeds, whereas the latter begin

[87] Al-Bakkī, *Taḥrīr al-maṭālib*, 40–41. For the popularity of the work, see the editor's introduction, pp. 19–20. This work has been consistently but wrongly attributed to al-Subkī; see, for example, al-Zabīdī, *Itḥāf al-sāda*, 2:14–15.

[88] For examples, see al-Bakkī, *Taḥrīr al-maṭālib*, 48, 59.

[89] For the classical view in Sunni Islam, see Adem, "Intellectual Genealogy of Ibn Taymīya," chaps. 2–5.

[90] Al-Bājūrī, *Tuḥfat al-murīd*, 56, 69.

[91] Al-Bājūrī, *Tuḥfat al-murīd*, 252.

[92] On al-Nābulsī, see Akkach, *Abd al-Ghani al-Nabulusi.*

> by reading books and seeking help from others in order to meet their needs. And the destination of the former is the presence of the living God, whereas the latter reach employment and positions, gathering shards that will not endure.
>
> So, there is no other path than that of the lords, masters, and leaders, and there is no other [true] belief than the unity of being correctly understood, as it corresponds to directly witnessed truth. And it is obligatory for everyone to search for this insight, explore its truths completely, hold on to its conviction, and abandon anything that contradicts it in the sayings of the theologians, because it is the truth, the correct belief. And it is also obligatory to protect it from the scorn of the critics and the censure of the ignorant, who discuss it without direct insight into it—those who are misguided and misguide others.[93]

Al-Nābulsī establishes a clear hierarchy between the recipients of inspiration, who depend only on God for their sustenance, and the critics of Ibn ʿArabī's cosmology, whom he depicts as relying on other people both for their livelihoods (such as salaries for teaching in madrasas) and for their knowledge, which they glean from reading books. He describes the former group as selfless and enlightened and the latter group as petty, limited, and tainted by their almost idolatrous dependence on their fellow humans. This dichotomy is immediately translated into a claim of authority and a demand for unquestioning acceptance.

Even disciplines as seemingly profane as literature and grammar were not immune to the influence of Neoplatonic Sufism. The Moroccan Sufi Ibn ʿAjība (1747 or 1748–1809) composed a commentary on the famous introductory grammar of Ibn Ājurrūm (d. 723/1323), but rather than dealing with grammar, he extracted Sufi wisdom from Ibn Ājurrūm's grammatical rules. In the introduction, Ibn ʿAjība stresses that grammar is only a preparatory subject; once one has mastered it, one can proceed to the study of logic and philosophy and finally reach the study of Sufism, which is the true science since it, once grasped, makes all other disciplines obsolete.[94]

Under the guise of spiritual unveilings and inspiration, the occult sciences, which had led only a marginal existence in the Islamic republic of letters, could now be justified and integrated into mainstream works, a process that has been described as an occultist renaissance.[95] Occultism offered the promise of predicting the future and affecting the physical and spiritual world not through the study of texts or reasoned argument but through the purposeful application of rules that were claimed to exist in nature, such as

[93] Al-Nābulsī, "Īḍāḥ al-maqṣūd," 262–63.
[94] Ibn ʿAjība, *al-Futūḥāt al-quddūsiyya*, 16.
[95] Melvin-Koushki, "Persianate Geomancy," 1.

the impact of the stars on fate (astrology), the meanings of patterns formed by tossed earth (geomancy), and the cosmological significance and uses of letters (letterism).

Letterism (*ʿilm al-jafr*) provides a good example of the spread of occultism. The roots of letterism in Islam appear to lie in esoteric Shiʿi currents, which believed, for example, that the Shiʿi Imams had inherited a book on the secrets of letters that Moses had buried and Muḥammad had rediscovered and handed to his son-in-law ʿAlī.[96] Possibly through the writings of the Brethren of Purity (Ikhwān al-Ṣafā), letterism came to Muslim Spain in the twelfth century and was adopted by the most important occultist writer in Islam, Aḥmad al-Būnī (d. 622/1225), and his fellow student Ibn ʿArabī.[97] The connection between Sufism and the pseudoscientific promises of occultism is visible in al-Būnī's work, where he describes occultism as the product of spiritual vision and as a necessary tool for reaching sainthood.[98] The power it contains, however, is not related to piety or even to divine favor. Whoever knows, for example, the "greatest divine name" will be able to fulfill wishes whether good or evil.[99]

Ibn ʿArabī's students took up the occult science of letterism as part and parcel of their master's teaching, and from them letterist ideas spread out to other Islamic disciplines, propagated by Sunnis and Shiʿis alike. Letterism was widely accepted among Ottoman scholars. The prominent Ottoman Sājaqlīzāde treated letterism as a legitimate discipline in his handbook for students but limited its application to saints who were recipients of divine inspiration, citing Ibn ʿArabī as his authority for this position.[100] Engagement with the occult sciences was so widespread that in nineteenth-century Bukhara, for example, 5 percent of all scholars were known to be practitioners, and judicial procedures such as the evaluation of witnesses and the adjudication of cases could be carried out not by means of the rational criteria that had been laid down in works of Islamic law a millennium earlier, but rather through occult practices such as calculating the respective numerical values of the parties' names to determine the truth value of their claims.[101] The British diplomat Paton, encountered in the preceding chapter visiting the Aḥmadiyya library in Aleppo, observed a heavy influence of letterism

[96] Al-Kulaynī, *Uṣūl al-Kāfī*, 172.

[97] Ibn Khaldūn, *al-Muqaddima* (al-Shidādī ed.), 3:119; Gardiner, "Forbidden Knowledge?," esp. 87–88.

[98] Al-Būnī, *Shams al-maʿārif*, 68. As Gardiner, "Forbidden Knowledge?," 101–5, has shown, the manuscripts of al-Būnī's work contain extensive later additions, so this statement could have been inserted by a subsequent hand, but this possibility does not detract from the widespread popularity of the work and the ideas it contained.

[99] Al-Būnī, *Shams al-maʿārif*, 69.

[100] Sājaqlīzāde, *Tartīb al-ʿulūm*, 112–13.

[101] Melvin-Koushki, "Persianate Geomancy," 154n134.

also on medical practice, describing the following scene in the office of a Damascene physician:

> When a patient presented himself, he would say, "What is your name?" Answer, for instance, "Halil." "And your father's name?" "Cassim." "Your mother's name?" "Fatimeh." He then calculated a number for each of these names, found out some conjunction of stars, felt the man's pulse, looked at his tongue, and after having made a short excursion through the signs of the Zodiac, out came the infallible recipe![102]

The challenge that the esoteric turn of the postclassical period posed to the classical written tradition of Islam lay in the core proposition that individual inspiration—whether received directly from God or through intermediaries such as Muḥammad, living or dead saints, or *jinnīs*—granted access to true knowledge, whereas book learning was superficial, futile, or at best a preparatory step to gaining real knowledge. Together with the scholasticism that permeated postclassical religious scholarship, this devaluation of book learning undermined the educational ideal of the widely read scholar who was intellectually at home in different periods and possessed a diachronic view of the literatures he studied. Instead, the postclassical period favored either a more pedantic model of scholastic erudition or the inscrutable aura of the inspired savant.[103] Both the pedant and the savant were self-contained in their knowledge; neither was driven to seek out old books, their authors, and their contexts, or to appreciate the breadth of the surviving literary tradition.

COUNTERCURRENTS: PUSHING BACK AGAINST SCHOLASTICISM AND ESOTERICISM

There were, however, dissenting voices—signs of unease with and critique of the constrained scope of postclassical book culture. Ḥasan al-ʿAṭṭār (1766–1835) was a scholar squarely in the postclassical mold, trained at al-Azhar and appointed its rector in 1830.[104] But in his own teaching, and particularly with his closest students, he drew on a far wider selection of topics and writings in history, geography, and literature than was common for Azhari scholars at the time.[105] In a gloss penned the year before his appointment as rector, he lauded the wide reading and knowledge of earlier scholars such as al-Qarāfī (d. 684/1285) and complained about the scholars of his own era:

[102] Paton, *Modern Syrians*, 197.
[103] On the latter ideal, see Gilsenan, *Saint and Sufi*, 12.
[104] Ḥasan, *Ḥasan al-ʿAṭṭār.*
[105] Al-Majdī, *Ḥilyat al-zamān*, 23–25; Mubārak, *al-Khiṭaṭ*, 13:53–54.

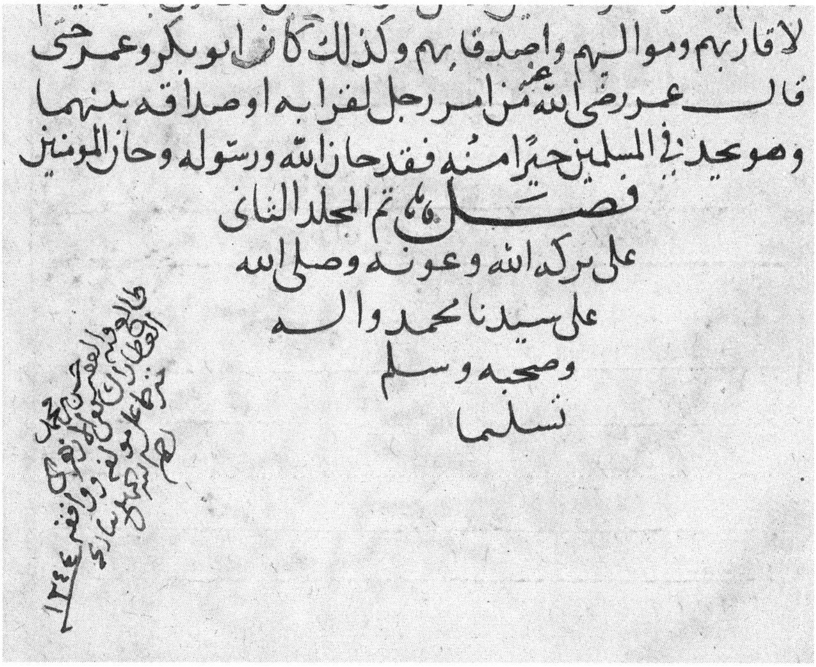
لاقاربهم ومواليهم واصدقايهم وكذلك كان ابو بكر وعمر حتى
قال عمر رضي الله عنه من امر رجلا لقرابة او صداقة بينهما
وهو يجد في المسلمين خيرا منه فقد خان الله ورسوله وخان المؤمنين
فصل تم المجلد الثاني
على بركة الله وعونه وصلى الله
على سيدنا محمد واله
وصحبه وسلم
تسليما

FIGURE 2.2. Al-ʿAṭṭār's note at the end of a manuscript of Ibn Taymiyya's *Minhāj al-sunna*, recording that al-ʿAṭṭār read and annotated the book in 1244/1828 or 1829. Courtesy of General Collection, Beinecke Rare Book and Manuscript Library, Yale University.

"We have confined ourselves to a limited corpus of books that later scholars have written . . . , and we reread these throughout our lives, having no ambition to look into others, as if all knowledge were contained in them."[106]

Al-ʿAṭṭār was not alone in his frustration with the narrowness of the postclassical textual corpus. From the late seventeenth century onward, we find a renewed interest in classical literature among a network of scholars that radiated out from the cities of Mecca and Medina in the Hijaz. This loose movement, formed of interconnecting scholarly circles, was characterized by certain key positions and preoccupations: a critique of contemporary Sufi practices, serious engagement with hadith, a historical consciousness, a willingness to challenge established doctrines of Islamic law on the basis of a reconsideration of the authoritative sources, and a rediscovery of the controversial fourteenth-century polymath Ibn Taymiyya, especially his

[106] Al-ʿAṭṭār, *Ḥāshiya ʿalā al-Maḥallī*, 2:225–26.

bibliographically rich and intellectually daring style.[107] The fact that the positions of individual scholars within this movement varied dramatically does not negate the existence of a discernible overall shift whose hallmarks were the emergence of a new philological sensitivity and an interest in classical works that had fallen out of the literary tradition.

A crucial link in this network of classically minded scholars was the Kurdish Ibrāhīm al-Kūrānī (d. 1101/1690).[108] At first glance, his autobiographical account of his intellectual formation appears to take the form of a stereotypical postclassical narrative of a Sufi quest for enlightenment. After moving to Baghdad, al-Kūrānī prays at the grave of the saint ʿAbd al-Qādir al-Jīlānī for guidance, and al-Jīlānī appears to him in a dream, pointing to the west. Subsequently al-Kūrānī moves to Damascus, where he becomes acquainted with Ibn ʿArabī's writings and visits his grave. He then encounters a book by a contemporary Sufi master residing in Medina, al-Qashāshī (d. 1071/1660). After reading it, al-Kūrānī declares that the work is probably just a reproduction of an earlier text, since its quality far transcends that of other contemporary works. But he soon discovers that his suspicion is unfounded and regrets his skepticism, realizing that spiritual enlightenment can be attained only by suspending one's doubts and thinking the best of people. After years of correspondence, al-Qashāshī orders al-Kūrānī to join him in Medina. On the way, al-Kūrānī passes through Cairo and decides to pause there to consult a copy of Sībawayh's (d. 180/796) foundational work on Arabic grammar, having earlier read a quotation from the work that he suspects is corrupted. He searches for the work and locates the only surviving copy in Cairo, and his suspicion is confirmed. However, he declines the opportunity to study the entire text with its owner, feeling guilty about engaging in such superficial pursuits of book learning while his master expects him in Medina.[109]

Al-Kūrānī's training in Medina under al-Qashāshī is reminiscent of al-Shaʿrānī's account of his own education a century earlier. Al-Kūrānī must enter a space of secluded meditation, where he spends seventy days. When he is released, he asks his shaykh why a fellow adept had had to spend only forty days in seclusion. Al-Qashāshī replies that the other adept had no previous schooling and was thus a blank slate, whereas al-Kūrānī's slate had still carried the imprint of writing from the superficial sciences, and this had to be erased first.[110]

In this narrative, the critical philological impulse is clearly depicted in negative terms. Al-Kūrānī's doubts about al-Qashāshī's authorship and his quest for Sībawayh's manuscript represent obstacles on the way to enlight-

[107] Dallal, "Origins and Objectives"; see also Dallal, *Islam without Europe*.

[108] Al-Murādī, *Silk al-durar*, 1:5–6.

[109] Al-ʿĪyāshī, *al-Riḥla*, 1:480–83.

[110] Al-ʿĪyāshī, *al-Riḥla*, 1:485–86.

enment and originate in the lower regions of the self. The prolonged length of his preparatory seclusion functions as a remedy for these habits of book learning. However, once al-Kūrānī established his own teaching circle in Medina, a keen critical philological interest resurfaced in both his teaching and his writing. For instance, al-Kūrānī sought to trace claims about authors and their positions back to the original source, as he had done with regard to Sībawayh's grammar. This approach marks his important defense of Ibn Taymiyya, who had been much maligned in the century before al-Kūrānī. The formative refutation of Ibn Taymiyya was that of al-Haytamī (d. 974/1566), who sought to deflect Ibn Taymiyya's critique of certain later Sufis, most prominently Ibn ʿArabī. Al-Haytamī's invective against Ibn Taymiyya is remarkably thin on reliable citation: although Ibn Taymiyya was one of the most prolific authors of Islamic intellectual history, al-Haytamī relied on hearsay and secondhand reports to portray Ibn Taymiyya as a deviant in all areas of religion.[111] Al-Kūrānī dedicated the conclusion of one of his works on theology to revisiting the position held by Ibn Taymiyya and his most famous student, Ibn Qayyim al-Jawziyya (d. 751/1350), on divine attributes; al-Haytamī had described their position as anthropomorphist. In contrast to al-Haytamī, al-Kūrānī made an effort to glean the views of these scholars from their own writings, and he managed to obtain three works by Ibn Taymiyya and two by Ibn al-Qayyim.[112] Over more than twenty pages, he then explained why the charge of anthropomorphism against the two scholars was impossible to sustain.[113] Al-Kūrānī's rehabilitation of Ibn Taymiyya on the basis of a methodologically sound reading of the works available to him had significant consequences for modern Islamic thought, as it lifted the stigma from what would become arguably the most influential classical author in the modern period. But it also set the stage for future conflicts once the discovery of additional works by Ibn Taymiyya forced scholars to grapple with his extensive critique of Ibn ʿArabī and popular Sufi practices.[114]

A second key node in the classical revival was Murtaḍā al-Zabīdī (1732–91), perhaps the greatest Arab philologist of the postclassical age. Al-Zabīdī

[111] Al-Haytamī, *al-Fatāwā al-ḥadīthiyya*, 114–15. See also El-Rouayheb, "From Ibn Ḥajar al-Haytamī to Khayr al-Dīn al-Ālūsī," 272.

[112] These works were Ibn Taymiyya's *al-Risāla al-tadmuriyya* and probably his *Sharḥ ḥadīth al-nuzūl* and *al-Risāla al-ḥamawiyya* (for the last two works, al-Kūrānī mentions only the contents, not the title), and Ibn al-Qayyim's *Kitāb al-Rūḥ* and *Shifāʾ al-ghalīl*; see al-Kūrānī, *al-ʿAyn wa-l-athar*, fol. 56a.

[113] Al-Kūrānī, *al-ʿAyn wa-l-athar*, fols. 56a–67b.

[114] On the effect of al-Kūrānī's reassessment of Ibn Taymiyya on the latter's reputation, see al-Kurdī, *al-Fawāʾid al-madaniyya*, 113–15; on al-Kūrānī's role in acquainting Shāh Walī Allāh of Delhi with Ibn Taymiyya, see al-Farīwāʾī, "Shaykh al-islām Ibn Taymiyya," 165. For extensive discussion of the fate of Ibn Taymiyya in later scholarship and his significance for reformist editors, see chapter 7.

is best known for his monumental Arabic dictionary, *Tāj al-ʿarūs* (The bridal crown), and for his commentary on al-Ghazālī's *Iḥyāʾ ʿulūm al-dīn* (Revival of the religious sciences), titled *Itḥāf al-sāda al-muttaqīn* (Gift of the god-fearing nobility). Both works show al-Zabīdī as a critical philologist who compares the manuscripts he uses and includes variant readings in the text.[115] In the dictionary, he even provides details on the manuscripts that he has used as sources, describing one, for example, as "consisting of five volumes; it is the draft version of the author, which was part of the endowment of the Sumaysaṭiyya Sufi lodge in Damascus but was later incorporated into the Ashraf [Barsbay complex] library in Cairo."[116] In his commentary, al-Zabīdī provides an extensive bibliography of the works he consulted directly; he quotes at least 115 works on hadith and history alone, going far beyond the usual works and commentaries of the postclassical curriculum.[117] The style of the commentary also diverges from the typical postclassical mode. For example, al-Zabīdī traces unacknowledged quotations by al-Ghazālī to earlier works,[118] which obviously requires an enormous amount of erudition. He also cites critiques of al-Ghazālī's positions and responds to them[119] and reproduces lengthy passages from a wide variety of other works to elaborate on al-Ghazālī's text.[120] Al-Zabīdī was a student of al-Kūrānī's students,[121] and he cites Ibn Taymiyya in a variety of contexts, showing impressive familiarity with his work.[122] Perhaps reflecting al-Kūrānī's rehabilitation of Ibn Taymiyya, al-Zabīdī refers to Ibn Taymiyya not only as an acceptable authority but as one of Islam's top intellects,[123] and he appeals to Ibn Taymiyya's analysis to dismiss certain reports attributed to Muḥammad as inauthentic.[124] Furthermore, he reproduces almost in full an epistle by Ibn Taymiyya on Quranic hermeneutics, which preserves a number of early exegetical opinions that have otherwise been lost.[125]

Possibly the most well-read Muslim scholar at the threshold of the print revolution was Muḥammad al-Shawkānī (1760–1834), who held the post of grand judge of Yemen for almost forty years and authored around 250

[115] See, e.g., al-Zabīdī, *Tāj al-ʿarūs*, 9:385, 404, 406, 528, 523.

[116] Al-Zabīdī, *Tāj al-ʿarūs*, 1:5.

[117] Al-Zabīdī, *Itḥāf al-sāda*, 1:3–4; Reichmuth, *World of Murtaḍā al-Zabīdī*, 298–303.

[118] Al-Zabīdī, *Itḥāf al-sāda*, 9:525–28.

[119] Al-Zabīdī, *Itḥāf al-sāda*, 1:35.

[120] Al-Zabīdī, *Itḥāf al-sāda*, 2:16, 278, 4:537–39. See also Reichmuth, *World of Murtaḍā al-Zabīdī*, chap. 5.

[121] Reichmuth, *World of Murtaḍā al-Zabīdī*, 20, 29, 32.

[122] In *Itḥāf al-sāda*, 1:176, al-Zabīdī praises Ibn Taymiyya for his two books against logic, *al-Radd ʿalā al-mantiqiyyīn* and *Darʾ taʿāruḍ al-ʿaql wa-l-naql*.

[123] Al-Zabīdī, *Itḥāf al-sāda*, 1:180.

[124] Al-Zabīdī, *Itḥāf al-sāda*, 1:449, 3:482.

[125] Al-Zabīdī, *Itḥāf al-sāda*, 4:537–39; compare to Ibn Taymiyya, *Muqaddima fī uṣūl al-tafsīr* (Zarzūr ed.), 35–47.

books.[126] In contrast to the esoteric dismissal of book learning, al-Shawkānī confidently celebrated his erudition. Most obviously, he dedicated his *Itḥāf al-akābir* (Gift of the greats) to an enumeration of all the books for which he possessed a continuous chain of transmission that reached back to the author. Such chains did not mean that al-Shawkānī had necessarily studied each book in detail with a teacher; in some cases, he had received permission to transmit a work as a token of recognition from a scholar who had likewise received such recognition from his own teacher. The number of books on al-Shawkānī's list is impressive: he cites 477 works, representing all Islamic disciplines as well as Arabic language and literature and including writings by both Sunni and Shiʿi authors.

Despite the length of the list, most of its works are later commentaries and teaching texts familiar from the widespread postclassical curriculum. But al-Shawkānī's handbook for students, *Adab al-ṭalab* (The know-how of learning), contextualizes these curriculum works within a much broader vision of education. Al-Shawkānī stresses the importance of a teacher's guidance at early stages of learning. A novice student ought to begin study of a subject by memorizing a basic text and then studying an appropriate commentary.[127] However, these works are not ends in themselves but rather constitute stepping-stones that enable the students subsequently to read higher-level works on their own. Such independent reading (*muṭālaʿa*) plays an essential role in the educational path that al-Shawkānī outlines. While the basic teaching texts familiarize students with key concepts, it is this further reading that provides depth. The first kind of depth is historical. Al-Shawkānī urges students to peruse the great biographical works, such as al-Dhahabī's fourteenth-century *Siyar aʿlām al-nubalāʾ* (Lives of distinguished scholars) and *Tārīkh al-islām* (History of Islam), which contain biographies of scholars and other prominent personalities from the beginning of Islam to the authors' times, as well as al-Ṭabarī's tenth-century history.[128] The second type of depth necessary for true learning consists of a critical attitude toward accepted positions. To achieve this depth in the field of law, al-Shawkānī recommends independent reading of the extensive works of scholars such as Ibn al-Mundhir (d. 318/930), Ibn Ḥazm, and Ibn Taymiyya, because these scholars practiced what al-Shawkānī calls verification (*taḥqīq*). Verification, in al-Shawkānī's usage, means examining the evidentiary basis of positions and subjecting received opinions within schools of thought to scrutiny by means of historical and rational evidence.[129] This definition contrasts starkly

[126] Haykel, *Revival and Reform*, 10–20.

[127] Al-Shawkānī, *Adab al-ṭalab*, 190.

[128] Al-Shawkānī, *Adab al-ṭalab*, 203.

[129] Al-Shawkānī, *Adab al-ṭalab*, 204–5. See also El-Rouayheb, "Opening the Gate of Verification," 265. Verification is also what al-Kūrānī's teacher Mullā Maḥmūd was said to have introduced in Damascus; see al-Muḥibbī, *Khulāṣat al-athar*, 4:330.

with the term's meaning in esoteric discourse, where verification denotes direct spiritual insight that circumvents the need for external evidence,[130] and it also differs from the scholastic usage of the term to refer to a process of rhetorical and logical analysis.[131] From al-Shawkānī's perspective, the positions enshrined in the tradition are not necessarily correct or exhaustive, and broad literary horizons thus provide a critical check and a reservoir of alternative readings.

Al-Shawkānī's educational ideal was a scholar who could interpret revelation unfettered and unmediated by precedent or earlier opinions—an independent scholar (*mujtahid*) who was familiar with the full sweep of the Arabo-Islamic literary tradition, not only the Islamic disciplines and the Arabic language but also literature. Al-Shawkānī thus rejected the claim, axiomatic in the postclassical view, that the mere possibility of reaching the status of a *mujtahid* had long been foreclosed.[132] Among postclassical scholars, the narrowness of the commentary tradition in religious scholarship was justified with reference to a theory of authority that invested the narrowed canon with the mantle of orthodoxy; the tradition embodied in the commentaries functioned as a benevolent hidden hand that both sustained truth and weeded out falsehood. But al-Shawkānī did not share this optimism. In his view, the postclassical structure of textual authority demanded and reproduced blind following (*taqlīd*), irrational partisanship to groups or individuals (*taʿaṣṣub*), and authoritarianism, in effect treating fallible human minds as infallible. As an alternative, al-Shawkānī proposed the goal of objectivity (*inṣāf*) vis-à-vis the corpus of ideas.[133] This position meant that all literature was potentially worth reading and considering. "As a general rule," al-Shawkānī concluded, "knowing any discipline is far better than being ignorant of it."[134]

Al-Shawkānī also departed dramatically from the postclassical mainstream in his insistence that the theological positions of Islamic sects be learned from each sect's own writings in order to ensure an accurate understanding of them.[135] He put this principle into practice in his work on legal theory, *Irshād al-fuḥūl* (The masters' guidance), which cites the opinions of more than four hundred Muslim scholars across a range of times, places, and

[130] See, for example, al-Shaʿrānī, *al-Ṭabaqāt al-kubrā* (al-Sāyiḥ and Wahba ed.), 2:92, where al-Shaʿrānī, like al-Muḥibbī, uses the term "gate of verification" but denotes esoteric insight thereby. For this usage among postclassical Sufis, see El-Rouayheb, *Islamic Intellectual History*, 236, 262–63.

[131] El-Rouayheb, *Islamic Intellectual History*, 26–36.

[132] Al-Shawkānī, *Adab al-ṭalab*, 205–6.

[133] Al-Shawkānī, *Adab al-ṭalab*, 86–89.

[134] Al-Shawkānī, *Adab al-ṭalab*, 207.

[135] Al-Shawkānī, *Adab al-ṭalab*, 196–98.

schools of thought.[136] He did not read the works of all of these theorists—he made use, inter alia, of the fourteenth-century encyclopedic work *al-Baḥr al-muḥīṭ* (The all-encompassing ocean) by al-Zarkashī (d. 794/1392)[137]—but he did consult a large number of foundational works directly.[138] The purpose of the impressive array of sources is to achieve objectivity (the term appears again in the introduction to the *Irshād*); that is, to consider the positions put forward by Muslim theorists throughout history and to select and defend the correct ones among them, without being constrained by adherence to any particular school or teacher.[139] Al-Shawkānī's works were influential for Muslim reformist thought in India and the Arab world. Within a century of his death, several of his works had been printed, and their circulation served to popularize his vision of immersion in the widest possible understanding of Arabo-Islamic literature.

* * *

Arabo-Islamic scholarship at the threshold of the print age was marked by two features that had significant ramifications for book culture. The first was the dominance of scholasticism, which manifested itself in the literary form of basic teaching manuals overlaid by a superstructure of numerous layers of postclassical commentary. And the second was the emergence of an esoteric intellectual ideal that disparaged book learning as inherently deficient in comparison with insight gleaned from direct divine inspiration or submission to an enlightened spiritual guide. The combined effect of these features was to undermine the continuity of postclassical Islamic thought with its classical predecessor.

My identification and discussion of these trends should not be read as a rehash of the nineteenth-century narrative of decline, which dismissed postclassical Islamic thought as a mere lifeless shell waiting to be revived and filled by European Enlightenment.[140] This narrative is untenable because its sweeping stigmatization of a period of several centuries as intellectually barren ignores actual historical variability and many instances of intellectual innovation. But we should not overcompensate for this caricature by treating any criticism of the postclassical intellectual framework as modernist slander. The available evidence does indicate that the supremacy of

[136] See al-Shawkānī, *Irshād al-fuḥūl*, index, 2:1203–22.

[137] Al-Shawkānī, *Irshād al-fuḥūl*, 1:196.

[138] These included al-Jaṣṣāṣ's *Fuṣūl*, al-Dabbūsī's *Taqwīm al-adilla*, and Ibn Ḥazm's *Iḥkām* from the tenth and eleventh centuries; see al-Shawkānī, *Irshād al-fuḥūl*, 1:211, 248, 254.

[139] Al-Shawkānī, *Irshād al-fuḥūl*, 1:54.

[140] On this debate, see, for example, Bauer, "In Search of 'Post-Classical' Literature"; Saliba, *Maʿālim al-aṣāla wa-l-ibdāʿ*; El-Rouayheb, *Islamic Intellectual History*, esp. introduction and conclusion; Dallal, *Islam without Europe*, introduction. I discuss the issue at greater length in the conclusion.

postclassical curriculum texts and the esoteric disdain for book learning, together with the dramatic loss of books from the Arabic-speaking lands discussed in the preceding chapter, had a significant constricting effect on the intellectual horizons of the Islamic literary tradition, especially by facilitating and accelerating the marginalization and loss of older works. Nevertheless, throughout the postclassical period there were scholars who resisted the shrinking of the literary horizon and insisted on engaging with as wide a range of literature as possible. These scholars actively sought out works that had lain outside the mainstream or had fallen out of use, and they embraced critical philological practices, carefully comparing manuscripts and tracing opinions back to their putative authors. Their struggle forms the backdrop for the embrace of printing by reformist scholars in the nineteenth century.

CHAPTER 3

The Beginnings of Print

If we envision Arabo-Islamic book culture as a type of memory that transcends generations and centuries, then maintaining this culture, whether by preserving books or by copying and distributing them, represents a constant struggle against oblivion. The preceding chapters have surveyed the challenges that the nineteenth century posed to the first goal of this struggle, that is, the maintenance and development of institutions of book preservation and access. This chapter turns to the changing means of cultural reproduction: the constitution of books as physical objects through the medium of print.

EARLY PRINTING IN THE ARABIC WORLD: LIMITED HORIZONS

The print revolution, inaugurated by Johannes Gutenberg (d. 1468), was central to the cultural formation of modern Europe. Within decades of Gutenberg's death, the technology of the printing press had also arrived in Istanbul, carried by Jewish refugees from Spain.[1] Arabic books were not, however, printed in the Middle East in significant numbers until the eighteenth century, and it was only in the nineteenth century that print came to dominate the production of Arabo-Islamic literature. To explain why print was not adopted earlier in the Islamic world, it is often claimed that two successive Ottoman sultans—Beyazid II (r. 1481–1512) and Selim I (r. 1512–20)—banned the printing of Arabic script within the empire in edicts issued in 1485 and 1515, respectively.[2] But as Kathryn Schwartz has shown, this claim is dubious; no direct documentation of such a ban exists.[3] Even if printing had indeed been prohibited by the authorities, the explanation would still be far from conclusive, since the fifteenth and sixteenth centuries witnessed several innovations that were initially banned by the Ottoman authorities but quickly became part and

[1]Block printing appears to have been used to print talismans in the tenth century CE in Egypt, Iraq, and Iran; see Bulliet, "Medieval Arabic *Ṭarsh*." Arabic works were printed in Europe already in the sixteenth century; see Roper, "History of the Book." On early efforts to print Christian works in Arabic in the Levant, see Walbiner, "Die Protagonisten."

[2]See, for example, Bloom, *Paper before Print*, 221.

[3]Schwartz, "Meaningful Mediums," chap. 2.

parcel of Middle Eastern culture—most notably, coffee, which arrived in the empire from Yemen via Egypt, and tobacco, which was brought from the Americas by European traders.[4] Therefore, we must still account for the lack of demand for printed books that would have made a ban so effective for more than two centuries.

On the demand side, past studies have suggested several practical factors that militated against the technology. Printing posed a threat to the scholarly conventions of scribal culture and consequently antagonized an influential segment of society; the nature of Arabic script, with its variable letter shapes and ligatures, made it difficult to reproduce in print form; and doubts regarding the ritual purity of the alien institution of the printing workshop were common.[5] But these explanations are speculative, and—as Schwartz has pointed out[6]—they are based on the deterministic assumption that as soon as a technology is available, it will be adopted; consequently, the "late" adoption of Arabic printing has to be explained with reference to factors such as state intervention, religious obscurantism, and technical limitations. Taking a broader view, it might be more fruitful to consider whether the existing system of scribes copying manuscripts by hand in fact served the reading public in Muslim societies well enough to preclude sufficient demand for printed books to overcome the various factors listed above that worked against the adoption of print.

It is important to recognize that the technologies of manuscript and print book production embody differing internal logics and cater to different types of reading audiences. Manuscript book cultures produce works as individual copies. Given the outlay of effort and expense involved in the production of each copy, works that do not have a guaranteed market as textbooks are unlikely to be copied without existing demand—that is, a specific request for a copy of a particular work from a prospective buyer. A printer, by contrast, faces substantial overhead costs in terms of the necessary machinery and, for each new book, the initial typesetting and proofreading, but after that every additional printed copy increases the printer's profit margin and reduces the unit cost. Printers thus have an incentive to print as many copies as they can hope to sell. As a consequence, while a manuscript book industry errs on the side of scarcity, relying on individual demand, printing tends toward (over)saturation. If the market for books is small, copying books by hand may indeed be more economical, since the limited demand would require printed books to be sold at a higher price in order to allow the printer to recoup the high initial production cost. It is only if the reading public is

[4] Michot, *Against Smoking*; Michot, *L'opium et le café*; and Hattox, *Coffee and Coffeehouses.*
[5] Roper, "History of the Book."
[6] Schwartz, "Meaningful Mediums," 23.

large enough to generate economies of scale that printing offers a financial advantage over copyist reproductions.

The Muslim world of the sixteenth to eighteenth centuries was home to a very small reading public for Arabic book-length prints. The centers of scholarship of the three major Muslim powers at the time—the Ottomans, the Safavids, and the Mughals—lay in non-Arabic-speaking lands, where Arabic was mastered only by religious scholars. Their Arabic was the dry language of the scholastic commentary tradition, which granted little attention or value to prose quality. In literature, the preferred languages were Persian and Ottoman Turkish. In the Ottomans' Arab provinces, the decline of educational institutions, discussed in chapter 1, had withered local religious scholarship, and the downgrading of erstwhile metropolises to the status of provincial towns had disbanded the Arabic-speaking scribal class that had been a pillar of Arabic literature and secular sciences in earlier centuries. As a result, the reading public of even an important Arab country such as Egypt probably numbered in the mere tens of thousands in 1800.[7]

When books in Arabic finally began to be printed in the eighteenth century, the technology was initially used either by non-Muslim communities (such as Levantine Christians, whose presses were, however, financed by European donations, not indigenous demand)[8] or for the printing of secular texts.[9] Islamic literature continued to be reproduced exclusively by hand. It was only in the nineteenth century—parallel to the rise of a new readership—that printing presses also began to produce Islamic literature. The central place for this development was Egypt.

The French troops who invaded Egypt in 1798 under Napoleon's command brought with them the tools of modernizing statehood, including a printing press by means of which French revolutionary propaganda could be addressed directly to the Egyptian people in their native Arabic tongue. Once

[7]There is no way of determining precisely the size of the reading public in Muslim countries before the later nineteenth century, especially since literacy is not a single state but rather encompasses various forms; a significantly greater number of people could read the Quran and carry out basic bookkeeping than could read a book cover to cover. This distinction is likely to explain the wide range of estimates—between 1 and 30 percent—of the literacy rate in Egypt around 1800, for example. If we take the lower end of the estimate range to indicate the potential audience for printed books, the reading public at the time might have consisted of a mere forty thousand people. See Hanna, "Literacy among Artisans and Tradesmen," 319 and 320. For Egypt's estimated population in 1800, see McCarthy, "Nineteenth-Century Egyptian Population," 6.

[8]Walbiner, "Christians of *Bilād al-Shām*," 11–12.

[9]For assessments of the work of Ibrahim Müteferrika in this field, see Sabev, "Waiting for Godot"; Reichmuth, "Islamic Reformist Discourse." For a reproduction of the official Ottoman permission for and religious fatwa on the printing of only nonreligious literature, see Müteferrika's print of the Turkish translation of al-Jawharī's eleventh-century dictionary *Tercüme-yi Sıhahu'l-Cevherī*, [2b–3a].

the French had gained control of the country, the press also began to publish regular newspapers and journals in French for the occupying forces. Although these uses were the primary reasons for the establishment of the press in Egypt, the trained Orientalists who staffed it, first among them Jean-Joseph Marcel, the book collector encountered in chapter 1, also saw its potential for remaking Arabic written culture. In 1801, the *Courier de l'Égypte* reported that when Khalīl al-Bakrī (d. 1808), an Egyptian scholar who had been appointed by the French to the Dīwān, or council, through which they governed Egypt, visited the French printing press in Cairo,

> he demanded to know what influence printing could have on the civilization of a people and seemed to understand and appreciate the reasons he was given, above all the following: first, the ease of multiplying and spreading a large number of copies of valuable works, which in manuscript form could be known only to a few; and second, the impossibility that all these copies could be lost or destroyed under any conceivable circumstances, which could happen to the best manuscripts. He then said that there were many valuable Arabic works whose publication would be infinitely useful in this country in which they were ignored by most people, and that he sincerely wished that they could be widely disseminated through printing.[10]

The French press did not and could not fulfill such a task. Apart from a small collection of Arabic wisdom literature that Marcel published both in the original and in French translation,[11] the French did not publish Islamic works in Egypt, and the editions of Arabo-Islamic literature that were subsequently produced in France remained little known in the Islamic world for another century. However, the technique and its potential were not forgotten. After the French withdrawal from Egypt in 1801, Muḥammad ʿAlī, an Albanian officer in the Ottoman army, succeeded in establishing himself as the unchallenged ruler of a de facto independent Egypt, and he set about building a modern state on the European model in Egypt. Integral elements of this state-building project were the training of military officers, doctors, and engineers; the formation of a governmental bureaucracy; and the establishment of a state educational system.[12] All of these ventures required means of disseminating information efficiently and on a large scale. Accordingly, in 1815 Muḥammad ʿAlī sent the fifteen-year-old Syrian Nīqūlā Massābikī (d. 1830) to Italy to learn the craft of printing.[13] Once Massābikī returned to Egypt four years later, he oversaw the establishment of a governmental printing

[10] *Courier de l'Égypte*, 24 Pluviose IX [February 13, 1801], 4.
[11] Marcel, *Fables de Loqman surnommé Le Sage*.
[12] See, for example, Fahmy, *All the Pasha's Men*.
[13] Al-Ṭahṭāwī, *Imam in Paris*, 17–22.

press in Bulaq, Cairo's port district.[14] The first work printed there, in 1822, was an Italian-Arabic dictionary.

Within the next twenty years, the Bulaq press published at least three hundred titles.[15] In terms of subject matter, the published books fell largely into the categories of military sciences, medicine, mathematics, and similar technical subjects, and they were often translations of works originally written in French and other European languages.[16] These works were intended to serve as textbooks for an emerging military and bureaucratic class that would form the bedrock of the Egyptian state. In addition, the launch of a government gazette and journal in 1828 (*al-Waqāʾiʿ al-miṣriyya*, "Egyptian affairs") opened a constant line of communication through which official decrees and ideas could be disseminated rapidly and widely.[17]

The printing of classical Arabic works or works on Islamic subjects had very low priority in this early phase.[18] Beyond selected sections of the Quran that were printed in 1833,[19] the few Arabic books to be published were mainly basic teaching texts on grammar and syntax. The most important of these were Ibn Ājurrūm's fourteenth-century grammar, printed in 1826 with a second edition in 1837; al-Kafrāwī's (d. 1788) commentary on Ibn Ājurrūm's grammar, printed in 1842; four prints of Ibn Ḥājib's (d. 646/1249) grammar with Jāmī's (d. 998/1492) commentary and various glosses;[20] and Ibn ʿAqīl's (d. 769/1367) commentary on Ibn Mālik's (d. 672/1274) *Alfiyya*, a versified Arabic grammar, which was printed in 1837. These works were made available in print because they were in consistently high demand as textbooks in the newly founded state schools. In 1834, for example, Muḥammad ʿAlī declared, "Given the necessity of teaching the *Alfiyya* and its commentary in the school of [the Nile delta city] Mansura and all other schools in the realm, and given that it is currently not available from the Bulaq printing house, notice is hereby given to those in charge to print sufficient numbers of this work to meet the demand."[21]

The only theological texts to be printed in this period were four succinct creedal primers that were part of the postclassical curriculum.[22] The press's

[14] The Bulaq press changed names (and ownership) several times in the course of the nineteenth century, so entries in the bibliography identify the publisher as simply "Bulaq." On the history of the press, see Ṣābāt, *Tārīkh al-ṭibāʿa*, 145–268.

[15] Bianchi, "Liste des ouvrages"; al-Shūrbajī, *Qāʾima bi-awāʾil al-maṭbūʿāt al-ʿarabiyya*; Schulze, "Birth of Tradition and Modernity," esp. 51–53.

[16] Heyworth-Dunne, "Printing and Translations under Muḥammad ʿAlī," 334.

[17] ʿImāra, *Rifāʿa al-Ṭahṭāwī*, 77–81.

[18] Riḍwān, *Tārīkh maṭbaʿat Būlāq*, 33.

[19] Albin, "Printing of the Qurʾān," 269–70.

[20] The base text was printed in 1831, and three commentary clusters in 1840.

[21] Riḍwān, *Tārīkh maṭbaʿat Būlāq*, 116.

[22] These were al-Laqqānī's seventeenth-century *Jawharat al-tawḥīd* (printed in 1825 and incorrectly described as a mystical work by Bianchi, "Liste des ouvrages"), al-Sanūsī's short

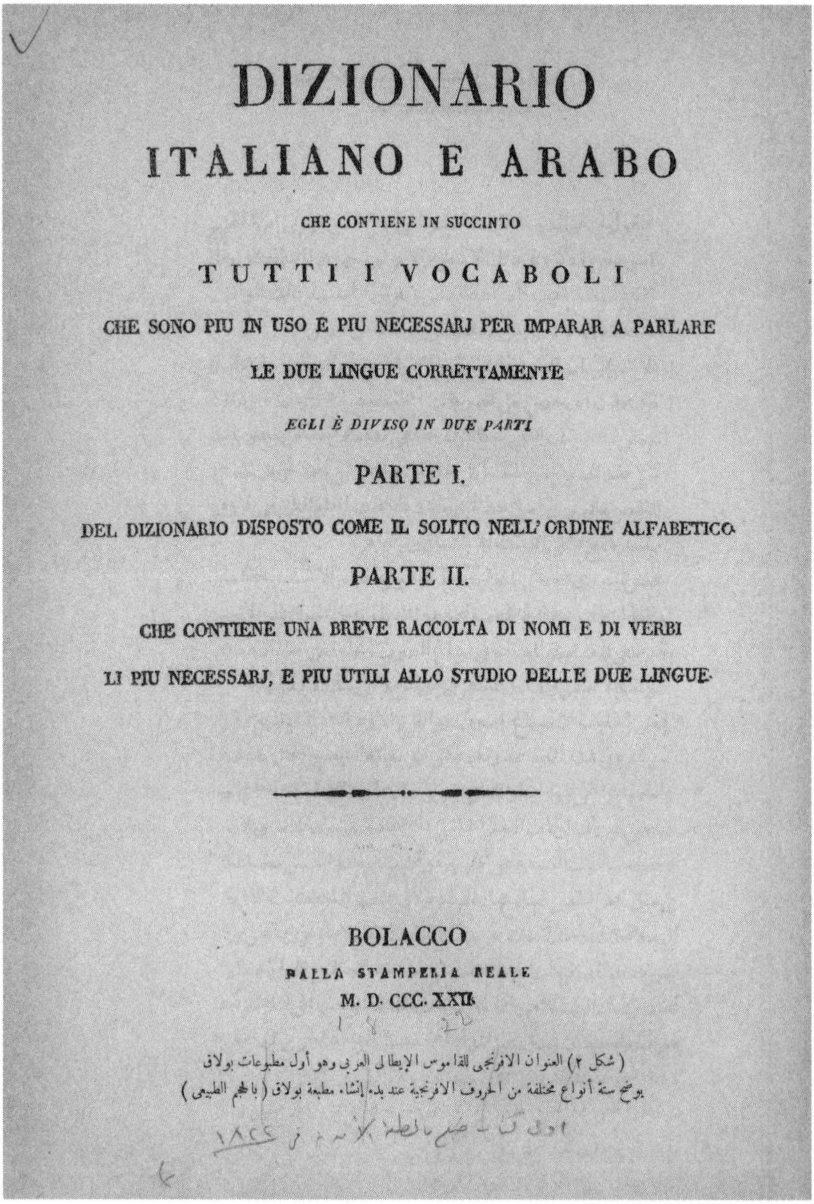

DIZIONARIO

ITALIANO E ARABO

CHE CONTIENE IN SUCCINTO

TUTTI I VOCABOLI

CHE SONO PIU IN USO E PIU NECESSARJ PER IMPARAR A PARLARE
LE DUE LINGUE CORRETTAMENTE

EGLI È DIVISO IN DUE PARTI

PARTE I.

DEL DIZIONARIO DISPOSTO COME IL SOLITO NELL' ORDINE ALFABETICO.

PARTE II.

CHE CONTIENE UNA BREVE RACCOLTA DI NOMI E DI VERBI
LI PIU NECESSARJ, E PIU UTILI ALLO STUDIO DELLE DUE LINGUE.

BOLACCO
DALLA STAMPERIA REALE
M. D. CCC. XXII.

(شكل ٢) العنوان الافرنجى للقاموس الإيطالى العربى وهو أول مطبوعات بولاق
يوضح ستة أنواع مختلفة من الحروف الافرنجية عند بدء إنشاء مطبعة بولاق (بالحجم الطبيعى)

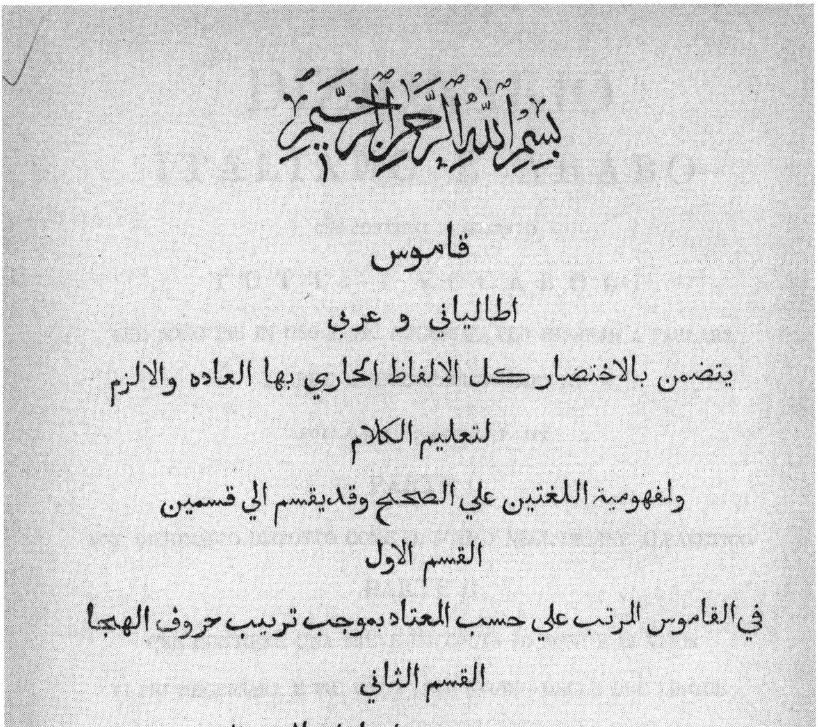

بسم الله الرحمن الرحيم

قاموس

اطالياني و عربي

يتضمن بالاختصار كل الالفاظ الجاري بها العاده والالزم

لتعليم الكلام

ولمفهومية اللغتين علي الصحح وقد يقسم الي قسمين

القسم الاول

في القاموس المرتب علي حسب المعتاد بموجب ترتيب حروف الهجا

القسم الثاني

ويتضمن مجموع مختصر من اسما وافعال من الاشد

الزام واكثر فايدة لدرس اللغتين

تم الطبع في بولاق بمطبعة صاحب السعاده

١٢٣٨

(شكل ١) العنوان العربي للقاموس الإيطالي العربي وهو أول مطبوعات بولاق

يوضح جمين من اول حروف عربية استعملت في بولاق وهي المصنوعة في إيطاليا (بالحجم الطبيعي)

Figure 3.1. Cover pages of Zākhūr's Italian-Arabic dictionary, Bulaq, 1822. Courtesy of Bibliotheca Alexandrina.

output in the field of philosophy was likewise modest and focused on post-classical teaching texts.[23] In Islamic law, two substantial texts in Arabic—recently written glosses on a commentary on a text on prayer[24] and on a commentary on a sixteenth-century compendium[25]—appeared in print before 1842.[26] The field of Sufism likewise saw the publication of a single Arabic work, Ibn ʿArabī's controversial *Fuṣūṣ al-ḥikam* (Bezels of wisdom), printed in 1838. The only work of Quranic exegesis to be printed in this period was an eighteenth-century text by Ismāʿīl Ḥaqqī of Bursa,[27] who was also the author of one of the several printed Turkish works on the life of Muḥammad;[28] the sole such work in Arabic to be published was that of al-Qāḍī ʿIyāḍ (d. 544/1149).[29] The only real Arabic-language reference work to be printed was Abū al-Baqāʾ's seventeenth-century lexicon.[30] In the field of literature, Turkish poetry and Turkish translations of Persian poetry dominated,[31] but original Persian works by Saʿdī and ʿAṭṭār were also published.[32] The few printed works of Arabic literature included works such as *Kalīla wa-Dimna* (Kalīla and Dimna), the famed collection of fables translated from Middle Persian into Arabic by Ibn al-Muqaffaʿ in the eighth century;[33] a collection of poetry attributed to Muḥammad's son-in-law ʿAlī b. Abī Ṭālib;[34] *The Thousand and One Nights* (*Alf layla wa-layla*);[35] and a commentary on al-Būṣīrī's (d. 695/1296) "poem of the cloak" (*Qaṣīdat al-burda*).[36] In sum, considering the voluminous

---

work on creed from the fifteenth century (printed in 1835), al-Samarqandī's tenth-century *al-Sawād al-aʿẓam* (printed in 1838), and *al-Tuḥfa al-Salīmiyya* by a certain Salīm Efendi (in Turkish, printed in 1841).

[23]The few publications in this field included al-Akhdarī's sixteenth-century poem on logic, *al-Sullam al-murawnaq/al-munawraq* (published in 1826), and an eclectic compendium on primarily philosophical topics by the eighteenth-century Ottoman poet, scholar, and statesman Ragıp Pasha (published in 1840).

[24]Mustafa Güzelhiṣarı's (fl. 1826) gloss, *Ḥilyat al-nājī*, on Ibrāhīm al-Ḥalabī's sixteenth-century commentary, *Ghunyat al-mustamlī*, on Sadīd al-Dīn al-Kashgharī's fifteenth-century *Munyat al-muṣallī*, printed in 1836.

[25]Aḥmad b. Muḥammad al-Ṭahṭāwī's (d. 1816) gloss on al-Ḥaṣkafī's seventeenth-century commentary, *Durr al-mukhtār*, on al-Timurtāshī's sixteenth-century *Tanwīr al-abṣār*, printed in 1836.

[26]There was also a small number of Turkish-language books on aspects of Islamic law.

[27]*Rūḥ al-bayān*, printed in 1839.

[28]*Sharḥ al-Muḥammadiyya*, printed in 1836.

[29]*Sharḥ al-Shifāʾ*, printed in 1841.

[30]*Al-Kulliyyāt*, printed in 1838 and again in 1840.

[31]A Turkish translation of Rūmī's thirteenth-century *Masnavī* appeared in 1836, a collection of poetry by Ragıp Pasha in 1837, and the *Dīwān* of Fuzūlī in 1838.

[32]Saʿdī's *Gulistān* and ʿAṭṭār's *Pand-nāmah* both came out in 1828.

[33]Published in 1836.

[34]*Dīwān ʿAlī b. Abī Ṭālib*, printed 1835.

[35]First issued in 1835 or 1836.

[36]Printed in 1841. There were a few additional publications on Islamic topics that do not fit neatly into a single genre. These include a Turkish commentary on and translation of Birgevi/

overall output of the Bulaq press in its two first decades, classical Islamic texts were only marginally represented,[37] and the same was true of Arabic literature, which was overshadowed by Persian and Turkish poetry.

THE EVOLUTION OF THE PUBLISHING INDUSTRY: EXPANDING POSSIBILITIES

The Egyptian publishing industry experienced a turning point in the late 1840s, both in terms of the number of books printed—which rose from an average of 31 titles per year before 1850 to an average of 191 titles per year between 1850 and 1900—and in terms of the language used. Whereas only about 55 percent of the books published before 1850 were in Arabic (36 percent were in Turkish and 3 percent in Persian), 88 percent of those issued between 1850 and 1900 were in Arabic (less than 2 percent were in Turkish and only 0.3 percent in Persian).[38] A typical print run before 1850 was between 500 and 1,000 copies.[39]

An important step was the Egyptian state's decision, made at some point in the 1830s, to permit private individuals (so-called commissioners, *multazimūn*)[40] to use the facilities of the Bulaq press to publish books of their choice; the opportunity was publicized through advertisements in the state newspaper, *al-Waqāʾiʿ al-miṣriyya*.[41] Several individuals, both Egyptians and non-Egyptians, took up the offer. For example, the retired Egyptian judge ʿAṭā Bey, who owned an autograph manuscript of a sixteenth-century work on Islamic law (*Multaqā al-abḥur* by Ibrāhīm al-Ḥalabī, d. 956/1549), had 500 copies of the work printed in 1847. In the same year, the Cairene bookseller Kāmil Efendi used the Bulaq press to publish al-Bayḍāwī's thirteenth-century Quranic exegesis together with a gloss, advertising the publication in the state newspaper.[42] This publication led to an early case of competition between an Egyptian and an Orientalist print of the same work. Fleischer, in Leipzig, had also edited

al-Birkawī's (d. 981/1573) treatise on Muḥammad's teachings (published in 1825 and 1841, respectively), and two works on the merits of *jihād* (published in 1826 and 1836, respectively).

[37] Reinhard Schulze has similarly noted a turn from postclassical to classical literature in the output of Arab presses around the middle of the nineteenth century; see his "Birth of Tradition and Modernity," 49–60; and "Mass Culture and Islamic Cultural Production," 194–97.

[38] ʿĀyida Nuṣayr has calculated that a total of 867 titles were published in Egypt before 1850 and a total of 9,538 titles between 1850 and 1900. Nuṣayr, *Ḥarakat nashr al-kutub*, 85–86, 166, 174.

[39] Nuṣayr, *Ḥarakat nashr al-kutub*, 90.

[40] Schwartz, "Meaningful Mediums," 200–201; Schwartz, "Political Economy."

[41] Riḍwān, *Tārīkh maṭbaʿat Būlāq*, 109.

[42] Riḍwān, *Tārīkh maṭbaʿat Būlāq*, 110. The exegesis was published together with a gloss as Shaykhzāde, *Ḥāshiya*.

al-Bayḍāwī's commentary (it was published in 1846–48), but when his student Wetzstein, the Prussian consul in Damascus whom we encountered as a manuscript collector and dealer in chapter 1, tried to market Fleischer's edition in Damascus, he could sell or barter only seven copies, because the German version was four times as expensive as the Egyptian one,[43] and its typeface was painfully awkward. Another commissioner who published several books through Cairene presses in the 1860s—mostly works by the sixteenth-century Sufi scholar al-Shaʿrānī (discussed at length in chapter 2)—was Ḥasan al-ʿIdwī al-Ḥamzāwī (1806–86).[44] Al-ʿIdwī was a committed Sufi and an enthusiastic admirer of al-Shaʿrānī; echoing the postclassical preoccupation with visions, he reported that al-Shaʿrānī had appeared to him in a dream and told him to spread his books far and wide, inspiring him to have al-Shaʿrānī's writings printed.[45]

The involvement of private individuals, particularly booksellers whose primary line of trade was the production and sale of manuscripts, in the publishing business initially led to a perpetuation of the preprint literary tradition in printed form. The majority of these publishers were businessmen, and they sought to supply books that the market knew and demanded. Such books are exemplified by the 1858 single-volume printing of a collection of basic teaching texts (*Majmūʿ al-mutūn*) traditionally taught as part of the postclassical curriculum, succinctly covering such subjects as creed, poetry in praise of Muḥammad, inheritance law, legal theory, hadith terminology, grammar, syntax, rhetoric, logic, philosophy, disputation, and Quranic recitation. This is the book that Ṭāhā Ḥusayn later reported being told to memorize in 1902 in preparation for attending al-Azhar.[46] Printed versions of required curriculum texts enjoyed a guaranteed clientele among students,[47] and their popularity is indicated by the fact that the 1858 *Majmūʿ al-mutūn* was reprinted at least twelve times in the nineteenth century.[48] By the time of the 1867 World Exposition in Paris, the Egyptian pavilion could host an exhibit of books taught at al-Azhar in which twenty-one of the fifty books on display were printed.[49]

43 Huhn, *Der Orientalist Johann Gottfried Wetzstein*, 123–24.

44 Al-Shaʿrānī's books published by al-ʿIdwī include his *al-Mīzān* (1862 or 1863), *al-Anwār al-qudsiyya* (1860), and *al-Jawāqit wa-l-jawāhir* (1860). On al-ʿIdwī's publishing activities, see Schwartz, "Political Economy."

45 Al-ʿIdwī, introduction to al-Bukhārī, *al-Jāmiʿ al-ṣaḥīḥ*, 1:2.

46 Ḥusayn, *al-Ayyām*, 1:67 (chap. 12).

47 See the observations of Goldziher in Mestyan, "Ignác Goldziher's Report," 457–58, and of Snouck Hurgronje in *Mekka*, 207.

48 It was printed in 1858, 1866, 1868, 1870, 1884, 1885, 1886, 1892, 1896, and 1897 in Cairo, plus in 1882 in Alexandria and in 1899 in Fez.

49 Edmond, *L'Égypte à l'Exposition universelle de 1867*, 368–70.

The existence of a state-owned printing press with de facto monopoly over the production of printed books raised the question of what works were fit to be reproduced and made available. According to a law promulgated in 1823, all materials to be printed in Bulaq by Europeans had to be inspected for their political and religious content. The law had been prompted by an incident in which an Italian teacher at a state school in Bulaq had attempted to print a poem entitled "The Oriental Religion" that denigrated Islam.[50] That the purview of the law came to be extended from foreigners to all petitioners seeking to use the press to publish works of their choice is evident from one of the earliest printed collections of fatwas, a seven-volume compilation of judgments issued by the Egyptian grand mufti Muḥammad al-ʿAbbāsī al-Mahdī (1827–97), which was published in 1887. The collection preserves two dozen fatwas containing al-Mahdī's verdicts on the permissibility of printing specific works by private persons and entrepreneurs, issued in response to inquiries from state organs between 1866 and 1884.[51] They demonstrate that one of al-Mahdī's key criteria in evaluating potential publications was that Quranic verses and the Prophet Muḥammad's sayings be treated with respect. He explicitly stipulates this as a condition of permission to print, referring to Muslim scholars' concerns that the large-scale reproduction of religious books and the involvement of non-Muslims in their printing and trade could expose the sacred texts to inappropriate handling. Nonetheless, he clearly accepts the technique of printing in itself.[52]

Al-Mahdī's responses to queries regarding the permissibility of particular works fall into three categories: explicit permission, explicit prohibition, and silence. The numerous requests to print the collection of teaching texts (*Majmūʿ al-mutūn*) mentioned earlier or the popular pietistic text *Dalāʾil al-khayrāt* (Guide to good deeds) are always granted, as are requests to print legal texts, commentaries, and works on the Arabic language. By contrast, al-Mahdī rejects repeated requests to print al-Būnī's thirteenth-century treatise *Shams al-maʿārif* (The sun of gnosis), explaining that the work contains esoteric teachings that direct readers to harm others and to degrade Quranic verses by using them as incantations for this purpose.[53] Finally, on occasion al-Mahdī appears to harbor reservations about a work but to see no legal reason to prohibit its printing, and in these situations he simply refrains from giving a judgment. For example, in 1875 the authorities presented to al-Mahdī an application from a Cairene bookseller to print a list of works that included *Dalāʾil al-khayrāt*, *Majmūʿ al-mutūn*, *The Thousand and One Nights*, a fictional

[50] Riḍwān, *Tārīkh maṭbaʿat Būlāq*, 100.

[51] Al-Mahdī, *al-Fatāwā al-Mahdiyya*, 5:292–97, 300–302; see also Peters, "Muḥammad al-ʿAbbās al-Mahdī," 77.

[52] Al-Mahdī, *al-Fatāwā al-Mahdiyya*, 5:294.

[53] Al-Mahdī, *al-Fatāwā al-Mahdiyya*, 5:292–94.

account of the Prophet's companion Muʿādh, a collection of invocations, a sixteenth-century commentary on Shāfiʿī law, a section of the Quran (the thirtieth *juzʾ*), and al-Thaʿlabī's eleventh-century compilation of stories about the prophets (*Qiṣaṣ al-anbiyāʾ*). In his response, al-Mahdī states that "there is no objection to the printing of"—and then names all the titles specified in the request except for *The Thousand and One Nights* and the fictional biography of Muʿādh.[54] Objections to such works were not new in Islamic thought, as already in the classical period, the use of historical figures in fictional narratives had been decried as lying and misleading the public.[55] *The Thousand and One Nights* had already been printed in 1835–36 and 1863 and would be printed again in 1885, and the fictional story of Muʿādh had been printed in 1859 and 1861.

The steady demand for postclassical teaching texts, popular devotional works, and entertainment literature meant that these types of texts were the first Arabic-language books to cross the watershed from manuscript to print (following the earlier printing of books that had been newly written or translated from other languages). They catered to an established audience and did not initially go beyond the horizons of the postclassical tradition. The few early works to be published before 1860 were texts that had always been part of active book culture, such as the Quran (printed in full in the 1850s)[56] and the hadith compilations of al-Bukhārī and Muslim (printed in 1850).[57] At first, then, it was only the form, not the content, of Arabic literature that changed. However, starting in the 1850s, print also began to be harnessed to challenge and broaden the scope of the available literature. Criticisms of the narrowness of the postclassical canon had been voiced already earlier by, for example, Ḥasan al-ʿAṭṭār, encountered in chapter 2, who had taken it upon himself to introduce his students to a wider range of writings, particularly classical works. His most prominent student, Rifāʿa al-Ṭahṭāwī, would carry this approach into print.

Al-Ṭahṭāwī had traveled to France as the imam of an educational mission of forty-four students, dispatched by Muḥammad ʿAlī in 1826 for the purpose of providing government experts with modern European training.[58] Al-Ṭahṭāwī proved a quick learner of French and an enormously gifted translator, and after his return to Egypt in 1831 he became the leader of a remarkable movement of translating works from European languages into Arabic, founding the School of Languages (Madrasat al-Alsun) in 1835 as the first

[54] Al-Mahdī, *al-Fatāwā al-Mahdiyya*, 5:297.

[55] Hirschler, *Written Word*, 168–69.

[56] Albin, "Printing of the Qurʾān," 271.

[57] Al-Bukhārī's and Muslim's compilations were published together with their commentaries in al-Qasṭalānī, *Irshād al-sārī*.

[58] Al-Ṭahṭāwī, *Imam in Paris*, 15–26.

كتاب الف ليلة وليلة
الطبعة الثانية
مقابلة وتصحيح الشيخ محمد
قطة العدوى
الجزء الرابع
طبع بمطبعة
عبد الرحمن رشدى بك
الكائنة ببولاق
سنة ١٢٧٩

Figure 3.2. An early print of *The Thousand and One Nights* corrected by Muḥammad Quṭṭa al-ʿAdawī, Bulaq, 1863.

FIGURE 3.3. Rifāʿa al-Ṭahṭāwī. Courtesy of Bibliotheca Alexandrina.

institution dedicated to training professional translators.[59] During his stay in Paris, he not only observed French culture, writing a justifiably famous description of it, but also gained a new perspective on his own cultural tradition. Thus, contemplating the Egyptian obelisk on the Place de la Concorde in Paris, he concluded that Egypt has a greater right than France did to the inheritance of Egypt's ancestors and that "any reasonable person must consider the gradual plunder of [Egypt's] heritage theft by a thief seeking to adorn himself with borrowed plumes."[60] Back in Egypt, he submitted to Muḥammad ʿAlī a plan for the systematic collection of all existing historical artifacts in Egypt and their centralized storage in his newly opened School of Languages,[61] a clear attempt to stem the continuing outflow of Egyptian artifacts.

[59] Under al-Ṭahṭāwī's leadership, this movement translated two thousand works into Arabic from French, English, and Italian as well as Ottoman Turkish; see the translator's introduction to al-Ṭahṭāwī, *Imam in Paris*, 46.

[60] Al-Ṭahṭāwī, *al-Aʿmāl al-kāmila*, 2:292.

[61] ʿImāra, *Rifāʿa al-Ṭahṭāwī*, 74–75; Reid, *Whose Pharaohs?*, 50–57.

While in Paris, al-Ṭahṭāwī also studied with the greatest Orientalist of his age, Antoine Isaac Silvestre de Sacy (1758–1838),[62] who seems to have mentored him as a cultural go-between given his role as a translator of French sciences into Arabic. Al-Ṭahṭāwī noted Silvestre de Sacy's inability to speak Arabic correctly but nonetheless praised his command of written Arabic and, in particular, his edition of al-Ḥarīrī's twelfth-century literary gem, *Maqāmāt*.[63] When al-Ṭahṭāwī passed his examinations in 1828, Silvestre de Sacy gave him a copy of his anthology of Arabic prose and poetry, which he had compiled for the benefit of French students of Arabic. The anthology was clearly also considered valuable by native speakers, and it was in fact later printed in Egypt in 1879. It contained, among other things, excerpts from Ibn Khaldūn's (d. 808/1406) *Muqaddima* ("Introduction," which formed part of a much longer historical work) on caliphal coinage and on the role of writing in human societies.[64] This was most probably not al-Ṭahṭāwī's first exposure to Ibn Khaldūn's masterpiece, which has been called both a philosophy of history and a foundational work of sociology. The previous generation of Egyptian bibliophiles, including the historian al-Jabartī[65] and al-Ṭahṭāwī's teacher al-ʿAṭṭār, had known and admired Ibn Khaldūn, and al-ʿAṭṭār's surviving manuscript copy of the work contains numerous notes written by al-ʿAṭṭār in the margins.[66] It is likely that the *Muqaddima* was one of the texts that al-Ṭahṭāwī read with al-ʿAṭṭār before going to Paris, and the sober and analytical style of his subsequent description of Paris and his acute social and societal sensibilities may well reflect this exposure.

Ibn Khaldūn was also admired among the Orientalists whom al-Ṭahṭāwī met in France. When al-Ṭahṭāwī read Montesquieu in Paris, his teachers referred to him as the French Ibn Khaldūn, and conversely to Ibn Khaldūn as the Montesquieu of the East.[67] The comparison had originally been coined by the Austrian Orientalist Hammer-Purgstall, who had become acquainted with the work in Istanbul.[68] The relative neglect of Ibn Khaldūn in the central Arab lands stood in sharp contrast to the high regard in which he was held among Ottoman intellectuals, for whom his ideas on the rise and fall of dynasties struck a chord. They not only read his work but also translated it into Turkish.[69] It is likely that the rediscovery of Ibn Khaldūn by early

[62] See al-Ṭahṭāwī, "al-Ibrīz," in *al-Aʿmāl al-kāmila*, 2:70, 213, 226.

[63] Al-Ṭahṭāwī, "al-Ibrīz," in *al-Aʿmāl al-kāmila*, 2:103–7.

[64] Silvestre de Sacy, *Chrestomathie arabe*, 2:106–33.

[65] Al-Jabartī, *ʿAjāʾib al-āthār*, 1:11.

[66] Kurd ʿAlī, "al-Khizāna al-Zakiyya."

[67] Al-Ṭahṭāwī, "al-Ibrīz," in *al-Aʿmāl al-kāmila*, 2:222.

[68] Hammer-Purgstall, *Erinnerungen und Briefe*, 2:854n1412.

[69] Fleischer, "Royal Authority, Dynastic Cyclism, and 'Ibn Khaldûnism.'" Hammer-Purgstall claims, in *Erinnerungen und Briefe*, 2:854, that the *Muqaddima* was widely read among the political elite in Istanbul.

nineteenth-century Egyptians (and certainly by the Orientalists) was inspired by his popularity among the Ottomans.[70]

Al-Ṭahṭāwī had experienced the modernizing state in both Egypt and France, and he adhered to a sociological outlook that viewed societies as historical entities, with pasts and futures that could be influenced and planned. These characteristics made him an ideal reformer. Further, his elite status as an alumnus of the educational mission to France allowed him to influence the powerful instruments of the Egyptian state, and his knowledge of classical writers such as Ibn Khaldūn provided him with indigenous literary resources that he could tap for the purpose of Egypt's cultural edification and development. In contrast to his predecessors, al-Ṭahṭāwī had the printing press at his disposal to advance his agenda of intellectual renewal, and he used his influence to promote the printing of books that were dictated neither by the government school curriculum nor by private profit considerations but rather by the goal of introducing forgotten but valuable ideas to the Arabic reading public.

Among the books that al-Ṭahṭāwī successfully lobbied to get printed in Bulaq were al-Maqrīzī's monumental fifteenth-century urban geography of Cairo, known as *al-Khiṭaṭ* (The quarters); the Quranic commentary of Fakhr al-Dīn al-Rāzī, the most extensive and oldest commentary printed at that time; al-Ḥarīrī's perennially popular *Maqāmāt*; two anthologies of Arabic poetry from the fifteenth and sixteenth centuries, respectively;[71] the tenth-century, twenty-volume *Kitāb al-Aghānī* by al-Iṣbahānī (which Seetzen had tried and failed to find in Egypt half a century earlier); and Ibn Khaldūn's history, including the *Muqaddima*.[72] With the exception of al-Ḥarīrī's *Maqāmāt*, which, as noted earlier, had been edited and published by Silvestre de Sacy in 1822, these works were published in full for the first time in Bulaq.

The Bulaq print of Ibn Khaldūn's *Muqaddima*, which appeared as a standalone volume in 1857 and as the first volume of the entire history in 1867, offers an example of the journey of classical texts from manuscript to printed form in the second half of the nineteenth century. Like the other texts whose publication al-Ṭahṭāwī organized, the *Muqaddima* was not part of the postclassical literary canon. Therefore, in contrast to curriculum texts, which existed in countless copies and featured continuous chains of transmission from their authors, the text of the *Muqaddima* was much more difficult to

[70]The dearth of manuscripts of Ibn Khaldūn's work in Egypt versus their abundance in Istanbul support this hypothesis. See also the discussion of the printing of the *Muqaddima* below.

[71]Ibn Ḥijja al-Ḥamawī's (d. 837/1434) *Khizānat al-adab* and al-ʿAbbāsī's (d. 963/1555 or 1556) *Maʿāhid al-tanṣīṣ*.

[72]Mubārak, *al-Khiṭaṭ*, 13:55–56; Verdery, "Publications of the Būlāq Press."

establish accurately and reliably and required considerable investigative work. Although al-Ṭahṭāwī played a crucial role in shepherding the book into print, there is no evidence that he participated in the philological work of establishing the text. This work was carried out by an employee of the Bulaq press, a so-called corrector (*muṣaḥḥiḥ*), in this case a certain Naṣr al-Hūrīnī (d. 1874), who was lauded by Ignaz Goldziher as one of the two leading correctors in Muslim lands (the other being Aḥmad Fāris al-Shidyāq).[73] But before we turn to al-Hūrīnī's labors, an introduction to the work of the *muṣahḥiḥ* is in order.

HOW PRINTING WORKED: THE ROLE OF THE CORRECTOR

The correctors who played an integral part in the production of printed versions of Islamic and Arabic books in the early stages of printing from roughly the 1850s to the 1930s are very little known, even among specialists.[74] One of the reasons for their obscurity is that their names did not typically appear at the beginning of the books they corrected—though there were exceptions, such as the 1905 print of Ibn Taymiyya's *Majmūʿ rasāʾil* (Collected epistles), which names the responsible *muṣaḥḥiḥ*, the Syrian scholar Muḥammad Badr al-Dīn al-Naʿsānī (1881–1943), on the title page.[75] Another reason is that they did not usually write introductions to the works they corrected. The only place in which the corrector's voice can be heard is generally the colophon, an addendum at the end of a book that is characteristic of the manuscript tradition. Although prints of newly written books featured introductions already in the early nineteenth century,[76] editions continued to favor colophons until the beginning of the twentieth century.

In a manuscript colophon, the copyist would record his name,[77] possibly the place and date of his copying of the work, and sometimes information regarding the manuscript that he had used—especially if it was an autograph copy, which naturally represented the gold standard. For example, in a colophon in a manuscript of the *Muqaddima* housed in the Egyptian National Library, a copyist by the name of Ḥasan b. Aḥmad announces that he completed his copy of the work in the month of Jumādā al-Ākhira in 1040 (February 1631)

[73] Mestyan, "Ignác Goldziher's Report," 456.

[74] Amīn, *Fayḍ al-khāṭir*, 3:51 (al-Shaykh al-Disūqī).

[75] The title page specifies that "its [the book's] correction was carried out by" (*ʿuniya bi-taṣḥīḥihi*) al-Naʿsānī.

[76] Nuṣayr, *Ḥarakat nashr al-kutub*, 336–37, 357. Nuṣayr provides a survey of the internal divisions of printed books in the nineteenth century at 321–58.

[77] I have found no record of a single female corrector, so for convenience my discussion of correctors uses only male pronouns.

٩٧٢

قال مترجمه العبد القليل العليل الكليل الآثم الغريق فى لجة المعاصى والمآثم ابو الكمال السيد احمد عاصم
عصمه الله تعالى فى حرزه الدائم فحمدا ثم حمدا ثم حمدا* لمن تيسيره بالختم ابدى هذا هو المرفاء لسفينة القلم
الجارية على البحر الخضم العيلم واليم الهقم الغطمطم الذى تقلو عن ادراك ساحله خلايا الاوهام فكانه
عنصر الماء البعيد الغور عن بلد العقول والافهام الا وهو الاوقيانوس البسيط فى ترجمة القاموس المحيط
والقابوس الوسيط وقد اتفق التوقف والاستواء على ميناء فرضة الانتهاء بشرطة التوفيق من مجرى
الرياح على وفق الاشتهاء فى اليوم الرابع عشر وهو يوم الاحد من ذى القعدة الشريف المنخرط فى سلك شهور سنة
خمس وعشرين ومأتين والف من هجرة من كمايرى من قدامه يرى من خلف وهى موافقة لحساب
كتبخانه علوم ١٢٢٥ ودقيقة هذا التاريخ غير مستتر على اصحاب الفهوم اللهم انفع بفوائده جميع
المسلمين ومتع من عوائده كافة الطالبين واجعله ذخر الاخرتى ولنسبة نبيك النبيه وسيلتى واعف
عنى ما صدر منى من زلاتى وصن وجهى يوم الحسرة عن ذلتى وهو يوم يندب فيه ويستغاث بندبة فياخجلتا
يا كربتا يا ندامتا على سوء اعمالى وهجنة حالتى واغفرلى ولوالدى ولجملة اصولى وفروعى وقرابتى واحبتى
واساتذتى ومشيختى ولجميع امة محمد عليه الصلوة والسلام بحرمة من به ختم مصحف الرسالة
وهو فاتحة الانبياء العظام وصلى الله عليه وعلى آله واصحابه وخلفائه واتباعه
واحبائه واشياعه وعلمائه وانصاره واوليائه وعلى قاطبة الانبياء
والمرسلين والملائكة اجمعين ماجرت جوارى الاقلام
فى عيالم عوالم العلوم موشيات المعالم
ومنشأت الاعلام

مم
م

تاريخ

ترجمة القاموس لما كملت مسكية الختم على خير الختوم ارختها للاسم وللاتمام قدتم الاوقيانوس بحر للعلوم

١٢٢٥

لله در العاصم الحبر الذى — ذاعت فضائله لدى الافاق
فاق الانام سيادة وزهادة — وعلا سناء مكارم الاخلاق
هو ترجم القاموس كشفا واضحا — من بحر علم ذاخر دفاق
حتى مأى فيه وحل رموزه — بتعمق خال عن الاغلاق
لا يبتغى الخيلاء من تصنيفه — الا رضاء القادر الخلاق
والله ينفد عند شخص ما اقتنى — اما لدى الرحمن فهو الباقى
لازال فى اوج السعادة صاعدا — وحسوده فى الخسف والاملاق

كتبه عثمان بن سليمان پناه
غفر لهما الاله

قد تم طبع الاوقيانوس البسيط * فى ترجمة القاموس المحيط * ورست جوارى اقلام طباعته على ساحل
الكمال * واستوت على جودى جود واجب الوجود المتعال * بعد ان شحنت من صحته بضايع
التحرير * وطرائف دقة النظر بحسب الامكان فى التدبر والتدبير * مثنية على المصنف
فى كل فن بكل لسان * مستمدة لروحه الشريفة من مولاه نفحات الروح والريحان *
سابحة فى بحار علومه بطلب رحمة له لا تتناهى * تالية بسم الله مجريها ومرسيها *
وكان ذلك فى استطلاع طلعة المحرم * مطلع سنة خمسين ومأتين
والف من هجرة خير العرب والعجم * ادام الله عليه تتابع
اكمل الصلوة والسلام * وعلى آله واصحابه
واشياعه
الكرام

Figure 3.4. A corrector's colophon from al-Fīrūzābādī, *el-Okyanus ül-basit*, 3:972.

and notes that he compared his copy against the "master copy" (*sulṭān al-nusakh*), namely, a copy that Ibn Khaldūn himself had declared accurate.[78] Correctors' colophons in printed works generally mention the name of the corrector, the printing house, and the date. They may also include the name of the current ruler (with extravagant praise), the name of the head of the press (with more praise), extremely ornate rhyming prose on the virtues of the work, and verse composed by the corrector celebrating the completion of the task, with the numerical value of the poem's last hemistich(s) adding up to the date on which the work was completed (a chronogram; see chapter 2). Such colophons typically contain no or only vague information on the manuscripts used for the print, and they do not attempt to contextualize the work meaningfully in its time, place, or genre.

The conventions of modern academic citation have sometimes led these correctors to be identified as editors (as Franz Rosenthal, for example, does in the introduction to his translation of the *Muqaddima* with reference to al-Hūrīnī).[79] However, this identification conceals the differences in the respective roles of the *muṣaḥḥiḥ* and the *muḥaqqiq*, or editor proper, a role that is attested only after 1911 and that is discussed in detail in chapter 5. More commonly, correctors are simply left out of bibliographic citations (as indeed they are in most references in this book's bibliography), which reinforces their obscurity.

The term *muṣaḥḥiḥ* as an occupational designation seems to have entered use alongside the adoption of print. It is tempting to see it as a simple translation of the European occupational title of the corrector (and its parallels in other European languages).[80] However, the term has its roots in Arabic written culture of the manuscript age: the verb "to correct" (*ṣaḥḥaḥa*) and the related verbal noun "correction" (*taṣḥīḥ*) are classical terms used for the task of weeding out mistakes from manuscript copies. For example, on the autograph copy of the *Muqaddima* mentioned earlier, Ibn Khaldūn wrote the following note: "I have compared it [against the original] and corrected it [*ṣaḥḥaḥtuhā*], and there is no copy more correct than this one. [This note was] written by its author, ʿAbd al-Raḥmān b. Khaldūn."[81]

It is important to remember that correctors in the age of print were not independent scholars but rather employees of the press who carried out necessary steps in the printing of any book, whether a classical or contemporary Arabic work or a translation from another language. The task of the corrector was primarily one of proofreading. First the handwritten script that formed

[78] Ibn Khaldūn, *al-Muqaddima* (MS Taymūr 355); see Badawī, *Muʾallafāt Ibn Khaldūn*, 59. The autograph he mentions is now located in Istanbul's Süleymaniye Library.

[79] Franz Rosenthal, introduction to Ibn Khaldūn, *The Muqaddimah*, x.

[80] On the European corrector, see Grafton, *Culture of Correction*.

[81] MS Atıf Efendi 1936, fol. 1a; Badawī, *Muʾallafāt Ibn Khaldūn*, 101.

the archetype for typesetting the pages had to be checked for errors, and then the typeset pages had to be checked against the script. Finally, when the base manuscript contained corrupted sections, the corrector had to do what he could to piece together the missing or problematic passages in order to produce a readable text.

The first known account of the role of the corrector in the printing of books was written in early 1930s India by the Yemeni corrector ʿAbd al-Raḥmān al-Muʿallimī (1895–1966).[82] While al-Muʿallimī's description obviously postdates the introduction of print in the Arabic world by a century, it can still serve as a useful guide to the general procedures that shaped the printing process. Al-Muʿallimī describes three stages of correction. At the beginning of the printing process, a new manuscript copy, which al-Muʿallimī calls the "draft copy" (*al-musawwada*), is made on the basis of an existing manuscript, the "source" (*al-aṣl*). The first step of correction is the collation (*taṣḥīḥ al-muqābala*) of the draft copy and the source to ensure that the former is an accurate reproduction of the latter. For this purpose, a lector reads out the source manuscript while the corrector follows the reading in the draft copy, correcting any errors along the way. The second step, which al-Muʿallimī calls "true" or "scholarly" correcting (*taṣḥīḥ ḥaqīqī* or *taṣḥīḥ ʿilmī*), involves comparing other manuscripts of the work with the draft copy in order to incorporate into the latter any superior readings, additional information, or helpful marginalia that the other manuscripts may contain. Once a set of pages has been typeset, proofs are printed, and these are again read by a lector to the corrector to allow the latter to spot any errors introduced in typesetting. This third step of correction al-Muʿallimī terms "print correction" (*taṣḥīḥ maṭbaʿī*). These different stages are sometimes reflected in the terms used for various correcting functions in early prints. For example, in the first edition of al-Jurjānī's *Dalāʾil al-iʿjāz, taṣḥīḥ al-aṣl* denotes the preparation of the source manuscript and thus corresponds most closely to what would later come to be called editing, whereas *taṣḥīḥ al-ṭabʿ* refers to proofreading at the typesetting stage.[83]

Al-Muʿallimī stresses that steps one and three (collating the draft manuscript copy against the existing source manuscript and collating the printed proofs against the draft copy) differ in nature from the second type of correction (comparison of the draft copy with other manuscripts). The former activities follow the rules and procedures that traditionally governed the work of scribes, aimed at the accurate reproduction of the original work and the avoidance of a variety of copyist errors. The task of the copyist or cor-

[82] The following description is derived from al-Muʿallimī's essay "Uṣūl al-taṣḥīḥ al-ʿilmī," in *Majmūʿ rasāʾil fī al-taḥqīq wa-taṣḥīḥ al-nuṣūṣ*, 17–31.

[83] Al-Jurjānī, *Dalāʾil al-iʿjāz* (ʿAbduh and al-Shinqīṭī ed.), title page. Al-Muʿallimī's theory of scholarly correcting is discussed further in chapter 8.

rector is mechanical, and he is not permitted to interfere with the text in order to improve it on the basis of his own knowledge of the subject matter or the Arabic language. By contrast, the second stage, that of "scholarly" correction, involves a different level of interaction with the text, calling for judgment (*ijtihād*) and intervention (*taṣarruf*) on the part of the corrector. At this stage the corrector takes an active role in establishing the text by deciding which textual variants to omit (in the case of obvious copyist mistakes), which to use as the main text, and which to record in the margin as possible or otherwise illuminating alternative readings.[84]

I am not aware of a similar theoretical account of the work of correctors in mid-nineteenth-century Egypt, but a comparable outline can be reconstructed from the fruits of their labor—that is, the printed books—and the surviving documents they used in the process of producing these books. The following is such an outline of Naṣr al-Hūrīnī's efforts to prepare the printed text of Ibn Khaldūn's *Muqaddima*.

Like Rifāʿa al-Ṭahṭāwī, al-Hūrīnī had studied at al-Azhar before being sent to France as the imam of an educational mission, in his case in 1844. After his return to Egypt, al-Ṭahṭāwī employed him as a translator at his School of Languages; subsequently al-Hūrīnī found employment as a corrector at the Bulaq press.[85] Parallel to his work at the press, he also worked for the wealthy book collector ʿAbd al-Ḥamīd Nāfiʿ Bey (discussed in the following chapter) to correct and annotate the manuscript copies Nāfiʿ commissioned for his personal library.[86] Al-Hūrīnī's professional life thus straddled the continuing manuscript culture and the nascent but rapidly growing print culture.

Al-Hūrīnī's first task as the corrector of Ibn Khaldūn's *Muqaddima* was to find a suitable manuscript or manuscripts to serve as the basis of the printed text.[87] By the mid-nineteenth century, most copies of the work were held in the libraries of Istanbul, though the oldest of them had in fact been produced in Egypt; some had been transferred from Cairo to Istanbul as early as in the sixteenth century.[88] Today, at least eleven manuscript copies of the *Muqaddima* can be found in Egyptian collections at the Egyptian National

[84]In the nineteenth century, prints produced in the Middle East followed the manuscript tradition by placing notes in the margins rather than in footnotes. This practice began to change in the twentieth century with the adoption of moveable type, but lithographs retained the aesthetic and layout of manuscripts. See Gacek, *Arabic Manuscripts*, 177–79.

[85]Al-Ziriklī, *al-Aʿlām* (2002 ed.), 8:29; al-Fiqī, *al-Azhar wa-atharuh*, 127–30.

[86]See, for example, the copy of a fifteenth-century geographical work on Egypt commissioned by Nāfiʿ and corrected and annotated by al-Hūrīnī: Ibn al-Jīʿān, *Kitāb mā bi-iqlīm Miṣr*, e.g., p. 16.

[87]For al-Rāzī's Quranic commentary, whose editing and publication al-Ṭahṭāwī also initiated, nine copies were gathered to solve the seriously difficult textual problems posed by that work; see the corrector's cryptic comments in al-Rāzī, *Mafātīḥ al-ghayb*, 6:688.

[88]These include the abovementioned MS Atıf Efendi 1936; see Franz Rosenthal, introduction to Ibn Khaldūn, *The Muqaddimah*, lxvii, xciv.

Library and the library of al-Azhar,[89] but neither library existed at the time when al-Hūrīnī set out to edit the work, and he seems to have been able to access only two copies. The absence of a central library or a catalog that could be consulted to locate manuscript copies was a key obstacle to efforts to print books that had fallen out of the literary tradition. As in Renaissance Europe, printers had to make decisions to print works without a comprehensive overview of the surviving manuscripts. In a written culture that had come to focus on either recent or very widely transmitted works, reconstructing rare and almost unknown texts posed a challenge. As al-Hūrīnī's fellow corrector Muḥammad Quṭṭa al-ʿAdawī (1795–1864) noted in 1853 in his colophon to al-Maqrīzī's *Khiṭaṭ* regarding that work, "The shroud of forgetting had descended over it, and its copies had become scarce in our lands, to the extent that it was almost not to be found. Its numbers are few; it has been abandoned and is no longer in use."[90]

A manuscript of the *Muqaddima* produced in 1854 (AH 1270) that survives in the Egyptian National Library clearly played a role in the Bulaq edition. This was probably what al-Muʿallimī called the draft copy (*musawwada*), because it also contains copious collation notes by al-Hūrīnī, including the information that he completed his reading of the manuscript in the month of Rajab in AH 1272 (March 1856). The inferior quality of the copy indicates that it was based on a recent manuscript, and al-Hūrīnī was thus required to correct numerous spelling mistakes, relying on his universally acknowledged mastery of Arabic. However, he also consulted a second copy of the work. On the margin of the printed text, al-Hūrīnī noted that the "the copy of a Moroccan dignitary" contained an addition to the introduction in which Ibn Khaldūn dedicates the work to the ruler of Tunis.[91] This alternative version of the text is shorter than the Fez version, on which al-Hūrīnī's draft copy was based (the latter is called the Fārisiyya version, because it was dedicated to the Marinid ruler Abū Fāris, r. 767–74/1366–72). There is also a third version of the text, dedicated to the Mamluk ruler Barqūq (r. 784–801/1382–99), which survives in Istanbul in a copy authorized by Ibn Khaldūn himself; this copy formed the basis of Quatremère's edition of the *Muqaddima*. But al-Hūrīnī had no access to manuscripts of this third version.[92] Although al-Hūrīnī distinguished between the Tunis and Fez versions, he did not conceive of them as historically distinct recensions but rather merged them into a combined hybrid of his own. In general, he mentioned the Tunis variants in the mar-

[89] Badawī, *Mu'allafāt Ibn Khaldūn*, 43–100; however, many of these were in fact copied in the mid-nineteenth century.

[90] Al-Maqrīzī, *al-Khiṭaṭ*, 2:520.

[91] Ibn Khaldūn, *al-Muqaddima* (Bulaq ed.), 6–8.

[92] On the different versions, see Badawī, *Mu'allafāt Ibn Khaldūn*, 37–40; and the critical edition of the earliest and latest recensions of the *Muqaddima* by ʿAbd al-Salām al-Shidādī (2005).

gins of the primary Fez text, but in one case he incorporated a whole chapter that was present in the Tunis version but absent from the Fez version, arguing that it rendered the text more logical.[93]

The numerous instances of textual corruption in his copy of the Fez version led al-Hūrīnī to look for help beyond Egypt in order to reconstruct the text. There is a two-page document drafted by al-Hūrīnī that lists textual problems in the *Muqaddima* and other parts of Ibn Khaldūn's history caused by lacunae in the copy available in Cairo. Al-Hūrīnī introduced the list with the following request: "This text lists the gaps in the copies of Ibn Khaldūn's history found in Egypt, in the hope that they will be filled in from the Tunisian shores."[94] It is not clear whether al-Hūrīnī in fact ever sent his list to Tunisia, nor whether he issued other, similar requests, but the problems listed in the document remain unfixed in the text that was eventually printed in Bulaq.[95] While the practice of integrating two distinct recensions of a text into a hybrid version, as al-Hūrīnī did, is philologically unacceptable today, many of the remaining textual problems in the Hūrīnī edition are products of the limited means at his disposal. In the absence both of properly cataloged libraries in Egypt and of institutional interlocutors abroad, the deficiencies of the draft copy could not be fully remedied. Since Ibn Khaldūn was of North African descent, al-Hūrīnī sought assistance from that region—examining a copy of the work in the possession of a Moroccan living in Egypt and drafting a request for assistance to someone in Tunisia. There is no evidence that he attempted to access any of the excellent copies of the *Muqaddima* available in Istanbul. He did, however, benefit from Ottoman scholarship on Ibn Khaldūn by drawing on the Turkish translation of the *Muqaddima* by Meḥmed Ṣāḥib Pīrīzāde (d. 1749), which was also published in Bulaq shortly thereafter,[96] particularly for help on the perennially difficult subject of non-Arabic place-names.[97]

Another problem inherent to the process of deciphering Arabic manuscripts is the ambiguity of the Arabic textual skeleton, in which many letters are distinguished from one another only through the placement of dots above or below the script. These dots are easily overlooked or misplaced; they may fade or be erased by damage; and many older texts do not include them in the first place or do so only erratically. For example, the numbers seven and nine are differentiated only by dots. Al-Hūrīnī's copy of the *Muqaddima* claimed that al-Bukhārī's ninth-century hadith compilation contained nine thousand hadith reports, but al-Hūrīnī noted in the margin that another

[93]Ibn Khaldūn, *al-Muqaddima* (Bulaq ed.), 110.

[94]The document is appended to the end of Ibn Khaldūn, *al-Muqaddima* (MS Taymūr 612) and reproduced by Badawī in *Mu'allafāt Ibn Khaldūn*, 64–71.

[95]See, for example, Ibn Khaldūn, *al-Muqaddima* (Bulaq ed.), 43.

[96]Fleischer, "Royal Authority, Dynastic Cyclism, and 'Ibn Khaldûnism,'" 200; Ibn Khaldūn, *Tercüme-yi Mukaddeme-yi İbn Haldun*.

[97]Ibn Khaldūn, *al-Muqaddima* (Bulaq ed.), 150 and 151.

work he had seen—al-Nawawī's thirteenth-century commentary on Muslim b. al-Ḥajjāj's ninth-century hadith collection—gave the number of reports in al-Bukhārī as seven thousand.[98] Al-Hūrīnī decided to let nine thousand stand in the main body of the text in spite of its divergence from the far more authoritative work by al-Nawawī (whose figure of seven thousand in fact is the approximate number of reports in al-Bukhārī's collection).

Al-Hūrīnī was confronting a dilemma born of what al-Muʿallimī, in his theoretical treatise on the corrector's work, would call the three concerns of a corrector: correspondence with reality, correspondence with the author's intention, and correspondence with the manuscript (see also chapter 8). Correspondence with reality would in this case have required acknowledgment of the fact that al-Bukhārī's collection contains seven thousand hadith reports. Correspondence with the author's intention would have consisted of reproducing Ibn Khaldūn's opinion on the matter—he might have been under the faulty impression that al-Bukhārī recorded nine thousand reports, possibly because of a copyist mistake in his own reading. Finally, correspondence with the manuscript meant following the wording of the draft copy, whether it reflected the author's intention or a later copyist error.[99] Al-Muʿallimī noted that these three concerns were often contradictory, but he argued that a printed book should seek to do justice to all three by recording as much information as could be gleaned from the available manuscripts and the expertise of the corrector. Presentation of this information in marginal notes or footnotes would allow readers to evaluate the editorial decisions made by the corrector, thus not leaving them at the corrector's mercy.

Such information was not, however, regularly provided in the Bulaq prints. Al-Hūrīnī's marginal notes in the 534-page print of the *Muqaddima* number barely two dozen; some record variants from the secondary manuscript or the Turkish translation, while others provide linguistic and other explanatory notes. The resulting edition served as the basis of all subsequent prints of the work in the Arab world until al-Shidādī's 2005 edition, but it was also subjected to significant criticism. For example, Aḥmad Shākir (1892–1958), one of the most important editors of the first half of the twentieth century (discussed further in chapter 8), included the following "advice to the reader" with reference to the Bulaq print of the *Muqaddima* in a footnote of his edition of Aḥmad b. Ḥanbal's hadith collection:

> This chapter of Ibn Khaldūn's *Muqaddima* is full of mistakes concerning both the names of individuals and the critiques leveled at their reliability, so let no one rely on this [work] for transmission. I do not believe that Ibn Khaldūn would have made such mistakes! Rather, in my opinion, they are the result of

[98] Ibn Khaldūn, *al-Muqaddima* (Bulaq ed.), 369.

[99] Al-Muʿallimī, *Āthār al-Muʿallimī*, 23:39.

copyist mistakes and correctors' negligence. I am still amazed that they could elude the knowledgeable Shaykh Naṣr al-Hūrīnī, God's mercy on him, who corrected this print at the Bulaq press.[100]

In defense of al-Hūrīnī, it must be noted that the reference works Shākir had at his disposal to call out al-Hūrīnī's mistakes were printed only in the decades after al-Hūrīnī's death in 1874, and we do not know whether any of them were available to him in manuscript form. Judging by al-Hūrīnī's marginal notes on the *Muqaddima*, he either had very limited access to reference works, especially comprehensive ones, or he lacked the time to make full use of them; he was, after all, an employee with a schedule of tasks to complete on a deadline.

The limitations under which correctors such as al-Hūrīnī worked are made clearer in the unusually rich colophon that al-Hūrīnī added to his 1866 edition of Ibn Shākir's (d. 764/1363) *Fawāt al-Wafayāt* (Addendum to "The obituaries [of eminent men]"). Al-Hūrīnī mentions the financer of the edition, then outlines the difficulties he encountered in locating complete and accurate manuscripts of the work, and finally describes his chance discovery of a manuscript in the Hijaz that allowed him to solve the problems in the manuscripts available in Cairo. I have translated the entire colophon below, omitting only the more elaborate and largely untranslatable eruptions of rhyming praise:

The master of arts and sciences, his excellency Muḥammad Pasha ʿĀrif, has been successful in reviving the fields of literature, linguistics, and exegesis through the multiplication of the [available] texts on these [subjects] and their dissemination through accurate prints. He has been particularly enthusiastic about the discipline of history, whose literature was investigated by the author of the [bibliographical work] *Kashf al-ẓunūn* and found to reach 1,300 works, among them this *Addendum*. Therefore, he [Muḥammad ʿĀrif] became interested in printing it after printing [Ibn Khallikān's] *Wafayāt* [*al-aʿyān*, "The obituaries of eminent men"]; but we did not manage to find [this book] except in an incomplete copy in the endowment of Muḥammad Bey Abū al-Dhahab[101] and another copy in the endowment of the Wafāʾiyya order,[102] and both copies contain copyist mistakes. Nevertheless, he insisted on beginning its printing at his own expense at the ʿĀmira press in Bulaq, Cairo, [a place of] blossoming virtues, its harbor characterized by justice, bestowing its bounty on the people, in the cooling shadow of the most generous felicity, the greatest khedive, lord of Egypt and unicum of the age, his grace, our Efendi, protected by God's providence—Ismāʿīl, son of Ibrāhīm, son of Muḥammad ʿAlī . . . [three

[100] Aḥmad b. Ḥanbal, *Musnad Aḥmad*, 3:493.

[101] On this institution, see Crecelius, "*Waqfīyah* of Muḥammad Bey Abū al-Dhahab."

[102] This library was part of the Wafāʾiyya mosque, built by ʿAbd al-Ḥamīd I and completed in 1199/1784.

> more lines of florid praise]. So I began correcting with the utmost effort the atrocious misspellings, until divine providence assisted me by directing me to the lands of the Hijaz to fulfill my legal obligation [to undertake the Ḥajj pilgrimage] and to visit the lord of the prophetic abode [i.e., Muḥammad's grave in Medina] in the year 1282 [1866 CE]. The head of this printing house, a man of great virtue, his excellency Ḥusayn Bey Ḥasanī . . . [a line of rhyming, untranslatable praise] . . . assisted me in this [endeavor] and agreed to charge the virtuous and learned litterateur Shaykh Zayn al-Dīn al-Ṣayyād al-Marṣafī with correcting the contracted text while I was away. In the noble city of Mecca I then found a Levantine copy [of the text] originating from Hama that had been copied from the autograph copy, and I borrowed it from the noble Miḥḍār al-ʿAlawī, may God reward him for the sake of this collation. So I collated against it the contracted printed [copy] from beginning to end, line by line, investing serious effort, with no obvious mistake [left] in the whole book. So praise be to God for guidance to what is correct. This work was completed at the beginning of Rajab 1283 of the Hijra [November 1866].[103]

The first interesting point in this description is its mention of Ḥājjī Khalīfa's seventeenth-century *Kashf al-ẓunūn* as a bibliographical reference work. We encountered the work already in chapter 1 as the archetype of ʿAlī Mubārak's imagined complete Orientalist library, and its importance to the printing movement cannot be overestimated: together with certain other works, such as Ibn al-Nadīm's tenth-century *Fihrist*, it provided Arab intellectuals and correctors such as al-Hūrīnī with a map to the ocean of Arabic manuscripts by situating works within their times and genres and by charting the intellectual affiliations of their authors, which the postclassical teaching tradition had forgotten or suppressed. The second noteworthy piece of information concerns the commissioner (*multazim*) of the print. This was Muḥammad ʿĀrif Pasha, a wealthy and politically powerful individual whose interest in the revival of Islamic literary classics led him to found Egypt's first scholarly society, described in chapter 4. It was ʿĀrif's insistence on publishing the *Addendum* that prompted the start of the project, even though only fragmentary or otherwise severely deficient manuscripts of the work could be found in Cairo. The Egyptian National Library had not yet been established, and the fact that al-Hūrīnī nonetheless managed to locate two copies of the work in the city's endowed libraries attests to considerable effort, since the libraries were scattered and disorganized, and information about and access to their collections was highly dependent on personal connections and expertise. The colophon also documents a stroke of good fortune that had a significant impact on the project, namely, al-Hūrīnī's fortuitous encounter, during the Ḥajj pilgrimage, with the owner of a copy of the

[103] Ibn Shākir, *Fawāt al-Wafayāt*, 2:411–12.

Addendum that had been checked against an autograph and the latter's lending of that copy to al-Hūrīnī for the purpose of collating it with his soon-to-be-printed version. This encounter, in turn, was made possible by the leave granted to al-Hūrīnī by the head of the press, Ḥusayn Bey Ḥasanī, who engaged another corrector, al-Marṣafī, to continue work on the project in al-Hūrīnī's absence.

Even though al-Hūrīnī is primarily remembered as a corrector at the government press in Bulaq, he also worked on projects for other presses. Probably most important of these was his correction of al-Suyūṭī's unrivaled sixteenth-century handbook of Quranic studies, *al-Itqān fī ʿulūm al-Qurʾān* (Mastery of the sciences of the Quran). The printing was undertaken in 1863 by one of the earliest private printing presses, the Kastaliyya Press,[104] with a relatively large planned print run of 3,300 copies.[105] The Kastaliyya publishing house was still a new venture at the time, which may explain why it had to hire a corrector from the government press, and the press's inexperience is evident in al-Hūrīnī's addendum to the print, in which he bemoans the catastrophic quality of the book's typesetting. It appears that al-Hūrīnī had corrected each quire of pages (consisting of sixteen octavo sheets)[106] as it was printed; when he reached number nineteen, he noticed that the typesetters had omitted almost an entire quire, requiring a reprint of three quires. All the other mistakes that he found were included in a twelve-page list of errata included in the printed book, and al-Hūrīnī suggests in the addendum that the reader use this list to make the required corrections to the main text. This suggests that the Kastaliyya Press's prints did not go through a proofs stage, in which typesetting errors could be identified by the corrector and corrected for the final print. Skipping proofs clearly yielded significant savings in terms of materials and wages, but it also significantly reduced the quality of the final product. The establishment of private presses thus exacerbated the financial constraints on printing, as private presses were under pressure to make a profit and therefore were willing to cut corners and compromise the scholarly standards of the government press in Bulaq.[107]

The project for which al-Hūrīnī is most famous, however, is his work on al-Fīrūzābādī's (d. 817/1414) *al-Qāmūs al-muḥīṭ* (The all-encompassing lexicon). The *Qāmūs*, one of the most important Arabic lexica, had already been printed in Calcutta in 1817, and the Bulaq press had published its Turkish translation

[104] On the Kastaliyya Press, see Schwartz, "Meaningful Mediums," 293–324; Schwartz, "Political Economy." The form of the press's name varied across its publications. Another work that al-Hūrīnī corrected for this press was al-Shaʿrānī's *Kashf al-ghumma* (published in 1864).

[105] See al-Suyūṭī, *al-Itqān*, 2:1.

[106] Known as *malzama*, pl. *malāzim*; see Wehr and Cowan, *Dictionary of Modern Written Arabic*, 1015.

[107] On the early history of private presses in Egypt, see Ṣābāt, *Tārīkh al-ṭibāʿa*, 145–268.

as early as in 1834,[108] but the print overseen by al-Hūrīnī and Muḥammad Quṭṭa al-ʿAdawī, completed in 1855 or 1856 (AH 1272), was a landmark scholarly achievement.[109] There were three reasons for the high quality of this edition. First, al-Hūrīnī was well trained in lexicography; his mastery of the subject was recognized even by the leading Orientalists of his time.[110] Second, lexicography was a discipline with a venerable pedigree in Egypt, and interest in the subject had further intensified with the great translation movement inaugurated by al-Ṭahṭāwī's School of Languages, where al-Hūrīnī had served as a teacher and a translator. And third, several extensive commentaries on the *Qāmūs* were available, written by Badr al-Dīn al-Qarāfī (d. 1008/1599), ʿAbd al-Raʾūf al-Mināwī (d. 1031/1622), and Murtaḍā al-Zabīdī. These commentators had enjoyed access to high-quality manuscripts and, at least in the case of al-Zabīdī, had been able to produce something approaching a critical edition, including notes on variants. While these manuscripts must also have contained copyist mistakes, the fact that the commentaries expanded on the text of the *Qāmūs* meant that any mistakes were much easier to spot.

The resulting printed text is highly accurate. Nevertheless, in terms of appearance, it looks more like a continuation of the premodern manuscript tradition than like a modern edition. Although al-Hūrīnī included in his introduction elements similar to those of modern editorial introductions, such as discussion of earlier literature on the subject, biographical information on the author, and explanation of the author's terminology,[111] the bulk of the introduction consists of a bona fide traditional commentary on al-Fīrūzābādī's own introduction to the *Qāmūs*, taking individual words and explicating them.[112] Al-Hūrīnī and Quṭṭa al-ʿAdawī also added extensive comments to the text, but again, these took the traditional form of marginalia rather than footnotes. Some of these comments are quotations of earlier commentaries; others are the correctors' own and clearly identified as such. The Hūrīnī/Quṭṭa al-ʿAdawī version of the *Qāmūs* went through numerous reprints[113] and spawned several monographs that fruitfully critiqued the edition and its content.[114]

Beyond his work as a corrector, al-Hūrīnī also authored books on various topics.[115] The sole book of his that was printed (and subsequently reprinted

[108] Al-Fīrūzābādī, *el-Okyanus ül-basit.*

[109] Al-Hūrīnī corrected the entries from *alif* to *ṭāʾ* and those from *nūn* to the end; Quṭṭa al-ʿAdawī corrected the entries from *ṭāʾ* to *nūn.*

[110] See Fischer, "Muzhir or Mizhar?," 550.

[111] Al-Hūrīnī, "Fawāʾid sharīfa."

[112] Al-Hūrīnī, "Sharḥ al-dībāja." Al-Hūrīnī also authored at least one traditional gloss himself: *Ḥāshiyat al-Hūrīnī ʿalā Sharḥ al-Yūsī ʿalā risālatihi fī ʿilm al-bayān.*

[113] It was reissued in 1865, 1872, 1884, 1913, and 1925.

[114] See, for example, Aḥmad Taymūr, *Taṣḥīḥ al-Qāmūs*; al-Shidyāq, *al-Jāsūs.*

[115] See al-Ziriklī, *al-Aʿlām* (2002 ed.), 8:29.

several times) was his work on orthographic problems.[116] Al-Hūrīnī wrote the book explicitly to serve as a handbook for printing workshops, explaining that although the subject of orthography had been discussed in the classical literature, no comprehensive and systematic handbook had ever been written. The classical works on which he drew for this book had not yet been printed, but we know that he had himself copied Ibn Qutayba's ninth-century treatise *Adab al-kātib* (The know-how of the scribe), the oldest work that he mentions in his list of classical treatments of the topic.[117] Despite the fact that Arabic orthography had remained overall remarkably stable in the 1,200 years before al-Hūrīnī, the manuscript tradition still contained significant variant spellings. Al-Hūrīnī's book laid down the orthographic rules that he had systematically collected as a scholar and a corrector steeped in the manuscript tradition, reflecting the way in which his identity and methods as a corrector were essentially extensions of the scribal practices of the manuscript age. It was the next generation of editors who would systematize modern orthography (with innovations such as punctuation marks) and introduce new practices and standards into the editing and printing of classical texts.

* * *

Print was adopted in Egypt not to replace the scribal culture that maintained the Arabo-Islamic literary edifice, but rather to meet the needs of modern administration for uniform instruction and communication. However, once a printing press had been set up, workers trained, and production procedures put in place, it was logical for the state to rent out the machinery's unused capacity to private individuals. Booksellers began to shift their trade from manuscript books to printed ones by commissioning prints of bestselling curriculum texts and familiar works of popular literature, genres for which a known market existed. But soon the new technology was also harnessed for a different use: to rescue from oblivion works that had fallen out of the active tradition. Printing allowed individuals with reformist agendas to bypass the slow-turning wheels of scribal reproduction and to bring forgotten works quickly to a large audience. So, while Ḥasan al-ʿAṭṭār in the early 1820s still had to rely on a handwritten copy of Ibn Khaldūn's *Muqaddima* to teach the text to his closest students, a generation later his star student, Rifāʿa al-Ṭahṭāwī, used his influential position in the Egyptian state to have the *Muqaddima* printed, making widely available a work of which a mere handful of manuscript copies existed in Egypt at the time.

[116] Al-Hūrīnī, *al-Maṭāliʿ al-Naṣriyya*, published for the first time in 1859.

[117] Al-Hūrīnī, *al-Maṭāliʿ al-Naṣriyya*, 30–35. Al-Hūrīnī's personal, handwritten copy of Ibn Qutayba's work was later used as the basis for its first edition; see Ibn Qutayba, *Adab al-kātib*, 229.

The people in charge of overseeing the accurate printing of books—whether newly written, translated, or older works—were the correctors. The procedural diligence of the correcting process at the Bulaq press (which often contrasted sharply with the more erratic practices of private presses) produced reliable editions of works that were known to nineteenth-century scholarship and attested by numerous manuscript copies. However, the printing of older works that were not part of the postclassical canon and survived in few, often ancient or corrupted copies posed significant challenges to the correctors—challenges that they lacked adequate means to resolve. First, information about extant manuscripts and their locations was difficult to obtain in the absence of easily accessible and systematically cataloged manuscript libraries (the subsequent establishment of such institutions is described in chapter 1). Second, reliable reference works for specialized vocabulary, especially names and places, were scarce. And third, a critical philology had yet to be developed to help solve the myriad textual problems (see chapter 8). But the most fundamental question confronting the printing of classical Islamic works was not how to establish the texts themselves, fraught with difficulty though that process was. It was whether there would be a reading public large enough and interested enough in the classical literature to make the enormous project of locating, editing, and printing these texts worthwhile. This newly emerging constituency is the subject of the following chapter.

CHAPTER 4

A New Generation of Book Lovers

In the early years of its adoption, printing by and large reproduced the existing textual canon. But major societal changes were afoot, and soon the technology of print began to be used to publish very different kinds of works, works that had been forgotten and even almost lost. In Egypt, the agents of this wave of nontraditional book printing and editing represented a new class of intellectuals: elite bibliophiles and scholars who had at most one foot in the old scholarly tradition and the other in the structures and discourses of the rapidly modernizing Egyptian state. This new class of scribal intellectuals inaugurated a culture that valorized high-level Arabic, rare manuscripts, and philological accuracy.

THE EGYPTIAN SCHOLARLY SOCIETY

By the 1860s, print had been in use for several decades in Egypt. Besides the state press in Bulaq, several private presses had sprung up, printing books, newspapers, and journals.[1] This was the heady reign of Muḥammad ʿAlī's sons Saʿīd (r. 1854–63) and Ismāʿīl (r. 1863–79), which saw Egypt transfigured by ambitious modernization projects including the construction of railways, telegraph lines, and, most iconically, the Suez Canal—projects that promised a strong and modern Egypt but unwittingly laid the basis for foreign influence and invasion by necessitating large and eventually unsustainable loans from European banks.[2] Behind these grand infrastructure projects, the Egyptian state was undergoing a fundamental transformation from an essentially premodern administrative structure headed by the extended household of the ruler to an organized bureaucracy of civil servants, most of whom were trained in the newly established public school system or in other nontraditional educational institutions.[3] The curricula in these schools, and thus the intellectual backgrounds of the civil servants, were very different from the

[1]For a survey of private presses in Egypt and the Levant in the second half of the nineteenth century, see Glaß, "Die *naḥda* und ihre Technik," 64–76.

[2]See Owen, *Middle East in the World Economy*.

[3]See Fahmy, *All the Pasha's Men*.

postclassical tradition of Islamic scholarship.[4] Most importantly, they typically incorporated works translated from European languages and encouraged students to explore writings beyond those taught in school, including classical literature.[5] The graduates from these schools belonged to the first generation of Egyptians to grow up in a world where printed books, and latterly newspapers and journals, were the proper vehicle for exchanging and spreading ideas in society.[6] The overwhelming dominance of printed literature in this period is illustrated by the combined print run of books published in just six years between 1872 and 1878: at 361,815 individual books, it was already many times larger than the entire corpus of manuscripts in Egypt at the time.[7] These graduates increasingly took up positions of influence in Egypt and subsequently played an active role in setting the country's cultural course.

It was in this intellectual climate that the Egyptian Scholarly Society (Jamʿiyyat al-Maʿārif al-Miṣriyya) was launched in 1868. The society was founded by Muḥammad ʿĀrif Pasha (d. after 1871), a high government official encountered in chapter 3 as the private commissioner of the 1866 print of Ibn Shākir's *Fawāt al-Wafayāt*, and it was under the symbolic tutelage of Tawfīq Pasha (1852–92), at the time the heir apparent and later the khedive of Egypt. The society's objective was to preserve important works through print—"one of the most potent means of protecting them against loss"—and to share them with "those seeking enlightenment through the light of knowledge."[8] It took the form of a cooperative: to become a member, one had to purchase a share, which then granted the member a discount on the works that the society published. The printing itself was carried out by the state press in Bulaq, the private Wahbiyya Press, or later the society's own press.[9] Hundreds joined the society in its first year, and by July 1870 the society had 1,100 members as well as representatives in Cairo, Alexandria, various cities

[4]Heyworth-Dunne, *History of Education in Modern Egypt*, chaps. 2–5.

[5]In the 1890s, the supervisor of Egyptian state schools explicitly requested a guide to printed books to assist students in finding Arabic books to read; see van Dyck, *Iktifāʾ al-qanūʿ bi-mā huwa maṭbūʿ*, 6.

[6]The collective mental transformation enabled by print is analyzed in Anderson, *Imagined Communities.*

[7]For the print run, see Sarkīs, *Muʿjam al-maṭbūʿāt*, 1: *alif.* According to Sayyid, in *Dār al-Kutub al-Miṣriyya*, 30–31, in the early twentieth century, the Egyptian National Library contained fewer than 20,000 manuscripts. He puts the total number of Arabic manuscripts in Egypt today at about 125,000.

[8]Al-Manīnī, *Sharḥ al-Yamīnī*, 1:[243] (page 6 of the insert). Timothy Mitchell misinterprets this society as "perhaps modelled on Lord Brougham's Society for the Diffusion of Useful Knowledge, the organisation set up to teach the values of self-discipline and industriousness to the working class of England"; see Mitchell, *Colonising Egypt*, 90.

[9]Al-Rāfiʿī, *ʿAṣr Ismāʿīl*, 1:245; Jurjī Zaydān, *Tārīkh ādāb al-lugha al-ʿarabiyya*, 4:80.

in the Nile delta, and Istanbul.[10] Considering both Egypt's relatively small population at the time (around six million) and its low literacy rate (perhaps about 5 percent), this is a very large number,[11] particularly for a society that primarily published works that were at least half a millennium old. The society's publications included al-Jāḥiẓ's ninth-century literary smorgasbord *al-Bayān wa-l-tabyīn* (The book of eloquence and expression), a twelfth-century commentary on the eleventh-century poet al-Maʿarrī's early work *Saqt al-zand* (Spark from the flint),[12] a biographical dictionary of the Prophet Muḥammad's companions written in the thirteenth century,[13] and a literary and scientific anthology from thirteenth-century Andalusia.[14] However, the society also printed more recent works, such as a gloss on Islamic law barely more than a century old, written by an otherwise unknown commentator.[15]

A near-complete membership list from 1870 provides a portrait of the likely audience for published classical works in this period.[16] The majority of the society's members were elite officials from all branches of the government and the ruling classes. They included members of the royal family, the Egyptian governor of Sudan, palace administrators, and bureaucrats from the ministries of finance, agriculture, and war, responsible for communications, railways, customs, and the police force. The second-largest group of subscribers consisted of individuals employed in occupations related to knowledge production, translation, and dissemination—teachers, correctors, writers, and editors of newspapers and journals. This group included the reformist intellectual Rifāʿa al-Ṭahṭāwī (on whom see chapter 3), the Levantine author and publisher Aḥmad Fāris al-Shidyāq,[17] the influential litterateur Ibrāhīm al-Muwayliḥī (1846–1906), several correctors at the Bulaq press, and the corrector at the military academy (Ḥasan al-Ṭawīl, about whom more later), as well as a translator of military works, the translator of Saʿdī's *Gulistān* from

[10] At some point still in 1868, the society had 384 members; see the membership roster printed in Ibn al-Athīr, *Usd al-ghāba*, 1:400. By December 1869, there were 980 members (Ibn al-Athīr, *Usd al-ghāba*, 4:438), and by July 1870, the number had risen to 1,100 according to the list included in the 1870 print of al-Balawī's *Kitāb Alif bāʾ*, 2:592. The information on representatives and my analysis of the society's members below is based on the membership list in al-Manīnī, *Sharḥ al-Yamīnī* (published in 1870), 1:[243–44] (pp. 6–18 of the insert), 417–19.

[11] McCarthy, "Nineteenth-Century Egyptian Population," 6; Issawi, *Economic History of the Middle East and North Africa*, 114; UNESCO, *World Illiteracy at Mid-Century*, 52.

[12] Khuwayyī, *Sharḥ al-tanwīr ʿalā Saqt al-zand*.

[13] Ibn al-Athīr, *Usd al-ghāba*.

[14] Al-Balawī, *Kitāb Alif bāʾ*.

[15] Al-Shurunbulālī, *Fatḥ al-muʿīn ʿalā sharḥ Fatḥ al-Kanz*.

[16] Al-Manīnī, *Sharḥ al-Yamīnī*, 1:[243–44], 417–19.

[17] Al-Shidyāq's Jawāʾib Press in Istanbul printed numerous important classical works, such as al-Hamadhānī's *Maqāmāt* (discussed in chapter 6). See Roper, "Fāris al-Shidyāq and the Transition."

Persian into Arabic, and a lecturer at the college of medicine. The third-largest group consisted of holders of high office in religious institutions, such as imams of prominent mosques (the mosque at the Cairo fortress and the mosque of al-Ḥusayn), the current and two future shaykhs of al-Azhar,[18] the leader of the local guild of the descendants of the Prophet (*naqīb al-ashrāf*), and the judge of the city of Mansura. Other interesting subscribers included the son of Naṣr al-Hūrīnī, the corrector discussed at the end of chapter 3; the son of the prominent Azhari shaykh Muḥammad ʿIlīsh (mentioned in chapter 2); the Medina-based manuscript collector Amīn al-Madanī (on whom see chapter 1); a shaykh from Sudan; a number of booksellers; Egyptian expatriates living in Paris; several Christians, among them the Catholicos of Azbakiyya; "a foreigner named Augustus"; and the head dragomans of the French and the English.

The first noteworthy feature of this list is the marginal presence of the carriers of traditional Arabo-Islamic learning, the scholars (*ʿulamāʾ*). Beyond half a dozen elite shaykhs, the list includes a single person described as an Azhari student. The limited financial means of Azhari students and even teachers provides a partial explanation. In addition, the dominance of upper-level government officials may reflect the role of the society's founders' elite networks in the recruitment of new members, either through personal contacts or through the government newspaper *al-Waqāʾiʿ al-miṣriyya*, in which the society was advertised. However, even with these caveats, the stark near-absence of Azhari scholars among the society's members supports my earlier argument regarding the narrow and conservative horizons of the religious curriculum in this period, which discouraged any interest in the rediscovery of earlier works.

Most remarkably, the list indicates the emergence of a new constituency interested in classical literature and thought, and willing and able to pay for printed versions of classical works. These readers' education had either taken place outside the seminary-based postclassical curriculum in the newly established government schools or combined the traditional curriculum with explorations of new kinds of topics and fields through the study of European literature, translations, and newly printed works. The new constituency of readers was closely connected to the emerging modern state with its extensive and growing bureaucracy, but in a sense it also harked back to the past, as government scribes had historically played an important role in Arabic literature, Islamic thought, historiography, and other classical fields. However, gradual vernacularization in non-Arabic-speaking areas, accelerated by the Mongol invasion of the East in the thirteenth century and the Ottoman conquests of the Arabic-speaking lands in the sixteenth century, naturally

[18] Al-ʿArūsī (in office 1864–70), al-Anbābī (in office 1882–96), and Ḥassūna al-Nawawī (in office 1896–1900).

eroded the connection between government officials and the Arabic language.[19] Especially in an intellectual metropolis such as Istanbul, government scribes continued to write important works, but they rarely wrote in Arabic (with important exceptions, such as the magnificent seventeenth-century bibliography of the Ottoman scribe Ḥājjī Khalīfa). In the Arabic-speaking Ottoman provinces, meanwhile, scribal culture both declined on account of the loss of political independence and experienced a shift in favor of Perso-Turkish culture; an echo of this trend remains visible in the early output of the Bulaq press, in which Turkish and Persian works far outnumber Arabic literature.

ʿABD AL-ḤAMĪD NĀFIʿ AND THE RACE FOR MANUSCRIPTS

An illuminating example of this new scribal class of Egyptian bibliophiles (and here Egyptian is strictly a geographic term, as many of these individuals were immigrants from other provinces of the Ottoman Empire or descendants of recent immigrants) is ʿAbd al-Ḥamīd Nāfiʿ Bey (d. between 1861 and 1863),[20] the brother-in-law of Muḥammad ʿĀrif, the founder of the Egyptian Scholarly Society. The following biographical sketch of Nāfiʿ shows that he belonged to the same elite class of non-*ʿulamāʾ* as the members of the society, and indeed, much of the society's subsequent output was based on his personal library, which ʿĀrif inherited after Nāfiʿ's early death:

> His father was Khalīl Efendi, one of the very rich of Cairo, who owned a palace in Shubrā surrounded by gorgeous gardens. He grew up in Cairo, becoming enamored with literature when he was in his youth, spending much time with its masters, and benefiting greatly from their company. He also acquired a love of buying precious books and spent considerable sums in the process; so he gathered a great library through the purchase and transcription of books. He relied on Shaykh Naṣr al-Hūrīnī to collate and correct these copies.[21] His competition with other wealthy book buyers was legendary. It attracted booksellers who supplied him from faraway places, and he treated them generously and did not try to bargain, so his library became proverbial. He competed with ʿAbd al-Ghanī Fikrī, who could hardly keep up with him, despite being famous for paying high prices.

[19] See Aubin, *Émirs mongols et vizirs persans.*

[20] I could not ascertain Nāfiʿ's precise death date. According to Aḥmad Taymūr, Nāfiʿ died during the reign of Khedive Saʿīd (r. 1854–63), but he was still alive in 1861 when he had a manuscript copied (see Hirschler, *Medieval Arabic Historiography*, 118).

[21] Examples of manuscripts belonging to Nāfiʿ and corrected by al-Hūrīnī include Yaḥyā Ibn al-Jīʿān's *Kitāb mā bi-iqlīm Miṣr* and Ibn Qarqamās's *al-Ghayth al-murīʿ* (for which see Landberg, *Catalogue de manuscrits arabes*, 122).

Then he became involved with music; he authored an epistle on it and learned to play the *qānūn* well. He read extensively in Arabic literature and works of poetry and attended numerous poetic exchanges and discussions, to the point that he developed considerable literary ability. His house became a meeting place of the distinguished, scholars, and men of letters, who met almost every Friday night, challenging each other in poetry and discussing scholarly questions that stimulated the mind.

He formed a close friendship with Ibrāhīm Efendi Ṭāhir, a talented poet, and they kept each other's company faithfully and loyally until death separated them. They had taken to giving classical nicknames based on famous personalities and poets to people they met, taking care to match the nickname to the character of the person named, and Shaykh Aḥmad al-Faḥmāwī has assembled a large collection of these that contains many delightful anecdotes.

As for his publications, apart from his epistle on music, he wrote *Tārīkh aʿyān al-qarn al-thālith ʿashar wa-baʿḍ al-thānī ʿashar* ["The history of prominent individuals of the thirteenth and part of the twelfth centuries of the Hijra"], [the manuscript of] which was sold when his books were sold and is now housed in Leiden, the Netherlands. He also collected the poetic oeuvre of Ṣafwat Efendi al-Sāʿatī in abridged form.

He did not live long, dying as still a young man in the reign of the Khedive Saʿīd, and Muḥammad ʿĀrif Pasha, his brother-in-law, took charge of his books. These gave him rich literary material, which he printed for the Scholarly Society. [Later] they were scattered and sold.[22]

According to this biography, Nāfiʿ developed a passion for Arabic literature, especially poetry, and for music (the instrument he played, *qānūn*, indicates that his interest lay in Eastern rather than Western music). His family's wealth allowed him to become a patron of intellectual activity. He amassed a distinguished library through buying and copying; he employed the leading corrector of his age to ensure the accuracy of his copies; he financed the printing of several literary and scholarly works, including Ḥājjī Khalīfa's bibliography[23] and al-Shirbīnī's satirical commentary *Hazz al-quḥūf fī sharḥ qaṣīdat Abī Shādūf* (Brains confounded by the ode of Abū Shādūf expounded);[24] and he facilitated and participated in intellectual society by hosting a regular salon. Of course, literary salons had existed throughout Islamic history,[25] but what distinguished these new gatherings was the rise of Arabic vis-à-vis Persian and Turkish, a growing emphasis on clarity of

[22] Aḥmad Taymūr, *Aʿlām al-fikr al-islāmī*, 204–5.

[23] See the corrector's colophon in Ḥājjī Khalīfa, *Kashf al-ẓunūn* (Bulaq ed.), 2: 438. This was the first printing of the work in the Arab world.

[24] The other work is Ibn al-ʿAfīf al-Tilmisānī's *Dīwān al-shāb al-ẓarīf.*

[25] Ali, *Arabic Literary Salons in the Islamic Middle Ages.*

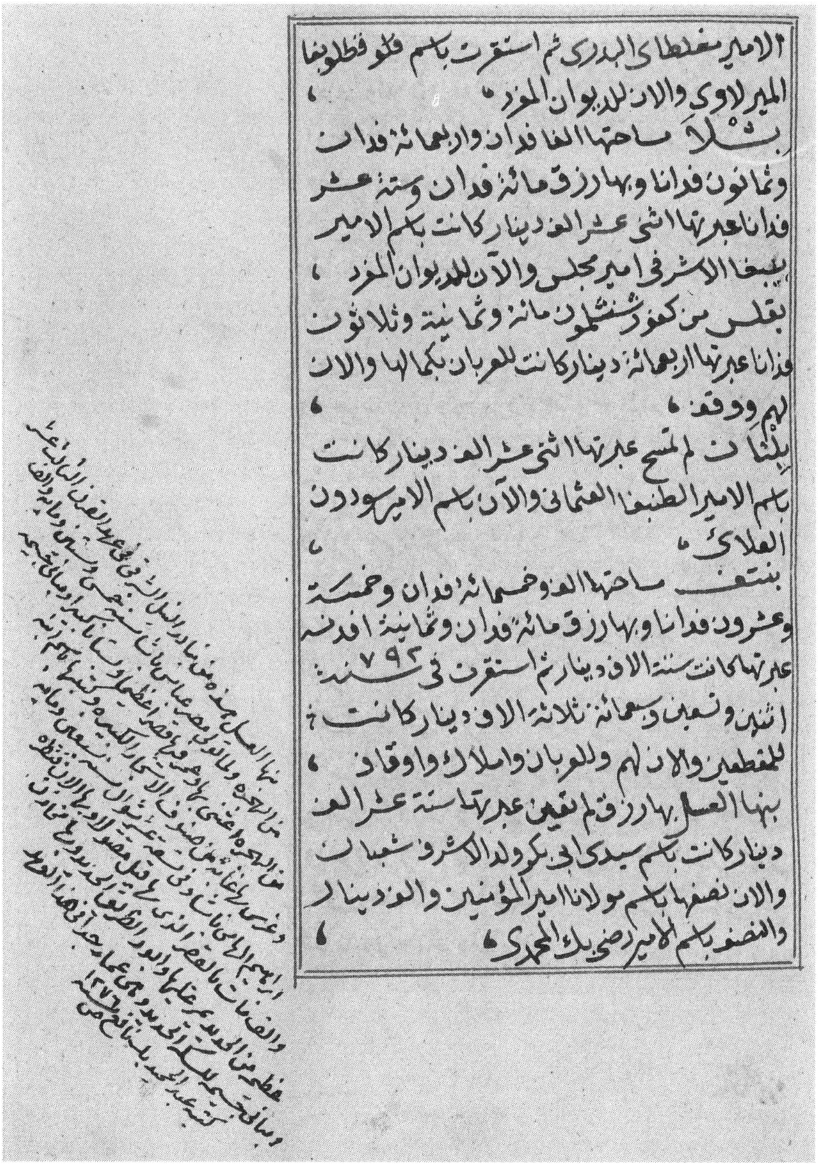

FIGURE 4.1. A signed marginal note by Nāfiʿ on a commissioned manuscript of Ibn al-Jīʿān's *Kitāb mā bi-iqlīm Miṣr*, fol. 45v, dated 1276/1859. Courtesy of General Collection, Beinecke Rare Book and Manuscript Library, Yale University.

expression and content, and a parallel impatience with the mannerisms of rhymed prose and with formalism in general.[26]

These tendencies both drew strength from and encouraged the printing of classical works that could function as sources of high-level Arabic. Whereas the German book collector Seetzen, as described in chapter 1, had not been able to find a single copy of al-Iṣbahānī's tenth-century *Kitāb al-Aghānī* in early nineteenth-century Egypt, half a century later the work's vast store of early Arabic poetry was available in thousands of copies through print and informed the literary debates of Cairene salons.[27] It is this intellectual and cultural context that gave Nāfiʿ's bibliomania its meaning: the discovery and systematic collection of manuscripts was part and parcel of a powerful cultural movement. The particular role that literature and its aesthetic and even ethical sensibilities played in the rediscovery of the classical heritage is explored in detail in chapter 6. For the moment, it suffices to say that Nāfiʿ and his fellow book-hunters in the second half of the nineteenth century were no antiquarians. Rather, they envisioned these works as the cultural lifeblood of a modernizing Egypt, as the model for a language that was far superior to postclassical Arabic, and as the source of aesthetic and ethical ideals fit for a modern society. The literary discoveries of this age allowed the participants in the literary salons to imagine themselves as playful reincarnations of classical figures. Nāfiʿ's habit of devising classical nicknames for his contemporaries would become a cultural fad and led to much poetry, fallings out, and public back-and-forth, particularly when the nickname was given with reference to physical appearance, as in the case of one intellectual figure who, known for his waddle, was nicknamed Ibn Baṭṭūṭa (after the famous fourteenth-century Moroccan traveler, but literally meaning "son of a duckling").[28] A generation later, Ṭāhā Ḥusayn (1889–1973) and his group of friends, still in their teens and enamored with poetry, adopted the names of classical authors as nicknames.[29]

The new fashion of book collecting and the premium that connoisseurs placed on rare exemplars of classical literature gave rise to high-profile rivalries, of which that between Nāfiʿ and ʿAbd al-Ghanī Fikrī (d. 1889) is among the most famous. Fikrī, a high-ranking bureaucrat and later civil court judge, was himself a litterateur and a poet, but most of his efforts seem to have been invested in buying manuscripts and searching for them in unknown or inaccessible libraries with the goal of obtaining copies of them. He had set up a small workshop in his house for binding books; he made the paper himself,

[26] See, for example, the style of Nāfiʿ's *Dhayl Khiṭaṭ al-Maqrīzī* and Mubārak's *al-Khiṭaṭ*.
[27] Aḥmad Taymūr, *Tarājim*, 94.
[28] Aḥmad Taymūr, *Tarājim*, 93, 112–14.
[29] Al-Zayyāt, "Wafāt al-ustādh Maḥmūd Ḥasan Zanātī" and "Maḥmūd Ḥasan Zanātī."

and he employed copyists who worked exclusively for him.[30] Aḥmad Taymūr recounts an anecdote in which a bookseller had imported a copy of the collected poems of the famous ninth-century poet al-Buḥturī to Cairo. In spite of al-Buḥturī's fame, his collected poems were unknown and unavailable in nineteenth-century Egypt, and Fikrī was thrilled by the news of the work's arrival. The bookseller, however, had promised to sell it to Fikrī's rival Nāfiʿ and did not intend to break his promise. Fikrī then proposed to rent the manuscript for one day and one night for an extorbitant sum, and the bookseller agreed. Fikrī took the manuscript home, cut open its binding, and distributed the constituent quires to his copyists, who set out to copy the work at a feverish pace. Once they were finished, Fikrī collated the copy and the original, then had the original rebound and returned it on time to the bookseller, who in turn delivered it to Nāfiʿ. When the latter, unaware of Fikrī's coup, proudly presented his copy of al-Buḥturī's collected works at his next literary salon, Fikrī haughtily pulled out his own copy and exclaimed, "Calm down, brother; we have already gorged ourselves on this!"[31]

Together with al-Ṭahṭāwī's collection, Fikrī's and Nāfiʿ's libraries appear to have been the largest private manuscript collections in Egypt during their lifetimes, but the latter two were scattered soon after their owners' deaths. As mentioned in Nāfiʿ's biography, Muḥammad ʿĀrif took over Nāfiʿ's library and began to publish some of its treasures, but both the society he founded and his library fell victim to politics. In the early 1870s, ʿĀrif aligned himself with Khedive Ismāʿīl's brother Ḥalīm against the monarch, and when the khedive prevailed ʿĀrif had to flee to Istanbul.[32] Without his presence, the society faltered, and ʿĀrif's library was eventually dispersed; its holdings ended up in places as far-flung as New Haven, Connecticut, and Patna, India.[33] Fikrī's library fared no better. Fikrī had planned a career in government service for his son Muḥammad Akmal (1863–1924), who attended the elite khedival school that trained top bureaucrats, but the son's hunchback appears to have prevented him from pursuing this path.[34] After Fikrī's death, Muḥammad Akmal sold off his inheritance, including his father's library. Most of its contents were bought by the Swedish Orientalist Carlo Landberg,

[30] On Fikrī, see Aḥmad Taymūr, *Tarājim*, 103–7.

[31] Aḥmad Taymūr, *Tarājim*, 106–7.

[32] Al-Rāfiʿī, *ʿAṣr Ismāʿīl*, 1:246. According to Goldziher, however, ʿĀrif's exile was prompted by the need to evade his debtors; Mestyan, "Ignác Goldziher's Report," 470.

[33] Nāfiʿ's copy of Ibn al-Jīʿān's (d. 885/1480) *Kitāb mā bi-iqlīm Miṣr* (see figure 4.1) was obtained by Yale University, and his copy of Abū Shāma's (d. 665/1268) *al-Rawḍatayn fī akhbār al-dawlatayn* found its way to the Khuda Bakhsh Oriental Public Library in Patna; see *Catalogue of the Arabic and Persian Manuscripts*, 15:146. Ibn al-Jīʿān's book has been published as *al-Tuḥfa al-saniyya bi-asmāʾ al-bilād al-miṣriyya*.

[34] Aḥmad Taymūr, *Tarājim*, 103–19.

who had already bought up some of Nāfiʿ's collection.[35] Landberg then resold the manuscripts. In 1884, 1,052 volumes passed to the Königlich Preußische Staatsbibliothek in Berlin,[36] and in 1900, with the mediation of the American philanthropist Morris Ketchum Jesup, a further 774 were sold to Yale University's Beinecke Library.[37] Al-Ṭahṭāwī's library, by contrast, was maintained by his family after his death and remains intact to this day. However, its inaccessibility has consigned it to obscurity, as it is housed in the family's hometown of Sohag, the capital of al-Ṭahṭāwī's home province in upper Egypt.[38]

AḤMAD TAYMŪR: NEW INTELLECTUAL OUTLOOKS

A towering figure in the emerging generation of elite, state-connected book collectors was Aḥmad Taymūr (1871–1930). Taymūr's biography and those of his teachers exemplify the shift from the preprint age of narrow postclassical scholasticism to the new interest in the ethical and aesthetic virtues of classical literature and the attendant movement to make this literature widely available through print.[39]

Taymūr hailed from a very distinguished family. His grandfather Muḥammad Taymūr Kāshif, a Kurd from the Mosul region, had served in the Ottoman army and arrived in Egypt together with Muḥammad ʿAlī after the French retreated from the country in 1801, and he became a close advisor to both Muḥammad ʿAlī and the latter's son Ibrāhīm.[40] Aḥmad's father, Ismāʿīl (1815–72), received a broad education through tutors in Persian, Turkish, and Arabic, covering literature, the Islamic sciences, and calligraphy.[41] His Turkish skills led to his appointment as the personal scribe of Muḥammad ʿAlī; he was subsequently appointed to various governorships, to the High Court of Justice (Jamʿiyyat al-Ḥaqqāniyya), and finally to the leadership of the office of the first lieutenant (Dīwān al-Katkhūda) of the khedive. Amid the demands of his government positions, Ismāʿīl derived deep pleasure from

[35]Landberg was the conduit for Ibn al-Jīʿān's *Kitāb mā bi-iqlīm Miṣr*, mentioned in note 33 above.

[36]Ahlwardt, *Kurzes Verzeichniss der Landberg'schen Sammlung*, iii.

[37]See Nemoy, *Arabic Manuscripts in the Yale University Library*, 8.

[38]For the catalog, see Yūsuf Zaydān, *Fihris makhṭūṭāt maktabat Rifāʿa Rāfiʿ al-Ṭahṭāwī.*

[39]For the political and cultural background of Taymūr and his contemporaries, see Gershoni, "Evolution of National Culture"; and Gershoni and Jankowski, *Egypt, Islam, and the Arabs.*

[40]Aḥmad Taymūr, *Tārīkh al-usra al-Taymūriyya*, 67–69.

[41]Aḥmad Taymūr, *Tārīkh al-usra al-Taymūriyya*, 77–84.

FIGURE 4.2. Aḥmad Taymūr. From *Majallat Majmaʿ al-lugha al-ʿarabiyya fī Dimashq*, special issue 4, 1927.

private reading (*muṭālaʿa*) and assembled a manuscript library by both buying manuscripts and having them copied. In addition, he hosted poets and scholars for discussion and intellectual company.[42]

This domestic environment appears to have nurtured a love of learning in Ismāʿīl's children. His daughter ʿĀʾisha (1840–1902), Aḥmad Taymūr's half-sister, refused to yield to her mother's demands that she learn embroidery and weaving and instead sought entry into the intellectual world of her father's salon. Ismāʿīl acquiesced and provided her with tutors to learn Persian, Turkish, and Arabic as well as Islamic law. Having been widowed in her thirties,

[42] Aḥmad Taymūr, *Tārīkh al-usra al-Taymūriyya*, 84.

ʿĀʾisha continued her literary education and eventually became a celebrated poet who wrote in all three languages.[43]

Aḥmad was Ismāʿīl's youngest child, born in 1871 barely a year before Ismāʿīl's death. Aḥmad learned Arabic, Turkish, French, and some Persian at home, then began his education at a French private school in Cairo.[44] After graduation, he did not enter government service but rather took private lessons on such diverse topics as the Quran and its recitation, logic, Arabic philosophy, Arabic rhetoric, and literature. In his later years, he gave an account of his early intellectual formation:

> At the age of twenty I graduated from modern schooling, having absorbed what there is to absorb of the usual sciences. My beliefs had been affected by the education in these schools. However, since childhood I had been fascinated by Islam and its virtues and by reading the biography of the Prophet and works on the Companions and the rightly guided caliphs. As a result, my heart had embraced some things but harbored doubts regarding others. I then compared what struck me as the virtues of the divine law and its aims with the innovations that people practiced, cherished, and considered the foundations of their faith. I found them to be at odds and contradictory. I therefore consulted the most senior scholars of al-Azhar and others, hoping to find a solution. However, I found them even more attached to these superstitions than were ordinary people, and I was on the verge of accepting them as part of the religion. The choice was, therefore, between two things: either the religion was a religion of superstitions and nonsense, which repelled any healthy disposition, or these things were correct, and it was a godlessness rooted in me that prevented me from accepting them.
>
> Then some friends referred me to the subject of this biography [Taymūr's teacher Ḥasan al-Ṭawīl]. I inquired about him among the people of knowledge, and they warned me about him, to the extent that one of them, may God give him what he deserves, accused him of hidden disbelief. I told myself: If I cannot get what I want from those described as pious and good, maybe I will find it among the heretics! So I went to meet him and asked to study texts with him and to receive his guidance. I studied with him the sciences of Arabic and logic, and particularly syntax and rhetoric. Then I read with him some philosophy, including parts of [Jalāl al-Dīn] al-Dawwānī's [d. 907/1501] commentary on al-Suhrawardī's *Hayākil al-nūr* ["Temples of light"], his commentary on [his own] *Risālat al-Zawrāʾ* ["Tigris epistle"], and other things. And when he saw that I was serious, he prescribed for me a second class, after the night prayer, on literature and similar things. Throughout this time, I asked him repeat-

[43] For an overview of ʿĀʾisha's career, see Hatem, *Literature, Gender, and Nation-Building.*

[44] For biographies of Aḥmad Taymūr and his family, see Aḥmad Taymūr, *Tārīkh al-usra al-Taymūriyya*, 89–92; Aḥmad Taymūr, *Tarājim*, 157–63; Schacht, "Aḥmed Pascha Taimūr"; Schaade, "Aḥmed Taimûr Paša."

edly to clarify for me what I found problematic, and he resolved everything for me. So, my meeting him and keeping his company were the greatest of blessings for me and my faith. . . . He was a Sunni in belief and a Sufi in orientation; he did not deviate from the law a hair's breadth, and he adopted Ibn Taymiyya's position against seeking assistance at graves and appealing to the dead for intercession.[45]

We can only speculate about what it was in his schooling that troubled Taymūr, but it is not surprising that attending a late nineteenth-century French private school could induce a sense of cultural schizophrenia in an intelligent Egyptian pupil. This sense of alienation compelled him to take a stance against phenomena of Egyptian popular religion—"superstitions" (*khuzaʿbalāt*) such as the cult of grave visitation and the related powers of the saints—that he found incompatible with his disposition and his understanding of Islam as formed through private reading. He found no relief among the scholars he consulted at al-Azhar: the postclassical literature with which they were familiar clearly endorsed a culture of charismatic popular religion in which living and dead saints played crucial roles for ordinary believers.

He finally found a kindred spirit in Ḥasan al-Ṭawīl (ca. 1834–99),[46] a man who straddled the worlds of al-Azhar and state bureaucracy. Born in a village in the Nile delta, al-Ṭawīl studied at al-Azhar but quickly made himself unpopular among teachers with his constant questioning of their teaching. His fortunes changed when Muḥammad Quṭṭa al-ʿAdawī, the Bulaq corrector, needed assistance in his work on the most important collection of prophetic traditions, that of al-Bukhārī (d. 256/870). Al-Ṭawīl got the job and was subsequently hired as a corrector for the publications of the ministry of war, a position that provided him with a stable source of income. He continued his studies, particularly in philosophy and mathematics, with Muḥammad Akram al-Afghānī (d. 1870), a scholar from India who had settled in Egypt. Al-Ṭawīl's interests were so varied and his reading so wide-ranging that Taymūr described him as an intellectually self-made man (*nasīj nafsih*). It was in this period that we find his name on the membership roster of the Egyptian Scholarly Society, subscribing to the latest editions of classical works. In 1867, al-Ṭawīl qualified as a teacher at al-Azhar, where he taught two generations of students, including two grand muftis of Egypt, Muḥammad ʿAbduh (see chapter 6) and Muḥammad Bakhīt al-Muṭīʿī (1854–1935). He then entered the service of the ministry of education as an inspector. In his final years, he taught at the new Dār al-ʿUlūm college, which had been founded in 1872 on ʿAlī Mubārak's initiative (like the Khedival Library had been in

[45] Aḥmad Taymūr, *Tarājim*, 126–27 (reading *istishfāʿ* for *istishfāʾ*).
[46] Aḥmad Taymūr, *Tarājim*, 120–29; Aḥmad Taymūr, *Aʿlām al-fikr al-islāmī*, 93–101.

1870) and which offered instruction in the Arabic and Islamic humanities in a modernized form.[47] There, again, al-Ṭawīl's students included important intellectuals of the next generation, such as Muḥammad al-Khuḍarī (1872–1927).

It is unlikely that al-Ṭawīl would have achieved the career he did without the availability of both governmental jobs and the newly emerging educational institutions that could accommodate a scholar whose drive to transcend the postclassical curriculum and the culture it entailed clearly sat uneasily with the Azhar mainstream. Taymūr, in his biography, reports having been warned of al-Ṭawīl as dangerous, but he also says that other Azharis drew on his broad reading to defend Islam against external challenges.

Taymūr's second major teacher was likewise an outsider: Muḥammad Maḥmūd al-Shinqīṭī al-Turkuzī (1829 or 1830–1904), who originated from Chinguetti, in present-day Mauritania. Mauritanians, and particularly scholars from Chinguetti, played an important role in late nineteenth- and early twentieth-century Arab scholarship. Their relative isolation, combined with robust educational institutions very different from those found in the Arabo-Islamic heartlands,[48] facilitated the preservation of knowledge that had become rare or extinct in other regions of the Islamic world. This is particularly true for poetry, of which al-Shinqīṭī had memorized copious amounts. His universally celebrated expertise, coupled with the direct and uncompromising personality of a desert dweller unaccustomed to the baroque niceties of nineteenth-century urban Middle Eastern society, led him to ecstatic receptions in Mecca, Istanbul, and Egypt, soon followed by quarrels, alienation, and personal and professional isolation.

After performing the pilgrimage to Mecca, al-Shinqīṭī settled in Medina and visited Istanbul several times to explore and copy important literary manuscripts.[49] He gained a reputation as an expert on the Ottoman manuscript holdings in Arabic literature, and in 1887 Sultan ʿAbd al-Ḥamīd II sent him on a special mission to England, France, and Spain to investigate European collections' holdings of works that were unavailable in Istanbul and should be copied. Al-Shinqīṭī's list of important works at the Escorial Library near Madrid is extant.[50] However, his relationship with the Ottoman sultan faltered when he consented to represent the sultan at the 1889 International Congress of Orientalists in Stockholm only on the conditition that the sultan restore some Mauritanian pious endowments in Medina.[51] ʿAbd al-Ḥamīd

[47] Ṭāhir, *Dār al-ʿUlūm.*

[48] See El Hamel, "Transmission of Islamic Knowledge"; see also al-Shinqīṭī's account of teaching in a tent in Mauritania in Aḥmad Taymūr, *Aʿlām al-fikr al-islāmī,* 369.

[49] E.g., the poetic anthology of al-Aṣmaʿī (d. 216/831), known as *al-Aṣmaʿiyyāt*; see al-Shallāḥī, "Qaṭf al-ʿanāqīd," 24.

[50] Al-Shinqīṭī, *Asmāʾ ashhar al-kutub al-ʿarabiyya.*

[51] Al-Shinqīṭī, *al-Ḥamāsa,* 2–3; Aḥmad Taymūr, *Aʿlām al-fikr al-islāmī,* 370.

found this demand unacceptable and dismissed al-Shinqīṭī. Settling in Egypt in 1889 or 1890, al-Shinqīṭī joined Muḥammad ʿAbduh's project of reintroducing the subject of literature into the Azhari curriculum and worked with ʿAbduh on the publication of ʿAbd al-Qāhir al-Jurjānī's (d. 471 or 474/1078 or 1081) *Dalāʾil al-iʿjāz* (Indications of miraculous form) and *Asrār al-balāgha* (The secrets of eloquence), as well as an edition of the topical literary dictionary *al-Mukhaṣṣaṣ* (The apportioned) by the eleventh-century Andalusian Ibn Sīdah, eventually published in seventeen volumes—al-Shinqīṭī's crowning scholarly accomplishment. Al-Shinqīṭī remained deeply focused on manuscripts, spending his days in the Egyptian National Library reading and copying manuscripts.[52] He even composed a poem of complaint when, in 1899 or 1900, the National Library, under the directorship of the German Orientalist Bernhard Moritz, forbade the copying of its manuscripts with ink (in order to protect the original manuscripts), with the result that al-Shinqīṭī's work on a copy of a tenth-century work on knowledge and its virtues could not proceed.[53] The move toward prioritizing the preservation of manuscripts over their continued use was an effect of a newly emerging vision of manuscripts as historical artifacts in a world increasingly dominated by printed books, but it angered and frustrated al-Shinqīṭī.

Al-Shinqīṭī died shortly after the publication of his edition of al-Jurjānī's *Dalāʾil al-iʿjāz*. In a playful inversion of the usual practice of eulogizing the dead, the Mauritanian, facing the end of his life far away from home, wrote a eulogy for himself, borrowing the initial hemistich from a seventh-century outlaw poet.[54] The eulogy demonstrates how central the work of editing classical books had been to his view of his life achievements:

> I thought of who would mourn me, yet could not find one
> Except books that will be scattered after I am gone, and my knowledge
> And other than the mufti Muḥammad ʿAbduh, my friend, upright and true
> in his affections and speech
> . . . .
> The printed *Mukhaṣṣaṣ* speaks eloquently
> Of the capacity of my memory in the face of omissions, gaps, and lacunae
> To this the mufti and those involved in its printing bear witness[55]

[52] Ḥusayn, *al-Ayyām*, 2:276 (chap. 19).

[53] Al-Shallāḥī, "Qaṭf al-ʿanāqīd," 36.

[54] This was Mālik b. al-Rayb, who had said, "I thought of who would mourn me, yet could not find one / except the sword and the spear"; al-Baghdādī, *Khizānat al-adab* (Hārūn ed.), 2:204.

[55] Al-Zayyāt, "Awwalu mā ʿaraftu al-Shinqīṭī," 247; for a longer version, see al-Shinqīṭī, *al-Ḥamāsa*, 14.

After his death, his son donated his manuscript collection, comprising 345 works, to the Egyptian National Library—thus preventing the dispersal of the library, which al-Shinqīṭī had feared.[56]

Al-Shinqīṭī mentored Taymūr in Arabic literature and acquainted him with the relevant manuscript tradition. For example, he advised Taymūr to read the tenth-century *al-Amālī* (Dictations) of al-Qālī and to ponder the work's literary content. It had not yet been printed,[57] so Taymūr had to copy lengthy sections by hand. The copying and the subsequent close reading of the text occupied Taymūr for several days, and his literary companions began to miss him. His friend and teacher Muḥammad Akmal (the son of the book collector Fikrī) composed a comical *zajal* poem that scolded both al-Qālī and al-Shinqīṭī for depriving Muḥammad of Taymūr's company. Another important text that Taymūr studied with al-Shinqīṭī was the "hanging odes," *Muʿallaqāt*, the most famous of the pre-Islamic Arabic poems that would so greatly excite the next generation of Arab intellectuals.

Taymūr came to share his teachers' dedication to books, to both their content and the material aspects of copying them. He annotated and corrected the manuscripts he owned, and he used his manuscript copies to correct already printed works. He published separate corrections of two of the most important published Arabic dictionaries (*Lisān al-ʿArab* and *al-Qāmūs al-muḥīṭ*).[58] This was an important service to the field of scholarship, since, as a contemporary magazine reviewer observed, correctors relied on these prints as reference works in editing other classical works.[59] Taymūr also compiled indexes for the most important of the works he owned, such as the seventeenth-century anthology *Khizānat al-adab* (Storehouse of literature) by al-Baghdādī—not for publication but for his own private use and for the use of those frequenting his library.[60] The books that he authored and that were published either during his lifetime or posthumously were highly learned storehouses of information in themselves, covering topics as diverse as the history of the Yazidi faith (practiced in the Kurdish homeland of his ancestors), the origins of the Islamic schools of law, biographies of doctors, Arab games, the history of the Ottoman flag, and relics attributed to Muḥammad; in addition, his reading notes were published after his death.[61]

Taymūr also participated in a venture for publishing classical Arabic and Islamic works, the Company for Printing Arabic Books (Sharikat Ṭabʿ

[56] Sayyid, *Dār al-Kutub al-Miṣriyya*, 31.

[57] The work was eventually published in 1906.

[58] *Taṣḥīḥ al-Qāmūs*, published in 1924, and *Taṣḥīḥ Lisān al-ʿArab*, published in 1916.

[59] Al-Khaṭīb, "Ḥarakat al-nashr wa-l-taʾlīf: Taṣḥīḥ al-Qāmūs," 402.

[60] Taymūr's indexes for this work were titled *Miftāḥ al-Khizāna* (The key to the storehouse), and they served as the basis for the later, published indexes to the *Khizāna*; see ʿAbd al-Salām Hārūn's introduction to the indexes in al-Baghdādī, *Khizānat al-adab* (Hārūn ed.), 12:10–11.

[61] For Taymūr's published works, see the bibliography.

al-Kutub al-ʿArabiyya), which was founded in 1897 with the goal of making "useful" works available in print.[62] This project was led by a committee that included Taymūr; ʿAlī Bahjat (1858–1924), the first indigenous head of the Museum of Arab Antiquities (Dār al-Āthār al-ʿArabiyya);[63] and Ḥasan ʿĀṣim (d. 1907), the director of the Department of Civil Affairs (Dīwān al-Khidīwī) and later the supervisor of the Islamic Charitable Society (al-Jamʿiyya al-Khayriyya al-Islāmiyya).[64] "Useful" could mean various things. In 1899, for example, the company published a one-volume handbook on Islamic law by the classical scholar al-Ghazālī. Al-Ghazālī was celebrated as the author of the ethical and pietistic *Iḥyāʾ ʿulūm al-dīn*, but his book on law had long been superseded as a teaching text by postclassical works. In the preface to the work, the executive committee of the company announced that it had decided to publish this work because of its clear and incisive content, the fact that it had not been printed previously, and their view that it could prove beneficial for both specialists and laypeople.[65] The mention of lay readers is interesting. The format of al-Ghazālī's book, which is neither a bare-bones teaching text nor an ornate commentary, makes it eminently readable and considerably more accessible for nonspecialist readers than the legal curriculum texts that had been printed by that time. Such readers could read al-Ghazālī's book by themselves, outside of the authoritive structure of a teaching institution.

The company also published, a year later, al-Balādhurī's famous ninth-century history of the Islamic conquests, *Futūḥ al-buldān*. The introduction explained that the executive committee had deemed the book to cover an important topic and to be written in elegant style. It admitted that the work had already been published twice in Europe, but pointed out that copies of these prints were no longer available; European prints of classical Arabic works were not only too expensive for wide distribution in the Arabic world but also often printed in such small numbers that they barely supplied Western libraries. In addition to responding to the unavailability of European prints, the project also had an aesthetic dimension. The 1866 Leiden edition by M. J. de Goeje was printed in a jarring, sharp-angled script, whereas the Egyptian company's 1901 version was both more readable and, with its elegantly rounded script, pleasing to the eye. Other books published by the company included classical histories of Saladin and of the Seljuk dynasty,[66] as

[62] Jurjī Zaydān, *Tārīkh ādāb al-lugha al-ʿarabiyya*, 4:81.

[63] Today's Museum of Islamic Art.

[64] Founded in 1892, the society sought to provide education and occupational training for Egypt's poor; Jurjī Zaydān, *Tārīkh ādāb al-lugha al-ʿarabiyya*, 4:89–90.

[65] Al-Ghazālī, *al-Wajīz*, 2.

[66] Ibn Shaddād's *Sīrat Ṣalāḥ al-Dīn* and ʿImād al-Dīn al-Iṣfahānī's *Tārīkh dawlat āl Saljūq*.

well as two classical works on government and politics.[67] All of these are, unsurprisingly, the kind of works that one would expect Taymūr and the other founders of the company to favor: political histories of famous rulers and dynasties, treatises on political theory, and an accessible work on law.

Taymūr's most important legacy, however, was his library. Located in Cairo's affluent Zamalek district, it was open to all interested researchers. It contained around fifteen thousand works,[68] roughly half of them manuscripts. The other half were works printed both in the Arabic world and in Europe. Taymūr's collection of Arabic printed works was so complete that the Syrian bureaucrat and writer Yūsuf Sarkīs (1856–1932) worked in Taymūr's library to write his comprehensive bibliography of Arabic books printed before 1919, and he consequently dedicated the work to Taymūr.[69] Another pathbreaking reference work that relied on Taymūr's library was Khayr al-Dīn al-Ziriklī's (1893–1976) *al-Aʿlām* (The luminaries), arguably the best modern Arabic biographical dictionary of prominent "Arabs, arabized individuals, and Orientalists" from the beginning of Islam up to the age of the author.[70] A particular feature of this work is that its biographies not only list the books authored by their subjects but also specify which are extant in manuscript form or have already been printed. In addition, they include images of the subjects' handwriting and other documents, which would provide twentieth-century Arabic-speaking students with their first exposure to manuscripts, embedded as these students were in a scholarly culture in which at least older manuscripts had ceased to be seen as usable objects and instead became targets of archival preservation or rarefied collection. The works of both Sarkīs and al-Ziriklī became indispensable references for subsequent research, but their composition was made possible only by the existence of libraries that were comprehensive (at least in ambition) and well cataloged, in this case by Taymūr himself.

Taymūr's library also played an important role in the rich intellectual culture that had blossomed in Arabic journals, because the rare and ancient works he collected fed directly into contemporary debates. Thus, for example, in 1925 a writer using the pseudonym Ibn al-Furāt began his article in the Egyptian journal *al-Zahrāʾ* with the following:

> Among the precious works that have recently been added to the Taymūr library in Cairo is *Tārīkh al-duwal wa-l-mulūk* ["History of dynasties and kings"]

[67] Ibn Qayyim al-Jawziyya's *al-Ṭuruq al-ḥukmiyya* and Ibn Ṭiqṭaqā's *al-Fakhrī fī al-ādāb al-sulṭāniyya*. For a list of works published by the company, see the list that follows the table of contents (no page number) in the company's print of al-Balādhurī's *Futūḥ al-buldān*.

[68] Aḥmad Taymūr, *Tarājim*, 159.

[69] Sarkīs, *Muʿjam al-maṭbūʿāt*, dedication (no page number). Sarkīs's project of a comprehensive inventory survived him; see Ṣāliḥiyya, *al-Muʿjam al-shāmil*.

[70] See the introduction to al-Ziriklī's *al-Aʿlām* (2002 ed.), 1:17.

by . . . Ibn al-Furāt (AH 735–807) [1334–1405 CE], reproduced photographically from the unique surviving manuscript in the Vienna library, in nine volumes. I will introduce it and its author to readers in the next issue of *al-Zahrāʾ*, God willing, but for now I will quote the history of Ibn al-Furāt on the Crusaders' burning the great library of the Banū ʿAmmār in Tripolis in the Levant in AH 503 [1109 CE].[71]

The arrival of a new manuscript copy in the Taymūr library could thus be an event—in this case, representing the recovery of a historical episode of contemporary relevance, since the wanton destruction of a significant library by the Crusaders held a particular significance in the age of colonialism. The unique manuscript of this work was held in the royal library in Vienna,[72] where it had served as a major source for Orientalist scholars' account of the Crusades but had been unavailable to Arab scholars. Taymūr employed the technology of photography to effectively recover works that had been lost to Middle Eastern scholars as a consequence of Western libraries' massive drive to acquire Arabic manuscripts in the nineteenth century.[73] Photography permitted the reproduction of manuscripts with complete accuracy in much less time than would have been needed to copy a text by hand. A significant part of Taymūr's manuscript collection in fact consisted of such photographic copies from libraries in Europe, including from the Vatican (probably facilitated by his connection to Sarkīs, who was an important supplier of Arabic books to the Vatican)[74] and Istanbul.[75]

AḤMAD AL-ḤUSAYNĪ'S RETURN TO THE CLASSICS

Another important Egyptian aficionado and collector of classical works in this generation (though in his case of works of primarily religious rather than literary nature) was Aḥmad Bey al-Ḥusaynī (1854–1914), the man whose writing first sparked my interest in book culture and early print (see the introduction). He was born in Cairo into an influential family that traced its genealogy all the way back to the Prophet Muḥammad. Al-Ḥusaynī's great-uncle (his paternal grandmother's brother) was Ḥasan al-ʿAṭṭār, mentioned earlier as a bibliophile, rector of al-Azhar, and teacher of al-Ṭahṭāwī.[76] Al-Ḥusaynī's father was the head of the coppersmiths' guild (*ṭāʾifat al-naḥḥāsīn*), and

[71] Ibn al-Furāt, "Iḥrāq dār al-ʿilm bi-Tarāblus al-Shām," 110.
[72] Flügel, *Die arabischen, persischen und türkischen Handschriften*, 2:46–49.
[73] For an example, see Wollina, "Tracing Ibn Ṭūlūn's Autograph Corpus," 319.
[74] Albin, "Sarkīs, Y. I.," 395.
[75] Al-Khaṭīb, "Faqīd al-ʿarabiyya wa-l-islām," 571.
[76] Al-Ḥusaynī, *Murshid al-anām*, 2:600.

al-Ḥusaynī inherited the position in his turn. At the same time, al-Ḥusaynī pursued a religious education at al-Azhar, where he became the favorite student and close confidant of Shams al-Dīn Muḥammad al-Anbābī (1824 or 1825–96). When the reformed national courts, which provided a formal role for lawyers, began operation in 1884, al-Ḥusaynī was among the first lawyers to practice in these courts. He became one of the most prominent lawyers of his time and was a founding member of the Egyptian lawyers' syndicate.[77]

At some point, al-Ḥusaynī retired from his occupation as a lawyer and dedicated himself to legal scholarship and book collection, devoting a large part of his efforts to procuring and copying manuscripts. Al-Ḥusaynī's father had been the legal guardian of Ḥasan al-ʿAṭṭār's descendants, and the family had witnessed firsthand the precariousness of manuscript libraries and the ease with which a lifetime's collection could be dispersed. Al-ʿAṭṭār's famous library had attracted the envy of several of his fellow Azharis, and after his death, they gathered a group of students and marched to his house, claiming that his books had been endowed to al-Azhar. The mob managed to remove a significant part of the library, depositing some of the volumes in the libraries of the various porticos of al-Azhar but keeping a large number for themselves.[78]

Al-Ḥusaynī's collecting efforts were not limited to Egypt. He traveled extensively in search of rare manuscripts, spending, in his own words, his "life and wealth" in their pursuit.[79] In addition to works of history and literature, al-Ḥusaynī sought out rare or even unique works on Islamic law, particularly pertaining to the Shāfiʿī school of law, to which he himself adhered. The resulting collection was the most significant library of Shāfiʿī texts of his time. Jurjī Zaydān (1861–1914), the great Levantine journalist, author of historical novels, and editor of the journal *al-Hilāl*, described it as a well-cataloged collection of 4,780 volumes of printed and manuscript works and lauded al-Ḥusaynī for placing it at the disposal of any interested reader.[80] Al-Ḥusaynī's intensive traveling and research seem to have taken their toll, however. His health began to fail when he was still in his late fifties, and in a 1911 book he confessed that his physical condition had not permitted him to fast more than three days during Ramaḍān. Al-Ḥusaynī died in Cairo in 1914, at the age of fifty-nine. His book collection was donated to the Egyptian National Library, at which point it contained 245 manuscripts, many of them comprising multiple volumes.[81]

[77] Ziadeh, *Lawyers, the Rule of Law and Liberalism*, 39.

[78] Although the incident must have taken place before al-Ḥusaynī's birth, during his lifetime his father was involved in trying to recover the misappropriated books, and al-Ḥusaynī refers to family lore on this matter; see *Murshid al-anām*, 2:608–9.

[79] Al-Ḥusaynī, *Murshid al-anām*, 1:19.

[80] Jurjī Zaydān, *Tārīkh ādāb al-lugha al-ʿarabiyya*, 4:115.

[81] Sayyid, *Dār al-Kutub al-Miṣriyya*, 32.

Like Taymūr, al-Ḥusaynī left behind an autobiographical description of his intellectual formation. He begins his account by tracing his scholarly genealogy back over more than a millennium. He lists his teacher, al-Anbābī, who served as rector of al-Azhar in 1882 and again from 1887 until 1895; then al-Anbābī's teacher, Ibrāhīm al-Bājūrī; then al-Bājūrī's teacher; and so on, the chain of teacher-to-student transmission leading back across time and space from Egypt to Syria, to Iraq, to eastern Iran, back to Iraq, and again to Egypt, where al-Shāfiʿī, the founder of the Shāfiʿī school of law, died in 204/820.[82] However, despite his in-depth studies with al-Anbābī and his sense of organic connectedness to the past, al-Ḥusaynī reports dissatisfaction with his studies, with many questions remaining unresolved in his mind. To resolve them, he turned to the works of "the ancients" (*al-mutaqaddimūn*), scholars from the first centuries of Islam:

> I sought out the books of the ancients from all regions and spent much money on acquiring them in order to collect volumes of great value, important in their field, until I had gathered—and this is a favor from God—more books by the ancients and the moderns alike than any library holds, spending in the process many years. Indeed, many of these books have not been read for centuries, and even the giants among the modern [i.e., postclassical] authors have not consulted them.[83]

It should be recalled that al-Anbābī's personal library, discussed in chapter 2, showed a marked focus on recently written works and the near-complete absence of early works on law and other subjects. By setting out to obtain and consult the works of the ancients, al-Ḥusaynī was thus deliberately breaking out of the confines of the tradition of his teachers. Al-Ḥusaynī artfully illustrates the breadth of his reading by integrating the titles of the works he had collected into his prose: "I became refined by the Revision [*al-Tahdhīb*] of the Revised [*al-Muhadhdhab*], in order to fulfill the Furthest Quest [*Nihāyat al-maṭlab*], and I made my Preparation [*al-ʿUdda*] to gain what is Reliable [*al-Muʿtamad*] and Comprehensive [*al-Shāmil*], and I was set aright by the Clarification [*al-Ibāna*] of Clarity [*al-Bayān*] and the Complete [*al-Kāmil*] and Comprehensive [*al-Majmūʿ*] Awakening [*al-Tanbīh*]."[84] Already this one

[82] Al-Ḥusaynī, *Murshid al-anām*, 1:13–16.

[83] Al-Ḥusaynī, *Murshid al-anām*, 1:17.

[84] Rearranged in order of authors' death years, the full list includes al-Buwayṭī's (d. 231/846) *Mukhtaṣar*; al-Muzanī's (d. 264/877 or 878) *Mukhtaṣar*; Ibn al-Qāṣṣ's (d. 335/946 or 947) *Talkhīṣ*; Abū al-Ḥasan al-Muḥāmilī's (d. 415/1024) or his grandson Abū Ṭāhir's (d. 528/1134) *Lubāb*; al-Bandanījī's (d. 425/1034) *Muʿtamad*; Abū Ṭayyib al-Ṭabarī's (d. 450/1058) *Sharḥ al-Muzanī*; al-Māwardī's (d. 450/1058) *Ḥāwī*; Abū al-Qāsim al-Fūrānī al-Marwazī's (d. 461/1069) *Ibāna*; probably Qāḍī Ḥusayn's (d. 462/1069) *Taʿlīqa*; Abū Isḥāq al-Shīrāzī's (d. 476/1083) *Muhadhdhab* and *Tanbīh*; Ibn al-Ṣabbāgh's (d. 477/1084) *Shāmil*; Imām al-Ḥaramayn al-Juwaynī's (d. 478/1085) *Nihāyat al-maṭlab*; al-Mutawallī's (d. 478/1086) *Tatimmat al-Ibāna*; Abū al-ʿAbbās

sentence contains the titles of eleven classical works of Islamic law, and the enumeration extends over a whole page.[85]

According to his own account, al-Ḥusaynī found the classical literature infinitely superior to the postclassical canon. He exclaims in rhymed prose, "In the works of the ancients are found profound investigations, . . . principles and their ramifications, . . . differences of opinion and argumentations, details and wider ruminations, which will make the modern books seem like a drop compared to the oceans."[86] Ironically, both the interweaving of titles and the use of rhymed prose are quintessential postclassical literary devices, but al-Ḥusaynī uses them here specifically to make a point about the inferiority of the postclassical tradition in terms of content. In his telling, his reading led him to view the scholarly practices of his own time in a newly critical light. Although postclassical scholars continued to cite and rely on the authority of classical authors, it became evident to al-Ḥusaynī that few had actually read these authors' works directly. Indeed, as seen in chapter 2, such direct engagement with the foundational literature was typically discouraged by the prevailing orthodoxy, which viewed the latest commentaries, glosses, and tertiary commentaries as the pinnacle of scholarly authority. As a consequence, later authors' grasp of the positions of and debates among the ancients was superficial at best and deeply erroneous at worst.[87] In his writings, al-Ḥusaynī details several instances in which faulty opinions had been misattributed to classical authors and the error had subsequently been reproduced for generations by successive authors citing only their immediate predecessors. For example, contemporary Shāfiʿī jurists considered the ear an opening to the body in the sense that water entering it would invalidate a person's fast. Al-Ḥusaynī traces this position, which was contradicted by common anatomical knowledge, through the school tradition and identifies its roots in textual corruption within the commentary tradition in the seventeenth century.[88]

As a first step toward remedying this situation, al-Ḥusaynī embarked on the publication of the foundational text of his own school of law, the Shāfiʿī school. This work or, more precisely, this cluster of works had been compiled by al-Shāfiʿī's students and given the overall title *al-Umm*, "The mother[book]." At this time, few foundational texts of Islamic law had been published,[89] and

---

al-Jurjānī's (d. 482/1089) *Taḥrīr*; Abū ʿAbd Allāh al-Ṭabarī's (d. 498/1105) *ʿUdda*; al-Rūyānī's (d. 502/1108) *Baḥr al-madhhab*; al-Ghazālī's (d. 505/1111) *Wajīz*, *Wasīṭ*, and *Basīṭ*; al-Baghawī's (d. 516/1122) *Tahdhīb*; al-ʿImrānī's (d. 558/1163) *Bayān*; and al-Nawawī's (d. 676/1278) *Majmūʿ*.

85 Al-Ḥusaynī, *Murshid al-anām*, 1:18.

86 Al-Ḥusaynī, *Murshid al-anām*, 1:26.

87 Al-Ḥusaynī, *Murshid al-anām*, 1:19.

88 Al-Ḥusaynī, *Nihāyat al-aḥkām*, 8; El Shamsy, "*Ḥāshiya* in Islamic Law," 299–300.

89 Two other works written by legal school founders, the *Muwaṭṭaʾ* of Mālik b. Anas (d. 179/795) and *Kitāb al-Kharāj* of Abū Yūsuf (d. 182/798), had been printed in 1864 and 1884/1885,

none of comparable length or scope, so the project was groundbreaking in a number of respects. The *Umm* had fallen out of continuous use and transmission for at least half a millennium.[90] Al-Ḥusaynī's first challenge was thus to gather a reasonably complete manuscript of the work.[91] Even though it had originally been compiled in Egypt, where al-Shāfiʿī had spent the last years of his life, the only two complete manuscripts in existence were held in the libraries of the Topkapı Palace in Istanbul, which were not accessible to the public at the time, and in the library of the Maḥmūdiyya madrasa in Medina.[92] In Cairo, only fragments of the work could be found. The National Library owned copies of two volumes (volume 8 and another volume whose number had been erased by damage to the manuscript),[93] and al-Ḥusaynī located a copy of the first volume in the Azhar mosque in the library of the North African portico (*riwāq al-Maghāriba*). The latter volume had belonged to his great-uncle Ḥasan al-ʿAṭṭār and appears to have been among the works looted from al-ʿAṭṭār's private library after his death, as described earlier.[94] Al-Ḥusaynī also traveled to Istanbul in 1902 and to Damascus in 1904 in search of manuscripts.[95]

Having assembled the text, he employed three experienced correctors to ensure the accuracy of the work.[96] The most senior of the three was Muḥammad al-Bulbaysī (d. unknown), who had two decades earlier (in 1882) corrected the famous Bulaq edition of the grand classical Arabic dictionary, the twenty-volume *Lisān al-ʿArab*. The second corrector was the younger Naṣr al-ʿĀdilī (d. unknown), who would a few years later correct the second printing of the most important classical work of Quranic exegesis, that of al-Ṭabarī (published in 1905–12);[97] and the third was the poet Maḥmūd Ḥasan Zanātī (d. 1949), who was part of a triumvirate of friends consisting of himself, Aḥmad Ḥasan al-Zayyāt (1885–1968, later the editor of the journal *al-Risāla*),

---

respectively. However, the former is primarily a work on hadith (and had relatively limited influence on the actual development of the Mālikī school according to Abd-Allah, *Mālik and Medina*, 77–78), and the latter's coverage is limited to taxation and fiscal issues. In addition, al-Shāfiʿī's epistle on legal theory (*al-Risāla*) had appeared in print in 1895.

90 Ibn Ḥajar, *al-Imtāʿ*, 103.

91 The text he assembled lacked a few folios; see the note by the later editor of *Umm*, Rifʿat Fawzī ʿAbd al-Muṭṭalib, in *al-Umm* (2001 ed.), 9:7–8. For al-Ḥusaynī's account of his search for the manuscripts, see *Murshid al-anām*, 1:20.

92 ʿAbd al-Muṭṭalib, introduction to *al-Umm* (2001 ed.), 1:30.

93 *Fihrist al-kutub al-ʿarabiyya al-maḥfūẓa bi-l-Kutubkhāna al-Khidīwiyya*, 3:264.

94 This volume did not find its way into the centralized Azhar library, and I was not able to establish its present whearabouts. See *al-Maktaba al-Azhariyya*, 2:446–47.

95 A copy of al-Buwayṭī's abridgment (*mukhtaṣar*) of al-Shāfiʿī's *Risāla* in Istanbul contains a note left by al-Ḥusaynī's copyist; for details, see the introduction to the present book. For al-Ḥusaynī's journey to Damascus, see Commins, *Islamic Reform*, 62.

96 Al-Shāfiʿī, *al-Umm* (Bulaq ed.), 4:413–16.

97 Al-Ṭabarī, *Jāmiʿ al-bayān* (Bulaq ed.), 30:232.

and Ṭāhā Ḥusayn, the doyen of Arabic literary studies in Egypt in the first half of the twentieth century.[98] In their separate colophons, the three correctors mostly adhere to the conventions of early print: they praise the current Egyptian khedive, ʿAbbās Ḥilmī II, and commemorate the work's completion with poems that conclude with chronograms. However, they also provide more details than previously customary on what they actually did on the text beyond simple proofreading. Al-ʿĀdilī and al-Bulbaysī specify that their work required them to decipher a text that lacked voweling and even, on occasion, the dots necessary to distinguish certain letters, as well as to correct textual corruptions inadvertently introduced by past scribes in the process of transmission, including misspellings, omissions, and jumbled word order.

The *Umm* was published by the state press in Bulaq in four composite volumes between 1903 and 1908. To cover the considerable cost of the publication, al-Ḥusaynī had to sell thirty acres (*faddān*) of agricultural land.[99] The title page and the correctors' colophons credit al-Husaynī with assembling the complete text and financing the entire printing and correcting process.[100] We see here the emergence of a new kind of role in the publication of Islamic literature: the discoverer and collector who is not employed by a press but has made the publishing of a specific work his intellectual project. Unlike Aḥmad Zakī (discussed in the next chapter), who actively oversaw the editing process of his projects, producing a critical apparatus and writing introductions, al-Ḥusaynī may not have actively participated in the editing itself. He clearly knew more about the topic of the work to be edited than did the correctors, but he was also still a practicing lawyer. The precise extent of the influence exerted by al-Ḥusaynī on the final edition became the topic of debate. In 1942, Muḥammad Zāhid al-Kawtharī (1879–1952), the famous Turkish scholar exiled in Cairo (and discussed in chapter 8), critized the edition for its correction of an alleged grammatical mistake by al-Shāfiʿī and accused al-Ḥusaynī of having changed the text.[101] In his rebuttal of al-Kawtharī's critique, the Yemeni corrector and philologist ʿAbd al-Raḥmān al-Muʿallimī (see chapters 3 and 8) pointed out that the correctors had more influence on issues of orthography and could have changed the text silently (a common practice) or, alternatively, that the correction might have been present in the manuscript itself.[102] This exchange illustrates the problems inherent in the prevalent editing practices in the Muslim world at this time: it was not

[98] For al-Bulbaysī and al-ʿĀdilī, see al-Ṭanāḥī, *Fī al-lugha wa-l-adab*, 2:635; for Zanātī, see Cachia, *Taha Husayn*, 49; and al-Zayyāt, "Maḥmūd Ḥasan Zanātī," 1754.

[99] Al-Ṭanāḥī, *al-Kitāb al-maṭbūʿ bi-Miṣr*, 52.

[100] Al-Shāfiʿī, *al-Umm* (Bulaq ed.), title page and 4:414.

[101] Al-Kawtharī, *Taʾnīb al-khaṭīb*, 49–50. The alleged mistake is quoted in al-Muzanī's *Mukhtaṣar*, which al-Ḥusaynī had printed on the *Umm's* margins.

[102] Al-Muʿallimī, *al-Tankīl*, in *Āthār al-Muʿallimī*, 10:690. On this debate, see also Khan, "Islamic Tradition," 63–71.

clear who was responsible for and had the final say on the textual form of the final product. Typically, the manuscripts used were not specified, editorial emendations were not marked, and no indication of textual variants was given.

The cover of the edition warns sternly, "No one is permitted to print this work from this copy. Anyone who prints it must either present a [manuscript] source for it or pay compensation."[103] The reason for this note is that in contrast to the majority of the printed legal works, which were popular teaching texts and consequently were available in numerous manuscript copies, the text of the *Umm* had had to be painstakingly reconstructed from fragments. Copying the printed version of the *Umm* would thus have constituted theft of significant intellectual and scholarly labor. But the warning was in vain: all subsequent prints of the *Umm* until the 2001 critical edition were pirated copies of the original Bulaq print.[104]

The publication of the *Umm* found a generally positive reception, but there were also dissenting voices. Al-Ḥusaynī describes the reactions to his project thus:

> I made it my intention to print it to propagate its benefits, and when I made my determination known, excitement spread among Muslims with the glad tidings of the realization of this hope. From all corners of the Islamic world requests poured in for this work, as well as letters in praise of the work, both in prose and in verse, with the exception of one person who wears the garb of a scholar but whose rigid insistence on the later glosses and immersion in the stupor of what he has read of the later authors are known. When the printing of this book was begun he committed disrespect of the "mother," even though, as the authentic prophetic tradition teaches us, she is most deserving of loving company. He argued his case shamefully and with great vigor.[105]

The unnamed opponent of al-Ḥusaynī's publishing project put forward four arguments. First, the *Umm* was an early work by al-Shāfiʿī and contained opinions that he had later abandoned and that should therefore be considered abrogated (al-Ḥusaynī remarks on this point that "he clearly knows nothing about the nature of this book"). Second, according to the sixteenth-century scholar al-Haytamī, one may not draw on works written before the two great synthesizers of the thirteenth century, al-Rāfiʿī and al-Nawawī ("a point on which [al-Haytamī] was mistaken"). Third, the nineteenth-century legal gloss of al-Bājūrī was more useful than the *Umm* could ever be ("a blatant lie"). And finally, the *Umm* was "an enigma that no human can solve or

[103] Al-Shāfiʿī, *al-Umm* (Bulaq ed.), 1:3.
[104] ʿAbd al-Muṭṭalib, introduction to his edition of *al-Umm*, 1:28–29.
[105] Al-Ḥusaynī, *Murshid al-anām*, 1:24.

comprehend."[106] The resistance of a mainstream scholar to the publication of the *Umm* is understandable. By accessing the early Shāfiʿī corpus directly, al-Ḥusaynī was effectively bypassing the bedrock of learning and authority held by the Shāfiʿī scholars of his time, whose acquaintance with these works was, at best, secondhand.

Al-Ḥusaynī's efforts to reinvigorate the legal discourse of his day were not limited to the publication of the *Umm*. He also wrote and published twelve monographs on diverse legal topics, ranging from the concept of intention and the rules of travel to the payment of alms on paper money and the prohibition of alcohol.[107] (In contrast to his assertion of copyright on the edition of the *Umm*, he explicitly permitted free reproduction of these works.) However, it is his last, unpublished work, a massive twenty-four-volume commentary on the ritual law section of the *Umm* that he completed only shortly before his death, that represents the culmination of al-Ḥusaynī's lifelong project of reviving the classical Shāfiʿī tradition. His reformist vision is laid out in the two-volume introduction to the commentary, from which the accounts quoted earlier of his intellectual trajectory and his project of publishing the *Umm* are also drawn. The aim of the commentary was to bring together the insights of all the great classical Shāfiʿī jurists into a single coherent debate that was centered on the original fountainhead of the Shāfiʿī school, al-Shāfiʿī's *Umm*. Instead of attempting the impossible task of editing separately the hundreds of volumes of classical works in his possession, al-Ḥusaynī laboriously synthesized their contents into a single work, seeking to represent fully the breadth of opinions and approaches within his vast material. The intended contribution of the work was thus both substantive, resurrecting the diversity of legal positions and arguments marginalized by postclassical myopia, and methodological, focusing attention once more on the superior legal argumentation of the early jurists of the school.

Aḥmad al-Ḥusaynī complicates the dichotomy between traditionalist and modernist religious figures that is often deployed to map the religious landscape of late nineteenth- and early twentieth-century Egypt. Al-Ḥusaynī proudly located himself within the Islamic intellectual tradition, happily and playfully employing its formal language of rhymed prose and wordplay and even following the postclassical habit of ending his work in a chronogram.[108] Upon completing a monograph, he continued a practice at least a half-millenium old[109] by inviting the scholarly elite of Cairo to his estate in Helwan and having the book read out loud to the assembled scholars. In response, some of the listeners composed, either individually or in groups, endorsements,

[106] Al-Ḥusaynī, *Murshid al-anām*, 1:25–26.
[107] See the bibliography for a list of al-Ḥusaynī's monographs.
[108] See, e.g., al-Ḥusaynī, *Dalīl al-musāfir*, 90; al-Ḥusaynī, *Nihāyat al-aḥkām*, 190.
[109] See Hans Rosenthal, "'Blurbs' (*Taqrîẓ*)."

or "blurbs" (*taqārīẓ*, sing. *taqrīẓ*), that were appended to the beginning and end of the printed text.[110] In spite of the profound challenge that his approach posed to the structure of legal authority in his time, his position on Islamic law and its dominant institutions—the four Sunni schools of law—was conservative. He believed staunchly in the schools' overall authority and sought to support, rather than undermine, their legitimacy, although he promoted a legal pragmatism that allowed the adherents of a particular school to adopt the positions of a different one in cases of hardship.[111] His dedication to the Shāfiʿī school of law is evident in his continuation of another venerable school practice—namely, the authoring of a complete biographical dictionary of the school's member jurists from the school founder to his own time.[112] What set him apart from his mainstream peers was both his insistence on the primacy of the classical "books of the ancients" and his openness to and reliance on modern scientific knowledge. His work on alcohol includes a detailed description of the chemical structure of alcohol and the effects it has on the human body, with citations of scientific studies on the subject. In his work on paper money, al-Ḥusaynī presents a study of global currencies, and in his "guide for the traveler" (*Dalīl al-musāfir*) he gives an introduction to modern geography as well as providing a list of coordinates for determining the correct prayer direction in countries on all seven continents.

In the intellectual historiography of Egypt, al-Ḥusaynī has been all but forgotten. This may seem odd, given his central role in the publication of al-Shāfiʿī's seminal work (the largest and most significant legal text to be published in Egypt until his time) and his authorship of what is, to my knowledge, the most extensive Sunni commentary on law written in the twentieth century. However, al-Ḥusaynī did not establish a continuing personal following: he held no religious office, wrote for no newspapers, and did not gather a circle of students around him. More significantly, his magnum opus was never published, most likely owing to its length, which would have made its printing prohibitively expensive at the time. Al-Ḥusaynī's legacy nonetheless lived on in the print of the *Umm*, which critically shaped modern views of the emergence of Islamic law;[113] in his manuscript library, which he bequeathed to the Egyptian National Library and which subsequently served as a key source for the textual reconstruction of the Shāfiʿī school; and in

[110] The scholars who wrote endorsements for al-Ḥusaynī's *Dalīl al-musāfir* include Muḥammad ʿAbduh (then grand mufti of Egypt, in office 1899–1905); Muḥammad Bakhīt (a member of the High Court of Sharīʿa, al-Maḥkama al-Ūliyya al-Sharʿiyya, and later the grand mufti from 1914 to 1921); ʿAlī al-Bablāwī (head of the Egyptian guild of the descendants of the Prophet, *naqīb al-ashrāf*); and Aḥmad al-Ṭūkhī (overseer of the Sharīʿa courts, *mufattish al-maḥākim al-sharʿiyya*); see al-Ḥusaynī, *Dalīl al-musāfir*, 2–3, 91–110.

[111] Ibrahim, *Pragmatism in Islamic Law*, 143.

[112] Included in al-Ḥusaynī's introduction to *Murshid al-anām*, 1:318–942 and 2:1–672.

[113] El Shamsy, "Al-Shāfiʿī's Written Corpus," 199–200.

٨٤ (تابع جدول سمت القبلة من الشمال نحو)

(أوروبـــــا)					(أمريكا الشماليه)					
(بلاد اسبانيا وجزائر باليار وبلاد البورتوجال وجزائر اسور وإسلندا)					(بلاد جرونلند وبلاد كندا وبلاد الممالك المجتمعة وكالي فورني وبلاد السكا ومكسيكا وجزائر انتيل)					
	أسماء البلدان	سمت القبله من الشمال نحو الشرق ″	′	°		أسماء البلدان	سمت القبله من الشمال نحو الشرق ″	′	°	
أسبانيا	الجزيرة ..	٢٩	٢٩	٩٧	جرونلند	بووين ...	٤٥	١١	٤٧	الشرق
	البكانت ..	•	•	•		جودهافن .	•	•	•	»
	ألمريا ...	٤٤	٢٩	١٠٠		جولينشاب	•	•	•	
	برسلونا ...	•	•	•		نيا كرنالك .	•	•	•	
	بامبولانا ..	•	•	•	كندا	تورونتو ..	•	•	•	
	توليدا ...	•	•	•		كبيك ...	١٠	٤	٦٠	»
	جبل الطارق	١٨	٣٢	٩٧		كرولك ...	•	•	•	
	سان سيباستيان	•	•	•		مونريال .	•	•	•	
	سان فرنندو	٢١	٢٢	٩٧		هالي فاكس	•	•	•	
	سفيل ...	•	•	•	الممالك المجتمعة وكالي فورني	البني	٥	١٦	٥٨	»
	فونت ارابي .	•	•	•		بالتيمور ..	•	•	•	
	فيرول ...	٤٠	٥٢	١٠٢		بوستون ..	•	•	•	
	قرطبه ...	•	•	•		سان فرانسسكوا	•	•	•	
	كارمونا ..	•	•	•		سنسيناتي .	٣٣	٤	٥١	»
	كارتاجين ..	١٤	٣٥	١٠٢		سالم	•	•	•	
	مدريد ...	١١	٣٣	١٠٣		شيكاجو ..	•	•	•	
	ملجا	١٣	٥٩	٩٨		فيلادلفي .	•	•	•	
	والنسيا ...	•	•	•		كامبريدج .	•	•	•	
جزائر باليار	بالما	•	•	•		نيورك ...	٤٦	٩	٥٨	»
	فورمانتيرا .	١٣	٥	١٠٦		واشنجتون	•	•	•	
	ماهون ..	•	•	•	السكا	خوديالك ..	•	•	•	
البورتوجال	ستوبال .	•	•	•		موجراف .	١٠	١	٠٠	الغرب
	فارو	٢٠	٤٣	٩٦	مكسيكا	الوارادو ..	•	•	•	
	كوامبر ...	•	•	•		جواد الاجارا	•	•	•	
	لسبون ..	٣٧	٣٠	٩٧		سان بلاس .	•	•	•	
	مافرا	•	•	•		ما زاتلان .	•	•	•	
جزائر أسور	انجرا ...	٣٨	٤٧	٨٥		ميكسيكو .	١٩	٤١	٣٩	الشرق
	أوبورتو ..	•	•	•	جزائر انتيل	بورت أوبرانس	•	•	•	
	سان ميجل .	•	•	•		فورد وفرانس	•	•	•	
إسلندا	ريكياويك	•	•	•		كينجستون	•	•	•	
	سكاجن ..	•	•	•		هاوان ...	٥٧	٤٥	٥٥	»

FIGURE 4.3. A page from al-Ḥusaynī's *Dalīl al-musāfir*, 84, with coordinates for the direction of prayer in cities in southern Europe and North America.

his fine monographs, such as his book on intention in Islamic law[114] and his work on anatomy, the latter of which the Syrian scholar ʿAlī al-Ṭanṭāwī (1909–99) memorably credited as his first lesson in sex education.[115] Even his "forgotten" commentary had an impact, as its introductory volumes served as important sources for the biographical works of Khayr al-Dīn al-Ziriklī and Yūsuf al-Marʿashlī (born 1952).[116] Finally, by donating a piece of Cairo real estate to a Kurdish immigrant, Faraj Allāh Zakī al-Kurdī (1882–1940),[117] al-Ḥusaynī enabled the foundation of what became an important publishing house specializing in classical works, the Kurdistān Press.[118] This press was active only for a short period, 1907–11, but in this time it published, in addition to several books by al-Ḥusaynī, more than a hundred important classical texts, including al-Ghazālī's *Miʿyār al-ʿilm* (Criterion of knowledge) on logic, published in 1911; al-Rāzī's work on divine transcendence, *Asās al-taqdīs* (The basis of sanctification), published in 1910; and several works by Ibn Taymiyya, most importantly his five-volume *Kitāb Majmūʿat fatāwā* (1908–11).

* * *

When Muḥammad ʿAlī began building a modern state in Egypt, the printing press represented a tool for the education of a new class of servants of the state. This new class of educated civil servants launched a cultural movement that adopted Arabic, rather than Ottoman Turkish or Persian, as the language of high culture and that sought to achieve a cultural renaissance through the rediscovery of texts—especially histories, ethical advice literature, and early works of poetry and prose—that had been largely forgotten because of their absence from the postclassical curriculum. These prominent individuals began to collect manuscripts in a systematic manner. They targeted rare and culturally significant works, arranged the publication of their discoveries, and injected them into cultural circulation through literary salons and the new media of journals and monographs.

The position of this class of intellectuals at the nexus of inherited wealth and the rapidly modernizing state gave them access to multiple avenues for obtaining manuscripts and for financing and publicizing their editions. Some, such as al-Ḥusaynī, used their personal assets to travel in search of important

[114] In 1997, Wahba al-Zuḥaylī complained that al-Ḥusaynī's book was the only modern work on the topic; see al-Zuḥaylī's *al-Fiqh al-islāmī wa-adillatuh*, 1:150.

[115] Al-Ṭanṭāwī, *Dhikrayāt*, 161.

[116] Al-Ziriklī, *al-Aʿlām* (2002 ed.), 1:94; al-Marʿashlī, *Nathr al-jawāhir*, 1:87–88.

[117] Al-Kurdī had been a student at al-Azhar before converting to Bahaism and becoming active in the printing of Baha'i literature, such as Abū al-Faḍā'il al-Īrānī's *al-Durar al-bahiyya*, in which al-Kurdī and Mīrzā Ḥasan are named as copyright holders. Muḥammad ʿAbduh and Rashīd Riḍā alerted the Azhari authorities to al-Kurdī's missionary activity at al-Azhar, which led to his being expelled. See Riḍā, *al-Manār wa-l-Azhar*, 28–29.

[118] The best study on the Kurdistān Press is Ra'ūf, *Maṭbaʿat Kurdistān al-ʿilmiyya*.

manuscripts and to underwrite the substantial expense of printing large-scale works. Other efforts were based on high-profile collaborations (such as the Company for Printing Arabic Books) or innovative crowdfunding schemes (as in the case of the Egyptian Scholarly Society). Further, the privileged backgrounds of these new bibliophiles, who enjoyed elite access to tutors and libraries as well as the new educational opportunities provided by emerging institutions such as state schools, enabled them to play an unprecedented role in the intellectual work of editing and correction. Aḥmad Taymūr sharpened the available scholarly tools through his published corrections of key reference works and his accessible, systematically ordered and indexed library. Aḥmad al-Ḥusaynī reconstructed a seminal, all-but-forgotten ninth-century legal text from fragments scattered across several countries, thus accomplishing a philological feat that would have been entirely beyond the capacity of a corrector but that still lacked a recognized position in the world of scholarship and print. It was al-Ḥusaynī's near-contemporary Aḥmad Zakī who finally gave a name to scholars of this kind by adopting the term *muḥaqqiq*, "editor."

CHAPTER 5

The Rise of the Editor

The challenges of publishing a classical work in the early twentieth century, discussed in the preceding two chapters, included locating and procuring a manuscript of the work, producing a sufficiently accurate version of the text to serve as the basis of the published book, and securing the funds to cover the costs of printing. These challenges are vividly illustrated in the career of Aḥmad Zakī Pasha (1867–1934), who, like Aḥmad Taymūr and Aḥmad al-Ḥusaynī, straddled the worlds of bureaucracy and scholarship. Zakī's efforts to raise the standards of Arabic scholarly publication inaugurated a host of enduring institutional and methodological developments. Most importantly, he established the model for a new, enormously significant cultural agent: the editor, *muḥaqqiq*.

AḤMAD ZAKĪ'S EARLY SCHOLARSHIP AND THE STATE OF THE FIELD

Aḥmad Zakī hailed from a humble Moroccan and Kurdish background,[1] but he was a gifted linguist and made a career in the Egyptian government as a translator from French to Arabic (he later added Spanish, Italian, and English to his linguistic repertoire). After graduating with a law degree in 1887, Zakī was hired as a translator for the government newspaper *al-Waqāʾiʿ al-miṣriyya*, and in 1889 he became the translator for the Egyptian cabinet. His bureaucratic skills earned him an appointment as secretary general of the cabinet in 1911, a position that he held until his retirement in 1921.[2]

Zakī's intellectual formation was strongly influenced by his brother Muḥammad Rashshād, thirteen years his senior, who became a judge. It was this brother's library that introduced Zakī to the wonders of books, and it was the gatherings hosted by Muḥammad that brought Zakī into contact with subjects ranging from geometry to the French language and Arabic literature.[3] Zakī's decision to study law was likewise due to his brother. At the

[1] Al-Jindī, *Aḥmad Zakī*, 268.

[2] Goldschmidt, *Biographical Dictionary of Modern Egypt*, 236; Kurd ʿAlī, "al-Khizāna al-Zakiyya."

[3] Al-Jindī, *Aḥmad Zakī*, 31.

FIGURE 5.1. Aḥmad Zakī in local dress on a visit to Yemen, 1906. Courtesy of Eltaher.org.

time, the study of law included a significant element of classical Arabic rhetoric, and Zakī attended the classes of a teacher who went on to become one of the greatest modern Arabic poets, Aḥmad Shawqī (1868–1932).[4] Another formative influence was the Khedival Geographic Society (established in 1875), which sparked Zakī's lifelong interest in the subject (he later translated Frederico Bonola's *L'Égypte et la géographie* into Arabic). He also became interested in pharaonic Egypt, becoming a member of the Institut d'Égypte in 1890 and interacting with, among others, the French archaeologist Gaston Maspero (1846–1916),[5] who had founded the French Institute for Oriental Archaeology (Institut français d'archéologie orientale) in Cairo. Zakī later combined these two interests in his 1899 Arabic and French *Qāmūs al-jughrāfiyya al-qadīma* (Dictionary of ancient geography).

Zakī inaugurated his scholarly career in 1890, at age twenty-four, with a bibliographical study on Arabic encyclopedias.[6] Published fifteen years after

[4] Al-Jindī, *Aḥmad Zakī*, 32.

[5] Al-Jindī, *Aḥmad Zakī*, 11, 23.

[6] *Mawsūʿāt al-ʿulūm al-ʿarabiyya = Étude bibliographique sur les encyclopédies arabes.*

the publication of Buṭrus al-Bustānī's groundbreaking Arabic encyclopedia *Dā'irat al-ma'ārif* (Circle of knowledge), Zakī's study aimed to uncover an indigenous Arabic encyclopedic tradition. He noted that the title of al-Bustānī's work was a literal translation of the Greek phrase *enkyklios paideia* (ἐγκύκλιος παιδεία), which had been contracted to form the term encyclopedia.[7] Zakī, however, was keen to discover an indigenous Arabic term for the genre of encyclopedias, and he believed to have found it in an article in the Beirut-based medical journal *al-Ṭabīb*, probably written by its editor Ibrāhīm al-Yāzijī (1847–1906).[8] The article translated the term encyclopedia as *mawsū'a*, drawing on the subtitle of the encyclopedic work *Miftāḥ al-sa'āda wa-miṣbāḥ al-siyāda fī mawsū'āt al-'ulūm* (The key to happiness and the lamp of mastery on the encompassment of the sciences) by the famous sixteenth-century Ottoman scholar Taşköprüzāde. The term *mawsū'a* seemed linguistically fitting, since the Arabic root *w-s-'* conveys a sense of encompassing, which matches the definition of an encyclopedia as a work that contains information on many topics, or on many aspects of a single topic. After the appearance of Zakī's monograph, the word *mawsū'a* became the primary term for encyclopedia in Arabic. (Al-Bustānī's literal translation *dā'irat al-ma'ārif*, meanwhile, was adopted into Persian.) However, the term *mawsū'a* appears to have been the product of an inadvertent but creative textual misreading: the actual subtitle of Taşköprüzāde's work is not *fī mawsū'āt al-'ulūm* but rather, in all published editions of the work, *fī mawḍū'āt al-'ulūm* (on the branches of the sciences).[9] The word *mawsū'a* denoting anything approaching the meaning of encyclopedia is not attested before al-Yāzijī's article. It seems, then, that in his search through classical Arabic manuscripts to find an indigenous term for a cutting-edge intellectual endeavor (a tactic used successfully already by al-Ṭahṭāwī in the mid-nineteenth century to avoid the need to arabize or invent translations for European terms), this editor of a medical journal unwittingly coined a pseudoclassical neologism. The misreading became universally accepted as the translation for the word encyclopedia both because of its (false) pedigree and because of its semantic felicity.

The main body of Zakī's bibliographical study on encyclopedias consists of lists of classical Arabic works that are either encyclopedic on a single topic or seek to encompass and represent all available knowledge. Zakī stresses the significance of encyclopedias with reference to Diderot's eighteenth-century

[7] Zakī, *Mawsū'āt al-'ulūm*, 8.

[8] [Al-Yāzijī], "Basṭ wa-īḍāḥ," 330.

[9] This argument regarding the origin of the term *mawsū'a* is strengthened by oral lore according to which either the printers of Ibrāhīm al-Yāzijī's article corrupted the word, or al-Yāzijī had consulted a library catalog in Istanbul and been misled by an entry in which a Turkish librarian had misspelled the title of Ṭaşköprüzāde's work because of Turkish pronunciation (replacing *ḍāḍ* with *sīn*). See al-Ṭanāḥī, *Fahāris kitāb al-Uṣūl fī al-naḥw*, 10; and Abū Zayd, *Fiqh al-nawāzil*, 1:104–5. I thank Saud al-Sarhan for the latter reference.

Encyclopédie in Western thought, namely, as a nexus at which particular knowledge is gathered, classified, and established to serve as a basis for further scholarship.[10] It should be remembered that encyclopedism—the effort to gather massive amounts of data in a given field—was still regarded as a cutting-edge scientific method in the nineteenth century. It yielded such monumental pieces of scholarship as the *Description de l'Égypte*, based on the material collected during Napoleon's Egyptian expedition (1798–1801) and published in twenty volumes between 1809 and 1828, and Alexander von Humboldt's encyclopedic account of his expedition to America, published in thirty volumes between 1805 and 1834. In his study, Zakī contends that in order to harness the intellectual promises of encyclopedism for Arabic intellectuals, the significant indigenous encyclopedic tradition has to be unearthed first to serve as the basis of further work.[11] The primary tools for starting such a project are bibliographic works that list the titles and subjects of classical works. Zakī, like other scholars of the nineteenth century, relied mainly on Ḥājjī Khalīfa's seventeenth-century *Kashf al-ẓunūn*,[12] which had been available in print since 1835, edited by Gustav Flügel and published in Leipzig, and had subsequently been published in Bulaq in 1858 in a cheaper but inferior edition. Zakī was also dimly aware of a much older bibliographical work, the tenth-century *Fihrist* of Ibn al-Nadīm,[13] which had been published in Leipzig in 1872 on the basis of the editorial notes left by Gustav Flügel. However, Zakī had no access to this work, nor does he seem to have known that it had been published; he had merely seen references to it in classical works.

From the information contained in a classical work on physicians, Zakī identified al-Fārābī's tenth-century *Iḥṣāʾ al-ʿulūm* (Enumeration of the sciences) as the earliest comprehensive Arabo-Islamic encyclopedia.[14] He knew of a surviving manuscript copy of this work in the Escorial Library in Spain, possibly thanks to the list made by Muḥammad Maḥmūd al-Shinqīṭī in 1887,[15] but was unaware that it had already been printed in Istanbul a decade earlier. Had he had access to it, he would have known that the work was merely an abridged overview of a handful of disciplines, consisting of no more than a few dozen pages in the printed version.[16] This error demonstrates the continuing challenges posed by the classical literary tradition at this time. Zakī faced insurmountable difficulties in gathering information

[10] Zakī, *Mawsūʿāt al-ʿulūm*, 11.
[11] Zakī, *Mawsūʿāt al-ʿulūm*, 4.
[12] Zakī, *Mawsūʿāt al-ʿulūm*, 24–29.
[13] Zakī, *Mawsūʿāt al-ʿulūm*, 29.
[14] Zakī, *Mawsūʿāt al-ʿulūm*, 13.
[15] Al-Shinqīṭī, *Asmāʾ ashhar al-kutub*, no. 132.
[16] See the editor's introduction to al-Fārābī, *Iḥṣāʾ al-ʿulūm*, 14.

regarding what books had been written, drawing conclusions on their contents on the basis of titles and short descriptions, and ascertaining which works were still extant in manuscript form and which had already been printed. He was also not aware of the work of the Austrian Orientalist Joseph von Hammer-Purgstall on Arabic encyclopedias, probably because it was written in German.[17]

Nevertheless, Zakī's *Mawsūʿāt al-ʿulūm* demonstrates considerable scholarly energy and ambition, and it set the course for his subsequent work. One of the largest encyclopedic works he mentions in the *Mawsūʿāt*, al-Nuwayrī's fourteenth-century *Nihāyat al-arab fī funūn al-adab* (The ultimate ambition in the branches of erudition), became one of Zakī's principal scholarly projects for the rest of his life, spawning a search for manuscripts of the work, schemes to finance its printing, and eventually, decades later, the beginning of its publication.[18]

The modest extent of the available literature in Egypt and the resulting constraints on scholarship are evident in Zakī's entry in the *Mawsūʿāt* on Quranic commentaries. As one of the most comprehensive such works he mentions the ninth-century commentary of al-Ṭabarī, which is today rightly considered the quintessential classical work of exegesis. Zakī, however, knew al-Ṭabarī's work only through al-Suyūṭī, having never seen it himself.[19] Given that for other works he explicitly mentions any extant manuscripts and specifies where they are housed, his omission of such information for al-Ṭabarī indicates that he was not aware of any surviving manuscripts. It was only more than a decade later, when it was finally printed for the first time in Cairo thanks to a manuscript imported from Najd in Arabia, that al-Ṭabarī's commentary could claim its position as an essential reference work.[20]

Zakī's attitude to the classical works he describes was *monumental* in the Nietzschean sense: it searched the past for what it could not find in the present, namely, a greatness that could serve as the foundation for struggles in the here and now.[21] For Zakī, a key struggle was to root modern institutions of knowledge in their classical context by engaging seriously with the often overlooked Arabo-Islamic literary heritage, instead of simply adopting Western institutions, ideas, and terminology as if this heritage did not exist. Accordingly, on the one hand, Zakī participated in the establishment of the first

[17] Hammer-Purgstall, *Encyklopädische Übersicht der Wissenschaften des Orients*; "Über die Encyklopädie der Araber, Perser und Türken."

[18] Zakī, *Mawsūʿāt al-ʿulūm*, 53–54. On the book itself and the fourteenth-century environment in which it was written, see Muhanna, *World in a Book*.

[19] Zakī, *Mawsūʿāt al-ʿulūm*, 62–63.

[20] Al-Ṭabarī, *Jāmiʿ* (al-Ghamrāwī ed.), title page. The Najdī manuscript, sent by the Āl Rashīd family, was collated with fragments found in Egypt. See also the editor's introduction to the 2001 edition, 1:63–110.

[21] See Nietzsche, "Vom Nutzen und Nachteil der Historie."

modern university in Egypt in 1908 (the Egyptian University, now Cairo University) and held the chair in Islamic civilization there; on the other, as described later in this chapter, he spent decades raising money and support for the systematic reconstruction and publication of two of the most extensive extant classical Arabic encyclopedias, whose rediscovery he saw as central to the project of indigenous modernization. Zakī also expended much energy in correcting references in the Egyptian press to foreign places whose names either were originally Arabic or had existed in arabized form in the classical age but were now simply transliterated from European languages. So, for example, a Moroccan town with the Spanish name Arzila was transliterated variously as Arzīlā, Arsīlā, ʿArzīlā, or even Arjīliyya instead of the town's real name, Aṣīla, as recorded already by the twelfth-century geographer al-Idrīsī.[22]

ENGAGEMENT WITH ORIENTALISM

Much of Zakī's preoccupation with the classics was directed at Europe and at the European Orientalist tradition, with which he had a complex relationship. In spite of his emphasis on the primacy and importance of the indigenous Arabo-Islamic scholarly tradition, evident in his work on encyclopedias, he was keenly interested in and impressed by the work of Orientalist scholars and sought to connect his work with theirs. He wrote several works in French, and even his Arabic works had French elements, such as an alternative title in French or an introduction in both Arabic and French.[23] The practice of authoring an introduction, as opposed to a traditional colophon, was likewise a feature he adopted from Orientalist scholarship.

The beginnings of Zakī's engagement with a European audience lay in his membership in the Khedival Geographic Society, but its high points were certainly his trips to several International Orientalist Congresses in Europe (London 1892, Geneva 1894, Hamburg 1902, and Athens 1912).[24] In 1892, he attended the congress in London as the representative of the Egyptian government. His presentation there consisted of three very different and disconnected parts. The first of these was an overview of the studies he was working on or had already concluded, including his work on encyclopedias, a dictionary of ancient place-names, and a Quranic concordance that was based on the work by Gustav Flügel as well as on indigenous Islamic works that he had found as manuscripts in the Egyptian National Library and in private

[22] Al-Jindī, *Aḥmad Zakī*, 173.

[23] Zakī's *Mawsūʿāt al-ʿulūm al-ʿarabiyya* carried the parallel title *Étude bibliographique sur les encyclopédies arabes*. For dual introductions, see, e.g., Zakī's edition of Ibn al-Kalbī's *Aṣnām*.

[24] On Zakī's congress trips, see Ryad, "'Oriental Orientalist.'"

libraries.[25] Second, Zakī presented an anthropological description of female mourners in contemporary Egypt. And third, he discussed a handful of manuscripts in the private collection of Sulaymān Abāẓa (which would become part of the Azhar Library a few years later), which the owner had opened up for Zakī upon learning of his travel to the conference.[26] This was the first time Zakī made a mark with the study of manuscripts, but these manuscripts still belonged to someone else; it was only afterward that he began to systematically develop his own library—a project made possible by the success of his career and consequent financial security.

In the course of his journey to the London congress, Zakī traveled through Italy, France, the United Kingdom, and Spain. He sent back a stream of reports that were printed in the Egyptian press. During his travels, he paid particular attention to libraries that contained Arabic manuscripts; one of his reports, for example, contains a substantial section on the Bibliothèque nationale in Paris.[27] Upon his return to Egypt, Zakī published his travel reports and the paper he had presented at the congress as a book with the title *al-Safar ilā al-muʾtamar* (The journey to the congress). The book had a pompous and narcissistic streak, which would remain a constant feature of Zakī's writing; it also foreshadowed another emerging characteristic, namely, a certain sycophancy in relation to Orientalist scholarship. Nevertheless, the book contained all the features that would come to define Zakī's intellectual project: a keen awareness of the institutions of book collection and production (for the latter, see, for example, his description of the French national printing press in Paris),[28] familiarity with Orientalist literature and with Arabic manuscript holdings in Europe as well as the Muslim world, the ambition to produce reference works as a foundation for subsequent scholarship on the Orient and its history, and a desire to bring Orientalist and Muslim scholarship into conversation. At the beginning of his presentation in London, Zakī made the reasonable, though nonetheless utopian, suggestion that the next International Congress of Orientalists be held in a Muslim country to allow Muslim scholars to participate.[29]

In 1896, Zakī became involved for the first time in editing and publishing a classical work, a fifteenth-century chronicle by al-Sakhāwī,[30] and the resulting book displays the clear influence of Zakī's exposure to Orientalist scholarship. The title page notes that Aḥmad Zakī financed both the correc-

[25] Zakī, *al-Safar ilā al-muʾtamar*, 457–63; Vollers, *Le neuvième Congres international des Orientalistes*, 14.

[26] Zakī, *al-Safar ilā al-muʾtamar*, 448–84.

[27] Zakī, *al-Safar ilā al-muʾtamar*, 274–81.

[28] Zakī, *al-Safar ilā al-muʾtamar*, 358.

[29] Zakī, *al-Safar ilā al-muʾtamar*, 455.

[30] Al-Sakhāwī, *Kitāb al-Tibr al-masbūk fī dhayl al-sulūk*.

(بسم الله الرحمن الرحيم)

اللهم صل على سيدنا محمد وآله وأصحابه وأزواجه وأنصاره وذريته وأهل بيته وسلم

الحمد لله العالم من القدم بما كان وما يكون والحاكم بما انبرم فى كل حركة وسكون أسر العالم
بأسره ونضد (١) العالم بأمره وأظهر الجميل باحسانه وستر زلة النبيل بامتنانه والصلاة
والسلام على أشرف رسله وخلقه وعلى آله وصحبه وأتباعهم القائمين بتمييز باطل ما نسب اليهم
من صدقه (وبعد) فعلم التاريخ فن من فنون الحديث النبوى وزين تقر به العيون
حيث سلك فيه المنهج القويم المستوى بل وقعه (٢) من الدين عظيم ونفعه متين فى الشرع
بشهرته غنى عن مزيد البيان والتفهيم إذ به (٣) يظهر تزييف مدعى اللقا وبيان (٤) ما صدر
منه من التحريف فى الارتقا اذ كان اختل عقله أو اختلط ولم يجاوز بلدته
التى لم يدخلها الطالب قط ويحفظ به الانساب المترتب عليها صلة الرحم والمتسبب عنها
الميراث والكفاءة حسبما (٥) قرر فى محله وفهم وكذا تعلم منه آجال الحيوف (٦) واختلاف
النقود والاوقاف التى ينشأ عنها من الاستحقاق ما هو معهود وينتفع به فى الاطلاع على
أخبار العلماء والزهاد والفضلاء والملوك والامراء والنبلاء وسيرهم وما أثرهم فى حربهم
وسلمهم وما أبقى الدهر من فضائلهم أو رذائلهم بعد أن أبادهم الحدثان وأبلى جديدهم
الاوان (٧) حيث تتبع الامور الحسنة من آثارهم ولا يسمع منهم فيما تنفر عنه العقول
المستحسنة من أخبارهم ويعتبر بما فيه من المواعظ النافعة واللطائف المفيدة لترويح
النفوس الطامعة مع ما يلتحق به من المسائل العلمية والمباحث النظرية والاشعار التى هى
جل مواد العلوم الادبية كاللغة والمعانى والعربية ولهذا صرح غير واحد من أهل الامانات
بأنه من فروض الكفايات ومن أحسن ما بلغنى من الشعر فى مدحه وأبين ما أعجبنى مما رغب
فى الاعتناء به وعدم طرحه قول القاضى الارجانى البديع الالفاظ والمعانى

---

(١) نضر (٢) رفعه (٣) ادسها (٤) وليت (٥) حيثما (٦) الحبوف (٧) لعلها الالوان

FIGURE 5.2. Zakī's footnotes in al-Sakhāwī's *Kitāb al-Tibr*, published in 1896.

tion and the printing of the work, but in fact his involvement went beyond simply paying the corrector and financing the printing. He supervised the editing process, but being a high government official rather than a paid corrector, he lacked an existing term to describe his role. The edition was based on the single, damaged manuscript available in Egypt (held in the National Library), so a critical edition was impossible, but in contrast to the old Bulaq editions, this edition clearly identified and described the manuscript used, and it contained footnotes that marked emendations to the text. As a scholar of classical works, Zakī was accustomed to Orientalist editing practices, including clear descriptions of the relevant manuscripts and a critical apparatus, and he wanted to implement these practices in the work he financed. In subsequent editions, as described later in this chapter, Zakī adopted the practice of using editorial footnotes to identify not only emendations but also textual variation between manuscripts. He also introduced a standardized system of punctuation marks and authored a short work on it.[31]

THE SYSTEMATIC COLLECTION AND PRESERVATION OF MANUSCRIPTS

With his government career taking off, Zakī began collecting books in earnest. As he would later recall, he began by reading the obituaries in the newspaper *al-Ahrām* to discover leads on private libraries he might be able to buy wholesale; he acquired at least half a dozen complete libraries in this manner.[32] He also traveled beyond Egypt to buy manuscripts, visiting the Levant, Yemen, and Istanbul.[33] What he could not buy he photographed.[34] The largest works that he pursued were al-Nuwayrī's abovementioned *Nihāyat al-arab* and al-ʿUmarī's *Masālik al-abṣār fī mamālik al-amṣār* (The routes of insight into the civilized realms). Both works had been authored by fourteenth-century government scribes in Egypt, and they constituted "vast, multi-themed collections spanning thousands of pages and containing material from a wide range of disciplines, from history and geography to cosmology, botany, ethics, and zoology."[35]

Zakī had already begun to look for al-Nuwayrī's *Nihāyat al-arab* in 1890, but for many years he was not able to find more than a single volume (volume 22) in Egypt, held at the National Library. In 1905, he published a pamphlet titled "The project to print the largest Arabic Egyptian encyclopedia,"[36] in

[31] Zakī, *al-Tarqīm fī al-lugha al-ʿarabiyya.*

[32] Al-Jindī, *Aḥmad Zakī*, 37 and 109–10.

[33] Al-Jindī, *Aḥmad Zakī*, chap. 7.

[34] Al-Jindī, *Ahmad Zakī*, 63–67.

[35] Muhanna, "Encyclopaedism in the Mamluk Period," 10. See also the table of contents for al-Nuwayrī's work in Muhanna, *World in a Book*, 153–57.

[36] *Mashrūʿ ṭabʿ akbar mawsūʿāt ʿarabiyya miṣriyya.*

which he announced the launch of a project aimed at publishing the *Nihāya* and the formation of a committee for the purpose. The committee was headed by Prince Ibrāhīm Ḥilmī (1860–1927), and its further members included senior Egyptian government figures (all at the high rank of Pasha) as well as a deputy general prosecutor as treasurer and Zakī himself as secretary; at this time the latter two held only the lower rank of Bey.[37] Zakī's formally subordinate position within the committee was clearly due to his rank, but in reality he was the driving force behind the project. The reason for the formation of such a committee at this point was that Zakī had found the first two volumes of the *Nihāya*, which had come into the possession of the head eunuch (Bāsh Āghā) of the khedival palace, and they were of excellent quality. The purpose of the pamphlet was to gain subscribers for the project: the last page contained a form to be filled in and mailed to the treasurer together with payment. Thirty volumes plus indexes were planned, and they were to cost five Egyptian pounds, an enormous sum in view of the fact that at the time one could buy an acre of prime agricultural land for seven pounds.[38]

In order to convince potential readers of the merits of the project, Zakī provides in the pamphlet a broad overview of the five areas covered by the *Nihāya*, as well as a detailed and descriptive table of contents for the first third of the work (covering heaven and earth, the human being, and animals and plants, with the remaining two-thirds of the work dedicated to history).[39] He then defends the importance of the work by citing other classical works (both published and as yet unpublished) that draw on the *Nihāya*, and he also lists fourteen Orientalists who had used the work extensively in their writings, including Silvestre de Sacy, Hammer-Purgstall, and Reinhart Dozy.[40] Zakī stresses that although the *Nihāya* had been written in Egypt, it had been plundered by successive conquerors and snatched away by foreign libraries, with the result that only fragments were still to be found in the land of its composition.[41] According to Zakī, the manuscript evidence indicated that the work had been popular in the fourteenth century, with numerous copies produced in Cairo and endowed for its mosques and madrasas, and now housed in Istanbul and Europe. Subsequently it had been subject to renewed interest among seventeenth- and eighteenth-century Ottoman bureaucrats. The two volumes owned by the Bāsh Āghā had originally been written for the Ottoman poet and statesman Ragıp Pasha (1698–1763), and the copy in the Köprülü Library in Istanbul had been produced for the grand vizier Köprülü

[37] Zakī, *Mashrūʿ*, 3.
[38] Hershlag, *Modern Economic History*, 113.
[39] Zakī, *Mashrūʿ*, 4, 9–31.
[40] Zakī, *Mashrūʿ*, 4–6.
[41] Zakī, *Mashrūʿ*, 1.

Mehmet Pasha (1575–1661). However, the latter copy had, according to Zakī, been ruined by the copyists, who were not proficient in Arabic.[42]

The 1905 initiative to publish al-Nuwayrī's *Nihāya* did not succeed. The reasons are not clear, but money seems to have been a major factor, suggesting that not enough people signed up to Zakī's subscription drive. In addition, he was still searching for better manuscripts of the work. In a 1911 letter, the German Orientalist Josef Horovitz (1874–1931) told Zakī about a copy of al-Nuwayrī's work that he had heard was in the possession of a family in Lebanon,[43] but there is no evidence that Zakī was able to consult this copy.

To advance his project, Zakī headed to Istanbul in 1909 to scour the city's rich manuscript libraries. Whereas the erosion of the classical library system in the Arab lands had necessitated the foundation of new institutions modeled on European libraries, the magnificent collections at the heart of the Ottoman Empire were still housed in functioning, centuries-old libraries—some attached to institutions such as mosques, madrasas, and Sufi lodges and others constituting self-standing public libraries, such as the seventeenth-century Köprülü and Atıf Efendi Libraries. And in contrast to the scarcity of manuscripts of nonmainstream works in places such as Egypt, the holdings of Istanbul's libraries were largely unscathed, boasting not only significantly larger numbers of Arabic manuscripts overall but also, more importantly, numerous old and rare works that were no longer available in the Arab provinces.[44]

Zakī was not the only Arab scholar to avail himself of the Ottoman libraries' bounty. Al-Ḥusaynī's and al-Shinqīṭī al-Turkuzī's trips to Istanbul were mentioned in chapter 4, and Aḥmad Taymūr, too, visited the city to look for manuscripts. He subsequently used the knowledge he had gained to advise Jurjī Zaydān, the author of historical novels, on works that the latter might find of interest for his writing (thus demonstrating a direct link between scholarly manuscript research and literature written for popular entertainment).[45] However, the number of Arab scholars who were able to benefit from Istanbul's library resources was generally small. In many cases, manuscript research was possible only on the margins of other, official activities. For example, the Baghdadi scholar Nuʿmān Khayr al-Dīn al-Ālūsī (on whom see chapter 7) visited Istanbul in 1885 to accept a political appointment and found and copied an important fourteenth-century theological commentary during his stay in the city,[46] and the Aleppine scholar Bashīr

[42] Zakī, *Mashrūʿ*, 2.

[43] Ryad, " 'Oriental Orientalist,' " 149.

[44] Beyond the libraries, a private market in Arabic manuscripts also flourished in the Ottoman capital; see Erünsal, *Osmalılarda sahaflık ve sahaflar.*

[45] Aḥmad Taymūr, *al-Mukhtār min al-makhṭūṭāt.*

[46] Specifically, the shorter of Ibn Taymiyya's two commentaries on al-Iṣbahānī's (d. 688/1289) theological handbook. For the work's eventual publication, see chapter 7. For al-

FIGURE 5.3. Beyazıt Library in Istanbul, 1880s. Courtesy of the Library of Congress.

al-Ghazzī (d. 1921) traveled to Istanbul during World War I to represent his hometown's political interests but amid his duties discovered an early text of Ḥanafī law that he then arranged to have printed.[47]

As a high government official in Egypt and a skilled networker, Zakī managed to secure the backing of the Ottoman grand vizier Ḥusayn Ḥilmī Pasha (1855–1922) as well as the support of the minister of education and the minister of endowments, and he plunged eagerly into the holdings of Istanbul's

Ālūsī's visit to Istanbul, see Nafi, "Abu al-Thana' al-Alusi," 481.

[47]This was al-Jaṣṣāṣ's *Aḥkām al-Qur'ān*, which was published in 1917–20. For al-Ghazzī's biography and stay in Istanbul, see al-Ṭabbākh, *I'lām al-nubalā'*, 7:574–83, esp. 580–81. For the immediate impact of the publication of al-Jaṣṣāṣ's work on political thought in India, see Zaman, *Modern Islamic Thought*, 228–29.

various libraries. However, despite his success in attracting support from high places, Zakī's enthusiasm quickly ran into practical obstacles. Between 1884 and 1896, the Ottoman state had, for the first time, published a catalog for the libraries of Istanbul, but it was barely more than an incomplete list of titles, copied from the first pages of manuscript volumes without verification of the title, the author's name, or the possible presence of other works within the same covers (a common occurrence).[48] Having visited more than forty public libraries in Istanbul, Zakī drafted a report concerning the state of Istanbul's libraries, including a ninety-six-point plan for improvement, and submitted it to the Ottoman government.[49] The report begins by arguing that libraries play a crucial role in the intellectual advancement of a society and that it was high time for the Ottomans to turn to their development, especially since the Istanbul library collections were so rich and precious. Zakī lists a host of problems with the present situation. It was time-consuming to rush from one library to the other, which was necessary because even different volumes of the same book could be scattered across more than one collection. Within libraries, books were arranged haphazardly, making it difficult to locate them. Catalogs were unsystematic and contained insufficient information, and they thus hampered efforts to find copies of the same book in different libraries. Books were stored in conditions that allowed damage from humidity and insects. Library hours of operation were limited and at the discretion of the librarians, who were underpaid and unqualified. It is therefore not surprising, argues Zakī, that the Bibliothèque nationale in Paris possesses numerous manuscripts bearing seals from Ottoman libraries; they were either sold by the librarians or stolen under their hapless eyes.

Zakī's extensive suggestions for improving the situation of the libraries include their consolidation into a single central library or at least the establishment of central libraries for specific fields (#1). The central library or libraries should be properly supervised by the ministry of education (#2) and staffed by librarians trained in Arabic, the language in which most manuscripts were written (#6), and these librarians should be adequately remunerated (#10). Opening hours should be fixed (#39), and access should be granted only to holders of a library card (#41). The central library should have a board responsible for having rare and important works printed or at least photographed (#12). The library should enter into relationships with other libraries worldwide and undertake, inter alia, the mutual exchange of catalogs

[48]Erünsal, "Brief Survey," 4. The forty volumes of this catalog, known as *Devr-i Ḥamīdī*, were published under the title *Defter Kütübkhāne* followed by the name of a specific library; for example, *Defter Kütübkhāne Esʿad Efendi*.

[49]Zakī, *Taqrīr muqaddam* (I am indebted to Amr Ryad for providing me with a copy of this work). The Ottoman Turkish version of the text was published by Erünsal in *Kütüphanecilikle ilgili Osmanlıca metinler ve belgeler*, 1:323–52. I am grateful to Ahmet Tunç Şen for help with this text.

(#14 and #15). The library's holdings should be properly cataloged and the entries ordered according to an ingenious system proposed by Zakī that would display not only fields and subfields but also a hierarchy of manuscripts. So, if an autograph exists, it is mentioned first, followed by any copies made of the autograph, and so on (##18–38). Zakī's proposal includes modern services for readers, including a separate room that would allow readers to photograph manuscripts (##78–85), but also modern restrictions such as forbidding readers to write on manuscripts (#55), thereby banning the traditional practice of correcting corrupted text while reading it.

Zakī's report appears to have convinced the Ottoman government to produce a central catalog that satisfied Zakī's standards. The first fascicle of the catalog was published in 1915, but World War I and the subsequent abolishment of the Ottoman Empire put an end to the project.[50] In fact, with the establishment of the Turkish republic and Atatürk's subsequent push to de-Orientalize the country, Istanbul's manuscript libraries were put even further out of reach for Arab scholars. Only in the late twentieth century did many of Zakī's suggestions become reality through the centralization of manuscript collections in the Süleymaniye Library, the compilation of modern catalogs, and the ease of acquiring reproductions (today in the form of digitized images).

Zakī's political connections appear to have opened for him a collection that was clearly not public but that would provide the most significant sources of his future scholarship: the libraries of the Topkapı Palace, the main residence of the Ottoman sultans from the mid-fifteenth to the mid-nineteenth century. In the wake of the 1908 Young Turk revolution, the grand vizier Ḥusayn Ḥilmī Pasha issued a decree (*firmān*) that permitted Zakī to explore the Topkapı's libraries. Zakī later claimed that he had been the first scholar in four hundred years to gain access to the literary treasures contained therein. According to his own account, Zakī spent all of his waking moments at the Topkapı for the next four months.[51]

The manuscript collection of the Topkapı Palace encompassed fourteen thousand Arabic, Persian, and Turkish works selected for their rarity, beauty, or age. Gathered from the various centers of the Muslim world by history's most powerful Muslim dynasty, they had in many cases been withheld from intellectual circulation for centuries.[52] The experience of suddenly being

[50]Erünsal, "Brief Survey," 4.

[51]De Tarrazi, *Khazāʾin al-kutub*, 1:255–56. On the Topkapı libraries, see Necipoğlu, "Spatial Organization of Knowledge," and the other articles in Necipoğlu, Kafadar, and Fleischer, *Treasures of Knowledge*.

[52]On the Topkapı's holdings, see the catalogs compiled by Fehmi Edhem Karatay. Unfortunately, access to the sultanic libraries remained problematic after Zakī's visit and even after the establishment of the Turkish republic, as the works contained therein were integrated into the Topkapı Museum and treated as museum artifacts to be preserved and displayed, not as books to be read.

confronted with these treasures was transformative for Zakī. First, it convinced him of the detrimental effect that the Ottoman conquest of Egypt had had on Egyptian and, more broadly, Arabic intellectual culture. After returning to Cairo, he penned an essay about the development of the arts in Egypt and depicted the Ottoman conquest and the subsequent transfer of books and objects to Istanbul as a prominent factor in what he called "the period of decadence" in recent Egyptian history.[53] Second, the unique manuscripts that Zakī discovered at the Topkapı and brought back to Egypt in the form of photographic copies fueled his scholarship for the rest of his life. For two years, he dedicated himself to editing three early works of Arabic advice literature, two by Ibn al-Muqaffaʿ and one attributed to al-Jāḥiẓ.[54] All three works comprised maxims and wisdom sayings regarding the virtuous life and correct behavior for sages, kings, and their subjects. Explaining his choice, Zakī stressed the value of manners and ethics in the constitution of societies and expressed hope that the publication of these forgotten classical works would contribute to the societal revival of Muslim peoples.[55] He even managed to convince the Egyptian ministry of education to incorporate the two works of Ibn al-Muqaffaʿ into the national preparatory school curriculum.[56] These two texts thus traveled, within three years, from the utter obscurity of the Ottoman sultan's library to the public school curriculum of the largest Arabic-speaking country.

THE ROLE OF THE EDITOR (*MUḤAQQIQ*)

These three works, published between 1911 and 1914, featured a crucial innovation: Aḥmad Zakī's name was prominently displayed on the cover of each, and his contribution was described by the term "verification" (*taḥqīq*). Subsequently, this and the related word *muḥaqqiq*, "verifier," became the standard terms for editing and editors, gradually replacing the corrector (*muṣaḥḥiḥ*) and his work of correction (*taṣḥīḥ*) as the primary interface between classical manuscripts and their printed manifestations. As noted in chapter 2, the word *taḥqīq* preceded the adoption of print by several centuries as a general term for exploring the evidentiary basis of claims and positions. Such exploration could consist either of scholarly efforts to evaluate opinions by means of rational or transmitted evidence, or of esoteric Sufi claims to direct experience of the truth. It is in the former sense that Zakī used the term for his own activity (he clearly had a strong epistemological

[53] Zakī, *Le passé et l'avenir*, 13–18.

[54] Ibn al-Muqaffaʿ, *al-Adab al-ṣaghīr* and *al-Adab al-kabīr*; al-Jāḥiẓ [attrib.], *al-Tāj*. The three works were contained in a single manuscript; see Zakī's introduction to *al-Tāj*, 26–28.

[55] Ibn al-Muqaffaʿ, *al-Adab al-ṣaghīr* (Zakī ed.), 1–7.

[56] See the note on the front cover of both works.

dislike of esotericism, evident in the suggestion, included in his proposal for the planned Istanbul central library, that works on magic and the occult be made accessible only with the library director's special permission).[57] Applied to editing, scholarly verification entailed evaluating manuscripts and variants against each other and against the editor's own knowledge. It should be noted that the term *taḥqīq* was not entirely unknown in the world of print before Zakī; for example, Muḥammad ʿAbduh's contribution to the earlier publication of a classical work on logic had also been described as *taḥqīq* on the edition's cover.[58] However, in that case the term appears to have denoted not the activity of modern editing but the explanatory notes that ʿAbduh added to the text, a usage that did not catch on.[59]

Zakī's long scholarly introduction to *Kitāb al-Tāj* (The book of the crown), attributed to al-Jāḥiẓ, breaks with the precedent of formulaic correctors' colophons by foregrounding Zakī's own authoritative voice.[60] Over fifty pages, he lays out precisely what the work of verification meant for him. The first point he sought to verify, he says, is the attribution of the work; the second is its title; and the third is the correctness of the individual words in the three manuscripts available to him. To settle the first two questions, Zakī reports tracing quotations of the work in other books, scouring bibliographical and biographical works in print and manuscript form for information that would link al-Jāḥiẓ to a work of that title and content, and undertaking a comparison between the style of al-Jāḥiẓ's known works and the text of *Kitāb al-Tāj*. The verification of individual words was done primarily by comparing the three manuscripts he had before him. Whereas earlier editions generally provide little to no information on the manuscripts used, Zakī includes ten pages of facsimile images of the manuscripts as well as details about their provenance.[61] In another significant departure from past practice, Zakī systematically recorded textual variants between the manuscripts and placed this critical apparatus in footnotes, thus clearly following Orientalist conventions over the traditional practice of writing notes in the margins. The same preference for Orientalist practices is apparent in his choice to write introductions rather than colophons for the editions.

[57] Zakī, *Taqrīr muqaddam*, #48.

[58] Al-Sāwī, *al-Baṣāʾir al-naṣīriyya*.

[59] ʿAbduh had copied the text by hand decades earlier when teaching in Beirut and then taught it at al-Azhar. The front cover identifies him as responsible for the book's *taḥqīqāt*. But the book's lack of a scholarly introduction, information on the manuscript, and a critical apparatus means that ʿAbduh did not "edit" the work in the way that Zakī would do with his editions.

[60] Al-Jāḥiẓ [attrib.], *al-Tāj*, i–xiv (French introduction), 24–72 (Arabic introduction).

[61] Al-Jāḥiẓ [attrib.], *al-Tāj*, 73–83. In addition to the Topkapı copy, Zakī used a manuscript from the Ayasofya Library in Istanbul and a further manuscript from Istanbul bought and brought to Cairo by a merchant called S. Sherman.

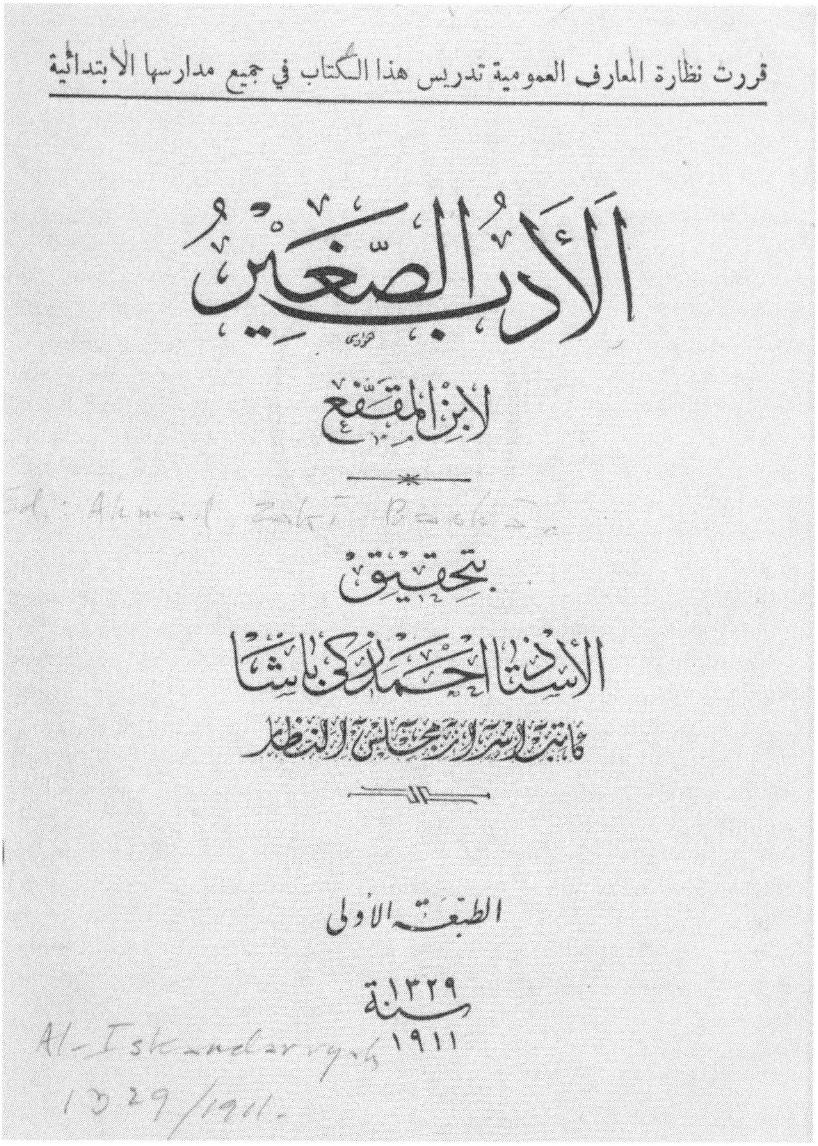

FIGURE 5.4. Cover page of Ibn al-Muqaffaʿ, *Adab al-ṣaghīr*, explicitly describing Aḥmad Zakī as responsible for the book's editing (*taḥqīq*).

By adopting the term "verification" for the role of the editor as a mediator between manuscript and print, Zakī created a new cultural figure: the editor as an expert scholar who employs a philological toolkit (the details of which were still in flux and subject to debate for another quarter-century; see chapter 8) and whose work is valued for reviving the classical heritage.

The editor as an expert thus contrasts sharply with the corrector, whose work was primarily seen to consist in the menial and occupational task of copying manuscripts in a printer's shop and catching mistakes made by typesetters.

Editing classical works takes time. In spite of his high-level government career, Zakī managed to find the time to edit the three abovementioned short treatises. Remarkably, he was also involved in another 1911 publication, al-Ṣafadī's fourteenth-century biographical dictionary of blind personalities in the Arabic and Islamic tradition.[62] When an international conference to improve conditions for the blind was planned in Cairo, the organizing committee asked Zakī to publish al-Ṣafadī's work, of which he had discovered several copies in Istanbul libraries, including a particularly valuable one in the Topkapı Palace.[63] The request was made late, leaving Zakī only twenty days to have the work printed. He met the deadline thanks to the help of two of his friends, the Syrian Ṭāhir al-Jazāʾirī (discussed in chapter 6) and a Mauritanian scholar, Aḥmad b. al-Amīn al-Shinqīṭī (ca. 1863–1913).[64] Zakī was so unhappy with the result of the rushed editing process that he named himself only as the financier of the work, not its editor, on the title page. He even had to publish his longer French introduction to the work separately.[65] In his Arabic introduction, Zakī described the manuscripts used, the time constraints that rendered the edition at best preliminary, and his efforts to include a critical apparatus and to vocalize the text, to which the printers were not used and in which they consequently made many mistakes. He also made the sensational claim for which this edition is remembered, namely, that the work shows that medieval Arabs had developed a script for the blind comparable to Braille.[66]

In addition to these four single-volume works that he published soon after returning to Cairo, Zakī also discovered hitherto lost parts of al-ʿUmarī's *Masālik al-abṣār* in the Topkapı Palace libraries.[67] The importance of this colossal political and historical geography had already been recognized by European scholars, who had analyzed the various fragments of the work

[62] Al-Ṣafadī, *Nakt al-himyān*; see also Zakī's French essay on this work, *Dictionnaire biographique des aveugles.*

[63] See the introduction to al-Ṣafadī, *Nakt al-himyān, alif.*

[64] Introduction to al-Ṣafadī, *Nakt al-himyān, jīm.*

[65] Zakī, *Dictionnaire biographique des aveugles.*

[66] Introduction to al-Ṣafadī, *Nakt al-himyān, jīm*, 207–8; see also Malti-Douglas, *Blindness and Autobiography*, 62; Ḥusayn, *al-Ayyām*, 3:505–6 (chap. 19). Zakī was not incorrect in noting that a blind scholar in Baghdad had used protruding letters to help him identify them on the page, but there is no evidence that this practice was used to reproduce whole books or that it was adopted by other blind readers.

[67] Al-ʿUmarī, *Masālik al-abṣār* (2010 ed.), 1:73. For a sketch of the available manuscripts and their history, see Krawulsky, "Masālik al-abṣār fī mamālik al-amṣār."

preserved in Paris, London, Manchester, and Madrid,[68] but it had never been studied or edited in its entirety. Zakī, too, had earlier found a substantial fragment of it in the library of Kara Çelebizade Hüsamettin (d. 1068/1658), which had originally belonged to the famed Maḥmūdiyya library in Cairo (see chapter 1),[69] but his Istanbul discovery offered the first chance of a complete edition. Zakī decided to make a second attempt at harnessing his government connections for the benefit of a large-scale project to publish an important classical work. In the fall of 1910, five years after his unsuccessful attempt to crowdfund the publication of al-Nuwayrī's encyclopedia, the Egyptian cabinet, including Khedive ʿAbbās Ḥilmī II, approved a project with the grand title "Revival of Arabic Letters" (Iḥyāʾ al-Ādāb al-ʿArabiyya). The project was formally proposed by the minister of knowledge and education (*wazīr al-maʿārif*), Aḥmad Ḥishmat (1858–1926), but its real originator was Zakī, who also put together the list of books to be published under its auspices. The project description lamented the postclassical decline of libraries in the Arab world; it hailed the establishment of the Egyptian National Library but noted the incompleteness of its holdings. Given this situation, the description explained, the Egyptian government had decided to commit more than nine thousand Egyptian pounds to the publication of twenty-seven classical works that Aḥmad Zakī had photographed in the libraries of Europe and Istanbul, ranging from al-Nuwayrī's and al-ʿUmarī's encyclopedias to works on literature and rhetoric, medicine, zoology, mineralogy, astronomy, geography, military sciences, musical theory, politics and governance, prophetic traditions, history, biography, travel, and ancient religions.[70] The challenges of the project were enormous, and Zakī would come to much grief in his efforts to bring it to fruition, but the plan nonetheless demonstrates a nexus of government policy and scholarly interest in publishing classical works. The project for the revival of Arabic letters was not uncontroversial. Some commentators criticized what they saw as a waste of government money for the sake of reviving "Arabic superstitions," while others decried it as too little investment, noting that the government had spent more money on supporting the production of foreign plays in Egyptian theaters than on publishing its own Arabic heritage.[71]

The first book to be published under this project appeared in 1914—a thin but historically enormously significant work, the ninth-century *Kitāb al-Aṣnām* (Book of idols) by Ibn al-Kalbī, which provided an unprecedented window into pre-Islamic beliefs as reconstructed and recorded in the early

[68] See the editor's introduction to al-ʿUmarī, *Masālik al-abṣār* (2010 ed.), 1:73–74.

[69] The Maḥmūdiyya's name and lending rules are visible on fol. 1a of the manuscript.

[70] Ḥishmat, "Iḥyāʾ al-lugha al-ʿarabiyya"; see also al-Jindī, *Aḥmad Zakī*, 60; Ḥishmat, "Iḥyāʾ al-ādāb al-ʿarabiyya."

[71] Riḍā, "Mashrūʿ Iḥyāʾ al-ādāb al-ʿarabiyya."

Islamic period.[72] Aḥmad Zakī had bought the work from his bibliophile friend Ṭāhir al-Jazāʾirī and presented it at the 1912 International Congress of Orientalists in Athens with a characteristic theatrical flourish: "Today, I can announce that I had the rare fortune to buy a very beautiful manuscript, paying its weight in gold: thirty small folios for thirty pounds sterling."[73] Zakī stressed that the copy he had bought was a unicum, which was true in that it was the only copy known at the time. (Two decades later, a further copy was discovered.)[74] Zakī himself edited the work; he displayed his name prominently on the title page as both editor and owner of the sole surviving manuscript and included an introduction in Arabic at one end of the book and a French introduction at the other end. The French introduction contains the paper that Zakī presented in Athens and reproduces remarks by Theodor Nöldeke (1836–1930), then the greatest living European scholar of pre-Islamic and early Islamic Arabia, regarding the importance of Zakī's find. The Arabic introduction is far more substantial, providing biographical information on the author, references to earlier authors who cited the *Aṣnām*, an analysis of the transmission of the manuscript, and reproductions of selected pages from the manuscript. The text itself, fewer than sixty pages long, is vocalized to facilitate understanding of the work's unusual and often archaic words and expressions. In addition, Zakī added an index of deities as well as a list of other pre-Islamic deities that were not mentioned in the text, increasing the edition's value as a reference work and establishing himself as an authority not simply on the philological dimension of the text but on its subject matter.

Over the following decade, Zakī focused his scholarly energy on al-Nuwayrī's and al-ʿUmarī's encyclopedias. He had managed to assemble a complete copy of the latter from fragments in the Ayasofya Library and the Topkapı Palace. One of the Topkapı fragments was particularly valuable, because it was the only known copy of the work's first volume (carrying a different title from the rest of al-ʿUmarī's work), and the copyist had read the volume aloud to al-ʿUmarī and incorporated the resulting corrections into the text. This first volume, dealing with geography, contained descriptions of Palestine, including the mosque of al-Aqṣā, and Zakī decided to compare the description against the original, traveling to Jerusalem in 1923.[75] When the first volume was published in 1924, Zakī was named as the editor on the title page, and he wrote the work's foreword as well as its philological footnotes and marginal summaries of and commentaries on al-ʿUmarī's text. A

[72] Nyberg, "Bemerkungen zum Buch der Götzenbilder."

[73] Zakī's French introduction to Ibn al-Kalbī's *Aṣnām*, ii.

[74] Spies, "Die Bibliotheken des Hidschas," 119.

[75] Al-ʿUmarī, *Masālik al-abṣār* (1924 ed.), editor's introduction.

striking feature of Zakī's comments is their occasionally culturally apologetic tone. When al-ʿUmarī reports that his teacher believed the earth to be round and other lands, plants, animals, and people to exist on the other side of the known world, Zakī takes this as evidence that Muslim scholars had theorized the existence of the new world a century and a half before Christopher Columbus.[76] Elsewhere, he argues that they had established the sources of the Nile centuries before the European discovery of them.[77]

Neither al-Nuwayrī's nor al-ʿUmarī's work was published in full during Zakī's lifetime. Before his death in 1934, Zakī saw the publication of the first seven volumes of al-Nuwayrī's work—barely a third of the total—and only the first volume of al-ʿUmarī's opus. It would take until 1997 and 2001, respectively, for the complete works to appear in print. It was not only the length of the works that thwarted his efforts; their complexity in terms of topics, people, and places discussed posed a daunting challenge, and reviews of the early volumes of al-Nuwayrī's work harshly criticized the profusion of misreadings in the edition.[78]

Zakī's means, connections, and travels also allowed him to facilitate the work of other Arab scholars who were interested in editing classical works but lacked his enviable resources. One such scholar was Muṣṭafā al-Qabbānī (d. 1918), a Damascene who emigrated to Cairo in the beginning of the twentieth century.[79] Al-Qabbānī's cousin ʿAbd al-Fattāḥ Qatlān cofounded the Salafiyya bookshop and printing house with al-Jazāʾirī's protégé Muḥibb al-Dīn al-Khaṭīb (on whom see chapter 6).[80] Beyond this sparse information, we know al-Qabbānī only through the books he corrected, which include works by al-Ghazālī on logic (*Miḥakk al-naẓar*, "The critical test"), the nature of belief and sectarianism (*Fayṣal al-tafriqa*, "The decisive criterion"), and natural theology (*al-Ḥikma fī makhlūqāt Allāh*, "The wisdom in God's creations"). He was also behind the 1905 publication of Averroes's *Metaphysics* (*Kitāb mā baʿd al-ṭabīʿa*), printed in Cairo by the Adabiyya Press with funding from al-Qabbānī and Muḥammad Amīn al-Khānjī (also discussed in chapter 6). The *Metaphysics* had previously been accessible only through its Hebrew and Latin translations, but al-Qabbānī found an Arabic manuscript of it in the Egyptian National Library.[81]

Other works were not so easily available, and the difficulties that al-Qabbānī faced in procuring copies of works to be published illustrate the

[76] Al-ʿUmarī, *Masālik al-abṣār* (1924 ed.), 31.
[77] Al-ʿUmarī, *Masālik al-abṣār* (1924 ed.), *dāl*, 68.
[78] See al-Karmalī's review in *Majallat Majmaʿ al-lugha al-ʿarabiyya fī Dimashq*.
[79] Kaḥḥāla, *Muʿjam al-muʾallifīn*, 12:269.
[80] Lauzière, "Construction of Salafiyya," 377.
[81] The print is based on MS Dār al-Kutub al-Miṣriyya, al-Ḥikma wa-l-falsafa 5. Arnzen, *On Aristotle's "Metaphysics,"* 11–12.

travails of an "ordinary" editor without Zakī's resources and social connections. In the introduction to his 1903 edition of al-Ghazālī's *al-Ḥikma fī makhlūqāt Allāh* (a work on natural features as signs of divine providence that is in close conversation with Galen's *De usu partium*, "On the usefulness of the body parts"),[82] al-Qabbānī describes at some length the process of obtaining an adequate copy of the text. He reports that after reading about the *Ḥikma* in other works,

> I wished to publish it for its renown among its author's works, . . . but unfortunately it had been lost, like others from the East, and had become, like the phoenix, a name without a reality. So I began to search for it in the catalogs of libraries in Istanbul and Syria and in the Khedival Library [in Egypt], but I found no trace of it, except in the catalog of the library in Berlin. Given the substantial expense, hardships, and long-distance travel that reaching it [there] would require, it became an unattainable dream. Yet my hopes still whispered to me of success in publishing it and reviving its text and its renown. Then God opened up His blessings to me in the form of a lover and publisher of knowledge, a supporter of its people, and a star of its venues—the famous and preeminent Aḥmad Zakī Bey, Second Cabinet Secretary. At the time he was about to depart for the Orientalist congress in Hamburg, Germany, in 1902, as the representative of the Egyptian state. I mentioned the issue to him, and he promised [to see what he could do], may God preserve him. He kept his promise and charged the learned shaykh Ḥāmid Wālī, a graduate of Dār al-ʿUlūm in Egypt and an Arabic teacher in Berlin, with copying the manuscript. He [Wālī], may God preserve him, spared no efforts in correcting [the copy he made] and collating it against [the manuscript] copy there.[83]

With no institutional channels or financial means at his disposal, al-Qabbānī had to rely on a chain of fortuitous coincidences to make his edition possible—in particular, Aḥmad Zakī's impending trip to an Orientalist congress in Hamburg and the latter's success in recruiting a willing and qualified copyist in Berlin. The growing public availability of catalogs from Western manuscript libraries in the Middle East meant that even non-elite editors such as al-Qabbānī were increasingly aware of the works available in libraries outside the region, but they relied on individuals such as Zakī to help them reach the manuscripts they had identified.

Upon his death, Zakī left behind several monographs and countless articles, both on classical Arabic culture and on contemporary Arab nationalist issues. His achievements in the revival of classical literature were not limited to the works he edited (or began to edit). His library, containing 1,482 manuscripts as well as 6,735 printed Arabic books and 3,014 books in non-Arabic

[82] El Shamsy, "Al-Ghazālī's Teleology."
[83] Al-Ghazālī, *al-Ḥikma fī makhlūqāt Allāh*, 1–2.

languages,[84] also made a lasting contribution. Zakī permitted public access to his library already in his lifetime, and after his death it became part of the Egyptian National Library.

* * *

The new interest in the revival of works that had fallen into oblivion faced significant philological challenges. In contrast to widespread curriculum texts, these works had survived only in small numbers, as unica, or even as mere fragments; they had a higher likelihood of damage by water or insects; and given their typically greater age, they were often written in an unusual script or had undergone numerous rounds of copying, thereby accumulating a larger quantity of scribal errors. As the works had been left out of the teaching curriculum, the terms, personal names, and place-names appearing in them may no longer have been known, and since the Arabic script omits short vowels and relies on easily overlooked or misplaced dots to distinguish certain letters, these texts inevitably contained textual riddles whose resolution needed tools that the early correctors at Arab presses simply did not possess. In particular, good reference works, including Arabic dictionaries, biographical dictionaries, geographical works, and works on the subject of the text to be edited, would have been indispensable. Early efforts to edit classical texts were thus hampered by a catch-22: the more rare or difficult a text, the more its editing depended on the availability of other, previously edited works whose editing would have been even more challenged by the absence of adequate reference material. It is for this reason that Aḥmad Taymūr's and Muḥammad al-Shinqīṭī's efforts to compile and publish corrections to complement previously printed reference works (discussed in the previous chapter) were so important.

The process of editing a work is significantly facilitated if the editor has recourse to multiple manuscripts of the work. To achieve such a desirable situation, however, the manuscripts must be held in libraries whose collections have been adequately cataloged, whose catalogs are available, and whose holdings can be accessed either in person, through agents, or by correspondence for the purpose of obtaining copies of the relevant works. All of these features were in short supply in the early stages of the print revolution. Furthermore, the editing process was initially in the hands of a press employee, the corrector, who usually lacked both the expertise and, most importantly, the time to search for and thoroughly compare variant manuscripts.

Wealthy individuals with interest and expertise in scholarly topics, such as Aḥmad al-Ḥusaynī, began to carry out crucial philological work on print-bound texts "behind the scenes," but it was only with Aḥmad Zakī that a fully formed role in the process of bringing classical works into print was

[84] Sayyid, *Dār al-Kutub al-Miṣriyya*, 60, 82.

established. Zakī was an expert scholar, a well-connected manuscript collector, and the owner of a significant library of his own. Through his engagement with Orientalist scholarship, he was exposed to Orientalist practices of editing and authorship, and he adopted these purposefully in his own work. This new approach to editing, inspired by Orientalists and drawing on specialized scholarship, differed in crucial respects from the work of the correctors of old. It came to be denoted by the term *taḥqīq*, hitherto meaning the evaluation of evidence but now endowed with the new technical meaning of applying philological standards to the editing of manuscripts for print.

CHAPTER 6

Reform through Books

The introduction of printing and the ensuing revolutions in book culture and the market for books opened up new horizons and possibilities not only for elite bureaucrats such as Aḥmad Zakī and Aḥmad Taymūr—the class of people known in Arabic as the "men of the pen"—but also for the "men of the turban," scholars trained in the religious sciences and immersed in the culture and discourses of Islamic scholarship. Confronted with a growing body of printed literature, including books translated from European languages as well as an increasingly diverse range of Arabic works, many of these scholars reacted with rejection, remaining focused on the conventional literary corpus. But some recognized the powerful potential of print to serve their objective of broad, indigenously rooted sociocultural change. Driven by lofty goals such as the renewal of the Arabic language, elevation of public discourse, and cultivation of ethical sentiments in society, these religious reformers excavated the classical tradition for forgotten books that could be harnessed as exemplars and disseminated across society thanks to print. This chapter focuses on two such reformers, the Egyptian Muḥammad ʿAbduh (1849–1905) and the Syrian Ṭāhir al-Jazāʾirī (1852–1920). As a reformer, ʿAbduh in particular has received a significant amount of scholarly attention. However, his contributions to the development of Islamic book culture in the service of language reform—the second of his self-identified life goals alongside religious reform[1]—remain little known, as do those made by al-Jazāʾirī.

MUḤAMMAD ʿABDUH AS A REFORMER OF LANGUAGE

The handsome 1919 textbook for Egyptian secondary schools and teaching colleges on the subject of Arabic literature and its history describes the preceding century as a time of revival (*nahḍa*). In the beginning of the century, the book reports, the standard of Arabic among the scribal classes had been abysmal, and even scholars trained in religious seminaries had incorporated Persianate features into their writings, adopting a style of rhymed prose that was affected, excessively florid, and enmeshed in formalities of language to

[1]See ʿAbduh's autobiographical sketch reproduced in Riḍā, *Tārīkh al-ustādh al-imām*, 1:11.

the detriment of content. According to the book's account, the situation had improved with the gradual shift from Turkish to Arabic as the language of the Egyptian government in its official newspaper (*al-Waqāʾiʿ al-miṣriyya*), especially once government schools began to produce graduates trained in Arabic. The Arabic of public exchange gradually shed its earlier artificiality. Additional factors were the spread of translations from Western languages into Arabic, since such translations lacked the ornateness and turgidity of postclassical Arabic writing, and the model of clear prose found in Ibn Khaldūn's *Muqaddima*, available in print since 1857 and wildly popular among teachers, readers, and newspaper editors.[2]

An important role in the revitalization of Arabic described in the textbook was played by a circle of Azhar students that formed in the 1870s, inspired by the activism of the originally Iranian Jamāl al-Dīn al-Afghānī (1838–97). The students began to participate in the public debates of the day by writing articles for newspapers and campaigning for educational, social, and political reforms and for independence from European influence. The most famous of these students was Muḥammad ʿAbduh, a native of the Nile delta who had transferred to al-Azhar in 1866 from a provincial seminary, the Aḥmadī mosque madrasa in the town of Tanta.[3] ʿAbduh contended that the task of the intellectual was not simply to call for remedying ills and improving conditions "out there" in society, but also to craft a language suited to such public discourse. The backwardness of Arab-Muslim societies was, in his view, partly rooted in the backwardness of their language. On a very basic level, the absence of scientific and social progress in the Arab lands meant that Arabic lacked the vocabulary to express and discuss discoveries, terms, and ideas that had been developed in more advanced societies. Translators faced the difficult task of forging Arabic words to represent the latest natural- and social-scientific knowledge, in the process expanding what could be said in Arabic.[4] On a higher level, ʿAbduh argued that the scholastic insistence on treating the postclassical intellectual tradition as authoritative without direct recourse to scripture had led to a decline in language. Whereas earlier scholars had debated the meaning of scripture and therefore sought to master its expressions, inter alia by studying literature to perfect their command of the language of revelation, later scholars accepted the scholastic tradition's imprimatur as a guarantee of truth. Therefore, the study of language was reduced to a formalistic analysis of the lexical meanings of individual words, their grammatical status, and their rhetorical uses, and this analysis was applied to a progressively narrowing corpus of recent texts. Such limited

[2] Al-Iskandarī and ʿInānī, *al-Wasīṭ fī al-adab al-ʿarabī wa-tārīkhuhā*, 265–82.

[3] On student life and the curriculum at the Aḥmadī mosque, see ʿAbd al-Jawād, *Ḥayāt mujāwir.*

[4] ʿAbduh, "al-Tuḥfa al-adabiyya."

FIGURE 6.1. Muḥammad ʿAbduh. Photograph from Album / Alamy Stock Photo.

intellectual ambitions amounted to lethargy and rigidity (*jumūd*) in the eyes of reformers such as ʿAbduh.[5]

When ʿAbduh began to teach at al-Azhar in 1877, he confined himself to the traditional curriculum in the classroom but offered additional classes in his home. In these classes, he taught books that lay outside the Azhari curriculum and that reflected and promoted his reformist objectives. ʿAbduh's reading list included both modern and classical works, as shown by the two titles named in his biography: one was Ḥunayn al-Khūrī's translation of François Guizot's 1846 *Histoire de la civilisation en Europe*,[6] and the other was *Tahdhīb al-akhlāq* (The refinement of character), a text on ethics by the

[5] ʿAbduh, "Mafāsid hādhā al-jumūd wa-natāʾijuhā."

[6] The translation was titled *al-Tuḥfa al-adabiyya fī tārīkh tamaddun al-mamālik al-urubāwiyya.*

tenth-century philosopher, historian, and court secretary Miskawayh, which was subsequently published by one of ʿAbduh's students.[7] In 1878, ʿAbduh was appointed to teach Arabic literature and history at the School of Languages (Madrasat al-Alsun) and at the Dār al-ʿUlūm college, which allowed him greater freedom to determine both the texts that he taught and the methods by which he taught them. One of the works he chose was Ibn Khaldūn's *Muqaddima*, which allowed him to introduce his students to history as developments between and within human collectives whose rise and fall are governed by intelligible laws, thereby instilling in them an indigenous sense of the political that was absent from the seminary curriculum. By contrast, when he attempted, a decade later, to incorporate the *Muqaddima* into the Azhari curriculum, the rector of al-Azhar, Shams al-Dīn al-Anbābī, rejected the proposal on the grounds that "it was not the tradition."[8]

In 1880, ʿAbduh became the editor of the state newspaper, *al-Waqāʾiʿ al-miṣriyya*, and he used his position to promote a political and linguistic-cultural agenda. During his editorship, the paper became both an instrument for holding government departments accountable through open criticism and a vanguard of the Arabic language. Under ʿAbduh's direction, the paper raised its own editorial standards and wielded its regulatory power over private newspapers to force them to employ competent editors and, if necessary, send them to evening classes on writing correct and clear Arabic.[9]

ʿAbduh was a supporter of the ʿUrābī revolt against the khedive and against European political encroachment in Egypt. When the movement was defeated by the British invasion of Egypt in 1882, he was sent into exile. He spent some time in Paris, publishing an anticolonial and religious reformist journal, *al-ʿUrwa al-wuthqā* (The strongest bond), with al-Afghānī, and then moved to Beirut, where he taught at the innovative Sulṭāniyya school from 1885 to 1888.[10] During this time, he discovered several classical texts, which he copied, supplied with explanatory notes, taught in his classes, and published in print. The first was the *Maqāmāt* (Assemblies) of the late tenth-century Badīʿ al-Zamān al-Hamadhānī, one of the greatest works of classical Arabic prose literature. The work had been edited and printed a few years earlier in Istanbul by al-Shidyāq, but it is not clear whether ʿAbduh knew this. In any case, ʿAbduh's edition was arguably superior: it was based on several manuscripts (though he does not, unfortunately, specify which ones), and it included ʿAbduh's straightforward gloss on difficult terms. In the introduc-

[7] Riḍā, *Tārīkh al-ustādh al-imām*, 1:135. *Tahdhīb al-akhlāq* was published by ʿAbduh's student ʿAlī Rifāʿa as Ibn Miskawayh, *Tahdhīb al-akhlāq wa-taṭhīr al-aʿrāq*; see Ẓaẓā, "Bāqa min al-falsafa al-islāmiyya."

[8] Riḍā, *Tārīkh al-ustādh al-imām*, 1:466 and 136.

[9] Adams, *Islam and Modernism in Egypt*, 47–48; al-Ṣāwī, "Muḥammad ʿAbduh and *al-Waqāʾiʿ al-Miṣrīyah*," 42–44.

[10] On the school, see Hanssen, *Fin de siècle Beirut*, 171–78.

tion, ʿAbduh admits frankly that he omitted certain parts of the text that he considered inappropriate for students.[11] The second literary work he edited was the *Nahj al-balāgha* (Pinnacle of eloquence), a collection compiled by al-Sharīf al-Raḍī (d. 406/1016) of sermons ostensibly given by Muḥammad's son-in-law and caliph ʿAlī b. Abī Ṭālib, who was famed for his eloquence. Again, ʿAbduh added a basic commentary to the text to help "the people of this age who have lost the connection to the roots of their language." In the introduction, ʿAbduh recounts his chance encounter with a manuscript of the work, describing the effect of reading ʿAlī's powerful words as akin to witnessing a ferocious battle in which the forces of truth and eloquence rout the forces of falsehood, doubt, and vice.[12] This image illustrates the close link that ʿAbduh saw between ethics and correct, articulate language. He viewed the study of language simply for the sake of formal correctness as frivolous and argued that it is only in the pursuit of truth that language becomes refined and *adab*—the Arabic term that refers to both literature and virtuous conduct—acquires meaning.[13]

During his sojourn in Beirut, ʿAbduh also visited Levantine Tripoli, where he met Rashīd Riḍā (1865–1935), the scion of a local scholarly family. Like ʿAbduh, Riḍā had received a traditional education, but he later made his mark in the publishing industry.[14] The journal he founded and edited, *al-Manār* (The lighthouse), became an internationally circulated platform on whose pages prominent figures debated the intellectual and religious issues of the day and classical works that served the reformist agenda were advertised and discussed. Equally significantly, Riḍā used his printing press to publish such classical texts, sometimes editing them himself and at other times printing editions that other scholars sent to him from all corners of the Muslim world. Several of the seminal classical publications discussed in this book were issued by Riḍā's Manār Press.

At the time of his first encounter with ʿAbduh, however, Riḍā was still in his early twenties, and the meeting launched a friendship that would endure until ʿAbduh's death. ʿAbduh and Riḍā discovered a shared unhappiness with the state of Islamic education and the absence of classical works from religious curricula. When ʿAbduh asked Riḍā which Quran commentaries he was studying in Tripoli, Riḍā replied that the sole text covered in his classes was the commentary of the eighteenth-century Ottoman scholar Ismāʿīl Ḥaqqī, which, he complained, was full of "fanciful stories and Sufi superstitions."

[11] See ʿAbduh, *al-Aʿmāl al-kāmila*, 2:408, where the introduction is reproduced. See also Pomerantz and Orfali, "Maqāmāt Badīʿ al-Zamān al-Hamadhānī," 46n23.

[12] See ʿAbduh, *al-Aʿmāl al-kāmila*, 2:409.

[13] ʿAbduh also discovered and edited a book on logic and later took it back to Egypt, where it was published after his death together with his notes: al-Sāwī, *al-Baṣāʾir al-naṣīriyya*.

[14] On Riḍā and his publishing activities, see, for example, Hamzah, "From *ʿIlm* to *Ṣiḥāfa*"; Ryad, "Printed Muslim 'Lighthouse.'"

FIGURE 6.2. Employees at Manār Press, 1926. Courtesy of Amr Ryad.

ʿAbduh recommended instead al-Zamakhsharī's twelfth-century commentary, praising its precise linguistic analysis. Riḍā further lamented that "the study of ethics has disappeared; neither students nor teachers can be found for it," to which ʿAbduh added, "This way religion disappears, too."[15] Both ʿAbduh and Riḍā were admirers of al-Ghazālī's *Iḥyāʾ ʿulūm al-dīn* as a masterpiece of virtue ethics and a paragon of elegant Arabic prose.[16] Later, when ʿAbduh met the Syrian scholar Jamāl al-Dīn al-Qāsimī (discussed in the following chapter) in Cairo in 1903, ʿAbduh advised al-Qāsimī to write an accessible abridgment of al-Ghazālī's work for use in schools, a suggestion that al-Qāsimī followed.[17]

ʿAbduh's interest in classical works was accompanied by a refined philological sense, and he was a critical reader of newly published works. In an article published in Beirut in 1886, he argued that one of the allegedly oldest historical texts in Arabic, a work on the conquests of Syria (*Futūḥ al-Shām*) attributed to al-Wāqidī (d. 207/823) and printed two decades earlier in Cairo,[18] could not in fact be by al-Wāqidī. ʿAbduh's argument was based on an analysis of the book's style, which reflected fourteenth- or fifteenth-century

[15] Riḍā, *Tārīkh al-ustādh al-imām*, 1:390.
[16] Riḍā, *al-Manār wa-l-Azhar*, 140, 142, 143, 147, 188.
[17] Jamāl al-Dīn al-Qāsimī, *Mawʿiẓat al-muʾminīn min Iḥyāʾ ʿulūm al-dīn*.
[18] Al-Wāqidī [attrib.], *Futūḥ al-Shām*.

Egypt, not eighth-century Hijaz, where al-Wāqidī had been born.[19] ʿAbduh's sophisticated critical approach contrasts sharply with that of his near-contemporary, ʿAbd al-Qādir al-Jazāʿirī (1808–83), the Algerian statesman in exile in Damascus. ʿAbd al-Qādir, too, was a learned scholar, but his scholarship was still steeped in the epistemological paradigm of esoteric inspiration. Thus, he grounded his argument against the authenticity of *al-Shajara al-nuʿmāniyya* (The blood-red tree), an occult work attributed to Ibn ʿArabī that predicts the Ottoman conquest of Arab lands that took place almost three centuries after Ibn ʿArabī's death, not in an analysis of the features of the text itself but rather in a vision he claimed to have had, in which he had asked Ibn ʿArabī about the work and the latter had replied, "Lies and forgery!"[20]

After his return to Egypt in 1888, ʿAbduh's career flourished again. In 1899, he was appointed grand mufti of Egypt, and he used his position to advocate for educational reforms. He played a key role in the establishment of a unified Azhar Library, as seen in chapter 1, and he was the driving force behind the introduction of Arabic literature as a subject at al-Azhar. According to the great Egyptian prose essayist and translator al-Manfalūṭī (d. 1924), who was a student at al-Azhar at the time, before ʿAbduh's reforms literature had been dismissed as a trivial pursuit at the seminary: finding their student with a book of poetry or prose literature, his teachers would react as if they had found "gold in the pocket of a thief, or an empty alcohol bottle in that of a young man, or a lover in a girl's bedroom."[21] Reflecting the intellectual preoccupations of the postclassical period outlined in chapter 2, al-Manfalūṭī describes an intellectual world in which scholars were experts in grammatical and rhetorical analysis but incapable of expressing ideas clearly and eloquently.[22] Like ʿAbduh, whose devoted student he became, al-Manfalūṭī saw literature as crucial for the development of the ethical individual, because it engendered human affects such as compassion and depicted embodied virtues. Furthermore, literature connected words to meanings, whereas moral decay was characterized by the separation of words and meanings, which allowed "generosity to be called wastefulness and self-control to be called cowardice."[23]

ʿAbduh achieved the hiring of two professors of Arabic literature at al-Azhar. The first was Sayyid b. ʿAlī al-Marṣafī (d. 1931), whose many illustrious students included Ṭāhā Ḥusayn. Ḥusayn later described al-Marṣafī as an

[19] ʿAbduh, "Kutub al-maghāzī wa-aḥādīth al-qaṣṣāṣīn," 212. For further discussion of this work, see chapter 8.

[20] ʿAbd al-Qādir al-Jazāʾirī, *al-Mawāqif*, 2:709; see also Gril, "L'énigme de la *Šaǧara al-nuʿmāniyya*," 140–42.

[21] Al-Manfalūṭī, *al-Naẓarāt*, 1:9–10.

[22] Al-Manfalūṭī, *al-Naẓarāt*, 1:24–27.

[23] Al-Manfalūṭī, *al-Naẓarāt*, 1:17–18.

inspirational teacher who rejected the hitherto dominant scholastic mode of instruction and encouraged his students to engage directly and critically with the authors they read and to strive to rival them in their own literary output.[24] Ḥusayn also provided an eloquent testimony of the impact that the new exposure to classical literature had on his generation of students, hitherto raised on the postclassical literary diet:

> When they read some literary texts that had originally appeared in the Abbasid era [750–1258 CE], they discovered a closeness to nature and a distance from artificiality; they discovered a role for feeling, sentiment, and intellect, and became aware of the distance between the lively literature they were now reading and the dead literature to which they had become accustomed; they also concluded that this ancient literature was in fact closer to their own sentiments and much more capable of expressing their emotions than the moribund "modern" [i.e., postclassical] literature which only managed to reflect its writers' ability to collect and distribute phrases.[25]

The second literature hire at al-Azhar was the Mauritanian scholar Muḥammad Maḥmūd al-Shinqīṭī al-Turkuzī, introduced in chapter 4 as the teacher of Aḥmad Taymūr.[26] Al-Shinqīṭī also played a role in the Society for the Revival of the Arabic Sciences (Jamʿiyyat Iḥyāʾ al-ʿUlūm al-ʿArabiyya),[27] an organization that ʿAbduh established in 1899 to edit and finance the publication of forgotten classical works.[28] Under the society's auspices, and at ʿAbduh's instigation, al-Shinqīṭī edited the monumental literary anthology *al-Mukhaṣṣaṣ* as well as two of the most important classical works on linguistics, *Asrār al-balāgha* and *Dalāʾil al-iʿjāz*, both written by the eleventh-century scholar ʿAbd al-Qāhir al-Jurjānī.

Al-Jurjānī's contributions to Arabic linguistics had never received much attention and by ʿAbduh's time had been all but forgotten.[29] But they were perfectly suited to promoting ʿAbduh's goal of reorienting the study of language to emphasize the expression of content: the two books defend the prioritization of semantics over the formal analysis of texts.[30] Accordingly, ʿAbduh made great efforts to accomplish the works' publication and popu-

[24] Ḥusayn, *al-Ayyām*, 2:280–85 (chap. 19).

[25] Translated in Allen, "Post-Classical Period," 15. According to Allen, the article from which the quotation is drawn was published in *al-Jadīd* in 1930 and reprinted in *Akhbār al-adab* in 1997.

[26] Al-Zayyāt, "Awwalu mā ʿaraftu al-Shinqīṭī."

[27] Also called the Society for the Revival of Arabic Books (Jamʿiyyat Iḥyāʾ al-Kutub al-ʿArabiyya). See Riḍā, *Tārīkh al-ustādh al-imām*, 1:753.

[28] ʿAbduh, *al-Aʿmāl al-kāmila*, 1:196–97.

[29] Noy, "Legacy of ʿAbd al-Qāhir al-Jurjānī."

[30] Versteegh, *Arabic Linguistic Tradition*, chap. 9.

larization.[31] Both he and al-Shinqīṭī owned manuscripts of *Dalāʾil al-iʿjāz*, but they were deficient, so ʿAbduh secured additional copies from Baghdad and Medina, and al-Shinqīṭī collated the four copies. Al-Jurjānī's other work, *Asrār al-balāgha*, was so obscure that ʿAbduh could not find a single copy in Egypt. He was eventually able to procure a copy from Tripoli thanks to Rashīd Riḍā, who told him of a friend there who had inherited a manuscript of the work. Having learned of the existence of a second manuscript in Istanbul, ʿAbduh sent one of his students there to collate the Tripoli copy. As soon as al-Jurjānī's pages came off the press, ʿAbduh began to teach the works to his students at al-Azhar; in the course of teaching, however, he discovered so many mistakes in the printed versions that he insisted that the binding of the books be halted until half a dozen errata pages for each book could be printed and incorporated.[32] It is not an exaggeration to say that the publication of these two works fundamentally changed the study of Arabic rhetoric.[33]

ʿAbduh's motivation for founding the Society for the Revival of Arabic Sciences lay in his frustration with the continuing unavailability of what he considered foundational works of Islamic thought and the continuing lack of interest not only among laypeople but even among Muslim scholars in these works. In his public exchange with the Syrian Christian intellectual Faraḥ Anṭūn (1874–1922) in 1902, he expressed his exasperation in the following words:

> The books of the ancients have been lost. Someone searching for the *Mudawwana* of Mālik or the *Umm* of al-Shāfiʿī or one of the early Ḥanafī tomes finds himself in the situation of a person looking for a Quran in the house of an atheist. Should you find one fragment here and another there, and finally put them together, the mistakes of the copyist will stand between you and your being able to benefit from the work. Muslims have neglected the sciences of their religion and consideration of the opinions of the early generations. . . . Many exegeses on the Quran were written in the third century [AH] and afterward, until the sixth century, such as the exegesis of al-Ṭabarī[34] . . . and many others. They contain the views and methods of these giants. . . . No student of the religious sciences can do without them. Is it possible for a serious

[31]The fact that Riḍā added forewords to later editions of these works has led Arab scholars to consider Riḍā the editor and to ignore ʿAbduh's role. See, for example, Maḥmūd Shākir's introduction to his editions of al-Jurjānī's *Asrār al-balāgha*, 5, and *Dalāʾil al-iʿjāz*, *yāʾ*.

[32]Al-Jurjānī, *Asrār al-balāgha* (ʿAbduh and al-Shinqīṭī ed.), Riḍā's introduction, *hāʾ*; al-Jurjānī, *Dalāʾil al-iʿjāz* (ʿAbduh and al-Shinqīṭī ed.), 403; ʿAbduh, *al-Aʿmāl al-kāmila*, 1:196.

[33]See Maḥmūd Shākir's introduction to his edition of al-Jurjānī's *Asrār al-balāgha*. For recent work on al-Jurjānī's contribution to the study of Arabic rhetoric, see Harb, "Poetic Marvels"; Noy, "Emergence of *ʿIlm al-Bayān*."

[34]ʿAbduh helped Naṣr al-ʿĀdilī prepare a second edition of al-Ṭabarī's exegesis to supersede the first, poorly done edition; see al-ʿĀdilī's colophon in al-Ṭabarī, *Jāmiʿ al-bayān* (Bulaq ed.), 30:232.

> researcher to find a reliable copy of these great works, except by accident and chance? Is it appropriate for a community that claims to uphold a religion and to follow their forebears in it to abandon the works of these forebears and to leave what they have written as food for worms and a resting place for dust?[35]

His prominent position enabled ʿAbduh to pursue texts globally. The last work that he helped publish was the *Mudawwana* of Saḥnūn (d. 240/854), a multivolume collection of the legal opinions of Mālik b. Anas that is both one of the earliest works of Islamic legal reasoning and a foundational text for the Mālikī school of legal thought.[36] Although the work had been written in Egypt by a Tunisian scholar, only fragments could be found in either Egypt or Tunisia. However, ʿAbduh heard that a complete copy was extant in the venerable Qarawiyyīn Mosque in Fez, Morocco. So he turned to the sultan of Morocco, Mulay ʿAbd al-ʿAzīz (r. 1894–1908), with a plea:

> I had hoped that Your Majesty would have an interest in the religious sciences, in the revival of what has withered among them, and in the publication of rare books on them, so as to refine souls with their literature and revive and connect hearts through them. Trusting in these noble aims, I am inspired to inform Your Highness that the Society for the Revival of the Arabic Sciences has been formed in Egypt. Its specific task is to search for early works that are on the verge of being lost, to correct their manuscript copies, and to print them, in order to recover what has been lost of the knowledge of the ancients and what has been hidden from us by the works of the recent [generations]. This society organized the printing of the book of ʿAlī b. Sīdah the Andalusian on language, titled *al-Mukhaṣṣaṣ*, which will be completed soon. It is now searching for copies of Imam Mālik's *Mudawwana* to procure a correct copy and print this precious work. A fragment of this work has been discovered in Egypt and another one in Tunisia, and they are in the society's possession. However, no complete and reliable copy has been found thus far. I have been assured that such a complete copy exists in the Qarawiyyīn Mosque. It would be easy for His Highness the Sultan—may God support him and through him the faith—to help us in this venture and support us in this beneficent effort by issuing an order to send us this copy either in its entirety—so we can collate it with what we have and thereby correct the deficiencies in our manuscripts before returning it and, upon the work's publication, sending ten copies to the mosque, God willing—or, alternatively, part by part, with us sending each part back as soon as the need has been met. Either way, we submit all due thanks to the Sultan for his attention.[37]

[35] ʿAbduh, "al-Islām wa-l-Naṣrāniyya," in *al-Aʿmāl al-kāmila*, 3:338, 359–60.
[36] See Abd-Allah, *Mālik and Medina*, 63–70.
[37] ʿAbduh, *al-Aʿmāl al-kāmila*, 2:362–63.

ʿAbduh's appeal seems to have been successful: a manuscript of the *Mudawwana*, written on gazelle skin, was sent from Morocco to Cairo. However, ʿAbduh died in July 1905, before the editing was finished, and the project was seen to completion by a group of Azhari scholars.[38] When the printed edition appeared in a series of volumes in 1905 and 1906, it made no mention of ʿAbduh's considerable contribution to its success; the colophon seems to strenuously avoid his name and instead heaps copious praise on conservative Azhari scholars not known to have had any interest in classical texts. This remarkable omission is illustrative of a wider problem with ʿAbduh's legacy at his alma mater. Although he enjoyed (and still enjoys) popularity in overall cultural discourse in Egypt and beyond, many of his conservative colleagues at al-Azhar saw his reformism as deeply suspicious and his interest in literature as diametrically opposed to religion, rather than, as ʿAbduh himself had seen it, as necessary for its ethical existence. Still in ʿAbduh's lifetime, ʿAbd al-Raḥmān al-Shirbīnī (d. 1908), the rector of al-Azhar, accused ʿAbduh of turning al-Azhar "into a school of philosophy and literature that wages war on religion and extinguishes its light."[39]

ʿAbduh's campaign against the baroque features of postclassical Arabic nevertheless bore fruit. A striking example is the genre of blurbs (*taqārīẓ*, sing. *taqrīẓ*), short texts that scholars wrote in support of works by their colleagues that were then attached to the works.[40] Postclassical blurbs had become formulaic exercises in praising the author and his book in rhymed prose or verse, usually with no indication of the work's actual content.[41] ʿAbduh repurposed the genre, composing blurbs in clear, uncluttered prose and discussing explicitly the contents of the book in question.[42] ʿAbduh's style proved influential on the generation that succeeded him.[43] Although the inclusion of blurbs in published works eventually went out of fashion, the genre was resuscitated by Riḍā, who appropriated the term as a heading for the book review section of his journal, *al-Manār*, inaugurating a practice that was subsequently adopted by another influential journal, *al-Muqtaṭaf*.[44]

[38] Saḥnūn, *al-Mudawwana*.

[39] Riḍā, *Tārīkh al-ustādh al-imām*, 1:503.

[40] See the example of al-Ḥusaynī's *Dalīl al-musāfir*, discussed at the end of chapter 4.

[41] The blurbs of Ḥasan al-ʿAṭṭār were a rare exception: although written in rhyming prose, they provided substantial information on the books in question. See two examples in Ḥasan, *Ḥasan al-ʿAṭṭār*, 107–8.

[42] Compare ʿAbduh's blurb against the others included in al-Ḥusaynī, *Dalīl al-musāfir*, 2–3, 91–110.

[43] For blurbs from the early 1930s, see, for example, Muḥammad Ḥabīb Allāh al-Shinqīṭī, *Zād al-muslim*, 6:999–1008. I am grateful to Matthew Steele for this reference.

[44] The Cairene journal *al-Muqtaṭaf*, edited by Yaʿqūb Ṣarrūf, titled its book review section "Blurb and Critique" ("al-Taqrīẓ wa-l-intiqād") from 1898 onward.

Al-Azhar had not been a source of editions of classical texts before ʿAbduh, and it did not become one after him. As a religious seminary, al-Azhar saw itself primarily as the upholder of a timeless religious tradition that could be mastered by studying the texts of its curriculum. From this perspective, the drive to discover and resurrect forgotten texts was inherently suspicious: if a text had fallen out of circulation, it had likely done so for a good reason, being inferior or deviant; and even if it was neither, the fact that it was no longer encased in a living interpretive tradition in the form of detailed commentaries meant that both the form and the content of the text were dangerously underdetermined. Reformist scholars who sought to expand the scope of the curriculum were implicitly denying the comprehensiveness of the tradition and trying to reinject into it ideas that it had already discarded.

Therefore, the task of editing classical works continued to be carried out mostly by intellectuals educated in nonseminary institutions—"men of the pen"—or by scholars with religious training who, for one reason or another, stood apart from the mainstream seminary system—individuals such as al-Shinqīṭī, the perennial outsider; Riḍā, who channeled his education and skills into the publishing industry; and the energetic reformer who was called "the Muḥammad ʿAbduh of Syria,"[45] Ṭāhir al-Jazāʾirī.

THE MULTIFACETED ACTIVISM OF ṬĀHIR AL-JAZĀʾIRĪ

We have already encountered Ṭāhir al-Jazāʾirī as the driving force behind the establishment of manuscript libraries in Damascus and other Levantine cities in chapter 1 and as Aḥmad Zakī's friend and helper in chapter 5. But al-Jazāʾirī's influence on modern Arabic book culture was far more extensive. His private manuscript collection, his notes on the holdings of the Ẓāhiriyya Library, and his role in the publication of several important classical works have left an enduring imprint on the landscape of classical Arabo-Islamic literature. Like ʿAbduh, al-Jazāʾirī believed in the potential of literature and ethical writings to contribute to communal improvement, but he was less a public intellectual than he was a scholar, possessing a deep familiarity with manuscript literature and steering the rediscovery of classical texts both openly and from behind the scenes.[46]

Al-Jazāʾirī was born in Damascus in 1852. His family had been part of a wave of Algerian immigrants that had arrived in Damascus in the wake of Amir ʿAbd al-Qādir's defeat by the French in 1847. His father became a prominent personality in Damascus and served as a judge. Ṭāhir al-Jazāʾirī's formal

[45] Escovitz, "'He Was the Muḥammad ʿAbduh of Syria.'"

[46] On al-Jazāʾirī's activism, see Weismann, *Taste of Modernity*, 283–91.

FIGURE 6.3. Ṭāhir al-Jazāʾirī. From al-Ziriklī, *al-Aʿlām*, plate 523.

education covered the Islamic disciplines, Arabic, Turkish, and Persian, as well as the natural sciences. After the completion of his schooling, the central figure in his further studies was ʿAbd al-Ghanī al-Ghunaymī al-Maydānī (1807–81), an early Syrian reformist scholar also known for sheltering Christian refugees during the 1860 massacres.[47] Al-Maydānī's reformism consisted of a staunch opposition to what he saw as superstition in popular religion.[48] Later, recalling his lessons in legal theory with al-Maydānī, al-Jazāʾirī marveled at his teacher's critical treatment of the various positions discussed.[49] Al-Maydānī had studied with the nineteenth century's greatest author of legal commentaries, Ibn ʿĀbidīn (d. 1836), and his writings show him engrossed in and limited to the postclassical literary horizon.[50] Nevertheless,

[47]Commins, *Islamic Reform*, 40–41.

[48]Kurd ʿAlī, *Kunūz al-ajdād*, 5–6.

[49]Al-Bānī, *Tanwīr al-baṣāʾir*, 74.

[50]See, e.g., al-Maydānī, *Sharḥ al-ʿaqīda al-Ṭahawiyya*, 74–75. For a list of the books he studied, see al-Maydānī, *al-Lubāb*, 1:39–44.

his personal library, to which al-Jazāʾirī had access, did contain older works, such as Ibn Fāris's *al-Ṣāḥibī*, an important tenth-century work on linguistics, which Ignaz Goldziher encountered on a visit to Damascus in 1873 and brought to the attention of Western academia.[51]

However, the unrivaled knowledge of classical texts for which al-Jazāʾirī would become renowned and his substantial private library originated not in his studies with al-Maydānī or other teachers, but in his experience as a bookseller. Already as a primary school student al-Jazāʾirī had begun to sell manuscripts in the vicinity of Saladin's mausoleum,[52] and by reading the works he sold, he expanded his interests to encompass classical literature of religious, historical, and literary nature alike. He took a particular interest in rare and early manuscripts, eventually compiling a list of the rarest and most significant manuscripts he had encountered in his life.[53] When al-Jazāʾirī met Goldziher on the latter's visit to Damascus, both men were in their early twenties. Al-Jazāʾirī introduced Goldziher to the intellectual life of the city, taking him to salons and bookshops. Goldziher subsequently recalled this period as the "most beautiful" of his life and considered the reformism he encountered among Syrian Muslim intellectuals a model to be emulated by modern Jews.[54] The two men remained lifelong friends.[55] Nearly three decades after the visit, Goldziher wrote a moving letter to al-Jazāʾirī:

> I hope that you still remember your Hungarian friend, who sought your hospitality in Syria in 1290 [1873 CE], gaining enlightenment from its scholars, frequenting its learned men and litterateurs—your friend becoming day by day more familiar with you in discussions. We—you and your servant, the writer [of these lines]—were young then, engrossed in the noble sciences, drowning in the seas of fine literature; now, how much has changed! After the passage of twenty-seven years, my bones are brittle and my hair is gray. But by God almighty, your memory has not faded from my soul or my mind, nor has the memory of the enlightened friends. And while "my patience has been reduced and my sorrows multiplied / yet the one in love excels in patience."[56]

In 1878, when al-Jazāʾirī was twenty-six, the Ottoman sultan appointed a new governor for Syria, the famous Midḥat Pasha. Midḥat Pasha had served as the grand vizier of the Ottoman Empire for a few months in late 1876 and early 1877, and he had been instrumental in the introduction of the first

[51]Ibn Fāris's (d. 395/1004) *Ṣāḥibī* was published in Cairo in 1910. For the episode, see Goldziher, *Tagebuch*, 58. For al-Maydānī's library, see al-Maydānī, *al-Lubāb*, 1:126–30.

[52]Kurd ʿAlī, *Kunūz al-ajdād*, 6.

[53]Ṭāhir al-Jazāʾirī, *Fihris muntakhabāt li-nawādir al-kutub.*

[54]Goldziher, *Tagebuch*, 64; van Ess, "Goldziher as a Contemporary," 507–8.

[55]Kurd ʿAlī, *Kunūz al-ajdād*, 15.

[56]Goldziher, "Min ʿālim gharbī ilā ʿālim sharqī," 321. The quoted line is from Saladin's court poet ʿArqala al-Kalbī (d. 567/1171); see Ibn Shākir, *Fawāt al-Wafayāt*, 1:147.

Ottoman constitution during his tenure. His zeal for reforming the Ottoman state proved to be his undoing, and his short stint as grand vizier ended in exile. But shortly thereafter he was dispatched to Syria, still an exile but now one with an official portfolio. In Syria, Midḥat Pasha immediately embarked on various reform projects, but his efforts were continuously frustrated by the central authorities in Istanbul.[57] Undaunted, Midḥat Pasha circumvented Ottoman obstructivism by embracing local reform initiatives. Many of these initiatives were spearheaded by Ṭāhir al-Jazāʾirī. They included the centralization of endowed libraries into the Ẓāhiriyya, discussed in chapter 1; support for a variety of Islamic charitable societies founded as counterweights to the newly established Western missionary schools; and efforts to combat illiteracy, including among women.[58] Al-Jazāʾirī, who had already begun to teach primary school students in the Ẓāhiriyya four years earlier, was a central figure in the educational reform movement. He became a champion of primary education in Syria, campaigning for parents to enroll their children in school, serving as the chief inspector of schools, and authoring textbooks for use in these schools.[59] One of these textbooks, which he published at the age of twenty-seven, adapted the postclassical genre of the *badīʿiyya* poem (in which each line contains a recognized Arabic rhetorical figure) for teaching use by interspersing its lines with straightforward explanations of the figures used.[60]

Al-Jazāʾirī was a significant force in Damascene intellectual life, participating actively in salons and study circles as well as hosting them, and he seems to have used this engagement as a vehicle of advancing his reformist agenda. The following account by his student Muḥammad Kurd ʿAlī illustrates his approach:

> It was the habit of the shaykh [al-Jazāʾirī] to keep the company of various different groups, whatever their intellectual tendencies—even atheists or members of Sufi brotherhoods. Once he encountered a group that had attached itself to a Sufi brotherhood, reciting its litany. He found in some of [the group's members] a readiness to learn. So he kept the company of their master, acting as his student, until he could convince the group to spend their time reading a work on Sufism that both was good literature and called for virtuous conduct. He had to endure suspicious looks, so he entered their gatherings claiming that he was

[57] See Midḥat, *Life of Midhat Pasha*, 176–80.

[58] Tibawi, *Modern History of Syria*, 156; Muḥyī al-Dīn, *al-Shaykh Ṭāhir al-Jazāʾirī*, 33–35.

[59] Escovitz, "'He Was the Muḥammad ʿAbduh of Syria,'" 294; Muḥyī al-Dīn, *al-Shaykh Ṭāhir al-Jazāʾirī*, 36–37; Kurd ʿAlī, *Kunūz al-ajdād*, 6–7. Muḥammad Kurd ʿAlī met al-Jazāʾirī for the first time when the former was a schoolboy and the latter the school inspector; see Kurd ʿAlī, *al-Mudhakkirāt*, 1:11.

[60] Ṭāhir al-Jazāʾirī, *Badīʿ al-talkhīṣ wa-talkhīṣ al-badīʿ*. This poem was one of the last representatives of the genre; see Bauer, "Die *Badīʿiyya*," 56.

seeking to learn, eager to listen to their master's lesson. Meanwhile, he brought manuscripts of the work to collate them with the printed copy [that they were reading]; then he tried to teach some of them how to use linguistic reference works, so misreadings could be corrected and the work would receive the service it deserved. In this way, he managed to bring those of them who were ready from books on Sufism to works on other Islamic sciences and literature. I heard that some of them [reached such a level of learning that they] tired of reading Ibn Jarīr al-Ṭabarī's *tafsīr* with its extensive exegesis of the Quran. Capable intellectuals emerged from this group, yet before that [intervention] they had been entirely occupied with inspirations, imaginings, and dreams.[61]

The only actual reformist intervention that al-Jazāʾirī undertook in this Sufi group, according to Kurd ʿAlī's anecdote, was to encourage the group's members to read good books and to provide these books with "the service they deserve" by reading the printed copies critically, collating them against manuscripts and making use of other tools, such as reference works, to weed out textual corruptions. Once these skills had been learned, al-Jazāʾirī then introduced the group members to classical works of both literature and Islamic scholarship, such as the great ninth-century Quran commentary by al-Ṭabarī, which had just been discovered and printed.[62] Al-Jazāʾirī's program, as reflected in this anecdote and the overall trajectory of his work and activism, appears to have been rooted in philological competence and care for texts, together with a humanistic embrace of literature and the promotion of education and wide learning. Like many of his fellow reformists, he dismissed the value of esoteric claims to knowledge and rejected their authoritarian implications.

Al-Jazāʾirī attracted a circle of students, whom he encouraged to pursue a variety of intellectual fields—from religious, literary, and philosophical study to the modern natural and social sciences.[63] One of these students was the thirteen-year-old Muḥibb al-Dīn al-Khaṭīb (1886–1969), whose father Abū al-Fatḥ had been the director of the Ẓāhiriyya Library from 1879 to 1897 and a close friend of al-Jazāʾirī's. After his father's death, Muḥibb al-Dīn became a de facto foster son to al-Jazāʾirī. The latter had him copy manuscripts housed in the Ẓāhiriyya Library, particularly works by Ibn Taymiyya, both to broaden his intellectual horizons and to earn money by selling the resulting copies.[64] Muḥibb al-Dīn went on to become an important publisher in Cairo.

[61] Kurd ʿAlī, *Kunūz al-ajdād*, 15.

[62] Al-Ṭabarī, *Jāmiʿ al-bayān*. Until shortly before its publication, this enormously important work was known only through mentions in later works; the work itself was presumed lost. See Zakī, *Mawsūʿāt al-ʿulūm*, 62–63.

[63] Kurd ʿAlī, *Kunūz al-ajdād*, 8–9.

[64] Rizvi, "Muhibb al-Din al-Khatib," 14–17. For example, Muḥibb al-Dīn al-Khaṭīb copied in 1901 Ibn Taymiyya's *Kitāb al-Istighātha/al-Radd ʿalā al-Bakrī* and sold it to Aḥmad Taymūr

Others of al-Jazāʾirī's students became scholars of Arabic literature, medicine, and natural sciences at the American University in Beirut.[65] In addition, his weekly salons were attended by some of the most influential Syrian intellectuals of the late nineteenth and early twentieth centuries.[66] Muḥammad ʿAbduh befriended al-Jazāʾirī during his years of exile in Beirut.[67]

In the 1890s, al-Jazāʾirī began to edit classical works of Islamic thought and literature. His focus on ethical and literary works mirrors and was probably inspired by the work of ʿAbduh and his circle to edit such works a decade earlier. Al-Jazāʾirī's editions reveal both a reformist drive to publish socially useful works and a philological concern with using the oldest and most reliable manuscripts available.

The nature and extent of al-Jazāʾirī's actual contribution to the work of editing these texts are not obvious and require some excavation to establish. His first project was a collection of the sermons of the classical orator Ibn Nubāta (d. 374/985), which he furnished with a biographical introduction and basic commentary in footnotes.[68] In both form and content, the edition is very similar to ʿAbduh's edition of ʿAlī b. Abī Ṭālib's sermons (*Nahj al-balāgha*). The title page describes al-Jazāʾirī's role only as that of the commentator, and it names him next to the commissioner (*multazim*) who financed the print; this was a certain ʿAbd al-Bāsiṭ al-Ansī (d. 1928), who belonged to a prominent Levantine Ottoman scholarly family.[69] The final page, however, reveals that al-Jazāʾirī also served as the corrector of the edition, and it claims that the underlying manuscript, dating from 589/1193, was copied from the original transcript of Ibn Nubāta's sermons.[70] This emphasis on the age of the manuscript and its pedigree as a direct copy of the original suggests that the entire editing process, beginning with the identification and procurement of the manuscript and culminating in the correction of the proofs, was carried out by the manuscript connoisseur al-Jazāʾirī himself.

(now included in the Taymūr collection at the Dār al-Kutub al-Miṣriyya, no. 281, under the title *Khulāṣat al-Radd Ibn Taymiyya ʿalā al-Bakrī fī al-istighātha*). See Ibn Taymiyya, *al-Istighātha* (al-Suhaylī ed.), 103–4.

[65] These former students included the physician and Arab nationalist politician ʿAbd al-Raḥmān Shahbandar (1880–1940) and the historian and litterateur Wajīh b. Fāris al-Kīlānī (1886–1934); Kaḥḥāla, *Muʿjam al-muʾallifīn*, 5:141, 13:160.

[66] In addition to Shahbandar (see previous note), they included the scholar and publisher Muḥammad Kurd Alī (1876–1953), the intellectual and political activist Rafīq al-ʿAẓm (1865–1925), the activist and later first Syrian president Shukrī al-Quwatlī (1891–1967), and the Christian intellectual and later Syrian prime minister Fāris al-Khūrī (1877–1962); Muḥyī al-Dīn, *al-Shaykh Ṭāhir al-Jazāʾirī*, 41–42.

[67] Kurd ʿAlī, *Kunūz al-ajdād*, 15.

[68] The work, *Dīwān khuṭab Ibn Nubāta*, was published in 1894.

[69] Al-Dughaym, "Dawr āl al-Ansī," 19.

[70] Ibn Nubāta, *Dīwān*, 528.

Al-Jazāʾirī's role is similarly obscure in his second classical publication, Ibn al-Akfānī's (d. 749/1348) philosophical treatise on the classification of the sciences.[71] The colophon names Muḥammad Salīm al-Āmidī al-Bukhārī (1851–1928), al-Jazāʾirī's student and lifelong friend, as the corrector,[72] but on the title page al-Jazāʾirī is quoted as saying, "I have encountered several copies of this original and beneficial work, but they are riddled with countless corruptions, distortions, replacements, additions, and omissions, so I set out to correct this version as well as possible, after gathering as many copies as I could and collating them and consulting many relevant reference works to fill in its lacunae and restore its structure."[73] Clearly, then, al-Jazāʾirī had a central part in establishing the text. Whereas the title of "corrector" likely reflected the institutional function of ensuring the correct transfer of an established text into print, primarily through proofreading, the bulk of the activity that later came to constitute the purview of the editor was performed by al-Jazāʾirī. At the end of the text, just before the four pages of errata, a note states that during the printing of the text, "I discovered a correct copy in the hand of my shaykh, the eminent scholar Muḥammad al-Ṭanṭāwī [d. 1889]";[74] the following errata, the note adds, thus contain not only typesetting errors but also better readings gleaned from the newly discovered manuscript. It is not clear whether the note was inserted by al-Bukhārī or al-Jazāʾirī, since both could have referred to al-Ṭanṭāwī as their teacher.

Like ʿAbduh's edition of al-Hamadhānī's *Maqāmāt*, al-Jazāʾirī's editions of Ibn Nubāta's and Ibn al-Akfānī's works had been preceded by earlier publications of the same texts; as in ʿAbduh's case, it is impossible to determine whether al-Jazāʾirī knew of these editions. Ibn Nubāta's sermons had been printed in Bombay, Ibn al-Akfānī's work in Calcutta (by the Austrian Orientalist Aloys Sprenger) and in Cairo (by Maḥmūd Bey Abū al-Naṣr, a lawyer, public intellectual, and journal editor). Al-Jazāʾirī's editions are superior to their predecessors, and they contain more information regarding the manuscripts used (the Bombay print of Ibn Nubāta and Sprenger's Calcutta edition of Ibn al-Akfānī contain none; the Abū al-Naṣr edition gives a vague hint).[75] It is also not obvious what role Abū al-Naṣr played in the editing of the text.[76]

[71]See Witkam, *De egyptische arts Ibn al-Akfānī*. On the Jazāʾirī/Bukhārī edition, see pp. 122–24.

[72]Ibn al-Akfānī, *Irshād al-qāṣid* (al-Jazāʾirī ed.), 139.

[73]Ibn al-Akfānī, *Irshād al-qāṣid* (al-Jazāʾirī ed.), 1.

[74]Ibn al-Akfānī, *Irshād al-qāṣid* (al-Jazāʾirī ed.), 144. On al-Ṭanṭāwī, see al-Bayṭār, *Ḥilyat al-bashar*, 3:1284–88.

[75]Abū al-Naṣr mentions that he discovered Ibn al-Akfānī's work (most likely the manuscript) by chance in the École des langues orientales in Paris; see Witkam, *De egyptische arts Ibn al-Akfānī*, 121.

[76]The title page states that he "attended to the print" (*iʿtanā bi-ṭabʿih*), which suggests that he merely initiated and financed the printing.

A third noteworthy edition by al-Jazāʾirī is the 1901/1902 print of al-Rāghib al-Iṣfahānī's eleventh-century work on ethics.[77] Like ʿAbduh before him (and Jamāl al-Dīn al-Qāsimī, discussed in detail in the following chapter, after him), al-Jazāʾirī believed that the resurrection of classical ethical texts could contribute greatly to the edification of Muslim society.[78] The edition is based on a manuscript housed in the Khālidī Library in Jerusalem—another institution in whose establishment al-Jazāʾirī had had a hand—and on a second manuscript written by the Aleppine scholar Raḍī al-Dīn b. Abī Bakr in the sixteenth century. The title page of the published edition describes the work as having been "corrected most precisely and with maximum care under the supervision of Shaykh Ṭāhir al-Jazāʾirī."[79]

Finally, al-Jazāʾirī also edited and published the small but significant ethical treatise by Ibn al-Muqaffaʿ that Aḥmad Zakī would likewise publish in Cairo three years later. The very different geneses of the two editions illustrate the respective approaches of the two scholars. Whereas Zakī, as described in the preceding chapter, found his manuscript of Ibn al-Muqaffaʿ's work in the course of his grand expedition to the Topkapı Palace libraries, a visit that was made possible by his extensive political connections and during which he relied on photography to harvest a large number of manuscripts with maximum efficiency, al-Jazāʾirī spent years frequenting public and private manuscript libraries, painstakingly copying works he liked by hand. In the introduction to his edition, he provides the following account of his discovery of the manuscript and his motivations for publishing it:

> When I went to Baalbek in the year 1323 [1905 CE] I saw at the house of a distinguished man a collection he had borrowed from a prominent local person, and in it I found the long lost and searched-for epistle *al-Adab al-ṣaghīr* of ʿAbd Allāh b. al-Muqaffaʿ, the author with the legendary eloquence. So I copied it in about a day in my own hand. I hope that it is possible to have it published by someone known for high-quality publishing, so that its benefits can spread.[80]

The text was published in the Damascene journal *al-Muqtabas*, at the time edited by al-Jazāʾirī's student Kurd ʿAlī, who went on to found the Academy of the Arabic Language in Damascus (Majmaʿ al-Lugha al-ʿArabiyya fī Dimashq).

Al-Jazāʾirī also wrote books of his own, drawing on his deep familiarity with the Islamic scholarly tradition. His output included textbooks for schools

[77] Al-Rāghib al-Iṣfahānī, *Tafṣīl al-nashʾatayn*.

[78] See al-Jazāʾirī's comments in Ibn Hibbān, *Rawḍat al-ʿuqalāʾ*, *bāʾ*. ʿAbduh had been involved in his student's publication of Miskawayh's *Tahdhīb al-akhlāq*, and al-Qāsimī wrote and published an abridgment of al-Ghazālī's *Iḥyāʾ ʿulūm al-dīn*, as noted earlier in this chapter.

[79] Al-Rāghib al-Iṣfahānī, *Tafṣīl al-nashʾatayn*, title page.

[80] Ibn al-Muqaffaʿ, *al-Adab al-ṣaghīr* (al-Jazāʾirī ed.), 4.

but also specialist treatises such as a work on hadith terminology[81] and another on textual riddles.[82] The German Orientalist Hellmut Ritter (1892–1971) credited the latter work with explaining a feature that had puzzled him for years: the variant of postclassical chronograms that concealed the date of, for example, a book's composition behind a tangle of fractions.[83]

Al-Jazāʾirī's bibliophilia had another long-lasting effect on Islamic book culture. His decades-long immersion in manuscripts yielded dozens of volumes of detailed notes, which became part of the Ẓāhiriyya Library's collection and have served other scholars as a map to the collection and a guide to its highlights ever since.[84] For example, on the front cover of the 1901 Beirut edition of Miskawayh's eleventh-century work on the proofs for God, the soul, and prophecy,[85] the unknown editor quotes the following endorsement of Miskawayh's book from al-Jazāʾirī's notebooks: "It is important and deserving of being printed and appropriate for the current age. It strengthens faith, and most of it is unobjectionable." The Ẓāhiriyya Library was not merely the product of an antiquarian effort to preserve old texts; rather, in combination with al-Jazāʾirī's notes, its collection constituted a reformist program waiting to unfold. In his notes, al-Jazāʾirī identified and described classical works that he deemed potentially useful for the task of intellectual and societal reform and quoted particularly pertinent passages from them.

A notable feature of al-Jazāʾirī's notes is his citation of scientific discussions to demonstrate that scientific insights were not alien to the Islamic tradition, even if they appeared so in the late nineteenth century. Whereas some contemporary Muslim scholars still insisted that the earth was flat,[86] al-Jazāʾirī quoted Ibn Taymiyya's fourteenth-century observation that the earth and all other planets are spherical.[87] Modernist reformers used this statement alongside modern scientific evidence to persuade flat-earthers of the wrongness of their views; for example, Taqī al-Dīn al-Hilālī (1893–1987), a Moroccan protégé of Riḍā, referred to it in his exchange with scholars in Medina in 1928.[88] In another instance, al-Jazāʾirī cited Ibn ʿArabī's thirteenth-century discussion on evolution from minerals to humans, in which Ibn ʿArabī claims, among other things, that apes constitute the link between animals

[81] Ṭāhir al-Jazāʾirī, *Tawjīh al-naẓar ilā uṣūl al-athar.*

[82] Ṭāhir al-Jazāʾirī, *Tashīl al-majāz ilā fann al-muʿammā wa-l-alghāz.*

[83] Ritter, "Philologika xii: Datierung durch Brüche." For an example of such a device, see chapter 2.

[84] Parts of these notes have been published in al-Jazāʾirī's *Tadhkira* and *Kunnāsha.* On the various topics covered in the notes, see Muḥyī al-Dīn, *al-Shaykh Ṭāhir al-Jazāʾirī*, 71–74.

[85] Miskawayh, *al-Fawz al-aṣghar.*

[86] Lauzière, *Making of Salafism*, 81.

[87] Ṭāhir al-Jazāʾirī, *Tadhkira*, 1:49.

[88] Al-Hilālī, *al-Daʿwa ilā Allāh*, 164.

and humans.[89] This note is clearly connected to the debates surrounding Darwin's thought in Arabic at the time.[90]

The notebooks show that al-Jazāʾirī read widely within Islamic literature. He discusses works on Arabic literature, Sufism, law, and theology, as well as the writings of Shiʿi thinkers such as the tenth-century Brethren of Purity (Ikhwān al-Ṣafā) and the seventeenth-century philosopher Mullā Ṣadrā.[91] Most notes do not betray any value judgment on the authors discussed, but certain preferences can be gleaned from al-Jazāʾirī's respective treatment of Ibn ʿArabī, a key originator of postclassical esotericism, and Ibn Taymiyya, the iconoclastic bugbear of postclassical Islamic thought. Regarding Ibn ʿArabī, al-Jazāʾirī quotes the Indian intellectual and reformer Ṣiddīq Ḥasan Khān (1832–90), who praises Ibn ʿArabī's stance against conformism and his insistence on evidence instead of the mere following of tradition but warns that many early scholars considered several of Ibn ʿArabī's ideas heretical. Therefore, Khān argues, his ideas must be examined closely prior to acceptance, and the most controversial must be interpreted in such a way as to preclude contradiction of scripture. On the question whether Ibn ʿArabī's ideas were outright heretical, Khān advises silence as the safest option. He also claims that Ibn Taymiyya's attacks on Ibn ʿArabī did not spring from a personal rivalry but rather from a principled critique of Ibn ʿArabī's positions.[92] Beyond this extremely cautious endorsement, al-Jazāʾirī quotes Ibn ʿArabī himself on a number of occasions, but these citations are dwarfed by the amount of material that he preserves from and about Ibn Taymiyya, including bibliographical lists of his works, lists of his supporters, biographical reports covering events such as his trial in Egypt, and descriptions of his surviving works.[93] In Damascus of al-Jazāʾirī's time, Ibn Taymiyya's name still carried such a stigma that reasonable public discussion of his views was impossible. So al-Jazāʾirī made handwritten copies of his works and sold them cheaply to the local manuscript booksellers in order to bring his actual ideas into wider circulation.[94] However, he did not publish any of Ibn Taymiyya's works himself. That movement would be started by his younger contemporaries, described in the next chapter.

In 1907, al-Jazāʾirī fled from Ottoman Syria to Egypt. His active intellectual circles, his support for greater Arab participation in the administration of the Arab Ottoman provinces, and his advocacy for religious reform had

[89] Ṭāhir al-Jazāʾirī, *Tadhkira*, 1:76.

[90] See Elshakry, *Reading Darwin in Arabic*.

[91] Ṭāhir al-Jazāʾirī, *Tadhkira*, 1:96 and 90–92.

[92] Ṭāhir al-Jazāʾirī, *Tadhkira*, 1:46–47. See Khān, *al-Tāj al-mukallal*, 168–69.

[93] Ṭāhir al-Jazāʾirī, *Tadhkira*, 1:198, 216–21, 351–52, 536, 553–82.

[94] See the next chapter for the example of Ibn Taymiyya's *Muqaddima fī uṣūl al-tafsīr*, which made its way from al-Jazāʾirī's library to that of Muḥammad Jamīl al-Shaṭṭī (1882–1959) and then into print.

prompted an escalating crackdown on the part of the authorities, culminating in a series of raids on his home in search of incriminating materials. Before leaving Damascus, al-Jazāʾirī sold his belongings, including many of his books, but he took the most precious and rare manuscripts with him.

In Egypt, al-Jazāʾirī received an enthusiastic welcome. In the early twentieth century, Cairo was the unquestioned center of Arabic printing in the world, but al-Jazāʾirī, now in his mid-fifties, did not get directly involved in the editing business. Instead, both to make a living and to secure the future of his library, al-Jazāʾirī began to sell off his most prized books, particularly to the great collectors Aḥmad Taymūr and Aḥmad Zakī, whose personal libraries were publicly accessible already in their lifetimes. In the process, al-Jazāʾirī rejected much higher offers for his books from European libraries, because he wished for them to remain in Arab-Muslim lands.[95] The unique copy of Ibn al-Kalbī's ninth-century work on pre-Islamic religions in Arabia (*Kitāb al-Aṣnām*) that al-Jazāʾirī sold to Zakī and that Zakī subsequently edited and published was mentioned in chapter 5, and several other works from al-Jazāʾirī's collection were equally significant. An example is a unique manuscript of the tenth-century theological polemic *Kitāb al-Intiṣār* (The book of triumph) of al-Khayyāṭ, which would become foundational to the study of early Islamic theology: the work provides rich and detailed information on the beliefs of early Muʿtazilī theologians as presented by one of their own, including details about previously unknown early theological controversies. Al-Jazāʾirī, through his student Kurd ʿAlī, had already publicized some of the book's contents on the forgotten history of Muʿtazilī thought,[96] and in 1910, he sold the manuscript directly to the Egyptian National Library. He tried repeatedly to interest Cairene publishers in printing the work, but although he had already written an introduction to the edition, no publisher took up the offer.[97] Five years after al-Jazāʾirī's death, the Swedish scholar Henrik Samuel Nyberg (1889–1974) finally published al-Khayyāṭ's text. Even though he acknowledges in his introduction that it had been al-Jazāʾirī who had discovered the text, reference works to this day claim that Nyberg "discovered and edited" it.[98]

Another important fruit of al-Jazāʾirī's collection is a compilation of three philosophical and theological epistles by Averroes, which had been edited by Marcus Joseph Müller and published in Munich in 1859.[99] Aḥmad Taymūr bought al-Jazāʾirī's copy of Müller's printed edition and added it to his library, where it was picked up by the Syrian publisher Muḥammad Amīn al-Khānjī (1860–1939), who had arrived in Cairo in 1885. Al-Khānjī wanted to reprint the work for the Arabic book market, because the public clash, a few years

95 Kurd ʿAlī, *Kunūz al-ajdād*, 12.

96 Kurd ʿAlī, "al-Muʿtazila." For the identity of the unnamed source for Muʿtazilī ideas in the article, see the reprint, "Aṣl al-Muʿtazila," 148.

97 Al-Khaṭīb, "Ḥarakat al-nashr wa-l-taʾlīf: Kitāb al-Intiṣār."

98 Holtzman, "Islamic Theology," 65. See also Larsson, "H. S. Nyberg's Encounter," 168.

99 In Marcus Müller, *Theologie und Philosophie von Averroes*.

earlier, between Faraḥ Anṭūn and Muḥammad ʿAbduh over Averroes's ideas about the relationship between religion and philosophy had aroused interest in Averroes's thought.[100] But al-Khānjī also noticed that al-Jazāʾirī had inscribed in the margins of one of the epistles Ibn Taymiyya's commentary on it, which al-Jazāʾirī had come across in a manuscript of Ibn Taymiyya's multivolume work *Darʾ taʿāruḍ al-ʿaql wa-l-naql* (Rejection of conflict between reason and revelation).[101] Al-Khānjī incorporated the otherwise unknown commentary into his reprint of the epistles. Al-Khānjī's "edition" has been ignored in Western scholarship as merely one of many Egyptian reprints of an Orientalist edition, but as a consequence, the existence of the commentary—the only one known to have been written on Averroes's epistle—has likewise been overlooked, and the information contained in it has never been integrated into the study of Averroes.[102]

Al-Khānjī also benefited from al-Jazāʾirī's expertise directly by taking lessons with him on *Rawḍat al-ʿuqalāʾ* (The garden of the wise), an anthology of citations that encourage virtuous conduct written by the hadith master Ibn Hibbān al-Bustī (d. 354/965). Afterward, al-Khānjī published the text, noting on the title page that he had copied the manuscript and then read the copy aloud to Ṭāhir al-Jazāʾirī in the presence of the Mauritanian scholar Aḥmad b. al-Amīn al-Shinqīṭī and the Aleppine scholar Maḥmūd al-Sankarī (fl. 1920s).[103] The note reflects a fusion of the classical practice and terminology of studying a book in person with a scholar, on the one hand, and the requirement for the printing process of an error-free, collated copy of the original manuscript text, on the other. Al-Jazāʾirī had not himself studied the work with a teacher—he had simply discovered it, only months earlier—so this auditory session represents something of a resuscitation of tradition. As such, it indicates that the modern technology of printing was, like the manuscript culture that preceded it, embedded in communal scholarly interaction: scholars from places as widely separated as Mauritania and Syria met in Cairo to read a millennium-old text on virtue ethics and, in the process, to prepare the text for publication and thus dissemination to an even wider audience. Al-Khānjī further notes that he had initially become aware of the work through al-Jazāʾirī's notes, in which al-Jazāʾirī explicitly calls for the work to be published, describing its potential for wide-reaching social benefits—not only for men, he specifies, but also for women.[104]

[100] The exchange, which began with Anṭūn's article, continued in a six-article response from ʿAbduh, and culminated in a book-length rejoinder by Anṭūn, is reproduced in its entirety in Anṭūn, *Ibn Rushd wa-falsafatuh*. ʿAbduh's responses have also been published separately as *al-Islām wa-l-Naṣrāniyya*. On Anṭūn, see Reid, *Odyssey of Faraḥ Anṭūn*.

[101] See al-Khānjī's introduction to Ibn Rushd, *Kitāb Falsafat Ibn Rushd*, 2. Ibn Taymiyya's commentary is included under the heading "al-Radd ʿalā falsafat Ibn Rushd al-ḥafīd," 3–11.

[102] See, for example, Belo, "Averroes (d. 1198)."

[103] Ibn Hibbān, *Rawḍat al-ʿuqalāʾ*, *alif*.

[104] Ibn Hibbān, *Rawḍat al-ʿuqalāʾ*, *bāʾ*.

Al-Jazāʾirī is an idiosyncratic figure. A lifelong bachelor, he is described as wearing tattered clothing and carrying paper, a pen, a small knife, and thread (for binding) in one pocket and bread and dry cheese in another. He was fond of swimming and long walks, and he reportedly spent his nights in discussions with his friends, followed by reading and writing until the morning prayer, after which he would finally go to sleep. He sustained his nocturnal habits through cigarettes and coffee, the latter of which he brewed a week's worth at once to save time.[105] As he himself acknowledged, al-Jazāʾirī did not have the patience to be a great editor; he did not believe in the value of spending years to produce the most accurate base text possible. He used to say, "Perfection has no limits, and mistakes are corrected with time."[106] This pragmatic position was, in part, rooted in the frustration of knowing about the staggering number of unpublished classical texts that, al-Jazāʾirī believed, should be disseminated to inform and shape society in that era of growing literacy and increasing circulation of rival philosophical and religious ideas. Al-Jazāʾirī's impatience was evident when Aḥmad Zakī was awarded a large grant by the Egyptian government to publish classical texts (see chapter 5) but used only a fraction of the available funds because his insistence on impeccable editing slowed him down so much that he managed to complete only a few of the planned editions by the time the project's backer, the education minister Aḥmad Ḥishmat Pasha, lost his position and the project was canceled.[107] Al-Jazāʾirī, furious, wrote to Zakī, "You have harmed the Arab nation with your sluggishness in publishing books for the people. If you claim that you meant only to publish them without errors, integrating the differences between the copies and notes—meticulousness has no end! It is enough for people to benefit from what is there."[108]

Al-Jazāʾirī returned to his native Damascus in the short window of independence between the end of World War I and the beginning of the French occupation in 1920. He was made an honorary member of the Academy of the Arabic Language, but he died soon after from what seems to have been lung cancer.[109]

* * *

Al-Jazāʾirī the bibliophile ascetic and ʿAbduh the political and religious reformer stand out in the landscape of Muslim scholars around the beginning of the twentieth century because of their keen awareness of the foundational cultural importance of disseminating classical works at a historical moment

105 Kurd ʿAlī, *Kunūz al-ajdād*, 21–22.
106 "Al-itqān la ḥadda lah, wa-l-aghlāṭ tuṣaḥḥaḥ maʿ al-zaman"; Kurd ʿAlī, *Kunūz al-ajdād*, 11.
107 Kurd ʿAlī, *Kunūz al-ajdād*, 18–19.
108 Kurd ʿAlī, *Kunūz al-ajdād*, 11.
109 Kurd ʿAlī, *Kunūz al-ajdād*, 14.

at which large-scale literacy was transforming Muslim publics across the Arab lands, and because of the impact of the various ventures to publish seminal classical texts in which they were involved. The rediscovery of forgotten literature was an integral part of their reform agendas: as Fazlur Rahman has pointed out with respect to ʿAbduh, "ʿAbduh contended not only for the introduction of modern Western learning into al-Azhar, but—what is not generally recognized or understood—for the revival of old and original Islamic classics. . . . Indeed, to rediscover 'modernity' in the original Islamic tradition itself was a cornerstone of ʿAbduh's reformist thinking."[110] Neither ʿAbduh nor al-Jazāʾirī was motivated by a merely antiquarian impulse to preserve manuscripts as artifacts of "national heritage"; rather, both saw classical literature as a reservoir of intellectual and ethical resources necessary for the development of Muslim societies. This "indigenous modernity" could be harnessed to combat the backwardness and superstition that early twentieth-century reformers saw in the postclassical tradition, and it offered a vantage point from which to engage with Western thought and its politico-cultural hegemony without losing one's identity. In addition, both al-Jazāʾirī and ʿAbduh were educators who spent much of their time and energy teaching students, founding institutions of learning, and reforming already existing institutions, as well as writing textbooks for teaching use.[111] This hands-on role allowed them to promote the newly discovered classical works and to spread their lessons on language and ethics. But the next step—printing even controversial classical texts for reformist religious purposes and using them to challenge directly the prevailing religious orthodoxies—was taken by a younger generation of scholars, who would establish broad networks for locating, circulating, and publishing classical works.

[110] Rahman, *Islam and Modernity*, 66–67.

[111] For example, ʿAbduh, *Risālat al-tawḥīd*; Ṭāhir al-Jazāʾirī, *Tamhīd al-ʿurūḍ*; Ṭāhir al-Jazāʾirī, *al-Jawāhir al-kalāmiyya*.

CHAPTER 7

The Backlash against Postclassicism

The nineteenth- and early twentieth-century drive to discover forgotten texts and reintroduce them into active cultural use was antitraditional in the sense that it implicitly alleged that the current tradition, embodied in the postclassical textual canon, had not succeeded in preserving all valuable knowledge in scholarly circulation. The scholars who participated in the publishing movement thus posed a revolutionary challenge: they claimed that the tradition could be enriched, complemented, and even critiqued and corrected by means of texts that had been culturally orphaned. Such texts had to be laboriously recovered by reassembling their manuscript fragments, deciphering their script, reconstructing their text, and understanding their context through an intimate conversation between author and reader, unmediated by the intervention of tradition.

For the Egyptian bureaucratic elite and early reformers such as Muḥammad ʿAbduh and Ṭāhir al-Jazāʾirī, the rediscovery of literary, historical, ethical, and encyclopedic works as well as advice literature was a priority, reflecting their belief in the capacity of such books to raise the public's moral and linguistic standards and thus to contribute to societal improvement. In this chapter, by contrast, the focus is on the search for and publication of writings specifically on religious thought and practice by reformist members of the Muslim scholarly class, the *ʿulamāʾ*. These reformist *ʿulamāʾ* were a small but active and intellectually high-powered group who diverged from the scholarly mainstream of their day by attacking esoteric Sufi beliefs and practices as superstitious, irrational, and contrary to Islamic ideals and by criticizing the Islamic legal status quo, which they saw as a fossilized doctrine unresponsive to the actual challenges Muslims were facing.[1]

At least from the early twentieth century onward, some of these reformers referred to themselves as Salafis, or those seeking to emulate the *salaf*—the exemplary early Muslims. But although the terms "Salafi" and "Salafiyya" have, in the course of the twentieth century, come to stand for extremely narrow notions of orthodoxy and orthopraxis and correspondingly limited literary horizons, a hallmark of the Salafism of the reformers discussed in this chapter was the breadth and eclecticism of their literary interests and publishing activities and their fearless, even eager engagement with diverse

[1]Commins, *Islamic Reform*, chaps. 5 and 6.

ideas.[2] Contrast, for example, the insistence of one of these early twentieth-century Salafis on the value of Muslim theological currents that Sunnism had always considered unorthodox with the stark condemnation of such currents as un-Islamic by a twenty-first-century Salafi author.[3] Like many modern-day Salafis, the early reformers disapproved of key features of the Sufi discourses of their day, but they were not primitivists or puritans desiring to purge all intellectual developments between their own time and the prophetic age. Rather, their book-collecting and publishing activities targeted classical works sidelined by the postclassical orthodoxy, works that they believed to hold ideas and doctrines that could reinvigorate Islamic thought.[4] Much of the attention of these reformers was focused on the work of the Damascene scholar Ibn Taymiyya, in whom they saw a kindred spirit, but they also published works by thinkers such as Avicenna, Miskawayh, al-Ghazālī, and Ibn ʿArabī—not because they necessarily agreed with all the ideas put forward by these authors, but because they were confident that truth would be distinguished from falsehood even in the absence of explanatory commentaries. The following sections introduce some of the key figures in the emerging networks of reformist *ʿulamāʾ*, in particular Maḥmūd Shukrī al-Ālūsī in Baghdad and Jamāl al-Dīn al-Qāsimī in Damascus, and describe their efforts and motivations in discovering, circulating, and printing classical books.

A TRANSNATIONAL NETWORK OF BOOK COLLECTORS

The classically inspired reform movement of the late nineteenth and early twentieth centuries relied on the efforts and cooperation of a network of like-minded scholars residing across the Middle East in Egypt, the Levant, Iraq, the Hijaz, and Yemen as well as beyond it, in places such as India and the Maghreb. One of the nodes in this network was the Indian scholar and government official Ṣiddīq Ḥasan Khān, whose assessment of Ibn ʿArabī was mentioned in chapter 6. Khān performed the pilgrimage to Mecca and Medina in 1869 and took the opportunity to search for and buy manuscripts of books that were not in wide circulation at the time, including works by the Yemeni reformer al-Shawkānī and by Ibn Taymiyya, even an autograph of

[2]For a debate on the continuities and discontinuities between early twentieth-century Salafism and later Salafism, see Lauzière, "Construction of Salafiyya"; Griffel, "What Do We Mean by 'Salafī'?"; and Lauzière, "Rejoinder."

[3]Jamāl al-Dīn al-Qāsimī, *Tārīkh al-Jahmiyya wa-l-Muʿtazila*; al-Rifāʿī, *al-Ṣawāʿiq al-mursala.*

[4]Schulze has likened them to the European classicists of the nineteenth century; see Schulze, *Modern History*, 18.

the latter's critique of the logicians (*al-Radd ʿalā al-mantiqiyyīn*).[5] Yet works that would become ubiquitous a century later were still out of his reach at this time; such works included Ibn Kathīr's (d. 774/1373) Quranic exegesis, which Khān knew of but could not obtain, despite his connections and personal wealth.[6]

Afterward, he maintained contacts with the Hijaz in order to acquire more manuscripts of classical works. One of his main suppliers was Aḥmad b. ʿĪsā (1837–1911), a scholar from southwestern Arabia who had settled in Mecca and earned his living as a merchant. Ibn ʿĪsā became an important source of classical literature for reformists such as Khān.[7] He would employ a copyist with good handwriting to make copies of selected works and then dispatch the copies to Khān in India by sea. In 1876, he sent Khān a set of books that included Ibn Taymiyya's magnum opus on the harmony between reason and revelation (*Darʾ taʿāruḍ al-ʿaql wa-l-naql*), his extensive critique of Twelver Shiʿi theology (*Minhāj al-sunna*), and his student Ibn Qayyim al-Jawziyya's Sufi commentary (*Madārij al-sālikīn*). The shipment also contained works by Aḥmad b. Ḥanbal (d. 241/855), al-Ṭabarī (d. 310/923), Muwaffaq al-Dīn b. Qudāma (d. 620/1223), and Abū ʿUthmān al-Ṣābūnī (d. 449/1057).[8]

Ṣiddīq Ḥasan Khān published more than two hundred books, epistles, and pamphlets in Arabic, Urdu, and Persian, written with the help of a staff of secretaries put at his disposal by his status as the husband of Shāhjahān, the ruler of the princely state of Bhopal.[9] Many of his writings summarize material that he found in the classical manuscript works he collected or provide abridged versions of books written by later classically minded scholars such as al-Shawkānī.[10] Khān's books were published by a variety of presses in India, Cairo, and Istanbul (including Aḥmad Fāris al-Shidyāq's Jawā'ib Press). In spite of his extensive collection and use of classical works in his own writings, however, Khān did not have any of the classical works printed. This step was taken by the next generation of reformist scholars, foremost among them Maḥmūd Shukrī al-Ālūsī (1856–1924).

Al-Ālūsī was the scion of a prominent scholarly family in Baghdad. His grandfather Maḥmūd Shihāb al-Dīn (1802–54) had composed a thirty-volume

[5] Preckel, "Islamische Bildungsnetzwerke," 162–63.

[6] Khān, *Qaṣd al-sabīl*, 14n1.

[7] Preckel, "Islamische Bildungsnetzwerke," 217–19.

[8] These books were Aḥmad b. Ḥanbal's *al-Radd ʿalā al-Jahmiyya*, al-Ṭabarī's *ʿAqīda*, Ibn Qudāma's *Ithbāt ṣifat al-ʿuluww*, and al-Ṣābūnī's *ʿAqīda*; see Khān and Ibn ʿĪsā, *al-Rasā'il al-mutabādala bayna al-shaykhayn*, 76, 78–79, 86.

[9] Preckel, "Islamische Bildungsnetzwerke," 42–43.

[10] Khān's *Ḥuṣūl al-ma'mūl min ʿilm al-uṣūl* is an abridgment of al-Shawkānī's *Irshād al-fuḥūl*, as Khān readily admits (p. 3). Khān had studied with Yemeni scholars who stood in the tradition of al-Shawkānī; see Preckel, "Islamische Bildungsnetzwerke," 127–34.

commentary on the Quran,[11] and his uncle Nuʿmān Khayr al-Dīn (1836–99) wrote a seminal defense of Ibn Taymiyya.[12] Al-Ālūsī's intellectual networks, through which he found and disseminated information on rare books, were extensive. He counted among his contacts Ṣiddīq Ḥasan Khān;[13] Aḥmad Zakī in Egypt;[14] an old Imāmī Shiʿi friend from Najaf, who alerted al-Ālūsī to an unnamed rare book by al-Ghazālī;[15] a scholar from the region of Ḥaḍramawt in Yemen;[16] the French Orientalist Louis Massignon (1883–1962), with whom he shared information and manuscripts relating to Massignon's principal work on the tenth-century Sufi al-Ḥallāj, and who sent him copies or photographic reproductions of manuscripts in European libraries in return;[17] and Anastās al-Karmalī (1866–1947), an Iraqi Carmelite priest who was the leading scholar of Arabic lexicography in his time and the founder of what would become the Iraqi National Library.

Al-Ālūsī wrote to al-Karmalī to inform him of manuscripts on Arabic dialects that he had discovered in a Baghdadi library, and he provided al-Karmalī with a manuscript that the librarian had let him borrow.[18] He also told him about surviving but difficult to obtain classical works on lexicography.[19] Many of the letters exchanged between al-Ālūsī and al-Karmalī express the enthusiasm of a shared passion for books. In one letter, dated June 5, 1901, al-Ālūsī writes, "I consulted some [manuscript] library catalogs and found the souls' desire and the eyes' delight with regard to books that would interest you," and then goes on to mention works by philosophers such as Ibn Ṭufayl (d. 581/1185), al-Fārābī (d. 339/950 or 951), Avicenna (d. 427/1037), Ibn Kammūna (d. 683/1284), and Mullā Ṣadrā (d. 1050/1640), regretting that most of these works could be found only in the libraries of Istanbul.[20] Numerous letters carry messages such as "Have you heard of book X? Where could I find a copy?" or "I found an interesting manuscript on topic Y; do you know of anyone who would like to publish it?"[21] In other letters, al-Ālūsī refers to Ottoman censorship of his work because of Iranian objections to its content,[22]

[11] Maḥmūd Shihāb al-Dīn al-Ālūsī, *Rūḥ al-maʿānī*.

[12] Nuʿmān al-Ālūsī, *Jalāʾ al-ʿaynayn*, discussed below.

[13] Khān and Ibn ʿĪsā, *al-Rasāʾil al-mutabādala bayna al-shaykhayn*, 62.

[14] *Al-Rasāʾil al-mutabādala bayna Aḥmad Zakī wa-Anastās al-Karmalī*, 13–15. On Zakī, see chapter 5.

[15] Al-ʿAjmī, *al-Rasāʾil al-mutabādala bayna al-Qāsimī wa-l-Ālūsī*, 194.

[16] Al-ʿAjmī, *al-Rasāʾil al-mutabādala bayna al-Qāsimī wa-l-Ālūsī*, 211.

[17] Al-ʿAjmī, *al-Rasāʾil al-mutabādala bayna al-Qāsimī wa-l-Ālūsī*, 47, 169–70, 200.

[18] ʿAwwād and ʿAwwād, *Adab al-rasāʾil*, 87–89, 91.

[19] ʿAwwād and ʿAwwād, *Adab al-rasāʾil*, 92–93.

[20] ʿAwwād and ʿAwwād, *Adab al-rasāʾil*, 95–96.

[21] ʿAwwād and ʿAwwād, *Adab al-rasāʾil*, 108–9.

[22] ʿAwwād and ʿAwwād, *Adab al-rasāʾil*, 98. The work in question, *Mukhtaṣar tarjamat al-Tuḥfa*, is a revised translation of Shāh ʿAbd al-ʿAzīz of Delhi's (1746–1824) refutation of Twelver Shiʿi theology. To evade Ottoman censors, al-Ālūsī had to have it printed in Bombay.

and mentions that he possesses a manuscript of al-Ashʿarī's *Maqālāt al-islāmiyyīn* (Doctrines of the Muslims), an encyclopedia of early Muslim theological opinions. According to al-Ālūsī, someone had wanted to print al-Ashʿarī's work, but the Ottoman ministry of education had objected to the publication; Muslim theological works had become a target of Ottoman censorship, because the Ottoman claim to the caliphate did not meet the classical requirements for the office set out in these treatises.[23]

Al-Ālūsī wrote several books himself, many of which remain unpublished.[24] Of his published works, his three-volume encyclopedia of the Arabs[25] stands out for its size and erudition. His three-part history of his hometown of Baghdad—focusing on its scholars, its mosques, and its characteristic proverbs, respectively—shows an interest in local history and the local vernacular that has parallels in the work of his contemporaries in other Arab countries, such as Aḥmad Taymūr in Egypt and ʿAbd al-Qādir Badrān (1846–1927) and Muḥammad Kurd ʿAlī in Syria.[26] Another contribution that indicates al-Ālūsī's reformist commitments is his refutation of his contemporary Yūsuf al-Nabhānī (1849–1932).[27] Al-Nabhānī was a Palestinian scholar who had received his education at al-Azhar and had worked as a corrector at al-Shidyāq's press in Istanbul, where he corrected, among other things, books by Ṣiddīq Ḥasan Khān.[28] In 1906, after a successful career as a Sharīʿa court judge in the Levant, he authored an antireformist work in which he criticized calls for legal reasoning unfettered by the established legal schools, rebutted Nuʿmān al-Ālūsī's rehabilitation of Ibn Taymiyya (discussed below), and defended the validity of shrine devotions.[29] He also provided an explicit justification for the scholastic concept of authority, arguing that the neglect of Ibn Taymiyya's writings in the postclassical period reflected a divine judgment on their contents. The legal reformist Aḥmad al-Ḥusaynī, whose radical but nonetheless conservative mission to revive the classical legal schools was

[23] ʿAwwād and ʿAwwād, *Adab al-rasāʾil*, 117. The *Maqālāt* was eventually published in Istanbul in 1929–33 after the end of the Ottoman Empire by the German Orientalist Hellmut Ritter. For further examples of Ottoman censorship of classical works dealing with the caliphate, see al-Nuʿmānī, *Riḥla*, 67; and Ibn al-Akfānī, *Irshād al-qāṣid* (al-Jazāʾirī ed.), 56, 59, and 61 (where omissions from the text are indicated by dotted lines). The latter instance was also noted by Witkam, *De egyptische arts Ibn al-Akfānī*, 124–25.

[24] See al-Atharī, *Aʿlām al-ʿIrāq*, 140–52.

[25] Maḥmūd Shukrī al-Ālūsī, *Bulūgh al-arab fī aḥwāl al-ʿArab*.

[26] The three parts of al-Ālūsī's *Akhbār Baghdād*, initially published separately, were titled *al-Misk al-adhfar*, *Tārīkh masājid Baghdād*, and *Amthāl al-ʿawāmm fī madīnat dār al-salām*, respectively. Compare with the works of Aḥmad Taymūr (*al-Amthāl al-ʿāmmiyya*), Badrān (*Munādamat al-aṭlāl*), and Kurd ʿAlī (*Khiṭaṭ al-Shām*) on similar topics.

[27] Maḥmūd Shukrī al-Ālūsī, *Ghāyat al-amānī*.

[28] See his blurb at the end of Khān's *Qurrat al-aʿyān*, 155–59.

[29] Al-Nabhānī, *Shawāhid al-ḥaqq*.

described in chapter 4, wrote a blurb in praise of al-Nabhānī's work;[30] meanwhile, Maḥmūd Shukrī al-Ālūsī's response to it was published by the printing house that al-Ḥusaynī had helped to establish, the Kurdistān Press. Al-Ālūsī had to publish his refutation under a pseudonym out of fear of Ottoman reprisal.[31]

Al-Ālūsī's arguments in his reply to al-Nabhānī exemplify the reformist agenda he shared with many of his contemporaries: he criticizes popular shrine veneration, defends Ibn Taymiyya, and justifies independent reasoning. He also comments scathingly on al-Nabhānī's attempted appropriation of divine sanction for the boundaries of postclassical discourse, pointing out that if a work's popularity were indeed a reflection of its value and usefulness, the merits of al-Shirbīnī's ribald satire *Brains Confounded*, manuscripts of which were ubiquitous, would clearly outweigh those of the foundational work of al-Shāfiʿī, to whose school al-Nabhānī belonged, since the latter had been all but lost. Al-Ālūsī dismisses this position as a product of "compromised rationality" and concludes sarcastically, "I can assure the respected Shaykh al-Nabhānī that the books of Ibn Taymiyya and his associates are about to be taken up by the publishing houses of Egypt and India, so that none will remain neglected."[32]

The reformist agenda thus also informed the editing activities of al-Ālūsī and his extensive network of contacts. They sought to resurrect works that could be used to bolster reformist arguments, and for this reason they circulated information on and copies of manuscripts, worked together to collate and edit the chosen texts, and helped each other locate publishers and funding to print them. In these endeavors, al-Ālūsī collaborated particularly closely with Jamāl al-Dīn al-Qāsimī (1866–1914), the Damascene student of Ṭāhir al-Jazāʾirī.

Al-Qāsimī was a third-generation Damascene scholar; his grandfather had worked as a barber, but then dedicated himself to scholarship.[33] Al-Qāsimī's tumultuous career illustrates the immense power of the postclassical orthodoxy in his time. In 1896, at the age of thirty, he cofounded, with a small group of friends, a regular salon for discussing the religious, intellectual, and social issues of the day. Shortly thereafter, someone accused the members of this gathering of engaging in independent legal thought (*ijtihād*) and thus of failing to follow the opinions of the four canonical schools of Islamic law. According to his own account, al-Qāsimī and his friends responded defiantly:

[30] See al-Nabhānī, *Shawāhid al-ḥaqq*, 261.

[31] See the editor's introduction to Maḥmūd Shukrī al-Ālūsī, *Ghāyat al-amānī* (al-Ghayhab ed.), 1:8.

[32] Maḥmūd Shukrī al-Ālūsī, *Ghāyat al-amānī* (al-Ghayhab ed.), 2:270–72.

[33] Al-ʿAjmī, *Āl al-Qāsimī*; Commins, *Islamic Reform*, 42–46; Weismann, *Taste of Modernity*, 291–98.

"Since when is a man's intelligence and the freedom of his thought something reprehensible?" They were summoned to court, where the grand mufti of Damascus claimed to have evidence that the group had "gathered to interpret the Quran and the sayings of Muḥammad according to their own reasoning, and to refute previous scholars." The mufti admonished the group: "Why are you interested in books of hadith? Stick to works of law. Reading books on hadith and exegesis is forbidden!"[34] The most concrete of the accusations was the claim that al-Qāsimī had issued a legal opinion according to his own personal school, which he denied. He was also accused of authoring a gloss on a sixteenth-century work of comparative law (the *Mīzān* of al-Shaʿrānī, discussed in chapter 2). Al-Qāsimī admitted to having done so, but he stressed that the gloss simply provided explanations for difficult phrases and contained no legal arguments.[35] The controversy vividly demonstrates how inflammatory the mere idea of discussing the foundational texts of Islamic law—the Quran and the hadith corpus—or engaging in reinterpretation of previous scholarship (on however modest a scale) had become. As seen in chapter 2, any direct engagement with the classical literature effectively circumvented the postclassical structure of scholastic authority, and it was thus seen as deeply threatening to the status quo.

Al-Qāsimī had his revenge a decade later, in 1906, when he successfully published two collections of texts on legal theory written between the tenth and sixteenth centuries.[36] Most of the authors of the assembled texts were claimed by the four schools of law as their own, but all of them theorized the law as deriving from jurists' direct engagement with the texts of revelation, unmediated by school precedent, along with their consideration of custom and of individual and communal benefit (*maṣlaḥa*). Especially the last point, the importance of benefit, made waves: one of the authors, al-Ṭūfī (d. 716/1316), put forward the radical claim that benefit was not only an important factor but in fact the primary overall aim of Islamic law. Al-Qāsimī had found al-Ṭūfī's discussion in a Damascene manuscript containing not law but a commentary on a selection of Muḥammad's sayings.[37] Later in the same year, the reformist publisher Rashīd Riḍā reprinted al-Ṭūfī's text in his journal, *al-Manār*.[38] Despite the subsequent publication of several complete works by al-Ṭūfī, this excerpt remains his best-known text, its popularity rooted in its encapsulation of the progressive-reformist idea of Islamic law as religiously grounded but not formalistically textual, its overall priority the promotion of benefit for the individual as well as society.

[34] Ẓāfir al-Qāsimī, *Jamāl al-Dīn al-Qāsimī wa-ʿaṣruh*, 45.
[35] Ẓāfir al-Qāsimī, *Jamāl al-Dīn al-Qāsimī wa-ʿaṣruh*, 46. For the entire episode, see 45–57.
[36] *Majmūʿ rasāʾil fī uṣūl al-fiqh* and *Majmūʿ mutūn uṣūliyya.*
[37] Al-Ṭūfī, *Risāla fī al-maṣāliḥ al-mursala*, 69.
[38] Al-Ṭūfī, "Bāb uṣūl al-fiqh."

FIGURE 7.1. Jamāl al-Dīn al-Qāsimī. From Ẓāfir al-Qāsimī, *Jamāl al-Dīn al-Qāsimī*, unnumbered plate.

Al-Qāsimī also published a collection of thirty epistles on philosophy, virtue ethics, theology, Sufism, and law by a wide variety of authors, including Avicenna, Ibn ʿArabī, Yaḥyā b. ʿAdī, Ibn Tūmart, Fakhr al-Dīn al-Rāzī, Abū Shāma, Ibn Taymiyya, and al-Ghazālī.[39] He had gathered the epistles from various sources, written them out by hand, and sent them to Cairo, where Kurdistān Press printed the collection. The range of included authors transcends any easy ideological classification, at least from today's perspective, but the overall motivation behind the volume is mentioned in the anonymous afterword (probably written by the collection's financial backer, Muḥyī al-Dīn Ṣabrī al-Kurdī):[40] "One of the primary reasons why the scholars in this day and age are so deficient is that the works of these *imāms* have become neglected and forgotten."[41]

[39] *Hādhihi majmūʿat al-rasāʾil.*

[40] Muḥyī al-Dīn Ṣabrī al-Kurdī (d. 1940) was a Kurdish scholar who worked as a corrector on numerous books published by the Kurdistān Press.

[41] *Hādhihi majmūʿat al-rasāʾil*, 631.

The path by which one of the epistles—that by Ibn Tūmart (d. 524/1130), the colorful founder of the North African Almohad movement—found its way into the collection illustrates the reach of the networks on which scholars such as al-Qāsimī depended for information and copies of classical works. Al-Qāsimī had asked the Tunisian scholar Muḥammad al-Bashīr al-Nayfar (1889–1974) for copies of any surviving works by Ibn Tūmart. Al-Nayfar could not find any trace of Ibn Tūmart's writings in Tunisia, but he wrote to a friend in Paris, who managed to obtain a copy of a work by Ibn Tūmart that had been published by a French colonial official in Algiers in 1903 on the basis of a unique manuscript housed in the Bibliothèque nationale in Paris (a second manuscript was discovered later). The Parisian friend sent the book to al-Nayfar, who forwarded it to al-Qāsimī in Damascus in February 1910; al-Qāsimī, who had already made contact with al-Kurdī in Cairo via Ṭāhir al-Jazā'irī, sent it on to Cairo, where it was printed within the year.[42]

The challenge of obtaining funding for prints of classical works was a perennial one for al-Qāsimī and al-Ālūsī. By the beginning of the twentieth century, the Egyptian printing industry had expanded considerably from its early stages, outlined in chapter 3, and it continued to dominate the Arabic-language publishing scene. New private presses had been established in response to the growth of the Egyptian reading public and the increasing reach of Egyptian publications further afield, and the printing of books, including classical works, had become a considerable business. Although Cairene publishers were now printing many classical works on their own initiative, expecting subsequent sales to be sufficiently robust to yield a profit for the press, the profit calculus was more fraught for works that were longer or, especially, extant only in fragmentary form. The publication of the latter required significant effort and philological attention to establish a complete and coherent text, and without additional subvention their production costs often threatened to exceed the likely sales proceeds.

Al-Qāsimī and al-Ālūsī relied on four individuals in particular to provide the funding necessary to finance the publication of classical works. The first was ʿAbd al-Qādir al-Tilmisānī (d. unknown), a wealthy textile trader from Jedda, who had been educated at al-Azhar and had contracted an enthusiasm for books from a fellow merchant-scholar, Aḥmad b. ʿĪsā—the procurer of manuscripts for Ṣiddīq Ḥasan Khān and al-Ālūsī.[43] The second was al-Tilmisānī's protégé Muḥammad Naṣīf (1885–1971), likewise a merchant based in Jedda, who would come to amass a large private library of printed and manuscript works.[44]

[42] Ẓāfir al-Qāsimī, *Jamāl al-Dīn al-Qāsimī wa-ʿaṣruh*, 573–74.

[43] On al-Tilmisānī, see Ibn Bassām, *ʿUlamāʾ Najd*, 1:438–40.

[44] On Naṣīf, see Aḥmad and al-ʿAlawī, *Muḥammad Naṣīf*; Freitag, "Scholarly Exchange and Trade."

FIGURE 7.2. Muḥammad Naṣīf. From al-ʿAlī, *Ẓill al-nadīm*, 215.

The third financier was Muqbil al-Dhakīr (d. 1923), originally from Najd, who made his fortune as a pearl trader in Bahrain, supplying, among others, the Parisian jewelry house Cartier. Finally, al-Ālūsī's and al-Qāsimī's efforts received support from Qāsim Āl Thānī (d. 1913), the ruler of the nominally Ottoman but practically independent Emirate of Qatar.[45] The frequency of the respective mentions of these four suggests that al-Dhakīr played the most active role, followed by Naṣīf, who had his own scholarly interests and often had two copies made of the Damascene or Iraqi manuscripts identified by al-Qāsimī and al-Ālūsī—one to be sent to Cairo for printing and another for his own library.[46]

[45]On al-Dhakīr and Amir Qāsim, see al-ʿAjmī, *al-Rasāʾil al-mutabādala bayna al-Qāsimī wa-l-Ālūsī*, 61, 64, 71.

[46]See the example of Ibn Taymiyya's *Sharḥ al-ʿaqīda al-Iṣfahāniyya* mentioned later in this chapter; see also al-ʿAjmī, *al-Rasāʾil al-mutabādala bayna al-Qāsimī wa-l-Ālūsī*, 77n1.

IBN TAYMIYYA AS A MODEL OF BROAD ERUDITION

Al-Qāsimī's skirmishes with the authorities over the permissibility of direct engagement with foundational legal literature point to a key preoccupation of the reformist *ʿulamāʾ* of this period: increasingly impatient with the rigid postclassical mindset, they sought to expand the vistas of Islamic thought both methodologically—by drawing on a much broader range of literature and evaluating ideas objectively on their own merits, regardless of their originators—and substantively, by (re)introducing new or forgotten arguments into scholarly discourse.[47] On both of these fronts, Ibn Taymiyya, the fourteenth-century Syrian polymath, played a central role for the nineteenth- and twentieth-century reformers, just as he had done for the seventeenth- and eighteenth-century ones discussed in chapter 2.

Until the early 1900s, almost none of Ibn Taymiyya's prolific writings had been printed,[48] and given his persistent reputation as a heretic (promoted especially by his principal sixteenth-century detractor, al-Haytamī), his works were by no means widely available. The rehabilitation of Ibn Taymiyya was begun by scholars such as the seventeenth-century Ibrāhīm al-Kūrānī, whose philologically rigorous defense was described in chapter 2, and it was continued in the nineteenth century by, inter alia, al-Ālūsī's uncle Nuʿmān Khayr al-Dīn al-Ālūsī.

Nuʿmān al-Ālūsī's seminal work on Ibn Taymiyya, titled *Jalāʾ al-ʿaynayn fī muḥākamat al-Aḥmadayn* (The eyes' clearing on the judgment between the two Aḥmads), is a careful weighing of the arguments of one Aḥmad (al-Haytamī) against those of another (Ibn Taymiyya). Nuʿmān implores his readers "not to let the affliction of blind imitation and preoccupation with current ideas" lead to the abandonment of objective judgment (*inṣāf*): "It is incumbent on everyone seeking success in this world and the next not to judge between two opponents until both have been heard; so here I have—with God's help—quoted the words of both scholars and consulted the texts of both parties without partisanship."[49] His method consists of citing opinions against and in favor of Ibn Taymiyya, providing biographical information on the scholars cited, and then quoting Ibn Taymiyya's own words on the relevant issue to the extent that he could access them in late nineteenth-century Baghdad. Al-Haytamī's primary charges against Ibn Taymiyya concerned the latter's critique of unnamed Sufi masters (particularly Ibn ʿArabī), his alleg-

[47] This impulse also manifested itself in al-Qāsimī's approach to Quranic exegesis; see Coppens, "Breaking with the Traditional Curriculum?"

[48] Salāma, *Muʿjam mā ṭubiʿa*, 35–37.

[49] Nuʿmān al-Ālūsī, *Jalāʾ al-ʿaynayn* (Āl Zahawī ed.), 557. On this work, see Nafi, "Salafism Revived."

edly anthropomorphist understanding of divine attributes, and his contravention of the normative consensus of legal scholars on certain issues. Across the board, Nuʿmān refutes al-Haytamī's claims, scoffing at al-Haytamī's failure to cite Ibn Taymiyya directly,[50] and defends Ibn Taymiyya's right to develop his own positions and to criticize those of others as long as the criticism is evidence-based.[51] The latter point applies specifically to Ibn Taymiyya's critique of Ibn ʿArabī; although Nuʿmān refrains from condemning Ibn ʿArabī himself, he notes that particularly early scholars had harbored serious reservations regarding the theological acceptability of Ibn ʿArabī's doctrines.[52]

The methodological hallmark of Nuʿmān al-Ālūsī's intervention is his insistence on objectivity—the impartial and accurate presentation of arguments with reference to their authors' original writings. He draws attention to his own precise citation and attribution of earlier opinions, contrasting it with al-Haytamī's secondhand polemics, and he juxtaposes his approach explicitly with the esoteric postclassical claim that divine inspiration renders the consultation of books superfluous.[53] In addition, he excavates something of a countertradition, a string of scholars who, in the centuries after Ibn Taymiyya's death and particularly since al-Haytamī's critique, had come across Ibn Taymiyya's work and found it very different from the picture drawn by al-Haytamī.

The movement started by Muḥammad b. ʿAbd al-Wahhāb (1703–92) in the Najd region of central Arabia represented an exception to the widespread stigmatization of Ibn Taymiyya. But despite the claims laid by the Wahhābīs to Ibn Taymiyya's legacy, the hopes held by scholars such as Maḥmūd Shukrī al-Ālūsī and al-Qāsimī of obtaining copies of his works from Wahhābī sources were repeatedly dashed. Al-Ālūsī writes,

> I wrote to several scholars in Najd to acquire copies; they promised but did not deliver. A descendant of Muḥammad b. ʿAbd al-Wahhāb, the shaykh of the people of Najd, wrote to me months ago, saying that they had books of the two scholars [Ibn Taymiyya and his student Ibn al-Qayyim] that no one else possessed and claiming that they would be happy to send me copies of any that I want. He asked me for some books, which I sent to him; but when I asked for copies of some works of Ibn Taymiyya, among them *al-Radd ʿalā al-Bakrī* ["Response to al-Bakrī"], he never replied.[54]

[50] Nuʿmān al-Ālūsī, *Jalāʾ al-ʿaynayn* (Āl Zahawī ed.), e.g., 114. Nearly three decades later, Nuʿmān's nephew Maḥmūd Shukrī attacked Nuʿmān's critic al-Nabhānī for precisely the same fault—relying on secondhand, and demonstrably false, attributions of heretical opinions to Ibn Taymiyya instead of reading the latter's own writings, which furthermore were increasingly available in print in al-Nabhānī's time. See al-Nabhānī, *Shawāhid al-ḥaqq*, 130; Maḥmūd Shukrī al-Ālūsī, *Ghāyat al-amānī* (al-Ghayhab ed.), 1:492.

[51] Nuʿmān al-Ālūsī, *Jalāʾ al-ʿaynayn* (Āl Zahawī ed.), 177.

[52] Nuʿmān al-Ālūsī, *Jalāʾ al-ʿaynayn* (Āl Zahawī ed.), 84–96.

[53] Nuʿmān al-Ālūsī, *Jalāʾ al-ʿaynayn* (Āl Zahawī ed.), 116.

[54] Al-ʿAjmī, *al-Rasāʾil al-mutabādala bayna al-Qāsimī wa-l-Ālūsī*, 182; see also 47 and 98.

In retrospect, it is clear that relatively few of Ibn Taymiyya's works actually survived in central Arabia. The followers of Ibn ʿAbd al-Wahhāb accessed Ibn Taymiyya's ideas primarily through the lens of Ibn al-Qayyim's polemical theological poem *al-Nūniyya*,[55] which was widely known in Najd.[56] The majority of the manuscripts of Ibn Taymiyya's works are today held in libraries in Damascus, Istanbul, and Cairo, as well as those in Europe and America.[57] The availability of these works in Arabia improved only in the twentieth century, when private collectors and subsequently public universities began to buy older copies of Ibn Taymiyya's writings or have manuscript copies made for themselves.[58]

The wave of prints of Ibn Taymiyya's works began with the publication of a selection of his epistles in 1900.[59] Over the next half-century, more than 130 of his books were printed in Egypt.[60] One of the earliest major works by Ibn Taymiyya to see print (in 1903–5) was an important multivolume theological work, *Minhāj al-sunna al-nabawiyya* (The path of the Prophet), in whose margins was printed a section of his equally significant treatise on the relationship between reason and revelation.[61] A generation earlier, Ṣiddīq Ḥasan Khān had still been able to obtain the latter work in its entirety, but by 1903 only a fragment was available in Cairo. The published text nevertheless proved influential. It featured in a 1906 exchange on the pages of the journal *al-Manār* between al-Qāsimī and ʿAbd al-ʿAzīz al-Sinānī (d. 1931 or 1932),[62] who was a student of both Maḥmūd Shukrī al-Ālūsī and al-Qāsimī, regarding the position of the late Egyptian reformist Muḥammad ʿAbduh on the relationship between reason and revelation.[63] Al-Qāsimī's contribution to the debate, like Nuʿmān al-Ālūsī's work, illustrates the intellectual ideals that the reformers drew from Ibn Taymiyya's example: al-Qāsimī stresses the necessity of reasoned argument and of thorough excavation of previous positions and their justifications, and he refuses to be bound by the legal schools'

[55]The name derives from the fact that every line of the poem ends in the letter *nūn*. The actual title of the poem is *al-Kāfiya al-shāfiya fī al-intiṣār li-l-firqa al-nājiya*. On its contents, see Holtzman, "Insult, Fury, and Frustration."

[56]See the editors' introduction to Ibn al-Qayyim, *al-Kāfiya al-shāfiya*, 1:26–33.

[57]See, for example, the holdings of Ibn Taymiyya's works in the library of the University of Leiden, described in Witkam, *Inventory of the Oriental Manuscripts*, esp. vols. 1–3.

[58]For example, the small endowment established by Fāḍila bt. Sinān in late nineteenth-century Najd, which included three works by Ibn al-Qayyim and one by Ibn Taymiyya; see Āl al-Shaykh, "al-Marʾa al-fāḍila Fāḍila bt. Sinān."

[59]*Maʿārij al-wuṣūl*, *al-Ḥisba fī al-islām*, and *al-Wāsiṭa*.

[60]Salāma, *Muʿjam mā ṭubiʿa*, 35.

[61]The fragment was given the title *Bayān muwāfaqat ṣarīḥ al-maʿqūl li-ṣaḥīḥ al-manqūl*. The complete work was eventually published under the now famous title *Darʾ taʿāruḍ al-ʿaql wa-l-naql*.

[62]Ibn Bassām, *ʿUlamāʾ Najd*, 3:503–4.

[63]Al-Sinānī and al-Qāsimī, "Taʿāruḍ al-ʿaql wa-l-naql," 613.

precedent. In addition to the impact of Ibn Taymiyya's own thought, the publication of his writings had important ripple effects by calling attention to the countless other scholars and works cited in them. For example, Muḥammad Muḥyī al-Dīn ʿAbd al-Ḥamīd (1900–1973), one of the most active editors between the 1920s and the 1960s, described reading the published *Minhāj al-sunna* and being struck by the range of authors and opinions with which Ibn Taymiyya engaged. He was particularly fascinated by Ibn Taymiyya's frequent references to al-Ashʿarī's tenth-century doxography and consequently decided to edit and publish the work.[64]

Al-Qāsimī and al-Ālūsī scoured manuscript collections in search of Ibn Taymiyya's writings as well as other interesting works. A major site in the rediscovery of works by Ibn Taymiyya and Ibn al-Qayyim was the Ẓāhiriyya Library in al-Qāsimī's hometown of Damascus. Although the Ẓāhiriyya was already two decades old, its holdings were still yielding major unexpected finds in the early 1900s. The most important source for these discoveries was a single work, titled *al-Kawākib al-darārī* (The shining stars), by Ibn ʿUrwa al-Ḥanbalī (d. 837/1434).[65] Ostensibly, the work merely reorders the hadith reports found in Aḥmad b. Ḥanbal's ninth-century collection according to the chapter division of the much more user-friendly collection of Ibn Ḥanbal's contemporary al-Bukhārī. However, Ibn ʿUrwa's work consists of more than 120 volumes—several times the length of the work it claims to reorder.[66] Closer examination reveals that Ibn ʿUrwa included extensive fragments of other works and even entire multivolume books in the text of his *Kawākib*. Several of these included works are by Ibn Taymiyya and Ibn al-Qayyim. The practice of incorporating into one's writings older works, particularly theological ones, that were on the verge of being forgotten was established among the Ḥanbalīs, to whom Ibn ʿUrwa belonged,[67] but it can also be observed among scholars belonging to other intellectual currents, such as the fourteenth-century Shāfiʿī jurist al-Subkī in his biographical dictionary and the eighteenth-century reformist Sufi al-Zabīdī in his commentary on al-Ghazālī.[68]

One of the important works recovered in part from Ibn ʿUrwa's *Kawākib* was a substantial fragment of Ibn Taymiyya's refutation of Fakhr al-Dīn al-Rāzī's twelfth-century *Asās al-taqdīs* (The foundation of transcendence), in which the latter had argued for the rational necessity of interpreting certain

[64] Al-Ashʿarī, *Maqālāt al-islāmiyyīn*, 1:3. Hellmut Ritter's 1929–30 edition of al-Ashʿarī's work remains the superior edition, but ʿAbd al-Ḥamīd's is more easily available and affordable and thus better known in the Arabic world. On ʿAbd al-Ḥamīd and his prodigious editorial output, see al-Ṭanāḥī, *Madkhal ilā tārīkh nashr al-turāth*, 70–80.

[65] On Ibn ʿUrwa, see al-Sakhāwī, *al-Ḍawʾ al-lāmiʿ*, 5:214–15.

[66] Ibn ʿUrwa, *al-Kawākib*. Most manuscripts of the work are held at the Ẓāhiriyya.

[67] A prominent example is Ibn Baṭṭa's (d. 387/997) *Ibāna*, which contains eighth- and ninth-century theological texts.

[68] E.g., al-Subkī, *Ṭabaqāt al-Shāfiʿiyya*, 5:209–18; al-Zabīdī, *Itḥāf al-sāda*, 2:16, 278, 4:537–39.

FIGURE 7.3. The reading room of the Ẓāhiriyya Library, 1920s. From Ḥassūn, *Kitāb Sūriya*. Courtesy of Special Collections, Fine Arts Library, Harvard University.

divine attributes figuratively.[69] Maḥmūd Shukrī al-Ālūsī was fascinated by the work. He considered Ibn Taymiyya's systematic historical philology—his meticulous tracing of al-Rāzī's divergence from earlier authorities and even from the theologian he purports to follow, al-Ashʿarī—a model of critical scholarship. When Muḥammad Bahjat al-Atharī (1904–96) sought to become a student of al-Ālūsī, the latter agreed only on the condition that al-Atharī copy Ibn Taymiyya's refutation by hand in order to learn "the fundamentals of knowledge, research, and how to argue."[70] Unfortunately, the work as found in the *Kawākib* is not complete and was therefore not printed until 1971. A complete manuscript was discovered in Leiden and published in a critical edition only in 2005.

Another work discovered in the *Kawākib* was the shorter of Ibn Taymiyya's two commentaries on al-Iṣbahānī's (d. 688/1289) abridgment on creed.[71]

[69] *Bayān talbīs al-Jahmiyya*. The fragment is found in volumes 39, 42, 46, and 47 of the *Kawākib* (nos. 567 and 570–72 in the Ẓāhiriyya Library), and it formed the basis of Ibn al-Qāsim's 1971 edition of the *Bayān*; see 1:39–40.

[70] Al-Atharī, *Maḥmūd Shukrī al-Ālūsī*, 126; and al-Atharī, *Aʿlām al-ʿIrāq*, 114. The Awqāf Library (Maktabat al-Awqāf al-ʿĀmma) in Baghdad contains a fragment of the work copied in 1920; this could be the copy of Muḥammad Bahjat al-Atharī. However, the editors of the 2005 edition claim that it was written by Muḥammad Bahjat al-Bayṭār (1894–1976); see Ibn Taymiyya, *Bayān talbīs al-Jahmiyya* (al-Hanīdī et al. ed.), 9:26–28.

[71] Ibn Taymiyya, *Sharḥ al-ʿaqīda al-Iṣfahāniyya*.

Al-Qāsimī wrote to al-Ālūsī in January 1909 to ask him about this work. He had read about it in Ibn al-Qayyim's theological poem *al-Nūniyya*, which contains a section in which Ibn al-Qayyim recommends certain books by Ibn Taymiyya for their specific content and qualities.[72] It is this bibliographical information that drove al-Qāsimī's quest to find Ibn Taymiyya's commentary.[73] Al-Ālūsī responded two months later, informing al-Qāsimī that a copy of the shorter commentary existed in Baghdad and that the longer might be found in Najd.[74] The Baghdad copy had in fact been brought there by al-Ālūsī's uncle Nuʿmān, who had copied the work during his visit to Istanbul in 1885.[75] Within a month, al-Qāsimī wrote back, announcing that he had discovered the text in the *Kawākib* manuscript in Damascus.[76] Al-Qāsimī had his student and go-to copyist Ḥāmid al-Taqī (1882–1967)[77] make two copies of this version. One he sent to Jedda to the abovementioned merchant and bibliophile Muḥammad Naṣīf, and the other to Cairo for printing.[78]

The work was published by the Kurdistān Press still in the same year on the basis of the Damascus and Baghdad copies as part of a collection of Ibn Taymiyya's writings.[79] The collection also included three volumes of Ibn Taymiyya's responses to questions asked of him and two volumes of monographs, including his powerful genealogical critique of Neoplatonic influences on Muslim thinkers such as Ibn ʿArabī.[80] It appears that it was Maḥmūd Shukrī al-Ālūsī who convinced Faraj Allāh Zakī al-Kurdī, the Baha'i owner of the press, of the value of this project.[81] Shortly before, several other works by Ibn Taymiyya had been published in Cairo by two of the most influential publishers of classical works, both originally hailing from Syria, Muḥammad Amīn al-Khānjī (on whom see chapter 6)[82] and Muṣṭafā al-Bābī al-Ḥalabī (d. unknown).[83]

[72] See Ibn al-Qayyim, *al-Kāfiya al-shāfiya*, lines 3653–66.

[73] Al-ʿAjmī, *al-Rasāʾil al-mutabādala bayna al-Qāsimī wa-l-Ālūsī*, 57.

[74] Al-ʿAjmī, *al-Rasāʾil al-mutabādala bayna al-Qāsimī wa-l-Ālūsī*, 61–62.

[75] Nuʿmān's copy was most probably based on a manuscript in the Laleli collection (Süleymaniye Library, no. 2324); see the editor's introduction to Ibn Taymiyya, *Sharḥ al-Iṣbahāniyya*, 92 and 95.

[76] Al-ʿAjmī, *al-Rasāʾil al-mutabādala bayna al-Qāsimī wa-l-Ālūsī*, 67.

[77] On al-Taqī, see al-Marʿashlī, *Nathr al-jawāhir*, 319.

[78] These are today housed in the collection of Muḥammad Naṣīf at King ʿAbd al-ʿAzīz University in Jedda and at the Egyptian National Library, respectively.

[79] Ibn Taymiyya, *Kitāb Majmūʿat fatāwā*. On the publication, see al-ʿAjmī, *al-Rasāʾil al-mutabādala bayna al-Qāsimī wa-l-Ālūsī*, 168.

[80] Ibn Taymiyya, *Bughyat al-murtād* (known as *al-Sabʿīniyya*).

[81] Al-ʿAjmī, *al-Rasāʾil al-mutabādala bayna al-Qāsimī wa-l-Ālūsī*, 48.

[82] Al-Khānjī financed the 1907 print of Ibn Taymiyya's *Kitāb al-Īmān*. On al-Khānjī, see al-Ṭanāḥī, *Madkhal ilā tārīkh nashr al-turāth*, 59–62.

[83] Muṣṭafā al-Bābī al-Ḥalabī, together with his two brothers, financed the printing of Ibn Taymiyya's *Minhāj al-sunna* in 1904–5. On the al-Bābī al-Ḥalabī family, see al-Ṭanāḥī, *Fī al-lugha wa-l-adab*, 1:660–61.

Finally, al-Qāsimī's research into the Damascus manuscript of the *Kawākib* unearthed one more work by Ibn Taymiyya, one that has not survived anywhere else: *Qāʿida jalīla fī al-tawassul wa-l-wasīla* (A lofty principle on seeking intermediaries). This work is Ibn Taymiyya's most sustained argument against ritual practices aimed at securing the intercession of, for example, dead saints as intermediaries between the believer and God. Al-Qāsimī's student ʿAbd Allāh al-Rawwāf (1875–1940) copied the work and brought it to Egypt, where Rashīd Riḍā edited the text and printed it at his Manār Press in 1909.[84]

Al-Qāsimī played an important role in the rediscovery of several other important works by Ibn Taymiyya and his followers. In 1911, browsing the private library of the Damascene scholar Muḥammad Jamīl al-Shaṭṭī (1882–1959),[85] al-Qāsimī came across Ibn Taymiyya's *al-Radd ʿalā al-Bakrī*, a work attacking the practice of invoking saints (or anyone other than God) for assistance. He had Ḥāmid al-Taqī copy the work and sold it to Muḥammad Naṣīf.[86] Another work by Ibn Taymiyya in the library of al-Shaṭṭī was his influential *Muqaddima fī uṣūl al-tafsīr* (Introduction to the principles of Quranic exegesis).[87] Al-Shaṭṭī had acquired the work in 1896 from Ṭāhir al-Jazāʾirī and corrected it from a second copy al-Jazāʾirī had found a few years later.[88] In a letter to al-Ālūsī, al-Qāsimī mentions that Rashīd Riḍā intended to publish the work, but apparently nothing came of the plan, and the text was printed only in 1936 in Damascus, edited by al-Shaṭṭī himself.[89] A year after these discoveries, in 1912, al-Qāsimī visited Aleppo and spent four days surveying two of its endowed libraries. In the library of the ʿUthmāniyya madrasa he discovered a theological work by Ibn al-Qayyim,[90] and in that of the Aḥmadiyya madrasa he found *al-Bidāya wa-l-nihāya* (The beginning and

[84] Al-ʿAjmī, *al-Rasāʾil al-mutabādala bayna al-Qāsimī wa-l-Ālūsī*, 56, 68. Al-Rawwāf originated from central Arabia but had traveled to Damascus to study; see Ibn Bassām, *ʿUlamāʾ Najd*, 4:27–31.

[85] On al-Shaṭṭī, see Weismann, *Taste of Modernity*, 232–33.

[86] Al-ʿAjmī, *al-Rasāʾil al-mutabādala bayna al-Qāsimī wa-l-Ālūsī*, 162. This copy is now part of the Muḥammad Naṣīf collection at King ʿAbd al-ʿAzīz University in Jedda. A shortened version of Ibn Taymiyya's *Radd ʿalā al-Bakrī* had already been published as *al-Istighātha* in the 1905 collection *Majmūʿat al-rasāʾil al-kubrā*. A longer version was printed separately on the basis of al-Taqī's manuscript as *Talkhīṣ kitāb al-Istighātha*, financed by the Saudi ruler ʿAbd al-ʿAzīz.

[87] Most of the text had already appeared in print in Murtaḍā al-Zabīdī's *Itḥāf al-sāda*, which reproduces almost the entire text. On the *Muqaddima*, see Saleh, "Ibn Taymiyyah and the Rise of Radical Hermeneutics."

[88] See the editor's introduction to Ibn Taymiyya, *Muqaddima fī uṣūl al-tafsīr* (Zarzūr ed.), 23–27.

[89] Muḥammad Yusrī Salāma has claimed that Riḍā published the work in 1930, but I have not found any evidence for this claim. See Salāma, *Muʿjam mā ṭubiʿa*, 178–79.

[90] This manuscript of Ibn al-Qayyim's *al-Ṣawāʿiq al-mursala* is today housed in Aleppo's Awqāf Library. A copy of the manuscript was sent to al-Ālūsī and is now part of the al-Ālūsī

the end), a universal history authored by Ibn Taymiyya's student Ibn Kathīr.[91] Each these finds would become the basis of the published version of the respective work.[92]

As noted earlier, the interest of reformers such as al-Qāsimī and al-Ālūsī in Ibn Taymiyya and his students was both methodological and substantial. They saw his writings as models of critical engagement and analysis, but they also harnessed the content of his works in service of their reformist agendas. An example is the issue of divorce, on which subject al-Qāsimī found a unique book by Ibn al-Qayyim, titled *Ighāthat al-lahfān* (The rescue of the regretful), in his own grandfather's private library.[93] Both Ibn Taymiyya and Ibn al-Qayyim had been concerned with the negative social consequences of allowing a man to divorce his wife irreversibly through a single utterance—the standard legal position in their time, as in that of al-Qāsimī—instead of requiring him to stagger the declaration of divorce over three months, thus avoiding divorces pronounced in anger or as part of oaths and giving the husband time to come to his senses or change his mind.[94] In the book discovered by al-Qāsimī, Ibn al-Qayyim argues that a divorce formula uttered in a fit of anger is not valid. Al-Qāsimī had the text copied, corrected the copy himself, and sent it to Egypt, where Riḍā's Manār Press published it.[95] Muslim reformers eagerly embraced this argument and used it to challenge the prevailing law of divorce as religiously questionable and socially damaging.[96] In a letter written shortly before the publication, al-Qāsimī exclaims, "I am overjoyed about the good news that it is being printed, given that it is so very effective for the reform of marriage and family life. . . . The happiness of the community's marriage life depends on clearly knowing when the marriage bonds have been dissolved and when they have not."[97] Al-Qāsimī's scholarship and his interest in classical books were thus not simply a form of ivory-tower philology; rather, they served his broader goal of

---

collection in the library of the Iraqi Museum; see the published edition of Ibn al-Qayyim's *al-Ṣawāʿiq al-mursala*, 129–31.

[91] Al-ʿAjmī, *al-Rasāʾil al-mutabādala bayna al-Qāsimī wa-l-Ālūsī*, 206. The manuscript of Ibn Kathīr's *al-Bidāya wa-l-nihāya* of the Aḥmadiyya collection is today found in the Maktabat al-Asad (formerly the Ẓāhiriyya Library).

[92] The abridgment of Ibn al-Qayyim's *al-Ṣawāʿiq al-mursala* by Muḥammad b. al-Mawṣilī (*Mukhtaṣar al-Ṣawāʿiq al-mursala*) was published in 1929; the original text appeared only in 1987. Ibn Kathīr's *al-Bidāya wa-l-nihāya* was published for the first time on the basis of the nine-volume Aleppo fragment in 1923. On later manuscript finds of this work, see Ibn Kathīr, *al-Bidāya wa-l-nihāya* (al-Turkī ed.), 1:46–74.

[93] Ibn al-Qayyim, *Ighāthat al-lahfān*. See al-ʿAjmī, *al-Rasāʾil al-mutabādala bayna al-Qāsimī wa-l-Ālūsī*, 75.

[94] See Rapoport, "Ibn Taymiyya on Divorce Oaths."

[95] Al-ʿAjmī, *al-Rasāʾil al-mutabādala bayna al-Qāsimī wa-l-Ālūsī*, 76, 94.

[96] See, for example, Aḥmad Shākir, *Niẓām al-ṭalāq fī al-islām*.

[97] Ẓāfir al-Qāsimī, *Jamāl al-Dīn al-Qāsimī wa-ʿaṣruh*, 607.

contributing to the reform of communal life. The reform of divorce law would remain a point of contention for the following generations, with intellectuals of various stripes drawing on a range of classical works in support of their competing positions.[98]

Al-Qāsimī's letters exude a sense of urgency and a clear focus on the transformative potential of print technology to support the struggle for reform. In a letter to al-Ālūsī, he exclaims, "By God, what have recent centuries inflicted on us, by impoverishing our lands of useful works and leaving us with nonsense and vacuities!"[99] To Naṣīf, he writes, "It is incumbent to revive the works of the ancients and to publicize them by means of print. . . . What is important is to use several printing presses to speed up the process of publishing these gems," including, he specifies, those in Damascus, where presses had also started to multiply.[100] According to al-Qāsimī, the printing of books represented the best way of reforming society, "since the impact of a book endures and it is read by both supporters and opponents [of its thesis]; I know of many previously narrow-minded folk who have found their way by means of what we have printed and published."[101]

While much of his correspondence with al-Ālūsī concerned significant, programmatically reformist texts targeted at a scholarly audience, al-Qāsimī also sought to publish classical texts suitable for younger students and school use. In 1908, he wrote to al-Ālūsī about this endeavor, connecting it explicitly to his overall reform agenda:

> This service is necessary these days given all the schools that are about to be opened; they cannot be established except with such [texts]. One that I have come to consider significant is al-Zarkashī's *Luqṭat al-ʿajlān* ["The quick find"], since it deals with the four [key] disciplines [of philosophy, logic, theology, and legal theory]. I also gave it a commentary in the modern style. A brother has printed it for us in Alexandria, and once I receive copies I will send you several, God willing. The idea is that in the present time it is obligatory for everyone to consider what they can contribute to the raising of the community. If people like us cannot bring about political reform, then at least intellectual reform.[102]

The inauguration of modern state schools in the nineteenth century created an opening that al-Qāsimī sought to exploit. In the postclassical madrasa context, there had been no space for the rediscovery of classical works. The curriculum was largely fixed and did not accommodate additions from

[98] Shaham, "Judicial Divorce."
[99] Al-ʿAjmī, *al-Rasāʾil al-mutabādala bayna al-Qāsimī wa-l-Ālūsī*, 86.
[100] Al-ʿAjmī, *al-Rasāʾil al-mutabādala bayna al-Qāsimī wa-l-Ālūsī*, 71.
[101] Al-ʿAjmī, *al-Rasāʾil al-mutabādala bayna al-Qāsimī wa-l-Ālūsī*, 71.
[102] Al-ʿAjmī, *al-Rasāʾil al-mutabādala bayna al-Qāsimī wa-l-Ālūsī*, 78–79. Al-Qāsimī had al-Zarkashī's *Luqṭat al-ʿajlān* printed in Alexandria in 1908.

outside the tradition that lacked a continuous chain of transmission back to the author, as Muḥammad ʿAbduh found when he tried to introduce Ibn Khaldūn's *Muqaddima* to the Azhari curriculum and was told by the rector that such a thing was not done there.[103] Modern schools, however, were not constrained by the requirement of chains of transmission, and new reading material could thus be introduced much more easily.

The texts that al-Qāsimī selected and printed for school use were written by classical authors such as Ibn Ḥazm and al-Suyūṭī.[104] In contrast to the early prints of commonly used postclassical teaching texts (*mutūn*), discussed in chapter 3, these texts were chosen not only for their content—specifically, the diverse range of schools of thought that they represented, including some that had died out[105]—but also for their lucidity. Al-Qāsimī avoided any texts written in verse[106] (a postclassical fashion that made writings much more difficult to understand), and—like ʿAbduh before him—he composed his commentaries in a "contemporary" style that contrasts sharply with the linguistic and scholastic commentaries characteristic of the postclassical tradition. His comments on the base texts are conversational in tone and focus on the substantial points made in the texts.

CONTESTING THE POWER OF SAINTS

Beyond the limited textual horizons of postclassical Islamic scholarship, a second key target of nineteenth- and early twentieth-century Muslim reformers was the status of and rituals surrounding saints (*awliyāʾ*). Although respect for saintly individuals and the custom of visiting their graves can be traced back to the early period of Islam, by the postclassical period the institutionalized veneration of saints, living and dead, and the ritual visitation of saints' tombs had become a major part of Muslim religious life. Saints' tombs hosted elaborate religious rituals: worshippers circled around the grave in analogy to the circumambulation of the Kaʿba in Mecca during the Ḥajj pilgrimage; they beseeched the dead saint for intercession with God and for the fulfillment of wishes;[107] and they brought animals to the tomb and sacrificed them in the saint's name.[108]

[103] Riḍā, *Tārīkh al-ustādh al-imām*, 1:426. See also chapter 6.

[104] The collection was titled *Majmūʿ rasāʾil fī uṣūl al-tafsīr wa-uṣūl al-fiqh*, and it was published for the first time in 1913.

[105] The collection also includes a text by the Andalusian Ẓāhirī jurist Ibn Ḥazm.

[106] Al-ʿAjmī, *al-Rasāʾil al-mutabādala bayna al-Qāsimī wa-l-Ālūsī*, 78.

[107] See, for example, ʿUways, *Rasāʾil ilā al-imām al-Shāfiʿī*; Nuʿmān al-Ālūsī, *Jalāʾ al-ʿaynayn* (Āl Zahawī ed.), 510.

[108] See the autobiographical account of an Egyptian journalist describing animal sacrifice at the grave of al-Badawī in Tanta: al-Jiddāwī, *Kuntu qubūriyyan*, 16–17. See also al-Jabartī,

FIGURE 7.4. Worshippers at the shrine of al-Sayyida Zaynab in Cairo, 2014. Photograph by Mosa'ab Elshamy. Courtesy of Mosa'ab Elshamy.

The cult of saints was not simply about the power of the dead; it also served the economic interests of the living. Sufi brotherhoods, headed by hereditary shaykhs, competed for control of lucrative shrines—their endowments and their collection boxes.[109] The brotherhoods were influential societal and political actors, their power rooted in their status as delegates and intermediaries between humans and the divine. A pedagogical anecdote told by the postclassical Sufi authority ʿAbd al-Ghanī al-Nābulsī illustrates the force of this intermediary role:

> Muḥammad al-Ḥanafī al-Shādhilī was on his way from Egypt to Medina, and he and his followers were walking on water. He said to them: "Say 'O Ḥanafī' and walk behind me, but beware of saying 'O God,' lest you drown." One of them disobeyed him and called out "O God"; his foot slipped and he sank into the water up to his beard. The shaykh turned to him and said: "My son, you do not know God, and therefore you cannot walk on water through his name. You have to wait until I have taught you the grandeur of God, and then you will need no intermediaries anymore."[110]

ʿ*Ajāʾib al-āthār*, 2:249. For a defense of this and other Sufi practices decried by the reformers, see Dīrshawī, *Rudūd ʿalā shubuhāt al-salafiyya*.

[109] Al-Jabartī, ʿ*Ajāʾib al-āthār*, 3:425–26.

[110] Al-Nābulsī, *Kashf al-nūr*, 21.

The influence of the Sufi cult of saints was due to the growing authority of esoteric Sufism in the postclassical period, described in chapter 2. Nuʿmān al-Ālūsī, who dedicated a lengthy section of his work on Ibn Taymiyya to the issue of grave visitation,[111] quotes his father, Maḥmūd Shihāb al-Dīn, on the practice and its esoteric justification:

> I have seen many who prostrate themselves on the thresholds of saints' tombs. Some of them assign power to all of them [the saints] in their graves, whereas the scholars among them limit the number [of saints with miraculous posthumous powers] to four or five. And if one asks how they know this, they answer that they know it through inspiration. May they drop dead; how ignorant they are and how many falsehoods they invent! And some of them believe that the saints can leave their graves and take on various forms. . . . All of this is nonsense and has no shred of basis in revelation or the sayings of the early Muslims. These [ideas] have ruined people's faith, making them a laughingstock to Jews, Christians, and materialists.[112]

The connection between the power of dead saints and the esoteric doctrine of divine inspiration was not a mere popular belief; it was explicitly theorized and endorsed by postclassical Sufi authors.[113] Claims that God had delegated his creative powers to the saints, who could consequently affect anything from life and death to the weather and wars, were not uncommon.[114] The prominent Sufi ʿAbd al-Wahhāb al-Shaʿrānī, discussed in chapter 2, celebrated the potency of sainthood by relating the story of a Sufi master, Yūsuf al-Kūrānī, who, after a period of seclusion, was so charged with spiritual energy that he turned a dog into a saint by simply looking at it. As a result, "people came to ask [the dog] for help in their affairs, and when the dog became ill, other dogs gathered around him, crying and displaying sadness. When he died, they cried and whined. God inspired some people to bury the dog, and dogs began to visit his grave."[115] The book containing this anecdote was published in 1882; by the early twenty-first century, the story had become so embarrassing that a new edition of the work omitted it.[116] A similar embarrassment seems to underpin Maḥmūd al-Ālūsī's concern, at the end of the passage quoted above, about the potential ridicule of non-Muslims. The statement may be merely a rhetorical flourish, but it could also reflect awareness

[111] Nuʿmān al-Ālūsī, *Jalāʾ al-ʿaynayn* (Āl Zahawī ed.), 423–513.

[112] Nuʿmān al-Ālūsī, *Jalāʾ al-ʿaynayn* (Āl Zahawī ed.), 478, quoting Maḥmūd Shihāb al-Dīn al-Ālūsī, *Rūḥ al-maʿānī* (1926 ed.), 17:213.

[113] See, for example, Qāwuqjī, *Hādhihi Istighātha*; and al-Nabhānī, *Shawāhid al-ḥaqq*. For discussion, see Maḥmūd Shukrī al-Ālūsī, *Tārīkh Najd*, 102.

[114] For a collection of such claims, see the polemical work *Taqdīs al-ashkhāṣ fī al-fikr al-ṣūfī* by Muḥammad Lawḥ, 1:134–72.

[115] Al-Shaʿrānī, *al-Ṭabaqāt al-kubrā* (al-ʿAjmāwī ed.), 2:91–91.

[116] Cf. al-Shaʿrānī, *al-Ṭabaqāt al-kubrā* (al-Sāyiḥ and Wahba ed.), 2:132–34.

of the Western gaze on Muslims in a time of acute European encroachment on Muslim lands.

The reformers' rejection of the power of saints and their ritual role in society was not simply a sign of puritanism. Rather, it was rooted in unease and alarm about the intellectually constraining effect of esoteric Sufi ideas on society. In the eyes of the reformers, charismatic Sufism entailed an abuse of power over ignorant commoners, who sought to gain control over their lives by buying into the superstitions proffered by the cult of saints, and it led to the distortion of Islamic doctrines to accommodate the routine appearance of divine inspiration and miracles.

Critiques of the veneration of saints are common in the autobiographical accounts of late nineteenth- and early twentieth-century Arab writers, who likewise denounce what they see as the irrationality, superstition, and chicanery of widespread Sufi practices. Ṭāhā Ḥusayn, for example, describes in his autobiography the visits of the head of a Sufi brotherhood to his family's home. Ḥusayn decries the mindless devotion of the shaykh's followers, who fought over the right to drink the water their leader had used for his ablutions and who took his incomprehensible mutterings for great wisdom, and he notes with scorn the gluttony and material greed of the shaykh and his followers in exploiting their hosts.[117] The social status and acceptance of saints was so strong that the "madman" whom Sayyid Quṭb recalls from his home village was considered a potential saint despite his habit of running around naked and caked in filth and attacking children. Quṭb recounts his bewilderment as a child on observing how the adults around him willfully ignored the man's behavior, choosing to see it as supernaturally inspired and thus beyond the norms applicable to normal social conduct.[118]

Rashīd Riḍā's formative experience of Sufism was similarly one of disillusionment. He attended a ceremony of the Mevlevi Sufi order in his native Tripoli in which young men in flowing garments whirled around, accompanied by music, reaching a state of ecstasy and eventually prostrating themselves before their Sufi master. Riḍā, who in his account of the event reports having just read the chapter on the individual's obligation to take action against evil in al-Ghazālī's *Iḥyā ʿulūm al-dīn*, found this mixture of ritual devotion, entertainment, and submission to a human being unbearable. He stood up and declared, "One cannot watch this and remain silent, because that would implicitly validate this behavior. God's statement 'those who take your religion for entertainment and sport' [Q 5:57] is applicable to people such as these. I have done my duty here. Leave now!" But when Riḍā subsequently met his teacher, the latter advised him never to criticize the Sufis

[117] Ḥusayn, *al-Ayyām*, 1:81 (chap. 15).
[118] Quṭb, *Ṭifl min al-qariya*, 8–15.

again, because they were different from ordinary people. When Riḍā inquired whether Sufis were subject to the same ethical rules as everyone else, his teacher affirmed that they were, but that their spiritual aims were higher than those of ordinary people, who listened to music for mere entertainment. Riḍā objected that the new ritual devotions developed by Sufis, such as the whirling dervish ceremonies, were in fact much worse than sitting in coffeehouses and listening to music for entertainment, because the Sufis considered these forms of worship more powerful and profound than the rituals prescribed by Muḥammad himself. His teacher simply repeated his advice to abstain from criticizing Sufis.[119]

The fact that the popular Sufism of saints and miracles played an important role in the intellectual formation of literate youth heightened the reformers' concern. Ṭāhā Ḥusayn reports that

> books on magic, the virtues of the righteous, and the miracles of saints would fall into their hands; they would read them and be affected by them and would try to translate what they had read into actions and experience. They would at once follow the path of the Sufis and engage in magical practices, and Sufism and magic would become mixed up and connected in their minds, becoming one thing—its aim being to make life easier and to bring them closer to God.[120]

The continued prevalence of popular Sufi practices and beliefs posed a particular challenge to students enrolled in modern schools, where they were introduced to scientific understandings of the world. The disjuncture that these students experienced led, for many, to a process of cultural alienation, as they juxtaposed popular religious practices, the most visible manifestations of Islam, with the scientific rationalism associated with the non-Muslim West. The ensuing crisis of identity is evident in, for example, the biography of Aḥmad Taymūr, whose account of his own education is quoted in chapter 4. Taymūr sought to have his growing religious doubts assuaged by the scholars of al-Azhar, but to his dismay these scholars adhered to the "superstitions" that troubled him even more fervently than did common people—unsurprisingly, in view of the influence of esoteric Sufi ideas on postclassical scholarship. Taymūr's crisis of faith was eventually resolved by the renegade figure Ḥasan al-Ṭawīl, who introduced him to classical works. These works were free of the esoteric epistemology that forestalled critical engagement and of the scholastic spirit that restricted every question to a mere handful of possible answers, each encompassing infinite further minutiae.

[119] Riḍā, *al-Manār wa-l-Azhar*, 172–73. See also Hourani, *Arabic Thought in the Liberal Age*, 225–26, 232.

[120] Ḥusayn, *al-Ayyām*, 1:83 (chap. 15).

The very fact that these works had been largely forgotten meant that they were unencumbered by the suffocating weight of the later interpretive tradition. They could thus be discovered and read afresh, with the particular challenges of the time in mind.

Here, again, the methodological and substantive goals of the reformers coincide: the classical literature whose rediscovery opened up the narrow confines of postclassical scholarship and injected a breath of fresh air into its ossified literary practices also carried arguments and positions that could be harnessed to combat what the reformers saw as the greatest problems of postclassical thought. It is for this reason that people such as al-Qāsimī and al-Ālūsī were so excited about the discovery of works such as Ibn Taymiyya's *al-Radd ʿalā al-Bakrī* and *Qāʿida jalīla*, which forcefully and eloquently critiqued the cult of saints and furthermore unveiled the long and rich genealogy of such critique.

Rejection of esoteric Sufi ideas and practices was voiced by reformist figures with widely varying perspectives, among them some who continued to claim a Sufi identity while criticizing certain Sufi rituals. In addition to the individuals already discussed, critics of Sufism in the eighteenth and nineteenth centuries included al-Shawkānī in Yemen,[121] Shāh Walī Allāh and later the Ahl-i Ḥadīth and Deobandi movements in India,[122] and Muḥammad b. ʿAbd al-Wahhāb in central Arabia.[123] Whereas most of the reformers called the practices in question un-Islamic and argued that they compromised the monotheism at the heart of Islam, Ibn ʿAbd al-Wahhāb deemed practitioners to be outright unbelievers and, in alliance with the house of Muḥammad b. Saʿūd (d. 1765), declared war on them both in his writings and on the ground.[124] It is on this point of anathematizing fellow Muslims and sanctioning violence against them that Ibn ʿAbd al-Wahhāb parted company with contemporary reformers, who criticized his willingness to do so while sharing the underlying critique of Sufi practices.[125] It is noteworthy that although Ibn ʿAbd al-Wahhāb and his followers drew on Ibn Taymiyya's attacks on popular religion (occasioning the modern image of Ibn Taymiyya as a conservative fanatic),[126] their reception is entirely devoid

[121] See al-Ṣanʿānī, *al-Inṣāf*, 60, 70; al-Shawkānī, *Qaṭr al-walī*, 446–49.

[122] Walī Allāh, *Ḥujjat Allāh al-bāligha*, 2:50–59. On the attitude of his successor, Shāh ʿAbd al-ʿAzīz, see Preckel, "Islamische Bildungsnetzwerke," 101–2; and on the Ahl-i Ḥadīth, see ibid., 434–38. On the Deobandis, see Metcalf, *Islamic Revival in British India*, 182.

[123] See Crawford, *Ibn ʿAbd al-Wahhab*, 83–85.

[124] Ibn Ghannām, *Tārīkh Najd*, 49–78, 226–42.

[125] See Ibn Ḥamīd, *al-Suḥub al-wābila*, 3:973, for the criticism of Ibn ʿAbd al-Wahhāb by Ibn Fayrūz (1729 or 1730–1801 or 1802). For his teacher Muḥammad b. Sulaymān al-Kurdī, see Daḥlān, *al-Durar al-saniyya*, 47. For al-Shawkānī, see Haykel, *Revival and Reform*, 129.

[126] For recent, more balanced re-evaluations of Ibn Taymiyya's philosophical thought, see Hoover, "Ibn Taymiyya as an Avicennan Theologian"; Adem, "Intellectual Genealogy."

of Ibn Taymiyya's constructive engagement with theology, philosophy, and Sufism.[127]

* * *

Around the turn of the twentieth century, reformist scholars in the Ottoman Arab provinces and elsewhere in the Muslim world were engaged in a breathless quest to rediscover what they saw as important classical works in manuscript form and to make them widely available in print. In these efforts, they created personal networks of like-minded bibliophiles, which also included adherents of other Muslim sects, European Orientalists, Arab Christians, and Baha'is. The works they discovered were printed mainly in Egypt, which by this time boasted the largest Arabic publishing industry, a substantial reading public, and much more liberal press laws than the Ottoman realm.

The twin targets of these reformers' efforts were the two pillars of postclassical Islamic thought described in chapter 2: the narrow and—in their view—stultifying scholastic orthodoxy, which severely constrained the scope of acceptable literature and admissible argumentation, and the religious practices that had grown out of esoteric Sufism, manifested most visibly in the cult of saints and shrine veneration. Their goal was not the re-establishment of a mythical, "pure" vision of Islam. Rather, they sought to expand the horizons of Islamic thought and practice beyond postclassical traditionalism by drawing on the resources contained in classical literature. They were optimistic about the capacity of human reason and confident that truth would be distinguished from falsehood, and they thus deliberately published writings by a wide variety of divergent authors. Al-Qāsimī's choice to edit works by figures such as Avicenna, Ibn Ḥazm, Ibn ʿArabī, Fakhr al-Dīn al-Rāzī, and Ibn Taymiyya was mirrored in the eclectic list of the Salafiyya Press of Ṭāhir al-Jazāʾirī's protégé Muḥibb al-Dīn al-Khaṭīb (see chapter 6), whose catalog included, alongside works by Avicenna and al-Fārābī, a translation of Descartes's *Discourse on Method*, a work by the last Ottoman Shaykh al-Islām Muṣṭafā Ṣabrī, and lectures on the development of the Arabic novel given by Maḥmūd Taymūr (the son of Aḥmad Taymūr, discussed in chapter 4).[128] Underpinning this diversity was a broader understanding of "the classics" and a trust that the best arguments would carry the day.

[127]See, respectively, Hoover, "Ibn Taymiyya as an Avicennan Theologian"; Adem, "Intellectual Genealogy"; and Homerin, "Ibn Taimīya's *al-Ṣūfīyah wa-al-Fuqarāʾ*."

[128]Avicenna, *Manṭiq al-mashriqiyyīn*; al-Fārābī, *Mabādiʾ al-falsafa al-qadīma*; Descartes, *Maqāl ʿan al-manhaj* (for this work's publication history, see chapter 8); Ṣabrī, *Qawlī fī al-marʾa*; Maḥmūd Taymūr, *Nushūʾ al-qiṣṣa wa-taṭawwuruhā*. I disagree with Henri Lauzière ("Construction of Salafiyya," 378) that the Salafiyya Press's publication of these works reflected mere "business flair" rather than the particular, expansive character of its "Salafi" agenda.

The reformers' most important inspiration was Ibn Taymiyya, because he offered not only a model of incisive and tireless scholarship but also a broad genealogical analysis of Islamic thought. They highlighted his willingness to engage with the ideas of every religion, philosophy, and theological school and his insistence on taking his opponents' views seriously—a practice that contrasted with that of his critics. For thinkers such as al-Ālūsī and al-Qāsimī, the example of Ibn Taymiyya thus offered a crucial lesson for the formation of the modern Muslim subject: not what to think, but how to argue.[129] Ibn Taymiyya was a forerunner of the edition movement in another sense, too. His textual analysis of the authenticity of the so-called Khaybar document[130] prefigured the discourse of critical philology, which would become a crucial site of the next stage of the Arabic print revolution.

[129]For a dramatic example of a difference in the respective theological beliefs of Ibn Taymiyya and al-Qāsimī, see the latter's *Tārīkh al-Jahmiyya wa-l-Muʿtazila*.

[130]Ibn Taymiyya's argument is preserved in Ibn Qayyim al-Jawziyya, *Aḥkām ahl al-dhimma*, 1:169–71. See also Noth's discussion of Ibn Taymiyya's analysis in "Minderheiten als Vertragspartner."

CHAPTER 8

Critique and Philology

World War I and its aftermath affected all areas of political and cultural life in the Middle East. As the Ottoman Empire dissolved, its Arab provinces were converted into protectorates of Britain and France, while the Anatolian heartland was transformed, under the leadership of Mustafa Kemal Atatürk, into modern Turkey. Atatürk's aggressive secularizing agenda involved the wholesale abolition of institutions of Muslim religious learning and the abandonment of the Arabic alphabet of Ottoman Turkish for the Latin script of modern Turkish—acts of literary iconoclasm that, within a generation, would render Ottoman book culture largely incomprehensible. The end of the Ottoman caliphate as a symbol of Muslim unity and the almost universal dominance of European powers across the Middle East cast Arabo-Islamic thought into turmoil, creating a climate of deep uncertainty but also making space for the articulation of diverse visions for the future of Muslim societies, the collective identities of their peoples, and the intellectual resources to be drawn on for their advancement.[1]

European hegemony and aggressive Westernization in the former Ottoman Empire formed the backdrop for the next stage in the evolution of Arabic print culture: fierce debates over philology and the critical method. What was at stake was how to critically read the Arabo-Islamic heritage that was becoming accessible at an accelerating pace through the printing press—how to assess the authenticity of writings attributed to particular periods and authors and how to draw on these materials judiciously in order to reconstruct the historical and literary past. The site of these debates was the growing corpus of printed classical works. Even the opponents of the editing and publishing vanguard described in the preceding chapters could no longer ignore the influence of this literature, and accordingly the divergent arguments were phrased overwhelmingly in the idiom of philology. European Orientalists had already for a generation applied philological methods

[1]For the relious and cultural changes caused by the abolition of the Ottoman Empire and the establishment of modern Turkey, see Lewis, *Emergence of Modern Turkey*, chap. 12. For differing visions of a reformed caliphate, see, for example, Schulze, *Modern History*, chap. 2; Haddad, "Arab Religious Nationalism"; Bechor, *Sanhuri Code*, 45–46.

developed for the study of Greco-Roman classics to the analysis of Arabic texts, and in this period Muslim scholars' direct exposure to these methods and the theories behind them—especially through university training under Orientalist professors—increased dramatically. But this was not an encounter between equals. Western philological methods carried the cachet of Europe's global hegemony and the promise of scientific certainty, and their luster led some Arab scholars to declare Western philology the one and only objective window into the Arabo-Islamic past. Others, meanwhile, recognized the dangers of granting imported methods a monopoly of access to the past and set out to resurrect an indigenous philological tradition suited to addressing the particular challenges of the Arabic written tradition. The ensuing philological advancements were brought to bear not only on the juxtaposition of Orientalist and indigenous philology but also on substantial religious issues of the time, including grave visitation, theological tenets, and legal debates.

HISTORICAL CRITICISM

In 1925, the sixteen-year-old Maḥmūd Shākir (1909–97) walked into Muḥibb al-Dīn al-Khaṭīb's Salafiyya bookshop in Cairo, located near the Egyptian National Library. Shākir was the son of Muḥammad Shākir (1866–1939), a prominent Azhari scholar with reformist leanings,[2] but he had chosen to attend a government school rather than a seminary in order to pursue his interest in mathematics. By the time of this bookshop visit, however, Shākir's interests had shifted toward classical Arabic poetry, which he had studied privately with Sayyid al-Marṣafī, the most influential teacher of Arabic poetry in Egypt at the time.[3]

Inside the shop, Shākir ran into his mentor, Aḥmad Taymūr, who handed him a copy of the most recent issue of the *Journal of the Royal Asiatic Society of Great Britain and Ireland.* The issue featured an article on the origins of pre-Islamic poetry written by David Samuel Margoliouth (1858–1940), Laudian Professor of Arabic at Oxford.[4] In the article, Margoliouth argued that contrary to received wisdom, no pre-Islamic poetry had survived, and that the poems attributed to pre-Islamic poets had in fact been composed in the second and third Islamic centuries. In a subsequent meeting, Taymūr inquired

[2] Aḥmad Shākir, Maḥmūd Shākir, and Usāma Shākir, *Min aʿlām al-ʿaṣr.*

[3] Maḥmūd Shākir, *al-Mutanabbī,* 8–9. Shākir studied two classical texts that al-Marṣafī had published or was about to publish with his own commentary, *Asrār al-Ḥamāsa* and *Raghbat al-āmil sharḥ al-Kāmil.*

[4] Margoliouth, "Origins of Arabic Poetry."

FIGURE 8.1. Maḥmūd Shākir, 1936. From al-ʿAlī, *Ẓill al-nadīm*, 221.

about Shākir's opinion of the article. With striking self-confidence, Shākir replied,

> I think this is extreme silliness concocted by a nonnative speaker, shameless as always. . . . I have no doubt that I know English better than this foreigner will ever know Arabic, several times over. . . . I could trace the development of English poetry from Chaucer to today objectively better than any account he could produce of Arabic poetry. Yet I do not have the impertinence and brazenness to think that I could publish a single letter on the development of English poetry. As it is, the whims of fate that raise some people and abase others have afflicted us, our language, and our literature with a condition that allows such a scoundrel and his peers among the Orientalists to discuss our poetry, literature, history, and religion and to find among us those willing to listen to them.[5]

A year later, Shākir enrolled at Cairo University to study Arabic literature, just in time to attend the series of lectures that his renowned professor, Ṭāhā Ḥusayn, subsequently published as a controversial monograph, *Fī al-shiʿr*

[5]Maḥmūd Shākir, *al-Mutanabbī*, 12.

al-jāhilī (On pre-Islamic poetry).[6] In the lectures and the book, Ḥusayn made the same claim as Margoliouth, triggering a scandal. Ḥusayn's thesis was widely discussed in public and even debated in the Egyptian parliament, and condemnations by religious institutions, even accusations of apostasy, prompted Ḥusayn to offer his resignation—though he ultimately emerged from the affair both employed and famous. The case came to be seen primarily as one pitting academic freedom against religious dogmatism, because one of the claims that Ḥusayn made in the book was that the Islamic narrative about Abraham and his son Ishmael building the Kaʿba in Mecca was a mythical fabrication.[7]

Beyond particular points of doctrine, however, it was Ḥusayn's methodological stance that proved deeply unsettling to many observers. In the introduction to his study, he divides contemporary Arab scholarship into two camps, the traditionalists (*anṣār al-qadīm*) and the modernists (*anṣār al-jadīd*), and characterizes the former as adopting blindly the positions of the Arabo-Islamic tradition, whether in law or the history of literature.[8] This critique itself was not new; it was shared by virtually all reformists of the period. It was Ḥusayn's next step that was radical: he argued that the entire Arabo-Islamic scholarly tradition was fundamentally subjective, skewed by ethnic and religious agendas and unable to perceive itself objectively. Only the kind of methodological skepticism developed by Descartes offered the possibility of truly objective study of not only philosophy but also history.[9]

Maḥmūd Shākir was incensed to hear his professor promote a thesis he had already determined—on the basis of his own study—to be unsustainable. The only other student in the class to harbor any doubts regarding the professor's teaching was Maḥmūd Muḥammad al-Khuḍayrī (d. unknown), a philosophy student. According to Shākir's account, after long discussions, the two renegade students agreed on four points. First, Ṭāhā Ḥusayn's thesis was a plagiarized version of Margoliouth's hypothesis, omitting some of Margoliouth's less convincing evidence and adding other material but never acknowledging the original. Second, Ḥusayn's knowledge of pre-Islamic poetry was limited. Third, Ḥusayn's ostensible use of Descartes's method was deeply problematic, since instead of testing tentative claims against certain facts, as Descartes had proposed, Ḥusayn was using some classical texts to dispute the authenticity of other classical texts. He had not examined the texts he was using systematically or critically but seemed to accept them simply because they supported his original hypothesis. And finally, serious study

[6] Ḥusayn, *Fī al-shiʿr al-jāhilī*. See also Cachia, *Ṭāhā Ḥusayn*, 60; Maḥmūd Shākir, *al-Mutanabbī*, 13.

[7] Ayalon, "Revisiting Ṭāhā Ḥusayn's *Fī al-Shiʿr al-Jāhilī*."

[8] Ḥusayn, *Fī al-shiʿr al-jāhilī*, 14–17.

[9] Ḥusayn, *Fī al-shiʿr al-jāhilī*, 23–26.

of the authenticity of pre-Islamic poetry would require comprehensive literary analysis of allegedly pre-Islamic and early Islamic poetry, a task that remained unattempted.[10]

Shākir confronted his professor, but Ḥusayn refused to acknowledge any merit to his criticism. Shākir then turned to two Orientalists teaching at Cairo University at the time, the Swiss Rudolph Tschudi (1884–1960) and the Italian Carlo Alfonso Nallino (1872–1938), but found that their overarching concern was to cover up the issue of Ḥusayn's plagiarism. In disgust, he abandoned his degree and academia in general.[11] Shākir went on to become one of Egypt's foremost literary critics and editors of classical works as a private scholar.[12] His fellow student al-Khuḍayrī published a summary translation of Margoliouth's article to expose the similarities to Ḥusayn's study and translated Descartes's *Discourse on Method* into Arabic to explicate Descartes's ideas.[13]

The usual framing of the controversy surrounding Ḥusayn's *On Pre-Islamic Poetry* as the struggle of a critical modernist scholar against religious conservatism obscures the fact that the scholarly study of Arabic poetry has sided not with Ṭāhā Ḥusayn, but with his recalcitrant teenage student, Maḥmūd Shākir.[14] Shākir's derision at Margoliouth's thesis and his horror at Ḥusayn's adoption of it were not due to a reluctance to examine Arabo-Islamic history critically; Shākir's later oeuvre would include some of the finest historical investigations of Arabic literature ever written.[15] Rather, he was reacting to the absolute gulf that Ḥusayn postulated between the irredeemably subjective world of the ancients and the objectivity of the moderns, who have overcome their subjectivity by adopting a quintessentially Western methodology. This radical vision echoed the state-implemented cultural amnesia of Atatürk's Turkey, where the replacement of the alphabet had rendered the past both figuratively and literally illegible. Ḥusayn's approach left open the possibility of reading the past, but it declared any continuing tradition and discourse with the past impossible. As a result of such wholesale dismissal of the indigenous historical tradition, Shākir lamented,

[10] Maḥmūd Shākir, *al-Mutanabbī*, 14–16.

[11] Maḥmūd Shākir, *al-Mutanabbī*, 17–19.

[12] On Maḥmūd Shākir's significant role in twentieth-century Arabic thought, see Sayyid et al., *Dirāsāt ʿarabiyya wa-islāmiyya*, and the 1997 special issue of *al-Adab al-islāmī* dedicated to him.

[13] Al-Khuḍayrī, "Raʾī al-ustādh Margoliouth"; Descartes, *Maqāl ʿan al-manhaj*. The author of the article on Margoliouth is identified only as "M. M. Kh.," apparently to conceal the identity of al-Khuḍayrī, who was only a second-year student at the time. Shākir identifies him clearly in *al-Mutanabbī*, 14.

[14] See Arberry, *Seven Odes*, 228–45; Monroe, "Oral Composition in Pre-Islamic Poetry"; Zwettler, *Oral Tradition of Classical Arabic Poetry*; Asad, *Maṣādir al-shiʿr al-jāhilī*. See also Maḥmūd Shākir, *Qaḍiyat al-shiʿr al-jāhilī*.

[15] E.g., his *al-Mutanabbī*, *Abāṭīl wa-asmār*, and *Qaḍiyat al-shiʿr al-jāhilī*.

"these foreigners and those who follow them study our literature, poetry, and history as if they were inscriptions on ancient graves, written in a dead language, of a people that perished long ago, covered in the dust of centuries."[16]

This perspective on the affair surrounding Ḥusayn's book helps explain the urgency of the debates over philology in the late 1920s and beyond. The burgeoning corpus of classical works, put into circulation enthusiastically but relatively uncritically, created an acute need for a critical method of evaluating the newly available material, but the primary methodology on offer was one that had been developed by Orientalist scholars—cultural outsiders with enormous prestige and institutional power in the peak years of European colonialism. The declining status of philology in our own age has contributed to obscuring the significance of the encounter between indigenous Arabic philology and Orientalist philology.

Postclassical Arab scholars left us with few explicit discussions on philology, but a keen interest in the authenticity and accuracy of texts is evident in the work of several scholars, such as Ibrāhīm al-Kūrānī in the seventeenth and Murtaḍā al-Zabīdī in the eighteenth century (both discussed in chapter 2). In the nineteenth century, Ḥasan al-ʿAṭṭār evinced a similar interest, describing his realization that all the Egyptian manuscripts of a work on logic on which he was commenting were corrupted and his subsequent success in borrowing an uncorrupted copy of the text from a visiting Bukharan scholar to establish the correct reading.[17] And Ismāʿīl Ḥaqqī of Bursa, who wrote in both Arabic and Turkish, was a meticulous philologist who noted textual variants in the margins of the texts he copied and used stylistic analysis to determine whether texts attributed to particular authors were likely to be authentic.[18]

But it was only with the adoption of print that philological debates emerged from the margins of manuscripts and commentaries into a distinct field of analysis, articulated in dedicated publications. Among the earliest such contributions was Muḥammad ʿAbduh's 1886 article, mentioned in chapter 6, in which he argued against the authenticity of a work on the Muslim conquests of Syria (*Futūḥ al-Shām*) attributed to the ninth-century historian al-Wāqidī. The work had been deemed authentic by the Cambridge professor Simon Ockley (1678–1720) and by its editor, the British officer and Orientalist William Nassau Lees (1825–89), who published it in Calcutta between 1854 and 1862.[19] On the other hand, already in 1825 the Dutch Orientalist Hendrik Arent Hamaker (1789–1835) had claimed that the work was not authentic, but he pro-

[16] Maḥmūd Shākir, *al-Mutanabbī*, 13.

[17] Al-ʿAṭṭār, *Ḥāshiya ʿalā al-Khubayṣī*, 121–22.

[18] Heinzelmann, *Populäre religiöse Literatur*, 170–77.

[19] For Ockley, see Farsani, "Text und Kontext," 56; for Lees, see the editor's introduction to al-Wāqidī [attrib.], *Conquest of Syria*, 1:xiv–xxiii.

vided no arguments or evidence for his claim.[20] In 1860, the German Catholic bishop and Orientalist Daniel Bonifacius von Haneberg (1816–76) also argued against the authenticity of the work on the basis of its portrayal of the Byzantine forces, which he deemed to reflect not late antique soldiers but Crusader-era knights.[21] However, Haneberg's arguments are highly speculative and ungrounded in textual evidence; for example, he asserts that the challenges to one-on-one combat in battle described in the work were unknown in early Islam, even though they are found in the earliest surviving sources.[22] It is difficult to imagine that ʿAbduh would have known about these Orientalist debates on the authenticity of the text, especially since they were written in Latin or German. His arguments are altogether different and more substantial. ʿAbduh argues that the work's "style is that of Egyptian storytellers from the eighth or ninth [fourteenth or fifteenth CE] centuries, and it does not resemble the early Medinan or Iraqi dialects; [but] the man [al-Wāqidī] was born in Medina, then settled in Iraq."[23] ʿAbduh provides no specific examples, but an examination of the text indeed reveals lexical usages that are alien to Arabic of the early Islamic period but highly reminiscent of the style of later oral storytellers, as displayed, for example, in *The Thousand and One Nights*.[24]

ʿAbduh's short article constitutes the most philologically grounded nineteenth-century judgment on the *Futūḥ al-Shām*. It reflects a critical reading informed by a sensitivity to historical lexical usage—in contrast to Haneberg's analysis, which is innocent of such stylistic appreciation and attempts to date the text via speculation regarding its narrative elements. Importantly, ʿAbduh connects his discussion of the phenomenon of pious and historical forgeries to methods developed by classical Muslim scholars to weed out such forgeries, particularly the techniques used by hadith scholars to evaluate reports attributed to Muḥammad. In other words, he traces the genealogy of

[20] Al-Wāqidī [attrib.], *Incerti auctoris liber de expugnatione Memphidis et Alexandriae*, ix.

[21] Haneberg, "Erörterungen über Pseudo-Wakidi's Geschichte," 129–31.

[22] See, for example, Ibn Hishām, *Sīra*, 1:625.

[23] ʿAbduh, "Kutub al-maghāzī," 212.

[24] The repeated use of rhyming prose fragments, such as the religious exclamation *bi-l-tahlīl wa-l-takbīr wa-l-ṣalā ʿalā al-bashīr al-nadhīr*, which is repeated twenty-six times in the *Futūḥ al-Shām*, seems to constitute what Milman Parry called a "formula," a phrase used by oral storytellers to help improvisation; see Monroe, "Oral Composition in Pre-Islamic Poetry," 7 (my count of the phrases is based on the 1997 edition of Dār al-Kutub al-ʿIlmiyya's al-Maktaba al-Shāmila database at http://shamela.ws). This particular phrase is not attested in early Arabic literature but appears frequently in later works that were composed as oral performances, which supports ʿAbduh's analysis. See the same formula repeated in *The Thousand and One Nights* (*Alf layla wa-layla*, Quṭṭa al-ʿAdawī ed.), 1:305, 314; *Hādhā kitāb Qiṣṣat al-Bahnasā*, 99. The most extensive study of the *Futūḥ al-Shām* to date, by Yoones Farsani ("Text und Kontext"), concludes that an authentic core by al-Wāqidī was later expanded by storytellers.

his critical stance regarding the authenticity of a classical text to approaches developed in the classical tradition itself.

Ṭāhā Ḥusayn's bold claim, a generation after ʿAbduh, that a truly critical stance toward the past could be achieved only through the uniquely objective methodology of European scholarship turned a blind eye to this native critical tradition. This historical myopia was facilitated by the still spotty familiarity of Arab intellectuals with the emerging classical literature. For example, the Lebanese intellectual Yaʿqūb Ṣarrūf (1852–1927), in his review of *On Pre-Islamic Poetry*, applied Ḥusayn's skeptical approach to the epic of ʿAntara, a famous tale about a pre-Islamic hero, which he had read as a teenager and regarding whose authenticity he entertained serious doubts.[25] What Ṣarrūf could not know, since the relevant texts were only then being discovered, was that classical philologists, such as Ibn Taymiyya and his students in the fourteenth century, had already critiqued the authenticity of the ʿAntara epic and even identified its original author.[26] This lack of awareness about indigenous critical scholarship contributed to the tendency to dismiss premodern historical writing as incurably corrupted. In a later discussion of Ibn al-Nadīm's foundational tenth-century bio-bibliography of Arabic literature (*al-Fihrist*), Ṣarrūf again pressed the point about the unreliability of Arab histories. He used the examples of a document attributed to Muḥammad's son-in-law ʿAlī, of which two very different versions exist, and of a Crusader-era autograph of the memoirs of the Arab warrior-gentleman Usāma b. Munqidh, to which sections had been added in another hand, to demonstrate the challenges of written transmission. Oral transmission, he argued, is even more perilous. If the earliest surviving Arabic manuscripts that he knew of (from the tenth century) were beset by such problems, what could possibly be known with confidence about events that took place even earlier?[27]

The Moroccan scholar and statesman ʿAbd al-Ḥayy al-Kattānī (1888–1962), the most important modern collector of Arabic manuscripts in North Africa,[28] reacted to Ṣarrūf's article with alarm:

> He casts doubt on everything written by Arab civilization. This attitude will necessarily destroy the field of history, since the events of the world cannot be proven when judged according to such a standard. We have seen among Western scholars those who even deny the historicity of Jesus, claiming that

[25] Ṣarrūf, "al-Taqrīẓ wa-l-intiqād: Fī al-shiʿr al-jāhilī."

[26] Ibn Taymiyya, *Majmūʿ al-fatāwā*, 4:493, 18:351; al-Dhahabī, *Tārīkh al-Islām*, 12:205; Ibn Kathīr, *al-Bidāya wa-l-nihāya* (Shīrī ed.), 9:365. See also Shoshan, *Popular Culture in Medieval Cairo*, 23. On Ibn Taymiyya as a master philologist, see Ibn Qayyim al-Jawziyya, *Aḥkām ahl al-dhimma*, 1:169–71; and Noth, "Minderheiten als Vertragspartner."

[27] Ṣarrūf, "al-Taqrīẓ wa-l-intiqād: Al-Juzʾ al-rābiʿ Khiṭaṭ al-Shām." On the alleged letter of ʿAlī, see al-Qāḍī, "Early Fāṭimid Political Document."

[28] On al-Kattānī's manuscript collection, see al-Sibāʿī, *Tārīkh al-Maktaba al-Kattāniyya*.

> "history does not support his mission, nor his very existence." . . . If we adopt this skeptical approach, the time will come when all historical reports, whether ancient or modern, will become untenable. How strange it is that some skeptics will trust the narrations of Ibn al-Nadīm but declare others unreliable for no consistent reason![29]

As in Shākir's case, al-Kattānī's concern about the potentially corrosive effects of indiscriminate skepticism vis-à-vis the Islamic past did not reflect resistance to a historical critical approach to texts per se. An illustrative example is provided by al-Kattānī's 1933 visit to Syria, where he was shown a manuscript of a Quranic commentary attributed to the "Saint of Baghdad," ʿAbd al-Qādir al-Jīlānī. Al-Kattānī examined it and then handed it to the Aleppine scholar Muḥammad Rāghib al-Ṭabbākh (1877–1951), asking him for his opinion of the work. Al-Ṭabbākh scrutinized the work in turn and concluded that its style was not that of the eleventh or twelfth century, that is, al-Jīlānī's lifetime, but of a later period, the sixteenth or seventeenth century. Al-Kattānī replied approvingly, "That is correct."[30]

The question of how the skeptical historical method proposed by Ṭāhā Ḥusayn would affect the body of classical literature animated Egyptian literary circles. In a literary salon, the writer ʿAbbās Maḥmuḍ al-ʿAqqād (1889–1964) quipped that if one were to apply Ḥusayn's skepticism to Ḥusayn himself, one would end up erasing him, as he had erased pre-Islamic poetry. Taking up the idea, his friend Ibrāhīm al-Māzinī (1889–1949) penned a humorous article in which a twenty-third-century Egyptian historian examines critically the historical figure of Ṭāhā Ḥusayn and reaches the conclusion that either there were several authors called Ṭāhā Ḥusayn or there was in fact no historical person named Ṭāhā Ḥusayn, only a pen name adopted by various writers. As evidence, al-Māzinī uses biographical information on Ḥusayn and the positions he took in his writings to paint a picture of contradictions. For example, if Ḥusayn was, as claimed, a graduate of the conservative al-Azhar, how could he be also an active proponent of cultural change in areas such as Arabic orthography? Furthermore, Ṭāhā Ḥusayn was reportedly blind; why would a blind man be interested in how words are spelled?[31] Behind its lampooning style, the article made the serious methodological point that if one adopts a skeptical attitude to a historical topic, one can always isolate pieces of information that can be interpreted as contradictory and thereby used to question the historicity of the issue in question. In this process of contradiction-making, historical skepticism demands a straightforwardness and a simplicity of historical phenomena that are not

[29] Al-Kattānī, *Ibn al-Nadīm wa-kitābuhu al-Fihrist*, 150–51. The book was originally published in 1931.

[30] Al-Ṭabbākh, "al-Sharīf al-Kattānī yazūru Sūriyā," 329.

[31] Al-Māzinī, "Ṭāhā Ḥusayn fī mīzān al-tashkīk."

observable in real, everyday experience: arguably, Ṭāhā Ḥusayn as a professor was an iconoclast in large part *because* of his conservative Azhari schooling, against which he rebelled.

PSEUDOPHILOLOGY

The impact of the editing and publishing movement and the challenge it posed to postclassical scholarly orthodoxies is nowhere more poignantly evident than in the resort of the defenders of the status quo to the same philological techniques and vocabulary in order to support their views. This phenomenon is illustrated by the public debate in which the editor and book collector Aḥmad Zakī, whose career was described in chapter 5, became involved in the final years of his life. The debate concerned the historical authenticity of one of the most important sites of popular piety in Cairo: the alleged grave of al-Sayyida Zaynab bt. ʿAlī, the granddaughter of the Prophet Muḥammad and the daughter of the fourth caliph, ʿAlī b. Abī Ṭālib. In September 1932, Zakī published an extensive article arguing that contrary to common belief, the popular shrine of al-Sayyida Zaynab did not in fact contain the remains of the Prophet's granddaughter. First, he argued, the known historical accounts of Zaynab's life make no reference to her ever having traveled to Egypt; and second, her putative grave is not mentioned by any classical historian of Cairo or any traveler's description of the city, even in works specifically listing gravesites of the pious and the famous. Zakī concluded that the grave might belong to a different, unknown Zaynab, later misidentified as the Prophet's granddaughter; or it may have no connection to any Zaynab, or not be a burial site at all. The idea that Muḥammad's granddaughter was buried at the site was in fact so recent that the mosque adjacent to the shrine had been built only in the eighteenth century.[32]

The shrine of al-Sayyida Zaynab was a popular site of visitation and miracles, and the still influential Sufi brotherhoods in Egypt held it in high esteem. In November 1932, a certain Muḥammad Ghālib ʿAbd Allāh responded to Zakī's article with one of his own, which begins with a biography of Zaynab and a description of her exemplary piety and then provides an account of her arrival in Egypt in the early eighth century. The narrative then leaps to the sixteenth century, when a shrine was built at her gravesite, followed by the construction of the mosque in the eighteenth century. The only sources cited in ʿAbd Allāh's article are three works by the sixteenth-century Sufi ʿAbd al-Wahhāb al-Shaʿrānī (discussed in chapter 2), whose Sufi master, al-Khawwāṣ, had told him that "the Sayyida Zaynab buried in the Qanāṭir al-Sibāʿ district

[32] Al-Jindī, *Aḥmad Zakī*, 145–47. The article originally appeared in the newspaper *al-Ahrām*.

[of Cairo] is, without doubt, the daughter of Imām ʿAlī."[33] Remarkably, this evidence, presented by ʿAbd Allāh to refute Zakī's argument, in fact serves to affirm it. It shows that in the sixteenth century the grave was known merely to house the remains of a "Lady Zaynab," but establishing this lady's identity as Muḥammad's granddaughter required the mystical insight of al-Khawwāṣ. Given that al-Khawwāṣ was illiterate and prided himself on his hostility to textualism, the source of his knowledge cannot have been a written text; in addition, al-Shaʿrānī himself had received a thorough education in the textual tradition and would presumably have been better placed than al-Khawwāṣ was to know of such a source. In other words, the attempted defense of the authenticity of al-Sayyida Zaynab's shrine was anchored purely in the postclassical authority of esoteric inspiration.[34]

The debate escalated when, three weeks later, an official from the interior ministry submitted a formal query to the former grand mufti of Egypt (and student of Muḥammad ʿAbduh) Muḥammad Bakhīt al-Muṭīʿī, seeking his judgment on whether al-Sayyida Zaynab was buried in the shrine attributed to her in Cairo and specifically asking for the pertinent historical evidence. Bakhīt replied in the classical format of a fatwa, diligently citing his sources. He concluded that the classical historians, as well as the nineteenth-century scholars al-Jabartī and ʿAlī Mubārak, agreed unanimously that Muḥammad's granddaughter Zaynab had never set foot in Egypt, and he noted that the contrary position was supported solely by Sufi claims of inspiration and therefore had no historical value.[35]

But the controversy did not end there. Two weeks later, on December 17, 1932, Ḥasan Qāsim, the editor of the history section of the journal that had published ʿAbd Allāh's article and Bakhīt's fatwa, published a bombshell article in which he countered the arguments of Zakī and Bakhīt by drawing on hitherto unknown and unpublished historical works. First, he cited the travelogue of al-Kuhaynī, a tenth-century Andalusian traveler who visited Zaynab bt. ʿAlī's shrine in Egypt; the manuscript of the travelogue, Qāsim reported, was held in the ʿĀrif Ḥikmat Library in Medina. And second, he quoted three histories that described Zaynab leaving Medina and settling in Cairo in the early eighth century: an otherwise unknown epistle by the sixteenth-century Syrian scholar Ibn Ṭūlūn; the monumental history of Damascus by the twelfth-century historian Ibn ʿAsākir, held in the Khālidī Library in Jerusalem; and a ninth-century treatise, *Akhbār al-Zaynabāt* (Reports on women called Zaynab), written by the genealogist Shaykh al-Sharaf

[33] ʿAbd Allāh, "al-Sayyida Zaynab."

[34] ʿAbd Allāh's reliance on evidence from inspiration is reminiscent of the esoteric argument that ʿAbd al-Qādir al-Jazāʾirī had used half a century earlier to challenge the authenticity of a work attributed to Ibn ʿArabī; see chapter 6.

[35] Bakhīt, "al-Asʾila wa-l-ajwiba."

al-ʿUbaydalī (d. 435/1043).[36] Until today, Qāsim's seemingly robust battery of historical evidence has formed the backbone of all subsequent arguments for the historicity of Zaynab's shrine in Cairo; it has been cited extensively in articles and books by Egyptians and non-Egyptians, Sunnis and Shiʿis, particularly after Qāsim edited and published the *Akhbār al-Zaynabāt* in the following year.[37]

On closer examination, however, Qāsim's defense of Zaynab's shrine turns out to be an elaborate piece of philological theater, designed to mimic the work of the scholars and editors who were reviving classical literature but in fact based on fabrications aimed at justifying postclassical shrine rituals. The putative travelogue of the otherwise unknown al-Kuhaynī is not found in the ʿĀrif Ḥikmat collection in Medina, nor have I located it in any other repository; the same applies to the epistle by Ibn Ṭūlūn, for which Qāsim provides no location information.[38] Ibn ʿAsākir's well-known history of Damascus, meanwhile, does not contain the claim that Qāsim ascribes to it, nor is it held in the Khālidī Library. Citing Ibn ʿAsākir's history was a clever strategy, given that the work was known for its enormous size (the edited versions comprise between sixty and eighty volumes), but at the time only an abridgment of it, covering no more than 10 percent of the original work, had been edited. Ibn ʿAsākir's work had gained fame through Muḥammad Kurd ʿAlī, who had used it (in manuscript) as a major source for his six-volume history of greater Syria.[39] Finally, Qāsim's pièce de résistance, the *Akhbār al-Zaynabāt*, appears to be entirely forged. In the introduction, Qāsim tells the story of how he obtained a copy of the manuscript from an unnamed friend in Syria who had discovered it in the library of a friend in Aleppo. The manuscript had been copied in AH 676 (1277 or 1278 CE) by a man named al-Biltājī from an earlier copy written in 483 (1090 or 1091) by a certain al-Ḥusaynī, resident of Hyderabad.[40] This narrative of discovery, with its detailed description of copyists' names and dates of copying, has a ring familiar from the introductions of other classical works rediscovered in this period, but it is marred by the fact that Hyderabad was founded in the sixteenth century and therefore cannot have served as the home of an eleventh-century copyist. An examination of the text itself, as carried out by the Iranian scholar Ḥasan Fāṭimī, reveals that much of it has been copied and pasted from classical histories with only the names of the transmitters replaced, often with

[36] Qāsim, "al-Sayyida Zaynab."

[37] (Pseudo-)ʿUbaydalī, *al-Sayyida Zaynab wa-akhbār al-Zaynabāt.* See, for example, Sanad, "al-Sayyida Zaynab"; al-Hindāwī, *Silsilat majmaʿ maṣāʾib ahl al-bayt,* 3:329–34; Bint al-Shāṭiʾ, *al-Sayyida Zaynab,* 155.

[38] Whereas Ibn Ṭulūn was a historical figure, I have found no evidence that al-Kuhaynī was.

[39] See, e.g., Kurd ʿAlī, *Khiṭaṭ al-Shām,* 1:154.

[40] (Pseudo-)ʿUbaydalī, *al-Sayyida Zaynab wa-akhbār al-Zaynabāt,* 9–11.

invented names.[41] The critical apparatus accompanying the text identifies lacunae and records variants, again giving the impression of a genuine edition[42]—but since the manuscript is explicitly described as a unicum, the inclusion of putative variants betrays the absurdity of Qāsim's claims. In the afterword, Qāsim forestalls the objection that al-ʿUbaydalī is not known to have written a book titled *Akhbār al-Zaynabāt* by providing a fabricated reference that attributes such as work to al-ʿUbaydalī.[43]

The laboriousness and elaborateness of Qāsim's apparent forgery demonstrates the magnitude of the challenge that the critical historical approach, wielded by the likes of Zakī and Bakhīt, posed to postclassical positions and the urgency with which the proponents of the latter sought to combat it, using the philological conventions of their opponents to lend credibility to their defenses. The other defensive strategy—doubling down on the authority of inspired visions and witnessed miracles as proof of the authenticity of saintly shrines—was also deployed,[44] but its effectiveness was on the decline. Reformist currents were gaining ground, fueled by the ever-growing body of classical literature as well as by newly authored and published works, and they were increasingly discerning and sophisticated in their critical use of historical material. Postclassical practices such as shrine veneration were inextricably wedded to the old orthodoxy of esotericism and willful historical amnesia, and as such they were inevitably undermined by the resurgence of classical texts in widely available printed form. Zakī himself issued the final salvo in the debate over the grave of al-Sayyida Zaynab in an article published in April 1933. "Islam is not built on superstitions and mythical stories, nor on the veneration of decayed bones, into which one has become deluded through deception and forgery," he declared, framing the issue as one of both epistemology and theology.[45] For Zakī, superstitious religious practices and uncritical acceptance of claims about the past went hand in hand.

Around the same time, Zakī also challenged the authenticity of another important shrine in Cairo, namely, the alleged burial site of the head of al-Ḥusayn, the grandson of the Prophet (and the brother of Zaynab), who was believed to have been martyred in late seventh-century Iraq. Al-Ḥusayn's shrine was a major center of veneration, and the adjacent mosque was a hub of popular religiosity and Sufi brotherhood activity. But Zakī described the

41 Fāṭimī, "Barrasī-yi iʿtibār-i kitāb-i Akhbār al-Zaynabāt." I am grateful to Hassan Ansari for this reference.

42 See (pseudo-)ʿUbaydalī, *al-Sayyida Zaynab wa-akhbār al-Zaynabāt*, 12, 17.

43 (Pseudo-)ʿUbaydalī, *al-Sayyida Zaynab wa-akhbār al-Zaynabāt*, 26. The reference is to *Uqnūm al-āthār fī al-kashf ʿan al-kutub* by Abū Yaʿqūb al-Āzmūrī al-Amghārī (Amghāzī?), but I have found no evidence for the existence of this work or its alleged author. For a book that was actually penned by al-ʿUbaydalī, see his *Tahdhīb al-ansāb*.

44 ʿAbd Allāh, "al-Sayyida Zaynab"; see also Sanad, "al-Sayyida Zaynab."

45 Zakī, "Istiftāḥ al-sana al-thāniya," 29.

story of the transfer of al-Ḥusayn's head to Cairo in the eleventh century as a "myth that has taken root in people's hearts and established itself in their minds, gaining strength over time, transmitted from generation to generation, with each generation accepting it from the previous one as a settled affair, allowing no criticism."[46] Ibn Taymiyya had pointed out, already in the fourteenth century, that the alleged shrine of al-Ḥusayn's head lacked any historical basis, but the weight of tradition and the pious stories promoted by Sufis had, according to Zakī, rendered the shrine sacrosanct and immune to historical critique.[47] Some doubts regarding the shrine's authenticity had been raised by an Azhari professor a century before Zakī, according to Edward Lane (1801–76), but they had been effectively assuaged by a dream experienced by one of the professor's students, in which the Prophet Muḥammad himself had assured the student that al-Ḥusayn's head was indeed buried in Cairo.[48]

Zakī's critique was again countered by Ḥasan Qāsim, but given the declining currency of visionary dreams as evidence, he had to take a more scientific-seeming approach. At the end of his editorial afterword to his edition of *Akhbār al-Zaynabāt*, Qāsim reproduces an eyewitness account of the transfer of al-Ḥusayn's head to Cairo in 548/1153, which, he says, comes from the account of a traveler that had been published in a journal shortly earlier.[49] However, he names neither the traveler nor the journal and says vaguely that the manuscript is located in either Barcelona or Seville. I have found no trace of such an account, and given the fictional nature of the rest of the work, this claim, too, ought to be considered false unless evidence for its authenticity is found.

The temptation to use the still largely untapped multitude of Arabic manuscripts as a smokescreen for polemical positions that were not supported by the evidence affected not only minor figures such as Qāsim, but even the most learned manuscript expert in the generation after Ṭāhir al-Jazā'irī: the Ottoman émigré Muḥammad Zāhid al-Kawtharī. Al-Kawtharī was a classically trained scholar, a star of the Ottoman seminary system who came of age in the final days of the empire. Facing the abolition of the seminary system after World War I and possible threats to his life, he left Istanbul in 1922 and settled in Egypt, but for the rest of his life he labored under the burden of maintaining a scholarly ideal and religious orthodoxy that had vanished in his homeland. He possessed an encyclopedic knowledge of the Istanbul manuscript collections, and once in Egypt, he buried himself in the Egyptian National Library. This work was punctuated by long stays in Damas-

[46] Al-Jindī, *Aḥmad Zakī*, 147–48.

[47] Ibn Taymiyya, *Majmūʿat al-fatāwā* (al-Jazzār and al-Bāz ed.), 27:257–59.

[48] Lane, *Manners and Customs*, 194–96.

[49] (Pseudo-)ʿUbaydalī, *al-Sayyida Zaynab wa-akhbār al-Zaynabāt*, 90–93.

FIGURE 8.2. Muḥammad Zāhid al-Kawtharī. Courtesy of Saud al-Sarhan.

cus, where, according to his student ʿAbd al-Fattāḥ Abū Ghudda, he became so immersed in the Ẓāhiriyya collection that he could not tear himself away even when his money ran out and he could no longer afford food.[50] Al-Kawtharī's recognized expertise made him a critical node in the networks of editing and publishing of his time. For example, in 1938, the Indian scholar Abū al-Wafāʾ al-Afghānī (1893–1975), wishing to edit an eleventh-century biographical dictionary,[51] wrote to the German Orientalist Hellmut Ritter in post-Ottoman Istanbul,[52] who sent him photographs of the manuscript; al-Afghānī transcribed them and then sent a copy to al-Kawtharī in Cairo, who collated it against the manuscript of the work held in the Egyptian National Library before sending it back to Hyderabad, where it was finally edited and

[50] Abū Ghudda, *Ṣafaḥāt min ṣabr al-ʿulamāʾ*, 252–53.
[51] Al-Ṣaymarī's *Akhbār Abī Ḥanīfa wa-aṣḥābih.*
[52] On Ritter, see van Ess, *Im Halbschatten.*

published.[53] On another occasion, al-Kawtharī had a Syrian student of his copy a tenth-century biography of al-Shāfiʿī in Aleppo and then gave this copy to a Cairene publisher, who printed it.[54]

Although conservative scholars were in general less involved than their reformist peers in the editing of classical works, al-Kawtharī participated actively in the movement.[55] However, he saw himself as a carrier of a clearly delineated orthodoxy that was under threat from some newly surfacing classical works, and he worked tirelessly to "correct" classical texts and bring them into line with his own legal and theological commitments using means that were sometimes heavy-handed and occasionally outright deceptive. His first method was to insert extensive footnotes into classical texts that he deemed to contain questionable statements. For example, in an effort to combat the spread of Ibn Taymiyya's ideas, he published al-Dhahabī's (d. 748/1348) *Bayān zaghal al-ʿilm* (Exposition of false knowledge), which contains a paragraph in which al-Dhahabī urges his readers to abstain from the study of theology and uses Ibn Taymiyya as a cautionary illustration of the potential of theological discussions to lead to acrimonious disputes and strife among Muslims. Unfortunately for al-Kawtharī, the rest of al-Dhahabī's text beyond this paragraph espouses ideas that al-Kawtharī found deeply offensive, causing him to fight a running battle with the author in his editorial footnotes to either refute or simply gainsay him.[56] In one instance, when al-Dhahabī states that members of the Ḥanafī school of law (to which al-Kawtharī belonged) sometimes prioritize the results of their own legal reasoning over the dictates of revelation, al-Kawtharī's footnote even disputes the authenticity of a well-known Ḥanafī work in order to avoid al-Dhahabī's charge.[57]

Some works could not be rescued doctrinally even through the addition of copious footnotes, and such works, al-Kawtharī believed, should be outlawed entirely. He petitioned al-Azhar to ban the publication of an early theological polemic by al-Dārimī (d. 255/869), a hadith scholar and student of Aḥmad b. Ḥanbal.[58] In al-Kawtharī's view, al-Dārimī's affirmation of certain divine attributes mentioned in the Quran and in prophetic statements amounted to

[53] Al-Ṣaymarī, *Akhbār Abī Ḥanīfa wa-aṣḥābih*, 10.

[54] Ibn Abī Ḥātim, *Ādāb al-Shāfiʿī wa-manāqibuh*, 6, 12–13.

[55] See al-Kawtharī, *Rasāʾil al-Kawtharī ilā al-Binnūrī*, for al-Kawtharī's correspondence with the Indian-Afghani scholar Muḥammad al-Binnūrī (1910–77) about locating and editing books for publication.

[56] In al-Dhahabī, *Bayān zaghal al-ʿilm* and *al-Naṣīḥa al-Dhahabiyya*, see, e.g., 14 (on Abū Ḥanīfa), 18 (on the Ḥanbalīs), 23 (on theology), 24 (on Ibn Taymiyya).

[57] The work in question is al-Shaybānī's *al-Makhārij fī al-ḥiyal*; see al-Qūnawī's comments in the introduction to his edition of al-Dhahabī, *Bayān zaghal al-ʿilm*, 19–20. On the authenticity of al-Shaybānī's work, see Schacht's introduction to his edition of it.

[58] See al-Kawtharī, "Namādhij mimmā fī 'Naqḍ al-Dārimī'" and "Khuṭūrat al-qawl." Al-Dārimī's *Radd ʿalā Bishr al-Marīsī* was nonetheless published in 1939.

anthropomorphism, making his doctrine idolatrous. The later Ashʿarī tradition, to which al-Kawtharī adhered, distinguished between divine attributes that could legitimately be affirmed at face value (mostly abstract ones such as knowledge, but also others such as sight) and those that had to be interpreted figuratively (such as God's possession of eyes, or His being positioned above His throne). Al-Kawtharī faulted al-Dārimī for contravening Islamic orthodoxy, but he defined the content of this orthodoxy on the basis of works written much later than that of al-Dārimī.[59] This strategy was made even more questionable by the fact that a book by the founder of the Ashʿarī school had recently been published in India, and it showed the positions of Abū al-Ḥasan al-Ashʿarī to have been surprisingly close to those of al-Dārimī on a number of the contested issues.[60] Al-Kawtharī attempted to mitigate this potential challenge to his own position by casting vague aspersions on the authenticity of al-Ashʿarī's book. He first claimed that it was an early work aimed at enticing contemporary anthropomorphists to return to the fold, and then asserted that anthropomorphists had tampered with and corrupted the text and that as a result it was unreliable and should be ignored whenever it appeared to disagree with the doctrines of later Ashʿarī theologians.[61] But al-Kawtharī offered no evidence for his bold claim that "the manuscript copy [of al-Ashʿarī's book] printed in India is corrupt, distorted, and criminally manipulated" and that the book "needs to be reprinted from a reliable copy."[62] In fact, the critical edition of the work, published in 1977, shows this charge to have been baseless.[63] The purpose of the claim of textual manipulation was thus simply to defuse the threat posed by the text to al-Kawtharī's specific view of orthodoxy, which was based squarely on the theological doctrines of the later Ashʿarīs.

The same strategy is apparent in al-Kawtharī's treatment of the voluminous Quran commentary of Maḥmūd Shihāb al-Dīn al-Ālūsī, whose criticism of the popular veneration of shrines was mentioned in chapter 7 in the context of the efforts of al-Ālūsī's son, the reformer Nuʿmān al-Ālūsī, to challenge the practice.[64] The commentary was one of the most substantial exegeses written in the Ottoman Empire, and Maḥmūd Shihāb al-Dīn had dedicated it to the Ottoman sultan ʿAbd al-Majīd (r. 1839–61). In a footnote attacking Nuʿmān al-Ālūsī's defense of Ibn Taymiyya, al-Kawtharī laments that worldly concerns had led Nuʿmān astray (suggesting that his intellec-

[59] Al-Kawtharī, "Khuṭūrat al-qawl," 269–72.

[60] Al-Ashʿarī, *al-Ibāna* (Hyderabad ed.); see, e.g., 7 on the issue of God's eyes.

[61] See al-Kawtharī's comments in al-Subkī, *al-Sayf al-ṣaqīl*, 91.

[62] See al-Kawtharī's comments in Ibn ʿAsākir, *Tabyīn kadhib al-muftarī*, 28. He repeated this charge in al-Bayhaqī, *al-Asmāʾ wa-l-ṣifāt*, 2:297 (on the issue of God's eyes).

[63] Al-Ashʿarī, *al-Ibāna* (Maḥmūd ed.), 18 (on the issue of God's eyes).

[64] Maḥmūd Shihāb al-Dīn al-Ālūsī, *Rūḥ al-maʿānī* (1926 ed.), 17:213; quoted in Nuʿmān al-Ālūsī, *Jalāʾ al-ʿaynayn* (Āl Zahawī ed.), 478.

tual positions had been "bought") and accuses Nuʿmān of having changed the text of his father's exegesis when he had it printed after Maḥmūd's death, claiming that "if somebody were to compare the printed version with the manuscript housed today in the Ragıp Pasha Library in Istanbul, which is the one the author gave to Sultan ʿAbd al-Majīd, he would find convincing evidence of this."[65] As in the case of al-Ashʿarī's book, al-Kawtharī seems here to be drawing on his expert familiarity with Ottoman manuscripts to provide critical and specific philological evidence of textual tampering by a cabal seeking to manipulate the Islamic tradition. His claim has been repeated ever since.[66] However, the 2010 edition of the exegesis was based on the copy that Maḥmūd Shihāb al-Dīn al-Ālūsī gave to the sultan in 1850 (housed not in the Ragıp Pasha Library but rather in the Ahmet III Library in the Topkapı Palace), and it found no evidence of doctrinally significant differences between the autograph and the first print.[67] Again, then, it seems that al-Kawtharī sought to neutralize the threat that a particular text posed to his notion of orthodoxy by dressing up a pious lie as textual criticism.[68]

Despite their feebleness, such arguments seem to have permitted al-Kawtharī and his numerous admirers credible denial of the content of classical works perceived as problematic. The immense bibliophilic energy that al-Kawtharī brought into these discussions is both awe-inspiring and exasperating; the mind-boggling number of works, particularly unpublished manuscripts, that he cites makes fact-checking his claims a herculean task. But the very urgency with which he strove to counter ideas and works that he deemed dangerous reveals his deep misgivings about the changing religious landscape of the post–World War I Islamic world. He continued to use his official title "assistant to the Shaykh al-Islām of the Ottoman Empire" even after the collapse of the empire, longing for an institutional structure, and the religious authority it represented, that had disappeared.[69] In this new world with scant institutional authority, books were being published by people who, in al-Kawtharī's eyes, lacked the appropriate scholarly training and respect

[65] Al-Subkī, *al-Sayf al-ṣaqīl*, 115–16n2.

[66] A 1968 study sought to discredit the claim, which it described as widespread, by examining the manuscript copy held in the Ālūsī family library in Baghdad, but its author had no access to the Istanbul manuscript; see ʿAbd al-Ḥamīd, *al-Ālūsī mufassiran*, 164–65.

[67] Maḥmūd Shihāb al-Dīn al-Ālūsī, *Rūḥ al-maʿānī* (Ḥabbūsh et al. ed.), 67–70.

[68] Additional examples of al-Kawtharī's use of this strategy could be given. Another one, mentioned in chapter 4, is his claim that Aḥmad al-Ḥusaynī tampered with the manuscript of al-Muzanī's *Mukhtaṣar* in order to conceal a grammatical mistake made by al-Muzanī's teacher al-Shāfiʿī in a passage quoted in the *Mukhtaṣar*; al-Kawtharī, *Taʾnīb al-khaṭīb*, 49–50. However, the text as printed by al-Ḥusaynī is attested in the oldest manuscript of the work in Egypt, so al-Kawtharī's statement appears to be another case of baseless polemic. Compare al-Muzanī, *Mukhtaṣar*, fol. 2b, with al-Shāfiʿī, *al-Umm* (Bulaq ed.), 1:9.

[69] Haykel, "Political Failure of Islamic Law," 8–11.

for tradition; worse still, they were using these books to challenge ideas that he held sacrosanct. Speaking of such an upstart—Maḥmūd Shākir's older brother Aḥmad, discussed later in this chapter—al-Kawtharī complained,

> It is enough for him to have the fatwas of Ibn Taymiyya printed by Faraj Allāh al-Kurdī[70] and to cite a couple of pages on the issue of divorce, for example, and to publish this in journals and newspapers, without feeling the need to ascertain the reliability of the publisher, or to make sure he did not add or delete anything, correcting and corrupting according to his whim, or to verify that the work corresponds to reality and that the author is truthful, reliable, and not deviant.[71]

The adoption of printing—both for the publication of classical works and for their discussion in secondary publications such as journals—entailed a loss of authority for individuals such al-Kawtharī, and his hyperphilology represented a way of compensating for this loss. His overwrought erudition produced many fine editions, scholarly articles, introductions, and commentaries;[72] but in some cases, he tried to use his authority as an expert to suppress certain texts either by advocating for their banning or by undermining trust in their authenticity. The result was a modified scholasticism that accepted the printing of classical works but continued to define the later curriculum texts, which it saw as uniquely reliable, as the yardstick of what is right and proper. Measured against this skewed standard, many classical texts obviously fell short. They were deemed potentially corrupted and in turn potentially corrupting for ordinary people, and they therefore had to be vetted and thoroughly annotated by experts such as al-Kawtharī in order to neutralize their threat to orthodoxy. Ironically, it was al-Kawtharī's paranoia about forgery perpetrated by the enemies of orthodox Islam that prompted his interventions, which themselves had the effect of distorting the classical textual tradition. As one of his friends remarked, "This is how partisanship always works: it distances one from truth, even great scholars such as our friend Shaykh Muḥammad Zāhid al-Kawtharī."[73]

[70] The founder of the Kurdistān publishing house; see chapter 4.

[71] Al-Kawtharī, "Kalima fī al-iftā'," 94.

[72] For al-Kawtharī's articles, see his *Maqālāt*; for his introductions, see *Muqaddimāt al-imām al-Kawtharī*.

[73] Al-Ghumārī, *Sabīl al-tawfīq*, 81.

TEXTUAL CRITICISM

The critical approach to reconstructing historical events from old texts is closely related to the critical study of the texts themselves, and this field, too, was heavily contested in early twentieth-century Arab and Muslim discourse. Western textual criticism in this period was deeply influenced by the slim handbook on the subject published in 1927 by the German classicist Paul Maas (1880–1964).[74] The seductive power of this work lies in the clarity with which it approaches the messy task of editing a text on the basis of different and differing manuscripts, reducing the process to a set of assumptions and procedures that allow the editor-critic to reconstruct, if not the original, then a version of the text that is closer to the original than is any one of the individual surviving manuscripts. Maas's work drew on methodological developments in the nineteenth century, particularly those associated with the German classicist Karl Lachmann (1793–1851).

Lachmann divided the task of the textual critic into two distinct stages: *recensio*, the assembly of variants of a text from the various surviving manuscripts, and *emendatio*, the formulation of a better reading that may not be found in the manuscripts. *Emendatio* involves judgment that requires acquaintance with the subject matter, familiarity with the author and the linguistic style of his or her epoch, knowledge of scripts and their development, and an awareness of the various types of possible copyist mistakes. It is thus an art, not a science, and therefore not subject to systematic progress.[75] Lachmann's innovation concerned not *emendatio* but *recensio*. He extended its scope and laid down rules that promised to elevate it to a precise science that could yield certain conclusions. His central idea was that the collected variants among the manuscripts could be used to establish genealogical relations between the manuscripts.[76] These can then be ordered into a graph resembling a family tree—a stemma.[77]

The two necessary assumptions for such a stemma are that the copyists copied their texts without consulting other copies of the same work, so that each manuscript is a descendant of only one earlier copy, and that they copied the texts without inserting their own speculative corrections into them. If these assumptions hold, a stemma allows the textual critic to narrow down the manuscripts that must be consulted by excluding all so-called descriptive copies—those that the stemma shows to be merely copies of other already

[74] Maas, *Textkritik*.

[75] Timpanaro, *Genesis of Lachmann's Method*, 43.

[76] See Lachmann, *Kleinere Schriften*, esp. 1:81–114 ("Der Nibelungen Lied; Der Edel Stein").

[77] The stemma is a visualization of the relationships among manuscripts that Lachmann theorized. Stemmata were not invented by Lachmann, nor did he ever produce one himself. See Timpanaro, *Genesis of Lachmann's Method*, 90–96.

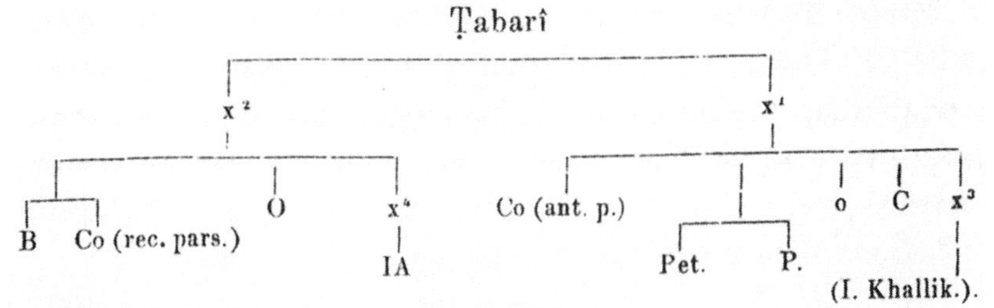

FIGURE 8.3. A Lachmannian stemma of the manuscripts of al-Ṭabarī's history, prepared by M. J. de Goeje (al-Ṭabarī, *Annales*, lxiii).

available or reconstructable copies. More importantly, the stemma provides a mechanical method of choosing between variants. If different branches of a stemma agree on a reading, this reading must have been present in their closest common ancestor, and this process of reasoning allows the critic to establish with certainty the content of an archetype. In the case of Greco-Roman, biblical, and other antique literature, the archetype is not the autograph but rather a later copy, given how many generations separate antiquity from the first surviving manuscript witnesses.[78] Once the archetype has been constructed through these objective criteria, the text has reached a state that is the closest to the original that can be achieved purely through the information contained in the manuscripts. The next step, then, is the inescapably subjective scholarly judgment of the *emendatio*.[79]

This high theory of textual criticism was developed in a European context in which classics had been printed for centuries, initially on the basis of recent, easily readable manuscripts. These vulgates were then improved in later editions by editors using either better manuscripts or their own learning to emend the text.[80] The systematic approach developed by Lachmann helped remedy the haphazardness of this strategy, but the effort required was so substantial that even Lachmann and other leading philologists of his time often fell significantly short in their practice of their own theoretical standards.[81] It is also not the case that Lachmann's method was immediately adopted by all of his contemporary philologist colleagues. Gottfried Hermann (1772–1848), a famed classicist at the University of Leipzig, for example, dedicated himself almost exclusively to *emendatio* of the printed vulgate versions

[78] Timpanaro, *Genesis of Lachmann's Method*, 85.
[79] Berschin, "Lachmann und der Archetyp."
[80] Timpanaro, *Genesis of Lachmann's Method*, 45–46.
[81] Timpanaro, *Genesis of Lachmann's Method*, 81, 90.

of classical texts by drawing on his profound knowledge of classical languages and literatures to solve textual problems in these versions.[82]

It was in this time of methodological innovation and flux that Orientalist scholars began to edit and publish classical Arabic texts in earnest.[83] Antoine Isaac Silvestre de Sacy in Paris and his student Heinrich Leberecht Fleischer in Leipzig, for instance, published foundational texts of Arabic literature and thought, but their editions contain very few text-critical elements: not only do they refrain from stemmatic analysis of the surviving manuscripts, but their editions do not even list textual variants between manuscripts.[84] This neglect of the *recensio* stage of editing appears to have been a deliberate methodological choice for these two scholars. Fleischer's student August Müller (1848–92) describes the notion of philology that Fleischer learned from Silvestre de Sacy as "nothing but the application of common sense to the transmitted material, combined with faithful, untiring striving for minute precision and completeness in the gathering and processing of what has been transmitted, excluding all witty arbitrariness," along with the conviction that proper method does not entail applying one mold to all types of texts.[85] Fleischer had also trained with Gottfried Hermann, whose philology consisted of meticulous *emendatio*. This theoretical posture was particularly appropriate for the types of texts that early Orientalist editors such as Silvestre de Sacy and Fleischer primarily edited—namely, classical works that had remained popular in the postclassical period as nuclei of extensive commentary traditions and that were consequently attested in countless manuscripts. For such works, a systematic examination of surviving manuscripts was (at least before the systematic global cataloging of Arabic manuscripts) both impossible and unnecessary.[86]

When the Bulaq press finally began to publish Arabic literature in the mid-nineteenth century (see chapter 3), there was initially little difference in the respective philological treatment that Orientalists and Egyptian correctors gave the texts they edited; the primary difference was rooted in the occupational fact that the correctors worked on a schedule and therefore had limited time to devote to individual works. Also, they did not themselves choose the texts they prepared for publication and therefore had to edit books

[82] Timpanaro, *Genesis of Lachmann's Method*, 75.

[83] See, for example, Fück, *Die arabischen Studien in Europa*, 147–50; al-Sayyid, *al-Turāth al-ʿarabī fī al-ḥāḍir*, 80–89.

[84] See, for example, the early Orientalist editions of al-Ḥarīrī's *Maqāmāt* (1822) and al-Bayḍāwī's *Tafsīr* (1846–48).

[85] August Müller, "Heinrich Leberecht Fleischer," 325–26.

[86] A century later, philological standards had changed so dramatically that Johann Fück (1894–1974) could not account for Fleischer's omission of a critical apparatus except by postulating that Fleischer must have been ignorant of the standards of classical textual criticism. See Fück, *Die arabischen Studien in Europa*, 171.

in fields with which they were not necessarily familiar. By the end of the nineteenth century, however, the picture had changed. Fleischer's student Müller's edition of Ibn Abī Uṣaybiʿa's biographical work on physicians and philosophers reflects a careful *recensio* of the significant number of manuscripts that Müller was able to gather, and it incorporates a separate, eighty-page critical apparatus (which his teacher Fleischer had still considered "philological trivialities").[87] Müller also produced a pathbreaking analysis of the philological challenges inherent in the editing of works that survive in several recensions.[88] The difference between Müller's edition and the native editions produced at the time is apparent in the contrast with Müller's initial publication of his edition two years earlier in Cairo.[89] Müller had originally decided to publish his edition at the Wahbiyya Press in Cairo in order to save money, as the proliferation of private printing presses and the growing Arabic reading public meant that a Cairo print incurred only a fraction of the costs of a print in Leipzig or Leiden.[90] As Müller had to find out, however, Muṣṭafā Wahbī (d. unknown), the owner of the press, did not have the technical means to print the complex critical apparatus Müller envisaged, nor was he willing to print the extensive indexes Müller had produced, which would have increased his own costs. Müller was so troubled by the quality of Wahbī's rushed product that he published an addendum to the work in Germany, containing an extensive introduction, a separate critical apparatus, and errata.

The differing audiences for classical works printed by Orientalists and by native presses—other Orientalists and a wider reading public, respectively—meant different priorities. The former valued scholarly precision and extensive recording of variants, whereas for the latter the production of a text that was both readable and affordable was paramount. A more significant difference between the two categories of editions, however, lay in the respective resources at the disposal of European Orientalists and their Arab counterparts. De Goeje's rightly famous edition of al-Ṭabarī's tenth-century history was underpinned by lavish funding and the collaboration of a network of scholars all over Europe, but it nonetheless took de Goeje two decades to locate and procure the surviving volumes of the work and another two decades to finish editing them using the latest philological tools, including the construction of a stemma.[91] No Arab editors had access to comparable financial and institutional support.

[87]See Ibn Abī Uṣaybiʿa, *ʿUyūn al-anbāʾ* (2nd ed.), xvi–xxxii (for the relationships between the manuscripts), xlvi (for Fleischer's attitude to Müller's philological work).

[88]August Müller, "Ueber Ibn Abi Oçeibiʿa."

[89]In this edition, Müller referred to himself playfully as Imruʾ al-Qays al-Ṭaḥḥān.

[90]Ibn Abī Uṣaybiʿa, *ʿUyūn al-anbāʾ* (1st ed.), v–vi.

[91]See al-Ṭabarī, *Annales*, 1:xxvii–lxiii. Even de Goeje, however, was unable to access the superior manuscript of the work at the Topkapı Palace that had originally belonged to Cairo's

By the 1930s, the poor quality of most locally printed classical editions was prompting growing unease among intellectuals in Egypt. The originally Syrian scholar Muḥammad Munīr Āghā (whose school experience was quoted in chapter 2) ran the Munīriyya Press, which printed numerous classics, and he bemoaned the general state of private printing in Egypt. According to Munīr Āghā, the industry was dominated by greedy men of little learning who were so focused on maximizing their profits that they were even willing to publish Ibn al-Jawzī's work on women under the similar but distinct name of Ibn Qayyim al-Jawziyya, since the latter, as a student of Ibn Taymiyya, was a more marketable author.[92] It is a striking illustration of the foundational nature of these early editions that this brazen misattribution continues to be perpetuated in both Arabic and Western scholarship.[93] In response to concerns over such unprofessional practices, the Egyptian historian Muḥammad ʿAbd Allāh ʿInān (1896–1986) suggested that the Egyptian state begin to supervise the quality of editions of classical works published by private presses.[94]

A prime example of what an editing project under official supervision could achieve is the so-called Sultanic edition of al-Bukhārī's ninth-century compilation of prophetic traditions.[95] The edition was commissioned by the Ottoman sultan ʿAbd al-Ḥamīd II in 1893 and was carried out in Egypt under the leadership of the rector of al-Azhar, Ḥassūna al-Nawawī, by a panel of sixteen Azhari scholars, including Aḥmad Taymūr's teacher Ḥasan al-Ṭawīl (on whom see chapter 4). The edition is noteworthy not only for its accuracy, which has made it the standard edition of the work until today, but also because of the fabled Yūnīnī manuscript on which it is based. Sharaf al-Dīn al-Yūnīnī (d. 701/1301), a leading hadith scholar in his time, had collected all the variants present in the manuscripts of al-Bukhārī's work that he could find and recorded them in the margins of his own copy. The resulting philological masterpiece is widely considered the most important manuscript of al-Bukhārī's famous collection. The Ottoman sultan sent the manuscript to Egypt to help in the edition of the text,[96] but somewhere along the way, it was lost; whether it ever made it back to Istanbul is unknown. The mystery of the manuscript is compounded by the fact that although the printed edition claims to have been based on the Yūnīnī manuscript, a comparison of

---

Maḥmūdiyya library.

[92] Munīr Āghā, *Namūdhaj*, 78–81. The work in question is Ibn al-Jawzī's *Akhbār al-nisāʾ*, and it was published under Ibn Qayyim al-Jawziyya's name in 1901.

[93] See, for example, Gordon and Hain, *Concubines and Courtesans*, 295; Booth, *Harem Histories*, 47; Ibn Qayyim al-Jawziyya [attrib.], *Akhbār al-nisāʾ* (Ḥalabī ed., 1997). However, more recently, note Ibn al-Jawzī, *Akhbār al-nisāʾ* (2000).

[94] ʿInān, "Turāthunā al-ʿarabī al-qadīm."

[95] Al-Bukhārī, *Ṣāḥīḥ al-Bukhārī* (al-Makkāwī et al. ed.).

[96] Al-Bukhārī, *Ṣaḥīḥ al-Bukhārī* (al-Makkāwī et al. ed.), 1:2–4 (al-Nawawī's introduction).

its text with an extant copy of the Yūnīnī text shows that the former lacks the majority of the recorded variants. The divergence suggests that the edition was in fact based on an abbreviated version of al-Yūnīnī's recension.[97] Nevertheless, even with this flaw, the edition is far superior to the Orientalist edition produced earlier by Ludolf Krehl (1825–1901) and Theodoor Juynboll (1802–61) as well as to many if not all later editions produced by Arab presses.

As seen in chapter 5, scholars such as Aḥmad Zakī, who had close contacts with European Orientalists, began to adopt the latter's editorial conventions in the early twentieth century, at a time when Orientalist philological practice still often fell short of the full-fledged Lachmannian theory.[98] But it is only in the 1930s, parallel to the growing criticisms of the "trade" editions produced by private presses, that an indigenous Arabic tradition of textual criticism began to be explicitly articulated and placed in juxtaposition to the Orientalist tradition. Perhaps the first to lay out the former was the Yemeni scholar ʿAbd al-Raḥmān al-Muʿallimī, who worked as a corrector at the Dāʾirat al-Maʿārif al-ʿUthmāniyya Press in Hyderabad, India, between 1927 and 1952 and whose procedural description of the correcting process was outlined in chapter 3. In the early 1930s, Al-Muʿallimī wrote a series of books on challenges, methods, and best practices in editing classical Arabic texts.[99]

In contrast to Maas's handbook on textual criticism, which opens with general and theoretical observations, al-Muʿallimī starts with the practical concerns of a corrector. He outlines two distinct tasks for the corrector: "scholarly correction," which consists of weeding out corruptions present in the available manuscripts, and "print correction," which is aimed at eliminating mistakes in the transfer of the text from the working copy written by the corrector to the typeset pages. Al-Muʿallimī is aware that scholarly correction has recently been termed "editing" (*taḥqīq*) in Egypt (see chapter 5), but he prefers to retain the older terminology.[100] He warns that scholarly correction must be completed before printing can commence. Correcting a few pages and having them typeset while subsequent pages are being corrected is not an acceptable procedure, first, because scholarly correction is slower than typesetting (al-Muʿallimī estimates one versus eight pages per day), and second, because a later section of the text can prompt the corrector to revise his earlier work, which is impossible if the earlier section has already been

[97] Aḥmad Shākir, *Jamharat maqālāt Aḥmad Shākir*, 1:125–38; Halal, "Taḥrīr al-aṣl al-muʿtamad."

[98] See, for example, the editions of Aloys Sprenger, such as the edition of Ibn al-Akfānī's fourteenth-century *Irshād al-qāṣid* (discussed in chapter 6), which contains neither variants nor information on the manuscript(s) used. See also Fück, *Die arabischen Studien in Europa*, 177.

[99] The books were published posthumously. For their dating, see the editor's introduction to al-Muʿallimī, *Majmūʿ rasāʾil*, viii.

[100] Al-Muʿallimī, *Majmūʿ rasāʾil*, 31.

printed. Al-Muʿallimī's "scholarly correction" is identical to Lachman's *emendatio*, requiring familiarity with the types of mistakes that copyists make when they misread or mishear words as well as a host of other unquantifiable qualities. "To put it concisely," al-Muʿallimī sums up the job, "it is about the quality of knowledge, the length of experience, careful procedure, and thoroughness."[101]

Then al-Muʿallimī considers the argument that it is sufficient to use a single manuscript as the basis of the edition of a classical work, since printing produces a thousandfold copy of the manuscript and thus makes it more widely available. Al-Muʿallimī objects to this argument on several fronts. First, once a work has been printed, there is little financial incentive to print it again in a more accurate form. Second, facsimile editions, such as the 1912 Orientalist print of a British Library manuscript of ʿAbd al-Karīm al-Samʿānī's twelfth-century genealogical dictionary,[102] reproduce the problems of manuscript culture, such as the occasional omission of the dots that disambiguate letters. And third, if the text is typeset on the basis of only one manuscript, readers may incorrectly assume that the text has been properly edited. Facing a manuscript, readers naturally adopt a critical stance toward the work of the individual scribe, but the impersonal nature of print imbues a book with an authority that might blind its readers to the shortcomings of the edition.[103]

The second approach that al-Muʿallimī describes is to use two manuscripts, the seemingly better one serving as the basis of the edition and the variants of the second one being noted in the margins. This method, too, al-Muʿallimī deems unacceptable. Since the corrector has not systematically evaluated the variants against each other but simply prioritized one manuscript wholesale, incorrect readings from that manuscript are given pride of place in the main text at the expense of better readings from the other manuscript, which are relegated to the margins.[104]

Finally, al-Muʿallimī rejects a third possible approach—consulting various manuscripts and correcting their mistakes (that is, engaging in both *recensio* and *emendatio*) but doing so silently, without indicating in the edition what each manuscript actually contained. This method renders the published text suspect in readers' eyes, since they know that unlike a copyist, who simply reproduces a text as is, the corrector has interfered with the text, but the extent of the corrector's interference is hidden. Furthermore, the corrector's emendations might be incorrect, and given that printed works in their multiplicity tend to survive longer than individual manuscripts do, the under-

[101] Al-Muʿallimī, *Majmūʿ rasāʾil*, 9–19, 29.

[102] Al-Samʿānī, *al-Ansāb* (Brill ed.). Compare this "edition" to al-Muʿallimī's thirteen-volume edition of the work.

[103] Al-Muʿallimī, *Majmūʿ rasāʾil*, 32–34.

[104] Al-Muʿallimī, *Majmūʿ rasāʾil*, 36.

lying manuscript containing the correct reading may well perish while the corrector's false emendation endures.

The method that al-Muʿallimī sanctions as the correct one is designed to ensure three levels of correspondence: the edition ought to correspond to the content of the manuscripts, to the intention of the author, and to factual reality. In the ideal case the three factors coincide, but in many cases one disagrees with the other two, and it is also possible that all three diverge. Contrary to the Lachmannian focus on the edition's correspondence with the text intended by the author, al-Muʿallimī argues that each level of correspondence is worthy of preservation. As an example, he observes that the first name of an early transmitter of prophetic reports, ʿUrābī b. Muʿāwiya, was seemingly misspelled as Ghurābī b. Muʿāwiya (the difference being a single dot over the first letter) by al-Bukhārī in his ninth-century biographical dictionary *al-Tārīkh al-kabīr*,[105] and in some later copies of the latter work the misspelling was further corrupted into ʿUzābī (by moving the dot from the first to the second letter). Recording all three spellings in an edition of al-Bukhārī's text preserves a historical depth that editorial prioritization of the "correct" spelling would obliterate. The only method that meets this standard is an edition with a critical apparatus that systematically records all significant variants and integrates them into the printed text.[106]

In his theoretical writings, al-Muʿallimī does not take the step of using variants to generate a stemmatic understanding of the relationships among the surviving manuscripts. His hierarchy of manuscripts in terms of their desirableness for editing grants primacy to the autograph copy, followed by a copy of the autograph that has been collated against the original with the participation of the author, then a copy of the autograph collated without the author's involvement, and so on.[107] The fact that accessing autographs was still a very real possibility for scholars such as al-Muʿallimī marks a significant difference between the Arabo-Islamic textual tradition and the Western classical tradition for which Lachmann's method was devised and in which there is no chance that any of the manuscripts available to the editor go back to the original author.[108]

Nevertheless, al-Muʿallimī's actual work as an editor-corrector demonstrates that he did develop ideas of genealogical relationships between manuscripts, and there is no indication that he adopted these ideas from Orientalist philology. In his introduction to his immensely influential edition of Ibn Abī Ḥātim al-Rāzī's biographical dictionary of transmitters of prophetic reports, al-Muʿallimī notes that in two of the three surviving manuscripts,

[105] Al-Bukhārī, *al-Tārīkh al-kabīr*, 7:112.

[106] Al-Muʿallimī, *Majmūʿ rasāʾil*, 39–42.

[107] Al-Muʿallimī, *Majmūʿ rasāʾil*, 8–9.

[108] This difference is discussed by Witkam in "Establishing the Stemma."

the ordering of the material varies, with certain chunks of text appearing to have been inserted at slightly different points in the text. He explains this phenomenon with reference to the author's method of collecting biographical information on the subjects of his work. He surmises that Ibn Abī Ḥātim wrote down each subject's name and whatever details he had and then left some blank space for future additions of information before moving on to the next entry. As new information accrued, the author gradually filled in the blank space and, once no space remained, expanded into marginal notes. The copyists who subsequently copied this autograph chose different places in which to insert the marginal information into the main text, producing slightly varying copies. Al-Muʿallimī concludes that the fact that two of the surviving manuscripts differ in this way in terms of ordering (but not in terms of content) indicates that they represent different and mutually independent manuscript branches whose common ancestor is the author's copy.[109] This sophisticated and convincing stemmatic interpretation demonstrates the high theoretical standard of al-Muʿallimī's work, based on his practical engagement with the specifics of the Arabo-Islamic textual tradition.

While al-Muʿallimī was writing his philological treatises in India, the German Orientalist Gotthelf Bergsträsser (1886–1933) gave a series of lectures at Cairo University in 1931 and 1932, which were eventually published as *Uṣūl naqd al-nuṣūṣ wa-nashr al-kutub* (The theory of textual criticism and book publishing).[110] A comparison of the respective theories and approaches of the two scholars reveals a surprising amount of overlap. In terms of *recensio*, Bergsträsser, like al-Muʿallimī, lays out a hierarchy of preferability for available manuscripts, although autographs or copies of autographs do not feature explicitly in Bergsträsser's list; he prioritizes completeness and readability over age and collation against other copies.[111] Both lay out techniques for ensuring accuracy, but whereas al-Muʿallimī stipulates three levels of desired correspondence—with the manuscript, with the author's intention, and with reality—Bergsträsser holds that the sole aim of an edition is to reconstruct the author's original text.[112] Bergsträsser's discussion of *emendatio* parallels al-Muʿallimī's arguments about the necessity of diligent scholarly judgment carried out on the basis of deep familiarity with the work's subject matter, the author, and the Arabic language in general, as well as the various types of copyist mistakes that occur in manuscripts.[113] What Bergsträsser does that al-Muʿallimī does not is describe in detail Orientalist edit-

[109] See al-Muʿallimī's introduction to Ibn Abī Ḥātim, *al-Jarḥ wa-l-taʿdīl*, 1: *kāf/alif–kāf/bā*.

[110] I am grateful to Josef van Ess for information on the background and nature of these lectures.

[111] Bergsträsser, *Uṣūl naqd al-nuṣūṣ*, 15.

[112] Bergsträsser, *Uṣūl naqd al-nuṣūṣ*, 39, 49–50.

[113] Bergsträsser, *Uṣūl naqd al-nuṣūṣ*, 50–88.

ing conventions, particularly the compilation of a scholarly apparatus, and explicitly address the construction and usage of a stemma with reference to Orientalist studies of the preceding decades.[114] He acknowledges the pervasiveness of the problem of "contamination" in the Arabic scribal tradition—that is, copyists drawing on more than one manuscript in their copies—and the challenge that it poses to the implementation of Lachmann's and Maas's methods, which were developed for writings emanating from a very different cultural context.[115]

Bergsträsser's lectures and the resulting book were a key vehicle in presenting the Orientalist philological tradition to Arab scholars, and their most distinctive feature was the concept of the stemma. However, the use of stemmata never caught on in a significant fashion among Arab editors. The Syrian scholar Ṣalāḥ al-Dīn al-Munajjid (1920–2010) included the technique in the handbook of textual criticism that he composed in the 1950s (which drew heavily on the French handbook of Blachère and Sauvaget).[116] But although al-Munajjid's text was reprinted repeatedly, stemmatic analysis found little reception in editorial practice or in subsequent theoretical treatments, such as the handbook of ʿAbd al-Salām Hārūn (1909–88), which was published a few years later and appears to have been far more influential.[117] There are likely to be multiple reasons for the sidelining of stemmata, not least the tension between the considerable time and effort required by their construction and the relatively modest resources available for such work in the Arab Middle East. But an important reason surely lies in the many differences between the textual corpus of classical European antiquity and the Arabo-Islamic tradition. Whereas a wide temporal chasm and countless generations of copyist monks working largely in isolation from one another typically separated early modern textual critics from the authors of classical Greek and Latin texts,[118] twentieth-century Arab editors stood much closer to the classical Arabo-Islamic authors, and the range of manuscripts at their disposal included autographs and copies collated with autographs, multiple versions and recensions issued by individual authors, and copies that drew on more than one *Vorlage* or had been silently emended by their copyists. All of these features make the straightforward application of stemmatic analysis to Arabic manuscripts in order to establish the "original" text problematic and in many cases impossible. Accordingly, Jan Just Witkam has cautioned

[114] Bergsträsser, *Uṣūl naqd al-nuṣūṣ*, 19–39.

[115] Bergsträsser, *Uṣūl naqd al-nuṣūṣ*, 26, 57; Maas, *Textkritik*, paras. 6, 9, 10, and 11.

[116] See al-Munajjid, *Qawāʿid taḥqīq al-makhṭūṭāt*, 3. See also Blachère and Sauvaget, *Règles pour éditions et traductions de textes arabes.*

[117] Hārūn, *Taḥqīq al-nuṣūṣ wa-nashruhā*. See also Maʿrūf, *Fī taḥqīq al-naṣṣ*.

[118] Greenblatt, *Swerve*, 28–29, 41. Copyist practices in European monasteries discouraged emendations and the use of multiple sources and thus produced "uncontaminated" copies that were ideally suited to stemmatic analysis.

that such analysis may create not an ordered family tree but rather only a "pile of twigs and branches, of which we will probably never know where in the tree(s) of transmission they had their place."[119]

Nevertheless, the Orientalist method outlined by Bergsträsser and, above all, the prestige attached to it exerted a profound influence on Arab scholarship. Their effects can be seen in a 1937 edition of a tenth-century poetic anthology, *Akhbār Abī Tammām* (The life and times of Abū Tammām). The work was edited by two Egyptians, Khalīl ʿAsākir and Muḥammad ʿAzzām, and an Indian, Naẓīr al-Islām; the former were students at Cairo University and the latter attended the University of Breslau in Germany. The editors were brought together by their respective professors, the Austrian émigré Paul Kraus (1904–44) in Cairo and Otto Spies (1901–81) in Breslau. The project marks a new phenomenon in Arabic editorial practice: an edition carried out under the auspices of a university. With the establishment of modern universities in the Middle East, beginning in the early twentieth century, editions of this type—theses or dissertations comprising a critical edition and an introductory study—became widespread, and, especially in the second half of the twentieth century, they came to account for a significant portion of all new editions of classical works.

In the introduction to the edition of ʿAsākir, ʿAzzām, and al-Islām, the supervisor of the first two editors, Aḥmad Amīn (1886–1954), praises their work as an exemplar of what graduates of the College of the Humanities at Cairo University can achieve, namely, "a truly scholarly edition of a classical text." He goes on to claim that it had been Orientalists who had been the first to produce such scholarly editions and who had laid down rules for them, explaining how to procure manuscripts from all over the world, which to exclude from consideration, and how to distinguish correct from incorrect readings. He mentions Bergsträsser's lectures as the pivotal point at which this superior method had become known in Egypt. By contrast, he dismisses previous Egyptian editions of classical works as products of unscrupulous and ignorant publishers, riddled with errors, often incomprehensible, and cranked out without the least scholarly care.[120] The Egyptian editors provide a parallel narrative, asserting that they had learned about textual criticism from Bergsträsser's lectures and a course taught by Paul Kraus. During their studies of classical texts, they write, "we came across works printed in Europe and others printed in Egypt and other Eastern countries. If we had to research a topic we would flock to the ones published in Europe; but if we

[119] Witkam, "Philologist's Stone," 34. See also Witkam, "Establishing the Stemma."

[120] Amīn's introduction to al-Ṣūlī, *Akhbār Abī Tammām*, i–iii. See also al-Ṣūlī, *Life and Times of Abū Tammām*, xxvi–xxvii.

found that only Egyptian editions were available, neither properly edited nor indexed, we would unwillingly turn to them."[121]

It seems fair to say that, as a general rule, Orientalist editions of classical texts were better than the average products of Egyptian publishing houses. This is unsurprising since there were comparatively few Orientalist editions, and, as noted earlier, their editors generally held academic positions that allowed them to spend years gathering manuscripts and editing a single text. However, the absolute distinction that Amīn and his students draw between scholarly Orientalist and unscholarly native editions is unjustifiably dogmatic. It appears particularly hyperbolic in the context of a work that had survived in a single manuscript and therefore lay beyond the scope of the quasi-scientific procedure of *recensio* that constituted the heart of modern textual criticism. The introduction therefore smacks of posturing by members of a new type of educational institution seeking to justify their professional position as an intellectual vanguard, wielding the tools of a cutting-edge method.

The sentiments expressed by Amīn and his students soon received a forceful reply from Aḥmad Shākir (1892–1958), the older brother of Maḥmūd, Ṭāhā Ḥusayn's youthful critic. At the time, Aḥmad Shākir was an Azhar graduate, a Sharīʿa court judge, and an active editor of classical texts. He wrote a forty-five-page essay on the nature of textual criticism and the Arabic and Orientalist philological traditions, which appeared as an introduction to his 1937 edition of al-Tirmidhī's ninth-century hadith collection.[122]

Shākir begins his introduction in a conventional manner by critiquing previous editions of the work at hand and specifically by decrying the unscholarly practices of private presses in his time. Al-Tirmidhī's text had been published twice before in Egypt, once by the government press in Bulaq in 1875 and again by two private presses in 1932–34.[123] Shākir notes the reliability of the former print, which was based on a single but high-quality manuscript, in contrast to the latter, which was replete with mistakes. He had lent his own copy of the Bulaq print to the editors of the new version and later realized that some of his own marginal notes on the copy had ended up in the edition, attributed to the ninth-century author.[124]

However, the bulk of Shākir's essay is devoted to a theoretical discussion of the state of philological scholarship on Arabo-Islamic literature. Throughout his analysis, Shākir acknowledges the strengths of the Orientalist phil-

[121] Al-Ṣūlī, *Akhbār Abī Tammām*, ix.

[122] Al-Tirmidhī, *al-Jāmiʿ al-ṣaḥīḥ*, 1:1–103. Pages 1:16–61 were reprinted separately as Shākir, *Taṣḥīḥ al-kutub*.

[123] The latter edition was included with Ibn al-ʿArabī's commentary on the text, *ʿĀriḍat al-aḥwadhī*.

[124] Shākir's introduction to al-Tirmidhī, *al-Jāmiʿ al-ṣaḥīḥ*, 1:7–8.

FIGURE 8.4. Aḥmad Shākir. From al-ʿAlī, *Ẓill al-nadīm*, 218.

ological tradition and expresses gratitude for its products. But he also problematizes the valorization of Orientalist philology on multiple fronts—by pointing out parallels in the classical Islamic tradition, by highlighting shortfalls in Orientalist editions, and, most significantly, by situating Orientalist scholarship and its relationship to indigenous scholarship within the broader context of colonialism. His overarching goal is to shear Orientalist scholarship of the mystique that his peers attribute to it by showing that beyond certain praiseworthy features, such as indexes, critical apparatuses, and information on the manuscripts used, Orientalist editions are subject to the same limitations and weaknesses that plague all philological endeavors.

According to Shākir, classical Muslim authors were clearly aware of philological challenges and developed practices to surmount them. The ninth-century linguist al-Akhfash observed that "a book copied but not collated [*lam yuʿāraḍ*] and then copied again but not collated will turn out gibberish," and his contemporary, the litterateur al-Jāḥiẓ, warned that it is easier to write ten pages of prose than to emend a single word in a corrupted copy of a text.[125] For this reason, Shākir argues, premodern Muslim scholars de-

[125] Shākir's introduction to al-Tirmidhī, *al-Jāmiʿ al-ṣaḥīḥ*, 1:16.

vised scribal conventions and procedures to prevent the corruption of texts in the copying process.[126] Another feature that he highlights is concern for reader accessibility. He lauds Orientalists for their custom of including indexes in their editions, which makes them more user-friendly, but he also goes to great lengths to show that classical Arabic authors, too, clearly sought to ensure the accessibility of their works, particularly through alphabetical ordering. In addition, he points out that Krehl and Juynboll's edition of al-Bukhārī's hadith compilation, for example, lacks an index even though the complex work is in dire need of one, whereas an Ottoman Muslim scholar, Muḥammad al-Sharīf Tūqādī, produced a separate index to al-Bukhārī's collection.[127] Responding to the dismissive statements of ʿAsākir, ʿAzzām, and Amīn (though not naming them explicitly), Shākir rejects the facile dichotomy between expert Orientalist editions and inferior native ones. Although he recognizes the weaknesses in the output of many private Arab presses, he defends the quality and reliability of prints produced by the old Bulaq press and by certain serious private presses, such as those of Muṣṭafā al-Bābī al-Ḥalabī and al-Khānjī.[128]

The comments of ʿAsākir, ʿAzzām, and Amīn are, for Shākir, symptomatic of a broader malaise in indigenous Arab scholarship: the methodological edge that Orientalists, on the whole, possess in the editing of classical works has led some of his contemporaries to accept anything that Orientalists say on Arabic or Islam, even when they contradict the greatest Muslim scholars, with a slavish and uncritical subservience. Yet Shakīr reminds his readers that Orientalists are not objective actors juxtaposed with inescapably subjective natives. Rather, they, too, have their own agendas. Some are missionaries or sympathetic to missionary activity, and their care in and dedication to editing texts are often accompanied by a tendentious interpretation of them. Others are not ideologically biased, but their scholarship may suffer from a lack of linguistic immersion, an insufficient knowledge of the subject matter, or excessive reliance on the work of earlier Orientalists whose conclusions could be mistaken.[129]

In Shākir's view, the unique authority that his contemporaries accord to Orientalist scholarship is not due to objective criteria but rather reflects the historical circumstances of colonialism: "We have been conquered in our homes, in ourselves, in our beliefs, and in everything that Islam holds sacred and that Muslims are proud of. Our people are weak, and the weak are always tempted to follow the strong and to glorify their deeds." As a scholar,

[126] Shākir's introduction to al-Tirmidhī, *al-Jāmiʿ al-ṣaḥīḥ*, 1:22–42.

[127] Shākir's introduction to al-Tirmidhī, *al-Jāmiʿ al-ṣaḥīḥ*, 1:43–60. For the Ottoman index, see Tūqādī, *Miftāḥ al-Ṣaḥīḥayn*.

[128] Shākir's introduction to al-Tirmidhī, *al-Jāmiʿ al-ṣaḥīḥ*, 1:17.

[129] Shākir's introduction to al-Tirmidhī, *al-Jāmiʿ al-ṣaḥīḥ*, 1:19.

Shākir maintains, "I have the strongest of loyalties to my religion and my language, and I know the meaning and proper limits of such loyalty. It does not mean hostility; but abandoning it entails humiliation and surrender. [Loyalty] means preserving and defending our achievements and glories."[130] Many of his fellow Arab Muslims, by contrast, are

> ignorant of the heritage of their ancestors and tempted by Europe's might and strength to the point of submitting to it and nearly forsaking their communal characteristics of religion, language, loyalty, and pride in order to become—as they claim—renewers and intellectuals. Their refrain is to celebrate the Orientalists: there are no emendations but those done by Orientalists; no indexes except those compiled by them; no knowledge save what they propound; no language except what they deem proper. The correct view on the Quran is theirs, and reliable hadith are only those that they deem reliable.[131]

Shākir thus sees two problems. First, the Orientalists' strengths in critical textual scholarship have morphed into a claim of superior and privileged access to and understanding of the Islamic tradition. And second, the context of colonialism with its structural inequalities between the colonizer and the colonized has led Arab intellectuals to internalize this claim, uncritically accepting the superiority of Orientalist methods and analyses. This inequality has distorted the discourse on textual scholarship. Instead of participating on a level playing field of scholarly arguments, Orientalist scholarship is automatically considered to produce objective results compared with "native" scholarship.

As an example, Shākir cites the project that would become his hallmark: the edition of al-Shāfiʿī's *Risāla* (Epistle), a foundational work on legal theory and hermeneutics written in the early ninth century. He complains,

> By God, I have spent many long days in convincing some of my colleagues that the ancient copy of al-Shāfiʿī's *Risāla* that is preserved in the Egyptian National Library was written entirely by the hand of al-Rabīʿ b. Sulaymān, al-Shāfiʿī's student, and that it was written during the author's [al-Shāfiʿī's] lifetime; I had to give them numerous arguments based on sound evidence before they were more or less convinced. And yet they possess sharp intellects and much learning and are not uncritical worshippers of the Europeans! All they had was the argument that the rules postulated by Orientalists for dating Arabic scripts were not compatible with my claims and that the Orientalist Moritz had dated this copy by means of the script to the mid-fourth century [mid-tenth century CE, i.e., a century and a half later]. It was difficult to convince them of something that contradicted these rules and the opinion of a single man, whom scores of

[130] Shākir's introduction to al-Tirmidhī, *al-Jāmiʿ al-ṣaḥīḥ*, 1:20.
[131] Shākir's introduction to al-Tirmidhī, *al-Jāmiʿ al-ṣaḥīḥ*, 1:60–61.

> others follow. This is the effect of blind following [*taqlīd*] and its allure, may God protect us and you from it. In the old days, al-Shāfiʿī said that "it was through blind following that the heedless became what they are."[132]

The German Orientalist and director of the Egyptian National Library Bernhard Moritz (1859–1939) had dated the National Library's manuscript of al-Shāfiʿī's *Risāla* using paleographic methods, but Aḥmad Shākir was skeptical of the precision of these methods and dated the manuscript on the basis of internal evidence to the lifetime of al-Shāfiʿī; the text claims to have been written by al-Shāfiʿī's student al-Rabīʿ, and it contains a permission to copy the text granted by al-Rabīʿ in his old age, shortly before his death.[133] Shākir's opinion seems convincing, particularly since recent studies of early Quranic manuscripts have indicated that Moritz's paleographic dating significantly underestimates the age of manuscripts when tested against radiocarbon dating.[134]

Like his brother Maḥmūd a decade earlier, Aḥmad Shākir describes a situation in which the Arabo-Islamic intellectual tradition that was being rediscovered was simultaneously being deconstructed by foreign scholars using speculative and often untested tools of analysis with a casualness and carelessness one applies only to the cultural phenomena of other peoples—especially if one does not consider their established opinions to have any scholarly value. Neither of the Shākir brothers was particularly bothered by this fact alone, but the historical moment of almost universal European domination meant that these foreigners found willing disciples among the Shākirs' countrymen, who fervently adopted the Orientalists' historical and textual methods, which they considered far superior to any indigenous ideas. Neither of the Shākirs was a traditionalist, in the sense of rejecting critical modes of inquiry. What they rejected was the new skepticism that did not grant any weight to indigenous scholarship, whether contemporary or classical, and thereby entrenched a cultural hierarchy that placed the West on top and Arabo-Islamic culture far below, unable to understand itself and therefore reliant on Orientalist analysis.

Aḥmad Shākir's 1940 edition of al-Shāfiʿī's *Risāla* became not just his personal editorial masterpiece but also a milestone of critical editing in the entire Arab world. It is prefaced by a hundred-page introduction on the author, the text, its manuscripts, and the textual history of the manuscripts. The book ends with sixty pages of painstakingly compiled indexes, and the text in be-

132 Shākir's introduction to al-Tirmidhī, *al-Jāmiʿ al-ṣaḥīḥ*, 1:61.

133 Shākir's introduction to al-Shāfiʿī, *al-Risāla*, 17–18. Compare this to Moritz, *Arabic Palaeography*, plates 117–18.

134 On the MS *Qāf* 47 Quranic manuscript in the Dār al-Kutub al-Miṣriyya, see Moritz, *Arabic Palaeography*, plate 44; and Marx and Jocham, "Zu den Datierungen von Koranhandschriften."

tween is beautifully typeset and of unmatched editorial quality.[135] Shākir's profound knowledge of al-Shāfiʿī and his work led him to choose readings that looked like copyist mistakes but have since been shown to be archaisms of early Hijazi Arabic.[136] Watching Shākir prepare his edition of the *Risāla* inspired his younger cousin ʿAbd al-Salām Hārūn to discover his own passion for classical texts.[137] Hārūn went on to produce countless seminal editions, which made him one of the foremost editors of the post–World War II generation.

* * *

Philology is not simply a critical way of treating texts; it also functions as a gatekeeper, determining which texts are released into the world, in what form they enter it, and what degree of authenticity—historical and textual—they are granted. In the initial stages of Arabic printing, the excitement of discovering long-lost riches and the enormity of the task of seeing them into print had relegated questions of historical and textual accuracy to a lower level of importance. But in the 1920s and 1930s, this heady rush gave way to a more mature, more critical, and less optimistic mood. Once the floodgates of classical literature had been flung wide open, the issue of how the newly accessible texts were to be used and treated asserted itself with greater urgency.

One axis of the discussion concerned method. The Lachmannian theory of textual criticism appeared to assuage the period's yearning for objectivity and scientific rigor, but its popularity overshadowed indigenous practices and standards of textual analysis, some of which were more appropriate to the material at hand. This imbalance was debated along the second axis, which concerned authority. At the same time as claims to authority rooted in inspired insight were disappearing, those justified by the prima facie superiority of Orientalist scholars and scholarship were consolidating interpretive authority in the hands of European outsiders and their native acolytes.

Amid these tensions, twentieth-century Arab editors produced editions of remarkable philological quality that remains in many cases unsurpassed.

[135] Both Rifʿat Fawzī ʿAbd al-Muṭṭalib, in his edition of al-Shāfiʿī's collected works, and Joseph Lowry, in his edition and translation of the *Risāla*, acknowledge this. See the introductions to al-Shāfiʿī, *al-Umm* (ʿAbd al-Muṭṭalib ed.), 1:37; and al-Shāfiʿī, *Epistle on Legal Theory*, xxxvi–xxxvii.

[136] Al-Ṭanāḥī, *Madkhal ilā tārīkh nashr al-turāth*, 92–94.

[137] Hārūn's introduction to Aḥmad Shākir, *Kalimat al-ḥaqq*, 4. The grandfather of Hārūn and the Shākir brothers, Hārūn ʿAbd al-Razzāq (1823–1918), participated in the Sultanic edition of al-Bukhārī's *Ṣaḥīḥ* (see al-Bukhārī, *Ṣaḥīḥ al-Bukhārī* [al-Makkāwī et al. ed.], 1:3) and assisted ʿAlī Mubārak in the writing of the latter's *Khiṭaṭ* (see al-Ṭanāḥī, *Fī al-lugha wa-l-adab*, 1:292), and Hārūn's father, Muḥammad Hārūn, edited Ibn al-Daybaʿ al-Shaybānī's *Taysīr al-wuṣūl* (1912). But these early editions were technically rudimentary compared to Aḥmad Shākir's work.

The text-critical method that they developed in the process is a hybrid one. A critical apparatus has become a standard feature of Arabic scholarly editions, whereas stemmatic analysis has not. The hallmarks of an expert editor today are mastery of Arabic, erudition in the subject at hand, thorough familiarity with the author, and impeccable judgment in choosing among variants assembled from multiple manuscripts. As such, editing is seen as a craft, not as a quasi-scientific application of Lachmannian rules.

The debates on historical criticism described in this chapter, particularly those elicited by the *On Pre-Islamic Poetry* affair, offer a window into how Arab intellectuals perceived and constructed their own past in the wake of the transformation of the textual landscape triggered by the rediscovery and printing of classical literature. But the methodological insights yielded by these debates are not only relevant to the intellectual history of twentieth-century Arabo-Islamic thought. Although they have been largely overlooked in Western scholarship, they speak directly to contemporary discussions on the methodology of writing early Arabic and Islamic history. Most importantly, they underscore the distinction between a critical stance and a skeptical one—between an approach that draws judiciously on the premodern textual heritage and one that treats this heritage as unreliable by its very nature.

Conclusion

By the middle of the twentieth century, the renaissance of classical Arabic literature through the vehicle of print had dramatically and irreversibly transformed the textual horizons of Islamic thought. The types of books that were read, taught, discussed, and circulated had changed, with a largely fixed curriculum of scholastic postclassical commentaries giving way to a diverse spread of works from all periods of Islamic history, particularly classical texts from the ninth to fifteenth centuries. The audience for books had changed, too. No longer dominated by traditional seminarians, the ranks of the Arabic reading public had swelled through rising literacy, state-sponsored modern education, and a growing bureaucratic and literary elite that ascribed primacy and prestige to eloquent Arabic expression and sought books—especially classical works, but also newly written texts and translations from European languages—that reflected this priority. Meanwhile, growing numbers of seminary-trained *ʿulamāʾ* had broken with postclassical orthodoxy and were using the emerging classical literature to critique and undermine it. In addition, the manner in which readers engaged with books had shifted. The practice of approaching a text through the mediation of interpretive authorities (ranging from written commentaries to Sufi shaykhs) was eclipsed by direct, unmediated engagement by readers sampling the full breadth of the textual corpus that was being reassembled in newly founded modern libraries and made widely available through print.

The course of this transformation was shaped by the purposeful actions of agents who selected, located, edited, circulated, and published classical works that met what they saw as the pressing needs of the age—whether the cultivation of ethical sentiments, the promotion of scientific and social-scientific inquiry, the combating of harmful superstitions, or the pursuit of historical accuracy. Some of these individuals are well known; most are obscure. But even in the former case, their role in the classical renaissance has been largely ignored.[1] The reason for the conceptual invisibility of their efforts to resuscitate the classical past is that these activities do not fit into the neat binary of forward-looking, Western-inspired modernity, on the one

[1]An important exception is the work of Maḥmūd al-Ṭanāḥī (1935–99), a dedicated student of Maḥmūd Shākir and himself a distinguished editor, who has explored the role of editors in a number of publications.

hand, and a continuous, undifferentiated, indigenous tradition, on the other. From the perspective of the scholars and editors discussed in this book, the tradition was far from monolithic. They saw a narrow postclassical tradition encased in curriculum commentaries and, beyond it, a largely forgotten and much more diverse classical tradition of scholarship. They rejected the idea that the former embodied unique authority and legitimacy as a continuously transmitted interpretive tradition, whereas the latter, precisely because it had been forgotten, represented at best unverifiable content and at worst valueless cultural refuse. For them, the tradition was a treasure trove to be mined for useful resources, not a straitjacket that determined what was and wasn't useful. By challenging the "naturalness" of the dominance of the postclassical corpus, they turned tradition from an unquestionable authority to something that could be negotiated and shaped—and themselves from subjects of tradition to its active makers. This stance can well be described as modern, but it did not entail an abandonment of the past.[2] Rather, as Ernst Cassirer has put it, "a new understanding of the past gives us at the same time a new prospect of the future, which in turn becomes an impulse to intellectual and social life."[3]

Although European political and cultural dominance was a constant backdrop to the lives and activities of the editors described in this book, their stories cannot be reduced to a reaction to colonialism, nor was Orientalism something they simply experienced passively. Instead, they excavated their own intellectual heritage for their own reasons, sometimes in dialogue with, informed by, or even in opposition to Western scholarship. It is true that Aḥmad Zakī, for example, adopted certain editorial conventions, such as footnotes, from Orientalists and that Orientalist scholars produced many early editions that Arab presses subsequently reprinted. But Orientalist and native editions were mostly carried out independently of each other, in pursuit of divergent interests and agendas. For example, in the area of Islamic law, Orientalist editions (which were often accompanied by translations) tended to focus on popular postclassical works that could serve as de facto handbooks for administering colonized Muslim populations,[4] whereas classical legal texts were mostly edited by Arab editors. Editions in fields such as history and early poetry were, at least in the nineteenth century, dominated by Orientalist efforts, while Arab editors led the way in lexicography and early Quranic exegesis.

My emphasis on the broadening and diversification of the Islamic intellectual tradition in the age of print overlaps unhappily with a thesis that has a deeply unsavory history: the so-called narrative of decline, which saw in

[2]Habermas, *Philosophical Discourse of Modernity*, 2.

[3]Cassirer, *Essay on Man*, 226.

[4]See, for example, Sachau, *Muhammedanisches Recht*; al-Nawawī, *Minhaj et Talibin*.

postclassical Muslim culture, in the words of the Scottish Orientalist Elias Gibb (1857–1901), a "moribund and hopeless age" yearning for revival by "the sun of the new culture, the culture of the West."[5] According to this narrative, "Islam" (treated as a unified cultural and historical phenomenon) had experienced a classical golden age but then descended into a decadence from which it could be revived only by a life-giving injection of Western culture. The political manifestations of this narrative—which was used first by colonialist powers to justify and naturalize European domination and then by Arab nationalists as evidence of the smothering of Arab genius by the Ottoman occupation—have rendered it legitimately toxic. Its intellectual implications are likewise untenable. The wholesale dismissal of postclassical cultural output ignores not only its scholarly merits when considered on its own terms but also the many instances of innovative scholarship produced in this period. Scholars such as Murtaḍā al-Zabīdī, Muḥammad al-Shawkānī, Shāh Walī Allāh, and al-Amīr al-Ṣanʿānī (1688–1768 or 1769), among many others, wrote important and original works in the eighteenth and nineteenth centuries,[6] and in logic and related fields, which I largely ignore in this book, the dominance of commentaries does not appear to have had the stultifying effect that it did in the realm of law, for example.[7] The very real contributions of postclassical scholars do not deserve the summary stigma of decline, nor should my generally bleak description of the literary output of this period discourage readers from appreciating delights such as al-Shirbīnī's seventeenth-century satire *Brains Confounded.*

However, I also reject the tendency to overcompensate for the pernicious stereotype of universal decline by denying the very real problems of postclassical scholarship and its significant discontinuities with classical scholarship. Recent efforts to rehabilitate the postclassical period parallel debates in European historiography, where from the 1970s onward the narrative of the fall of Rome and the ensuing Dark Ages has given way to a vision of late antiquity that minimizes the significance of Rome's collapse.[8] This shift has brought to light many interesting phenomena that had seemed insignificant in the context of a perspective that saw the period primarily as the aftermath of a catastrophe. But it comes with its own blind spots, such as an inability to acknowledge catastrophic change where it did occur and to understand what gave rise to the idea of the Dark Ages in the first place.[9] Similarly, the turn against the decline narrative in the study of Arabo-Islamic intellectual history in recent decades has produced valuable studies that have

[5] Gibb, *History of Ottoman Poetry,* 1:5, cited in Bauer, "Die *Badīʿiyya,*" 88.

[6] See, in particular, Reichmuth, *World of Murtaḍā al-Zabīdī*; Dallal, *Islam without Europe.*

[7] These fields are the focus in El-Rouayheb, *Islamic Intellectual History.*

[8] Ward-Perkins, *Fall of Rome,* 1–10.

[9] Ward-Perkins, *Fall of Rome,* part 2, "The End of Civilization."

begun to give texture to the terra incognita between the classical and modern periods. Yet this trend has also had the effect of silencing Muslim reformists' critique of postclassical thought and casting it simply as a reaction to Western charges of stagnation in the Muslim world, as a result of Orientalist propaganda, as a timeless Middle Eastern topos, or as a self-serving claim designed to further the reformists' agenda.[10]

I believe that this development is unfortunate, because the reformists' criticisms in fact address genuine features of postclassical Islamic thought—in particular, its scholasticism, which focused intellectual energies on a limited corpus of books and valorized formalistic (especially rhetorical and logical) modes of analysis, and its acceptance and even prioritization of esoteric knowledge. The unifying factor behind these trends was, as Khaled El-Rouayheb has convincingly argued, a drive for verification (*taḥqīq*), which took distinct forms in different fields.[11] In the formal scholarly realm, verification was pursued through the deployment of logic and rhetoric, which yielded increasingly fine-grained analysis of a fixed number of issues without usually expanding the range of questions asked. Meanwhile, the epistemic elevation of direct inspiration as the path to mystical verification offered the possibility of certain knowledge but, when applied to the mainstream rational and religious disciplines, inevitably undermined the evidentiary standards that had governed these fields in the classical period. We can reasonably see the reformist attacks on claims to "inspired" historical or textual expertise as modern, but it is not justifiable to attribute them simply to Western influence,[12] as if the reformers had no intellectual or aesthetic sensibilities of their own; on the contrary, they were clearly harking back to precedents within their own tradition. Today's newfound appreciation for the formal playfulness of postclassical writing reflects a broader renewal of interest in such aesthetics, but this appreciation should not preclude sympathy with Arab intellectuals on the cusp of the twentieth century who found the baroque formality of rhymed prose and *badīʿiyya* poems, like the ossified doctrines of the legal schools, inadequate for grappling with the dramatic societal changes that they were witnessing around them. It is surely for similar reasons that romantic poetry lost much of its appeal in Europe after the experience of the two World Wars. As I have sought to demonstrate in this book, the neoclassical refom of Islamic scholarship and Arabic literature was, for its proponents, a project of ethical reinvigoration at the communal

[10] See, e.g., Aydin, *Idea of the Muslim World*, 72, 75; El-Rouayheb, *Islamic Intellectual History*, 19, 361; Bauer, "Die *Badīʿiyya*," 83–87; Schulze, "Mass Culture and Islamic Cultural Production," 189–91.

[11] El-Rouayheb, *Islamic Intellectual History*, 28 and passim (see index).

[12] This seems to be the explanation suggested by Thomas Bauer in his otherwise outstanding "Die *Badīʿiyya*," 84–88.

and individual levels, and I believe it is difficult to dispute that for such a task postclassical literary forms were ill suited.

Although these features of postclassical thought were neither universal nor inescapable, they were common enough to mark the era's scholarship in distinct and recognizable ways. It is likely that they contributed, together with the decline of educational institutions and libraries, to the decreasing availability of classical works in the Arabic-speaking world, which further constrained intellectual production by reducing the resources at scholars' disposal. In their righteous zeal, the reformists may well have exaggerated the intellectual weaknesses of their age, but the sincerity of the feeling of liberation and optimism with which they reached into the classical tradition for tonics for present maladies should not be doubted.

* * *

Since the middle of the twentieth century, the perception of the Islamic intellectual tradition among scholars and intellectuals in the Muslim world and the West alike has been largely constituted by the products of this movement to resurrect, edit, and print Arabo-Islamic classics. The postclassical curriculum texts have remained relevant in contexts in which the age-old tradition of personal teacher-student bonds in teaching and textual transmission is still cultivated, primarily in the old Islamic universities (such as al-Azhar) and in "traditional" madrasas worldwide. But scholarly discourse has come to focus overwhelmingly on works written in the classical period, as well as on the writings of a relatively small number of later scholars, many of whom had been marginal before the introduction of print. However, we would do well to keep in mind the contingency of this largely print-defined body of classics. Al-Ṭabarī's ninth-century exegesis of the Quran was entirely unknown in the 1890s, but once the text was rediscovered and printed in 1903, it became the quintessential classical exegesis. The exegesis of al-Ṭabarī's contemporary al-Māturīdī, by contrast, remains obscure, not because of its inferior quality but because of its unlucky publishing history. The first volume was printed in 1971 and again in 1982. The first complete (but poor) edition appeared in 2004, but a critical edition was not published until 2011. The coincidence of precedence has elevated al-Ṭabarī's work into the pantheon of classics, while al-Māturīdī's is only beginning to find a readership.[13] Another telling example is the 1922 publication of Ibn al-Jawzī's (d. 597/1201) critique of certain Sufi rituals, *Talbīs Iblīs* (The devil's deception), which made his name permanently synonymous with fierce condemnation of Sufism. The much later publication of his *Baḥr al-dumūʿ* (Sea of tears), which revealed that in spite of his disapproval of what he saw as the excesses of some

[13] Saleh, "Rereading al-Ṭabarī through al-Māturīdī."

Sufis he had himself been an engaged Sufi, failed to dislodge this simplistic reputation.[14]

Today, the editing, publication, and study of classical Islamic texts are no longer the exclusive province of established scholars and publishing houses. Orientalists have largely abandoned the business of editing classical texts, with certain notable exceptions,[15] but the growing practice in recent decades of graduate students in the Arabic-speaking world as well as Turkey and Iran editing substantial classical works as part of theses and dissertations has brought a large number of such works into the public realm. Meanwhile, the Arabic printing industry has expanded far beyond its original heartlands. Presses in Iran, for example, were producing lithographic prints of classical Arabic works already in the nineteenth century, but their small print runs constrained their impact. However, the twentieth century has seen numerous high-quality Iranian editions of classical Arabic works. Another noteworthy development has been the growing participation of women. Whereas my research on the period up to the mid-twentieth century unearthed not a single significant female editor of classical works, more than a few of the editions produced under the auspices of modern universities across the Islamic world have been done by female scholars.[16] Important examples of such editors are ʿĀʾisha ʿAbd al-Raḥmān (1913–98), better known under her pen name Bint al-Shāṭiʾ;[17] Fawqiyya Maḥmūd, professor at ʿAyn Shams University in Egypt;[18] and my predecessor at the University of Chicago, Wadad Kadi (Wadād al-Qāḍī).[19]

The post–World War II period has also seen the establishment of important new institutions for the preservation and publication of classical manuscripts. In 1946, shortly after the inauguration of the Arab League, the Institute for Arabic Manuscripts (Maʿhad al-Makhṭūṭāt al-ʿArabiyya) was founded in Cairo. The aim of the institute was to index Arabic manuscript collections around the world and to publish a union catalog of these manuscripts. For these purposes, it dispatched expeditions to both Arab and non-Arab countries to survey the holdings of libraries that had not yet been cataloged and to preserve the rarest manuscripts on microfilm. These copies were then deposited at the institute's headquarters.[20] The institute's journal, *Majallat Maʿhad al-makhṭūṭāt al-ʿarabiyya*, was launched in 1955 as an arena

[14] See Held, "Ḥanbalite School and Mysticism."

[15] For example, the considerable editorial output of Sabine Schmidtke and her collaborators.

[16] Al-Ṭanāḥī, "Bint al-Shāṭiʾ wa-taḥqīq al-turāth."

[17] See, for example, Bint al-Shāṭiʾ, *al-Ghufrān: Dirāsa naqdiyya*, as well as her editions of Ibn Sīdah's *Muḥkam* and Ibn al-Ṣalāḥ's *Muqaddima*.

[18] See, for example, her editions of al-Ashʿarī's *Ibāna* and al-Juwaynī's *Kāfiya*.

[19] See, for example, her editions of al-Tawḥīdī's *al-Baṣāʾir wa-l-dhakhāʾir* and al-Qāḍī Nuʿmān's *Risālat iftitāḥ al-daʿwa*.

[20] Al-Ṭanāḥī, *Madkhal ilā tārīkh nashr al-turāth*, 133–38.

for discussion of the material and philological aspects of editing Arabic manuscripts. Other grand editing ventures in this period included the delegation sent by the Egyptian ministry of education to Yemen in 1951–52 to microfilm unique manuscripts in the grand mosque of Sanaa. The delegation discovered the writings of the Muʿtazilī theologian Qāḍī ʿAbd al-Jabbār (d. 415/1024 or 1025), and over the next two decades the discovered texts were gradually edited and published, producing the textual corpus that has dominated our view of this important school of Islamic theology until the present day.[21]

The Internet, aided by lax copyright laws and enforcement, has caused a revolution in the availability of edited texts: the vast majority of published premodern Arabic works can now be found online, on websites and in chat rooms dedicated to specific disciplines, authors, or theological orientations.[22] Free and open digital databases (such as al-Maktaba al-Shāmila) have made large corpora of classical texts easily searchable. Even the scholastic stronghold of al-Azhar, which continues to rely on postclassical commentaries in formal instruction, has begun to publish video recordings of lectures in which scholars explain these texts, thus dramatically increasing their accessibility. As a result of these developments, the opportunity for a comprehensive engagement with the Islamic tradition has been diffused to the level of the individual almost anywhere in the world. Indeed, the audience maps and counters on websites that host edited works indicate that they receive millions of hits annually, with visitors from virtually every country in the world.

Only a century and a half ago, such abundance of easily accessible classical texts would have seemed an impossible dream—and were it not for the tireless efforts of the individuals described in this book, as well as many others unmentioned on these pages, it might well have remained so. Their collective labors constituted a vibrant cultural movement that left the imprint of its values and priorities on the body of classics that it created. As a result, even today we see the classical past through the eyes of the editors of the nineteenth and twentieth centuries—a fact whose recognition is essential to a truly informed and critical view of these classics.

[21] For the delegation's report, see Nāmī, *al-Baʿtha al-miṣriyya*. On the editions yielded by the expedition, see Madelung, "ʿAbd-al-Jabbār b. Aḥmad."

[22] As of the writing of this book, some popular sites are waqfeya.com, alfeker.net, and shiabooks.net.

Bibliography

The Arabic article "al-" is ignored in alphabetization.

Al-ʿAbbāsī, ʿAbd al-Raḥīm b. ʿAbd al-Raḥmān. *Maʿāhid al-tanṣīṣ (Sharḥ shawāhid al-Talkhīṣ)*. Bulaq, 1274/[1857].

ʿAbd Allāh, Muḥammad Ghālib. "Al-Sayyida Zaynab." *Al-Islām*, November 12, 1932, 15–18.

Abd-Allah Wymann-Landgraf, Umar Faruq. *Mālik and Medina: Islamic Legal Reasoning in the Formative Period.* Leiden: Brill, 2013.

ʿAbd al-Ḥamīd, Muḥsin. *Al-Ālūsī mufassiran.* Baghdad: Maṭbaʿat al-Maʿārif, 1968.

ʿAbd al-Jawād, Muḥammad. *Ḥayāt mujāwir fī al-Jāmiʿ al-Aḥmadī.* Cairo: Dār al-Fikr al-ʿArabī, 1947.

ʿAbduh, Muḥammad. *Al-Aʿmāl al-kāmila.* 4 vols. Beirut: Dār al-Shurūq, 1993.

ʿAbduh, Muḥammad. "Al-Islām wa-l-Naṣrāniyya maʿ al-ʿilm wa-l-madaniyya." Part 5, *al-Manār* 5, no. 14 (1902): 521–45. Part 6, *al-Manār* 5, no. 15 (1902): 561–80. Reprinted as *al-Islām wa-l-Naṣrāniyya maʿ al-ʿilm wa-l-madaniyya.* Cairo: Maṭbaʿat Majallat al-Manār, 1903. Reprinted as "al-Radd ʿalā Faraḥ Anṭūn," in ʿAbduh, *al-Aʿmāl al-kāmila*, 3:257–368.

ʿAbduh, Muḥammad. "Kutub al-maghāzī wa-aḥādīth al-qaṣṣāṣīn." *Thamarāt al-funūn* 12, no. 587 (1886): 210–12. Reprinted in *al-Manār* 3, no. 31 (1901): 755–65.

ʿAbduh, Muḥammad. "Mafāsid hādhā al-jumūd wa-natāʾijuhā." *Al-Manār* 5, no. 14 (1902): 526–28.

ʿAbduh, Muḥammad. *Risālat al-tawḥīd.* Bulaq, 1315/[1897].

ʿAbduh, Muḥammad. "Travels in Europe." Translated by Tarek El-Ariss in *The Arabic Renaissance: A Bilingual Anthology of the* Nahda, edited by Tarek El-Ariss, 164–69 and 173–76. New York: Modern Language Association of America, 2018.

ʿAbduh, Muḥammad. "Al-Tuḥfa al-adabiyya." *Al-Ahrām*, July 28, 1877. Reprinted in ʿAbduh, *al-Aʿmāl al-kāmila*, 3:23–24.

Abū al-Baqāʾ. *Al-Kulliyyāt.* Bulaq, 1253/[1838].

Abū al-Faḍāʾil al-Īrānī. *Al-Durar al-bahiyya fī jawāb al-asʾila al-hindiyya.* Cairo: Maṭbaʿat al-Mawsūʿāt, 1900.

Abū Ghudda, ʿAbd al-Fattāḥ. *Ṣafaḥāt min ṣabr al-ʿulamāʾ.* Beirut: Dār al-Bashāʾir al-Islāmiyya, 2009.

Abū Yūsuf. *Kitāb al-Kharāj* [with al-Shaybānī's *al-Jāmiʿ al-ṣaghīr*]. Bulaq, 1302/[1884 or 1885].

Abū Zayd, Bakr. *Fiqh al-nawāzil.* 2 vols. Beirut: Muʾassasat al-Risāla, 1996.

Al-Adab al-islāmī 4, no. 16 (1997), special issue, "al-Ustādh Maḥmūd Muḥammad Shākir: Fāris al-turāth."

Adams, Charles C. *Islam and Modernism in Egypt.* New York: Russell and Russell, 1968.

Adem, Rodrigo. "An Intellectual Genealogy of Ibn Taymīya." PhD diss., University of Chicago, 2015.

Ahlwardt, Wilhelm. *Kurzes Verzeichniss der Landberg'schen Sammlung arabischer Handschriften.* Berlin: A. W. Schade's Buchdruckerei, 1885.

Aḥmad, Muḥammad Sayyid, and ʿAbduh al-ʿAlawī. *Muḥammad Naṣīf, ḥayātuhu wa-āthāruh*. Beirut: al-Maktab al-Islāmī, 1994.

Aḥmad b. Ḥanbal. *Musnad Aḥmad*. Edited by Aḥmad Muḥammad Shākir. 15 vols. Cairo: Dār al-Maʿrifa, 1946–56.

Ahmed, Asad. "Post-Classical Philosophical Commentaries/Glosses: Innovation in the Margins." *Oriens* 41, nos. 3–4 (2013): 317–48.

Al-ʿAjmī, Muḥammad b. Nāṣir. *Āl al-Qāsimī wa nubūghuhum fī al-ʿilm wa-l-taḥṣīl*. Beirut: Dār al-Bashāʾir al-Islāmiyya, 1999.

Al-ʿAjmī, Muḥammad b. Nāṣir. *Imām al-Shām fī ʿaṣrihi Jamāl al-Dīn al-Qāsimī: Sīratuhu al-dhātiyya bi-qalamih*. Kuwait: Wizārat al-Awqāf wa-l-Shuʾūn al-Islāmiyya, Idārat al-Thaqāfa al-Islāmiyya, 2009.

Al-ʿAjmī, Muḥammad b. Nāṣir, ed. *Al-Rasāʾil al-mutabādala bayna Jamāl al-Dīn al-Qāsimī wa-Maḥmūd Shukrī al-Ālūsī*. Beirut: Dār al-Bashāʾir al-Islāmiyya, 2001.

Al-Akhdarī, ʿAbd al-Raḥmān. *Al-Sullam al-murawnaq*. Bulaq, 1241/[1826].

Akkach, Samer. *Abd al-Ghani al-Nabulusi: Islam and the Enlightenment*. London: Oneworld, 2007.

Al-Akwaʿ, Ismāʿīl. *Ḥijar al-ʿilm wa-maʿāqiluhu fī al-Yaman*. 6 vols. Damascus: Dār al-Fikr, 1995–2003.

Āl al-Shaykh, ʿAbd al-Muḥsin. "Al-Marʾa al-fāḍila Fāḍila bt. Sinān wa-waqfuhā li-l-makhṭūṭāt." *Al-Jazīra*, March 29, 2015. http://www.al-jazirah.com/2015/20150329/wo1.htm.

Albin, Michael. "Printing of the Qurʾān." In *Encyclopaedia of the Qurʾān*, edited by Jane Dammen McAuliffe, 4:264–76. Leiden: Brill, 2004.

Albin, Michael. "Sarkīs, Y. I." In *Encyclopedia of Library and Information Science*, edited by Allen Kent, Harold Lancour, and Jay E. Daily, vol. 39, suppl. 4, 394–96. New York: Marcel Dekker, 1985.

Alf layla wa-layla. Bulaq, 1251/[1835 or 1836].

Alf layla wa-layla. Corrected by Muḥammad Quṭṭa al-ʿAdawī. 4 vols. Bulaq, 1280/[1863].

Ali, Samer M. *Arabic Literary Salons in the Islamic Middle Ages: Poetry, Public Performance, and the Presentation of the Past*. Notre Dame, IN: University of Notre Dame Press, 2010.

Al-ʿAlī, Wijdān. *Ẓill al-nadīm: Awrāq wa-asmār shaykh al-ʿarabiyya Abī Fihr Maḥmūd Shākir raḥimahu Allāh allatī lam tunshar min qabl*. Beirut: ʿĀlam al-Adab, 2016.

Allen, Roger. "The Post-Classical Period: Parameters and Preliminaries." In *Arabic Literature in the Post-Classical Period*, edited by Roger Allen and D. S. Richards, 1–24. Cambridge: Cambridge University Press, 2008.

Al-Ālūsī, Maḥmūd Shihāb al-Dīn. *Rūḥ al-maʿānī*. 9 vols. Bulaq, 1301–10/[1883 or 1884–1892].

Al-Ālūsī, Maḥmūd Shihāb al-Dīn. *Rūḥ al-maʿānī*. 30 vols. Cairo: Idārat al-Ṭibāʿa al-Munīriyya, 1926.

Al-Ālūsī, Maḥmūd Shihāb al-Dīn. *Rūḥ al-maʿānī fī tafsīr al-Qurʾān al-ʿaẓīm wa-l-sabʿ al-mathānī*. Edited by Māhir Ḥabbūsh, ʿAmmār Bakkūr, Zuhayr al-Qāsim, Anwar Ṭālib, Muḥammad Karīm al-Dīb, Fādī al-Maghribī, Sayyid ʿAbd al-Rashīd, et al. 30 vols. Beirut: Muʾassasat al-Risāla, 2010.

Al-Ālūsī, Maḥmūd Shukrī. *Amthāl al-ʿawāmm fī madīnat dār al-salām*. Baghdad: Dār al-Shuʾūn al-Thaqāfiyya, 2009.

Al-Ālūsī, Maḥmūd Shukrī. *Bulūgh al-arab fī aḥwāl al-ʿArab.* 3 vols. Cairo: al-Maṭbaʿa al-Raḥmāniyya, 1924.
Al-Ālūsī, Maḥmūd Shukrī [Abū al-Maʿālī al-Shāfiʿī al-Salāmī, pseud.]. *Ghāyat al-amānī.* 2 vols. Cairo: Maṭbaʿat Kurdistān al-ʿIlmiyya, 1325–27/[1907–9].
Al-Ālūsī, Maḥmūd Shukrī. *Ghāyat al-amānī.* Edited by Ghayhab b. Muḥammad al-Ghayhab. 2 vols. Alexandria: Dār Iḥyāʾ al-Sunna al-Nabawiyya, 1391/[1971 or 1972].
Al-Ālūsī, Maḥmūd Shukrī. *Al-Misk al-adhfar.* Baghdad: Maṭbaʿat al-Ādāb, 1930.
Al-Ālūsī, Maḥmūd Shukrī. *Mukhtaṣar tarjamat al-Tuḥfa al-ithnā ʿashariyya.* Bombay: al-Maṭbaʿa al-Mujtabāʾiyya, 1884.
Al-Ālūsī, Maḥmūd Shukrī. *Tārīkh masājid Baghdād.* Baghdad: Maṭbaʿat Dār al-Salām, 1927.
Al-Ālūsī, Maḥmūd Shukrī. *Tārīkh Najd.* Edited by Muḥammad Bahjat al-Atharī. Baghdad: Dār al-Warrāq, 2007.
Al-Ālūsī, Nuʿmān Khayr al-Dīn. *Jalāʾ al-ʿaynayn fī muḥākamat al-Aḥmadayn.* Bulaq, 1298/[1881].
Al-Ālūsī, Nuʿmān Khayr al-Dīn. *Jalāʾ al-ʿaynayn fī muḥākamat al-Aḥmadayn.* Edited by al-Dānī b. Munīr Āl Zahawī. Beirut: al-Maktaba al-ʿAṣriyya, 2006.
Amīn, Ahmad. *Fayḍ al-khāṭir.* 10 vols. Cairo: Maktabat al-Nahḍa al-Miṣriyya, 1953.
Anderson, Benedict. *Imagined Communities: Reflections on the Origin and Spread of Nationalism.* London: Verso, 1983.
Anṭūn, Faraḥ. *Ibn Rushd wa-falsafatuh.* Alexandria: Jāmiʿat al-Iskandariyya, 1903.
Arberry, Arthur John. *The Seven Odes: The First Chapter in Arabic Literature.* London: Allen and Unwin, 1957.
Arnzen, Rüdiger. *On Aristotle's "Metaphysics": An Annotated Translation of the So-Called "Epitome."* Berlin: de Gruyter, 2010.
Asad, Nāṣir al-Dīn. *Maṣādir al-shiʿr al-jāhilī wa-qīmatuhā al-tārīkhiyya.* Cairo: Dār al-Maʿārif, 1956.
Al-Ashʿarī, Abū al-Ḥasan. *Al-Ibāna ʿan uṣūl al-diyāna.* Edited by Fawqiyya Maḥmūd. Cairo: Dār al-Anṣār, 1977.
Al-Ashʿarī, Abū al-Ḥasan. *Kitāb al-Ibāna ʿan uṣūl al-diyāna.* Published together with al-Māturīdī's *Sharḥ al-Fiqh al-akbar,* al-Maghnīsāwī's *Sharḥ al-Fiqh al-akbar,* Mullā Ḥusayn's *al-Jawhara al-munīfa,* al-Ḥaydarābādī's *Ḍamīmat kitāb al-Ibāna,* Ibn Dirbās's *Risāla fī al-dhabb ʿan al-Ashʿarī,* and al-Ḥaydarābādī's *Ḍamīma ukhrā li-kitāb al-Ibāna.* Hyderabad: Dāʾirat al-Maʿārif al-Niẓāmiyya, 1903.
Al-Ashʿarī, Abū al-Ḥasan. *Kitāb Maqālāt al-islāmiyyīn wa-ikhtilāf al-muṣallīn.* 3 vols. Edited by Hellmut Ritter. Istanbul: Maṭbaʿat al-Dawla, 1929–33.
Al-Ashʿarī, Abū al-Ḥasan. *Maqālāt al-islāmiyyīn wa-ikhtilāf al-muṣallīn.* Edited by Muḥammad Muḥyī al-Dīn ʿAbd al-Ḥamīd. 2 vols. Cairo: Maktabat al-Nahḍa al-Miṣriyya, 1950–54.
Atçıl, Abdurrahman. "*The Kalām* (Rational Theology) Section in the Palace Library Inventory." In *Treasures of Knowledge: An Inventory of the Ottoman Palace Library (1502/3–1503/4),* edited by Gülru Necipoğlu, Cemal Kafadar, and Cornell H. Fleischer, 1:367–88. Leiden: Brill, 2019.
Al-Atharī, Muḥammad Bahjat. *Aʿlām al-ʿIrāq.* Cairo: al-Maṭbaʿa al-Salafiyya, 1345/[1926 or 1927].
Al-Atharī, Muḥammad Bahjat. *Maḥmūd Shukrī al-Ālūsī wa-arāʾuhu al-lughawiyya.* Cairo: Jāmiʿat al-Duwal al-ʿArabiyya, Maʿhad al-Dirāsāt al-ʿArabiyya al-ʿĀliya, 1958.

ʿAṭṭār, Farīd al-Dīn. *Pand-nāmah*. Bulaq, 1243/[1828].

Al-ʿAṭṭār, Ḥasan. *Ḥāshiyat al-ʿAṭṭār ʿalā sharḥ al-Khubayṣī*. Cairo: Dār Iḥyāʾ al-Kutub al-ʿArabiyya, 1960.

Al-ʿAṭṭār, Ḥasan. *Ḥāshiyat Ḥasan al-ʿAṭṭār ʿalā sharḥ al-Jalāl al-Maḥallī ʿalā Jamʿ al-jawāmiʿ li-l-imām Ibn al-Subkī*. 2 vols. Cairo: al-Maṭbaʿa al-ʿIlmiyya, 1316/[1898].

Aubin, Jean. *Émirs mongols et vizirs persans dans les remous de l'acculturation*. Paris: Association pour l'avancement des études iraniennes, 1995.

Avicenna. *Manṭiq al-mashriqiyyīn wa-l-Qaṣīda al-muzdawaja fī al-manṭiq*. Cairo: al-Maktaba al-Salafiyya, 1328/[1910].

ʿAwwād, Kūrkīs, and Mīkhāʾīl ʿAwwād, eds. *Adab al-rasāʾil bayna al-Ālūsī wa-l-Karmalī*. Beirut: Dār al-Rāʾid al-ʿArabī, 1987.

Ayalon, Yaron. "Revisiting Ṭāhā Ḥusayn's *Fī al-Shiʿr al-Jāhilī* and Its Sequel." *Die Welt des Islams* 49, no. 1 (2009): 98–121.

Aydin, Cemil. *The Idea of the Muslim World: A Global Intellectual History*. Cambridge, MA: Harvard University Press, 2017.

Al-ʿAẓm, Jamīl Bey. *Al-Ṣubābāt fīmā wajadtuhu ʿalā ẓuhūr al-kutub min al-kitābāt*. Beirut: Dār al-Bashāʾir al-Islāmiyya, 2000.

Badawī, ʿAbd al-Raḥmān. *Muʾallafāt Ibn Khaldūn*. Cairo: Dār al-Maʿārif, 1962.

Badr, Hamza ʿAbd al-ʿAziz, and Daniel Crecelius. "The Awqaf of al-Hajj Bashir Agha in Cairo." *Annales islamologiques* 27 (1993): 291–308.

Badrān, ʿAbd al-Qādir. *Munādamat al-aṭlāl*. Damascus: al-Maktab al-Islāmī, 1985.

Al-Baghdādī, ʿAbd al-Qādir. *Khizānat al-adab*. 4 vols. Bulaq, 1299/[1882].

Al-Baghdādī, ʿAbd al-Qādir. *Khizānat al-adab*. Edited by ʿAbd al-Salām Muḥammad Hārūn. 13 vols. Cairo: Dār al-Kitāb al-ʿArabī li-l-Ṭibāʿa wa-l-Nashr, 1967.

Bagnall, Roger S. "Alexandria: Library of Dreams." *Proceedings of the American Philosophical Society* 146, no. 4 (2002): 348–62.

Al-Bājūrī, Ibrāhīm. *Ḥāshiyat al-Bājūrī ʿalā sharḥ al-ʿallāma Ibn Qāsim al-Ghazzī ʿalā matn Abī Shujāʿ*. Edited by Maḥmūd al-Ḥudaydī. 4 vols. Jedda: Dār al-Minhāj, 2016.

Al-Bājūrī, Ibrāhīm. *Ḥāshiyat al-imām al-Bayjūrī ʿalā Jawharat al-tawḥīd, al-musammā Tuḥfat al-murīd ʿalā Jawharat al-tawḥīd*. Edited by ʿAlī Jumʿa. Cairo: Dār al-Salām, 2002.

Bakhīt al-Muṭīʿī, Muḥammad. "Al-Asʾila wa-l-ajwiba: Al-Sayyida Zaynab, wa-hal dufinat fī Miṣr?" *Al-Islām*, December 3, 1932, 15–17.

Al-Bakkī, Muḥammad b. Abī al-Faḍl. *Taḥrīr al-maṭālib*. Edited by Nazzār Ḥammādī. Beirut: Muʾassasat al-Maʿārif, 2008.

Al-Balādhurī, Aḥmad b. Yaḥyā. *Futūḥ al-buldān*. Corrected by Muḥammad al-Mahdī. Cairo: Maṭbaʿat al-Mawsūʿāt for Sharikat Ṭabʿ al-Kutub al-ʿArabiyya, 1901.

Al-Balādhurī, Aḥmad b. Yaḥyā. *Liber Expugnationis Regionum*. Edited by M. J. de Goeje. Leiden: Brill, 1866.

Al-Balawī, Abū al-Ḥajjāj. *Kitāb Alif bāʾ*. 2 vols. Cairo: al-Maṭbaʿa al-Wahbiyya for Jamʿiyyat al-Maʿārif, 1287/[1870].

Al-Bānī, Muḥammad Saʿīd. *Tanwīr al-baṣāʾir bi-sīrat al-Shaykh al-Ṭāhir*. Damascus: al-Maṭbaʿa al-ʿArabiyya al-Sūriyya, 1920.

Al-Barbīr, Aḥmad. *Al-Mufākharāt wa-l-munāẓarāt*. Edited by Muḥammad al-Ṭayyān. Beirut: Dār al-Bashāʾir al-Islāmiyya, 2000.

Bashir, Shahzad. *Sufi Bodies: Religion and Society in Medieval Islam*. New York: Columbia University Press, 2011.

Bauer, Thomas. "Die *Badīʿiyya* des Nāṣīf al-Yāziǧī und das Problem der spätosmanischen arabischen Literatur." In *Reflections on Reflections: Near Eastern Writers Reading Literature*, edited by Angelika Neuwirth and Andreas Christian Islebe, 49–118. Wiesbaden: Reichert, 2006.

Bauer, Thomas. "In Search of 'Post-Classical' Literature: A Review Article." *Mamluk Studies Review* 11, no. 2 (2007): 137–67.

Al-Bayḍāwī, ʿAbd Allāh b. ʿUmar. *Tafsīr al-Bayḍāwī = Beidhawii Commentarius in Coranum*. Edited by Heinrich Leberecht Fleischer. 2 vols. Leipzig: F. C. G. Vogel, 1846–48.

Al-Bayḍāwī, ʿAbd Allāh b. ʿUmar. *Tafsīr al-Bayḍāwī*. Published together with Shaykhzāde's gloss *Ḥāshiyat Shaykhzāde ʿalā tafsīr al-Qāḍī al-Baydāwī*. Bulaq, 1263/[1847].

Al-Bayhaqī, Abū Bakr. *Al-Asmāʾ wa-l-ṣifāt*. 2 vols. Cairo: al-Maktaba al-Azhariyya, n.d.

Al-Bayṭār, ʿAbd al-Razzāq. *Ḥilyat al-bashar fī tārīkh al-qarn al-thālith ʿashar*. 3 vols. Beirut: Dār Ṣādir, 1993.

Bechor, Guy. *The Sanhuri Code, and the Emergence of Modern Arab Civil Law (1932 to 1949)*. Leiden: Brill, 2007.

Behrens-Abouseif, Doris. *The Book in Mamluk Egypt and Syria (1250–1517): Scribes, Libraries and Market*. Leiden: Brill, 2018.

Belinkov, Yonatan, Alexander Magidow, Maxim Romanov, Avi Shmidman, and Moshe Koppel. "Shamela: A Large-Scale Historical Arabic Corpus." In *Proceedings of the Workshop on Language Technology Resources and Tools for Digital Humanities (LT4DH)*, Osaka, Japan, December 11–17, 2016, edited by Erhard Hinrichs, Marie Hinrichs, and Thorsten Trippel, 45–53. Osaka: COLING 2016 Organizing Committee, 2016.

Belo, Catarina. "Averroes (d. 1198), *The Decisive Treatise*." In *The Oxford Handbook of Islamic Philosophy*, edited by Khaled El-Rouayheb and Sabine Schmidtke, 278–95. Oxford: Oxford University Press, 2017.

Bergsträsser, Gotthelf. *Uṣūl naqd al-nuṣūṣ*. Edited by Muḥammad Ḥamdī Bakrī. Cairo: Wizārat al-Thaqāfa, 1969.

Berschin, Walter. "Lachmann und der Archetyp." In *Theoretical Approaches to the Transmission and Edition of Oriental Manuscripts: Proceedings of a Symposium Held in Istanbul, March 28–30, 2001*, edited by Judith Pfeiffer and Manfred Kropp, 251–57. Beirut: Orient-Institut, 2007.

Bevilacqua, Alexander. *The Republic of Arabic Letters: Islam and the European Enlightenment*. Cambridge, MA: Belknap Press of Harvard University Press, 2018.

Bianchi, Thomas-Xavier. "Liste des ouvrages turcs, arabes et persans imprimés à Boulac depuis 1238 de l'Hégire (1822) jusqu'à ce jour." *Journal Asiatique*, 4th ser., 1 (1843): 31–61.

Bint al-Shāṭiʾ (ʿĀʾisha ʿAbd al-Raḥmān). *Al-Ghufrān: Dirāsa naqdiyya*. Cairo: Dār al-Maʿārif, 1954.

Bint al-Shāṭiʾ (ʿĀʾisha ʿAbd al-Raḥmān). *Al-Sayyida Zaynab: ʿAqīlat Banī Hāshim*. Cairo: Dār al-Kitāb al-ʿArabī, 1972.

Bint al-Shāṭiʾ (ʿĀʾisha ʿAbd al-Raḥmān). *Turāthunā: Bayna māḍin wa-ḥāḍir*. Cairo: Maʿhad al-Buḥūth wa-l-Dirāsāt al-ʿArabiyya, 1968.

Blachère, Régis, and Jean Sauvaget. *Règles pour éditions et traductions de textes arabes*. Paris: Les belles lettres, 1953.

Bloom, Jonathan. *Paper before Print: The History and Impact of Paper in the Islamic World*. New Haven, CT: Yale University Press, 2001.

Bonola, Frederico. *L'Égypte et la géographie; sommaire historique des travaux géographiques éxecutés en Égypte sous la dynastie de Mohammed Aly.* Bulaq, 1889.

Bonola, Frederico. *Kitāb Miṣr wa-l-jughrāfiyā: Wa-huwa khulāṣa tārīkhiyya ʿan al-aʿmāl al-jughrāfiyya allatī anjazathā al-ʿāʾila al-Muḥammadiyya al-ʿAlawiyya bi-l-diyār al-miṣriyya.* Translated by Aḥmad Zakī. Bulaq, 1310/[1892].

Booth, Marilyn. *Harem Histories: Envisioning Places and Living Spaces.* Durham, NC: Duke University Press, 2010.

Bronner, Yigal. *Extreme Poetry: The South Asian Movement of Simultaneous Narration.* New York: Columbia University Press, 2010.

Brown, Jonathan A. C. *Hadith: Muhammad's Legacy in the Medieval and Modern World.* London: Oneworld, 2009.

Al-Bukhārī, Muḥammad b. Ismāʿīl. *Al-Jāmiʿ al-ṣaḥīḥ.* Published together with Ḥasan al-ʿIdwī's commentary *al-Nūr al-sārī.* Lithograph. 10 vols. Cairo: n.p., 1279/[1863].

Al-Bukhārī, Muḥammad b. Ismāʿīl. *Ṣaḥīḥ al-Bukhārī = Kitāb al-Ǧāmiʿ al-Ṣaḥīḥ: Recueil des traditions mahométanes.* Edited by Ludolf Krehl and Theodoor W. Juynboll. 4 vols. Leiden: Brill, 1862–1908.

Al-Bukhārī, Muḥammad b. Ismāʿīl. *Ṣaḥīḥ al-Bukhārī.* Corrected by Muḥammad Quṭṭa al-ʿAdawī. 3 vols. Bulaq, 1280/[1863].

Al-Bukhārī, Muḥammad b. Ismāʿīl. *Ṣaḥīḥ al-Bukhārī.* 9 vols. [Edited by] ʿAlī al-Makkāwī, Ḥasan al-Ṭawīl, Hārūn ʿAbd al-Razzāq, Salīm al-Bishrī, ʿAlī al-Bablāwī, Ḥamza Fatḥ Allāh, Muḥammad Ghānim, et al. ["Sultanic edition"]. Introduction by Ḥassūna al-Nawawī. Bulaq, 1311–12/[1894–95].

Al-Bukhārī, Muḥammad b. Ismāʿīl. *Al-Tārīkh al-kabīr.* Edited by ʿAbd al-Raḥmān al-Muʿallimī, Hāshim al-Nadwī, Aḥmad Allāh al-Nadwī, et al. 9 vols. Hyderabad: Dāʾirat al-Maʿārif al-ʿUthmāniyya, 1941.

Bulliet, Richard. "Medieval Arabic *Ṭarsh*: A Forgotten Chapter in the History of Printing." *Journal of the American Oriental Society* 107, no. 3 (1987): 427–38.

Al-Būnī, Aḥmad b. ʿAlī. *Shams al-maʿārif al-kubrā.* Beirut: Muʾassasat al-Nūr, 2005.

Al-Būṣīrī, Sharaf al-Dīn Muḥammad b. Saʿīd. *al-Burda.* Bulaq, 1257/[1841].

Al-Bustānī, Buṭrus. *Dāʾirat al-maʿārif: Encyclopedie arabe.* 6 vols. Beirut: n.p., 1876–82.

Al-Buwayṭī, Abū Yaʿqūb. *Mukhtaṣar.* Manuscript. Istanbul: Süleymaniye, Murad Molla, no. 1189.

Al-Buwayṭī, Abū Yaʿqūb. *Mukhtaṣar.* Manuscript. Cairo: Dār al-Kutub al-Miṣriyya, Fiqh Ṭalaʿat 208.

Cachia, Pierre. *Ṭāhā Ḥusayn: His Place in the Egyptian Literary Renaissance.* London: Luzac, 1956.

Cassirer, Ernst. *An Essay on Man.* New York: Doubleday, 1954.

Catalogue of the Arabic and Persian Manuscripts in the Oriental Public Library at Bankipore. Vol. 15, *History,* prepared by Maulavi Muinuddin Nadwi. Calcutta: Baptist Mission Press, 1929.

Chartier, Roger. *The Order of Books: Readers, Authors, and Libraries in Europe between the Fourteenth and Eighteenth Centuries.* Translated by Lydia Cochrane. Stanford, CA: Stanford University Press, 1994.

Chassebœuf, Constantin François de, comte de Volney. *Travels through Syria and Egypt, in the Years 1783, 1784, and 1785.* 2 vols. London: G. G. J. and J. Robinson, 1787.

Chittick, William C. "The Circle of Spiritual Ascent according to al-Qūnawī." In *Neoplatonism and Islamic Thought*, edited by Parviz Morewedge, 179–210. Albany: State University of New York Press, 1992.

Chodkiewicz, Michel. *An Ocean without Shore: Ibn Arabi, the Book, and the Law*. Albany: State University of New York Press, 1993.

Commins, David Dean. "ʿAbd al-Qādir al-Jazāʾirī and Islamic Reform." *Muslim World* 78, no. 2 (1988): 121–31.

Commins, David Dean. *Islamic Reform: Politics and Social Change in Late Ottoman Syria*. New York: Oxford University Press, 1990.

Coppens, Pieter. "Breaking with the Traditional Ottoman *Tafsīr* Curriculum? Al-Qāsimī's *Tamhīd Khaṭīr fī Qawāʿid al-Tafsīr* in the Context of Late-Ottoman Arabism." In *Ottoman Tafsir: Scholars, Works, Problems*. Istanbul: İSAR, forthcoming.

Crawford, Michael. *Ibn ʿAbd al-Wahhab*. New York: Oneworld, 2014.

Crecelius, Daniel. "The Waqf of Muhammad Bey Abu al-Dhahab in Historical Perspective." *International Journal of Middle East Studies* 23, no. 1 (1991): 57–81.

Crecelius, Daniel. "The *Waqfīyah* of Muḥammad Bey Abū al-Dhahab." Part I, *Journal of the American Research Center in Egypt* 15 (1978): 83–105. Part II, *Journal of the American Research Center in Egypt* 16 (1979): 125–46.

Al-Dabbūsī, Abū Zayd. *Taqwīm al-adilla*. Edited by Khalīl Mays. Beirut: Dār al-Kutub al-ʿIlmiyya, 2001.

Daftary, Farhad, ed. *Fifty Years in the East: The Memoirs of Wladimir Ivanow*. London: I. B. Tauris, 2015.

Daḥlān, Aḥmad b. Zaynī. *Al-Durar al-saniyya fī al-radd ʿalā al-Wahhābiyya*. Beirut: al-Maṭbaʿa al-ʿUthmāniyya, n.d.

Dallal, Ahmad. *Islam without Europe: Traditions of Reform in Eighteenth-Century Islamic Thought*. Chapel Hill: University of North Carolina Press, 2018.

Dallal, Ahmad. "The Origins and Objectives of Islamic Revivalist Thought, 1750–1850." *Journal of the American Oriental Society* 113, no. 3 (1993): 341–59.

Al-Dārimī, ʿUthmān b. Saʿīd. *Radd al-imām al-Dārimī ʿUthmān b. Saʿīd ʿalā Bishr al-Marīsī al-ʿanīd*. Edited by Muḥammad Ḥāmid al-Fiqī. Cairo: Matbaʿat Anṣār al-Sunna al-Muḥammadiyya, 1939.

Davidson, Garrett. "Carrying on the Tradition: An Intellectual and Social History of Post-Canonical Hadith Transmission." PhD diss., University of Chicago, 2014.

Davidson, Herbert A. *Alfarabi, Avicenna, and Averroes on Intellect: Their Cosmologies, Theories of the Active Intellect, and Theories of Human Intellect*. New York: Oxford University Press, 1992.

De Bruijn, J. T. P. "Chronograms." In *Encyclopaedia Iranica*, online edition. Last updated October 20, 2011. http://www.iranicaonline.org/articles/chronograms-pers.

De Jong, Frederick. Ṭuruq *and* Ṭuruq*-Linked Institutions in Nineteenth Century Egypt: A Historical Study in Organizational Dimensions of Islamic Mysticism*. Leiden: Brill, 1978.

De Jong, Frederick, and Jan Just Witkam. "The Library of al-Šayk̲ K̲ālid al-Šahrazūrī al-Naqšbandī (d. 1242/1827): A Facsimile of the Inventory of His Library (MS Damascus, Maktabat al-Asad, no. 259)." In Frederick de Jong, *Sufi Orders in Ottoman and Post-Ottoman Egypt and the Middle East: Collected Studies*, 55–78. Istanbul: Isis Press, 2000.

De Tarrazi, Philippe. *Khazāʾin al-kutub fī al-khāfiqayn*. 3 vols. Beirut: Wizārat al-Tarbiya wa-l-Funūn al-Jamīla, 1947–51.

Defter Kütübhāne Esʿad Efendi. Istanbul: Maḥmūd Bey Maṭbaʿası, n.d.

Dehérain, Henri. "Asselin de Cherville, drogman du consulat de France en Égypte et orientaliste." *Journal des savants* 14, no. 4 (1916): 176–87.

Déroche, François. *La transmission écrite du Coran dans les débuts de l'islam: Le codex Parisino-petropolitanus*. Leiden: Brill, 2009.

Descartes, René. *Maqāl ʿan al-manhaj li-iḥkām qiyādat al-ʿaql wa-li-l-baḥth ʿan al-ḥaqīqa fī al-ʿulūm*. Translated by Maḥmūd Muḥammad al-Khuḍayrī. Cairo: al-Maṭbaʿa al-Salafiyya, 1348/[1930].

Description de l'Égypte. 23 vols. Paris: Imprimerie impériale, 1809–28.

Al-Dhahabī, Shams al-Dīn. *Bayān zaghal al-ʿilm*. Edited by Abū al-Faḍl al-Qūnawī. Damascus: Dār al-Maymana, 2013.

Al-Dhahabī, Shams al-Dīn. *Bayān zaghal al-ʿilm* and *al-Naṣīḥa al-Dhahabiyya li-Ibn Taymiyya*. Annotated by Muḥammad Zāhir al-Kawtharī. Damascus: Maktabat al-Qudsī, 1928.

Al-Dhahabī, Shams al-Dīn. *Tārīkh al-Islām wa-wafayāt al-mashāhīr wa-l-aʿlām*. Edited by Bashshār ʿAwwād Maʿrūf. 15 vols. Beirut: Dār al-Gharb al-Islāmī, 2003.

Di-Capua, Yoav. "*Nahda*: The Arab Project of Enlightenment." In *The Cambridge Companion to Modern Arab Culture*, edited by Dwight F. Reynolds, 54–74. Cambridge: Cambridge University Press, 2015.

Dīrshawī, Muḥammad Nūrī al-Shaykh Rashīd al-Naqshabandī. *Rudūd ʿalā shubuhāt al-salafiyya*. Kuwait: Maktabat Dār al-Albāb, 1987.

Al-Disūqī, Muḥammad b. Muḥammad ʿArafa. *Ḥāshiyat al-Disūqī ʿalā sharḥ al-Taftāzānī ʿalā matn al-Talkhīṣ*. Corrected by Muḥammad Quṭṭa al-ʿAdawī. 4 vols. Bulaq, 1290/[1873].

Al-Dughaym, Maḥmūd. "Dawr āl al-Ansī fī nashr al-funūn al-adabiyya wa-l-thaqāfa al-ʿarabiyya wa-l-ʿuthmāniyya al-turkiyya." *Al-Ḥayāt*, July 1, 2006. http://www.alhayat.com/article/1299382.

Dyab, Hanna. *D'Alep à Paris: Les pérégrinations d'un jeune syrien au temps de Louis XIV*. Translated from the Arabic by Paule Fahmé-Thiéry, Bernard Heyberger, and Jérôme Lentin. Paris: Sindbad, 2015.

Edmond, C. *L'Égypte à l'Exposition universelle de 1867*. Paris: Dentu, 1867.

Eisenstein, Elizabeth L. *The Printing Press as an Agent of Change: Communications and Cultural Transformations in Early-Modern Europe*. 2 vols. Cambridge: Cambridge University Press, 1979.

El Hamel, Chouki. "The Transmission of Islamic Knowledge in Moorish Society from the Rise of the Almoravids to the 19th Century." *Journal of Religion in Africa* 29, no. 1 (1999): 62–87.

El Shamsy, Ahmed. "Al-Ghazālī's Teleology and the Galenic Tradition." In *Islam and Rationality: The Impact of al-Ghazālī*, vol. 2, edited by Frank Griffel, 90–112. Leiden: Brill, 2016.

El Shamsy, Ahmed. "The *Ḥāshiya* in Islamic Law: A Sketch of the Shāfiʿī Literature." *Oriens* 41, nos. 3–4 (2013): 289–315.

El Shamsy, Ahmed. "Islamic Book Culture through the Lens of Two Private Libraries, 1850–1940." *Intellectual History of the Islamicate World* 4, nos. 1–2 (2016): 61–81.

El Shamsy, Ahmed. "Rethinking *Taqlīd* in the Early Shāfiʿī School." *Journal of the American Oriental Society* 128, no. 1 (2008): 1–23.

El Shamsy, Ahmed. "Al-Shāfiʿī's Written Corpus: A Source-Critical Study." *Journal of the American Oriental Society* 132, no. 2 (2012): 199–220.

El-Ariss, Tarek, ed. *The Arab Renaissance: A Bilingual Anthology of the* Nahda. New York: Modern Language Association of America, 2018.

El-Rouayheb, Khaled. "From Ibn Ḥajar al-Haytamī (d. 1566) to Khayr al-Dīn al-Ālūsī (d. 1899): Changing Views of Ibn Taymiyya among Non-Ḥanbali Sunni Scholars." In *Ibn Taymiyya and His Times*, edited by Yossef Rapoport and Shahab Ahmed, 269–318. Karachi: Oxford University Press, 2010.

El-Rouayheb, Khaled. *Islamic Intellectual History in the Seventeenth Century: Scholarly Currents in the Ottoman Empire and the Maghreb.* New York: Cambridge University Press, 2015.

El-Rouayheb, Khaled. "Opening the Gate of Verification: The Forgotten Arab-Islamic Florescence of the 17th Century." *International Journal of Middle East Studies* 38, no. 2 (2006): 263–81.

El-Rouayheb, Khaled. "Rethinking the Canons of Islamic Intellectual History." In *Studying the Near and Middle East at the Institute for Advanced Study, Princeton, 1935–2018*, edited by Sabine Schmidtke, 154–63. Piscataway, NJ: Gorgias Press, 2018.

El-Rouayheb, Khaled. "The Rise of 'Deep Reading' in Early Modern Ottoman Scholarly Culture." In *World Philology*, edited by Sheldon Pollock, Benjamin A. Elman, and Ku-ming Kevin Chang. Cambridge, MA: Harvard University Press, 2015.

Elshakry, Marwa. *Reading Darwin in Arabic, 1860–1950.* Chicago: University of Chicago Press, 2013.

Erünsal, İsmail E. "A Brief Survey of the Development of Turkish Library Catalogues." *Libri* 51, no. 1 (2001): 1–7.

Erünsal, İsmail E. *Kütüphanecilikle ilgili Osmanlıca metinler ve belgeler.* 2 vols. Istanbul: İstanbul Üniversitesi Edebiyat Fakültesi Matbaası, 1982.

Erünsal, İsmail E. "Murad Molla." In *Türkiye Diyanet Vakfı İslam Ansiklopedisi*, 31:188. Istanbul: Türkiye Diyanet Vakfı, 1988–2013.

Erünsal, İsmail E. *Osmalılarda sahaflık ve sahaflar.* Istanbul: Timaş, 2013.

Erünsal, İsmail E. *Ottoman Libraries: A Survey of the History, Development and Organization of Ottoman Foundation Libraries.* Cambridge, MA: Harvard University, Department of Near Eastern Languages and Literatures, 2008.

Escovitz, Joseph H. " 'He Was the Muḥammad ʿAbduh of Syria': A Study of Ṭāhir al-Jazāʾirī and His Influence." *International Journal of Middle East Studies* 18, no. 3 (1986): 293–310.

Evans, Gillian Rosemary, and Philipp W. Rosemann. *Mediaeval Commentaries on the Sentences of Peter Lombard: Current Research.* 3 vols. Leiden: Brill, 2002–15.

Evliya Çelebi. *An Ottoman Traveller: Selections from the "Book of Travels" of Evliya Çelebi.* Translated with commentary by Robert Dankoff and Sooyong Kim. London: Eland, 2011.

Fahmy, Khaled. *All the Pasha's Men: Mehmed Ali, His Army and the Making of Modern Egypt.* Cambridge: Cambridge University Press, 1997.

Al-Fārābī, Abū Naṣr. *Iḥṣāʾ al-ʿulūm*. Edited by ʿAlī Bū Malḥam. Beirut: Dār al-Hilāl, 1996.
Al-Fārābī, Abū Naṣr. *Mabādiʾ al-falsafa al-qadīma*. Cairo: al-Maktaba al-Salafiyya, 1910.
Al-Farīwāʾī, ʿAbd al-Raḥmān. "Shaykh al-islām Ibn Taymiyya: ʿUlūmuhu wa-maʿārifuhu wa-daʿwatuhu fī shibh al-qāra al-hindiyya." *Majallat al-buḥūth al-islāmiyya*, no. 42 (Rabīʿ al-Awwal 1415/[1994]): 163–89.
Farsani, Yoones. "Text und Kontext des al-Wāqidī zugeschriebenen *Futūḥ aš-Šām*: Ein Beitrag zur Forschungsdebatte über frühe *Futūḥ*-Werke." PhD diss., Georg-August-Universität Göttingen, 2017.
Fāṭimī, Ḥasan. "Barrasī-yi iʿtibār-i kitāb-i Akhbār al-Zaynabāt." *Kitābhā-yi islāmī*, no. 21 (2005): 63–76.
Fihrist al-kutub al-ʿarabiyya al-maḥfūẓa bi-l-Kutubkhāna al-Khidīwiyya al-Miṣriyya al-Kubrā al-kāʾina bi-Saray Dār al-Jamāmīz bi-Miṣr al-maḥrūsa. 8 parts in 7 vols. Cairo: al-Maṭbaʿa al-ʿUthmāniyya, 1883–89.
Filipovic, Nenad, and Shahab Ahmed. "The Sultan's Syllabus: A Curriculum for the Ottoman Imperial *Medreses* Prescribed in a *Fermān* of Qānūnī I Süleymān, Dated 973 (1565)." *Studia Islamica* 98, no. 1 (2004): 183–218.
Al-Fiqī, Muḥammad Kāmil. *Al-Azhar wa-atharuhu fī al-nahḍa al-adabiyya al-ḥadītha*. Cairo: Maṭbaʿat Nahḍat Miṣr, 1965.
Al-Fīrūzābādī, Muḥammad b. Yaʿqūb. *El-Okyanus ül-basit fi tercemet il-Kamus il-muhit*. Translated from Arabic to Ottoman Turkish by Ahmet Efendi Asım. 3 vols. Bulaq, 1250/[1834].
Al-Fīrūzābādī, Muḥammad b. Yaʿqūb. *Al-Qāmūs al-muḥīṭ*. [Edited by] Aḥmad b. Muḥammad Shirwānī. 2 vols. Calcutta: printed by the editor, 1817.
Al-Fīrūzābādī, Muḥammad b. Yaʿqūb. *Al-Qāmūs al-muḥīṭ*. 4 vols. Corrected by Naṣr al-Hūrīnī and Muḥammad Quṭṭa al-ʿAdawī. Bulaq, 1272/[1855 or 1856].
Fischer, August. "Muzhir or Mizhar?" *Zeitschrift der Deutschen Morgenländischen Gesellschaft* 54 (1900): 548–54.
Fleischer, Cornell. "Royal Authority, Dynastic Cyclism, and 'Ibn Khaldûnism' in 16th Century Ottoman Letters." *Journal of Asian and African Studies* 18, nos. 3–4 (1983): 198–220.
Flügel, Gustav. *Die arabischen, persischen und türkischen Handschriften der Kaiserlich-Königlichen Hofbibliothek zu Wien*. 3 vols. Wien: Kaiserlich-Königliche Hof- und Staatsdruckerei, 1865–67.
Freitag, Ulrike. "Scholarly Exchange and Trade: Muḥammad Ḥusayn Naṣīf and His Letters to Christiaan Snouck Hurgronje." In *The Piety of Learning: Islamic Studies in Honor of Stefan Reichmuth*, edited by Michael Kemper and Ralf Elger, 292–308. Leiden: Brill, 2017.
Fück, Johann. *Die arabischen Studien in Europa bis in den Anfang des 20. Jahrhunderts*. Leipzig: Harrassowitz, 1955.
Fuzūlī, Muḥammad b. Sulaymān. *Dīwān*. Bulaq, 1254/[1838].
Gacek, Adam. *Arabic Manuscripts: A Vademecum for Readers*. Leiden: Brill, 2009.
Gardiner, Noah. "Forbidden Knowledge? Notes on the Production, Transmission, and Reception of the Major Works of Aḥmad al-Būnī." *Journal of Arabic and Islamic Studies* 12 (2012): 81–143.
Gershoni, Israel. "The Evolution of National Culture in Modern Egypt: Intellectual Formation and Social Diffusion, 1892–1945." *Poetics Today* 13, no. 2 (1992): 325–50.

Gershoni, Israel, and James Jankowski. *Egypt, Islam, and the Arabs: The Search for Egyptian Nationhood, 1900–1930.* New York: Oxford University Press, 1987.
Al-Ghazālī, Abū Ḥāmid. *Al-Ḥikma fī makhlūqāt Allāh.* Corrected by Muṣṭafā al-Qabbānī. Cairo: Maṭbaʿat al-Nīl, 1903.
Al-Ghazālī, Abū Ḥāmid. *Miʿyār al-ʿilm fī fann al-manṭiq.* Cairo: Maṭbaʿat Kurdistān al-ʿIlmiyya, 1329/[1911].
Al-Ghazālī, Abū Ḥāmid. *Al-Munqidh min al-dalāl.* Edited by Maḥmūd Bījū. Damascus: Maṭbaʿat al-Ṣabāḥ, 1990.
Al-Ghazālī, Abū Ḥāmid. *Al-Wajīz fī fiqh madhhab al-imām al-Shāfiʿī.* Cairo: Maṭbaʿat al-Ādāb for Sharikat Ṭabʿ al-Kutub al-ʿArabiyya, 1317/[1900].
Al-Ghumārī, ʿAbd Allāh b. al-Ṣiddīq. *Sabīl al-tawfīq fī tarjamat ʿAbd Allāh b. al-Ṣiddīq.* Cairo: Maṭbaʿat al-Bayān, 1985.
Gibb, Elias John Wilkinson. *A History of Ottoman Poetry.* 6 vols. London: Luzac, 1900–1909.
Gilsenan, Michael. *Saint and Sufi in Modern Egypt: An Essay in the Sociology of Religion.* Oxford: Oxford University Press, 1973.
Glaß, Dagmar. "Die *naḥda* und ihre Technik im 19. Jahrhundert: Arabische Druckereien in Ägypten und Syrien." In *Das gedruckte Buch im Vorderen Orient*, edited by Ulrich Marzolph, 50–84. Dortmund: Verlag für Orientkunde, 2002.
Goldschmidt, Arthur. *Biographical Dictionary of Modern Egypt.* Boulder, CO: Lynne Rienner, 2000.
Goldziher, Ignaz. "Min ʿālim gharbī ilā ʿālim sharqī." *Al-Zahrāʾ* 1, no. 5 (Jumādā al-Ūlā 1343/1924): 321–23.
Goldziher, Ignaz. *Tagebuch.* Edited by Alexander Scheiber. Leiden: Brill, 1978.
Gordon, Matthew, and Kathryn A. Hain. *Concubines and Courtesans: Women and Slavery in Islamic History.* New York: Oxford University Press, 2017.
Grafton, Anthony. *The Culture of Correction in Renaissance Europe.* London: British Library, 2011.
Greenblatt, Stephen. *The Swerve: How the World Became Modern.* New York: W. W. Norton, 2011.
Griffel, Frank. "What Do We Mean by 'Salafī'? Connecting Muḥammad ʿAbduh with Egypt's Nūr Party in Islam's Contemporary Intellectual History." *Die Welt des Islams* 55, no. 2 (2015): 186–220.
Gril, Denis. "L'énigme de la *Šağara al-nuʿmāniyya fī l-dawla al-ʿuṯmāniyya*, attribuée à Ibn ʿArabī." In *Les traditions apocalyptiques au tournant de la chute de Constantinople*, edited by Benjamin Lellouch and Stéphane Yerasmos, 133–52. Paris: L'Harmattan, 1999.
Gubara, Dahlia E. M. "Al-Azhar in the Bibliographic Imagination." *Journal of Arabic Literature* 43, nos. 2–3 (2012): 299–335.
Guizot, François. *Al-Tuḥfa al-adabiyya fī tārīkh tamaddun al-mamālik al-urubāwiyya.* Translated by Ḥunayn al-Khūrī. Alexandria: Maṭbaʿat al-Ahrām, 1877.
Habermas, Jürgen. *The Philosophical Discourse of Modernity: Twelve Lectures.* Translated by Frederick Lawrence. Cambridge: Polity Press, 1987.
Haddad, Mahmoud. "Arab Religious Nationalism in the Colonial Era: Rereading Rashīd Riḍā's Ideas on the Caliphate." *Journal of the American Oriental Society* 117, no. 2 (1997): 253–77.

Hādhā kitāb Qiṣṣat al-Bahnasā al-gharrā' wa-mā fīhā min al-ʿajā'ib wa-l-gharā'ib wa-mā waqaʿa li-l-ṣaḥāba fīhā. Cairo: al-Maṭbaʿa al-Wahbiyya, 1290/[1873].

Hādhihi majmūʿat al-rasā'il. Corrected by Muḥyī al-Dīn Ṣabrī al-Kurdī and Muḥammad Ḥusayn Nuʿaymī al-Kurdī. Cairo: Maṭba'at Kurdistān al-ʿIlmiyya, 1328/[1910].

Ḥājjī Khalīfa. *Kashf al-ẓunūn = Lexicon bibliographicum et encyclopaedicum.* Edited by Gustav Flügel. 7 vols. in 4. London and Leipzig: Oriental Translation Fund, 1835–58.

Ḥājjī Khalīfa. *Kashf al-ẓunūn.* Corrected by Muḥammad al-Sharīf al-Adkāwī. 2 vols. Bulaq, 1274/[1858].

Ḥājjī Khalīfa. *Sullam al-wuṣūl ilā ṭabaqāt al-fuḥūl.* Edited by Maḥmūd ʿAbd al-Qādir al-Arnā'ūṭ. 6 vols. Istanbul: IRCICA, 2010.

Halal, Ṣalāḥ Fatḥī. "Taḥrīr al-aṣl al-muʿtamad fī al-ṭabʿa al-sulṭāniyya min Ṣaḥīḥ al-Bukhārī." Research paper no. 3, Institute of Arabic Manuscripts (Maʿhad al-Makhṭūṭāt al-ʿArabiyya), Cairo, May 2018.

Al-Hamadhānī, Badīʿ al-Zamān. *Maqāmāt Abī al-Faḍl Badīʿ al-Zamān al-Hamadhānī.* Istanbul: Maṭbaʿat al-Jawā'ib, 1298/[1881].

Al-Hamadhānī, Badīʿ al-Zamān. *Maqāmāt Badīʿ al-Zamān al-Hamadhānī.* Corrected and commented on by Muḥammad ʿAbduh. Beirut: al-Maṭbaʿa al-Kathūlīkiyya, 1306/[1889].

Hamilton, Alastair. "'To Divest the East of All Its Manuscripts and All Its Rarities': The Unfortunate Embassy of Henri Gournay de Marcheville." In *The Republic of Letters and the Levant,* edited by Alastair Hamilton, Maurits van den Boogert, and Bart Westerweel, 123–50. Leiden: Brill, 2005.

Hammer-Purgstall, Joseph von. *Encyklopädische Übersicht der Wissenschaften des Orients aus sieben arabischen, persischen und türkischen Werken übersetzt.* Leipzig: Breitkopf und Härtel, 1804.

Hammer-Purgstall, Joseph von. *Erinnerungen und Briefe: Briefe von 1790 bis Ende 1819.* Edited by Walter Höflechner and Alexandra Wagner. 3 vols. Graz: Akademische Druck- und Verlagsanstalt, 2011.

Hammer-Purgstall, Joseph von. "Über die Encyklopädie der Araber, Perser und Türken." *Denkschriften der Kaiserlichen Akademie der Wissenschaften,* philosophisch-historische Classe, 7 (1856): 205–32; 8 (1857): 106–22; 9 (1859): 1–44.

Hamzah, Dyala. "From *ʿIlm* to *Ṣiḥāfa* or the Politics of the Public Interest (*Maṣlaḥa*): Muḥammad Rashīd Riḍā and His Journal *al-Manār* (1898–1935)." In *The Making of the Arab Intellectual (1880–1960): Empire, Public Sphere and the Colonial Coordinates of Selfhood,* edited by Dyala Hamzah, 90–127. London: Routledge, 2013.

Haneberg, Daniel Bonifacius von. "Erörterungen über Pseudo-Wakidi's Geschichte der Eroberung Syriens." *Abhandlungen der Königlich-Bayerischen Akademie der Wissenschaften,* Philosophisch-philologische und historische Classe, 9, no. 1 (1860): 128–64.

Hanna, Nelly. "Literacy among Artisans and Tradesmen in Ottoman Cairo." In *The Ottoman World,* edited by Christine Woodhead, 319–31. Milton Park: Routledge, 2012.

Hanssen, Jens. *Fin de siècle Beirut: The Making of an Ottoman Provincial Capital.* Oxford: Clarendon Press, 2005.

Harb, Lara. "Poetic Marvels: Wonder and Aesthetic Experience in Medieval Arabic Literary Theory." PhD diss., New York University, 2013.

Al-Ḥarīrī, Abū Muḥammad al-Qāsim. *Maqāmāt.* Manuscript. Paris: Bibliothèque nationale de France, Arabe 5847.

Al-Ḥarīrī, Abū Muḥammad al-Qāsim. *Maqāmāt = Les séances de Hariri*. Edited by Antoine Isaac Silvestre de Sacy. Paris: Imprimerie royale, 1822.

Al-Ḥarīrī, Muḥammad. *Durrat al-ghawwāṣ fī awhām al-khawwāṣ*. Edited by ʿArafāt Muṭrajī. Beirut: Muʾassasat al-Kutub al-Thaqāfiyya, 1998.

Hārūn, ʿAbd al-Salām. *Taḥqīq al-nuṣūṣ wa-nashruhā*. Cairo: Muʾassasat al-Ḥalabī, 1965.

Ḥasan, Muḥammad ʿAbd al-Ghanī. *Ḥasan al-ʿAṭṭār*. Cairo: Dār al-Maʿārif, 1968.

Ḥassūn, ʿĀmir Badr. *Kitāb Sūriya: Ṣuwar min al-ḥayāt al-sūriyya*. Damascus: Markaz al-Fawāl, 2000.

Hatem, Mervat Fayez. *Literature, Gender, and Nation-Building in Nineteenth-Century Egypt: The Life and Works of ʿAʾisha Taymur*. Basingstoke: Palgrave Macmillan, 2011.

Hattox, Ralph. *Coffee and Coffeehouses: The Origins of a Social Beverage in the Medieval Near East*. Seattle: University of Washington Press, 1985.

Haykel, Bernard. "The Political Failure of Islamic Law." Yale Law School Legal Scholarship Repository, Occasional Papers, no. 12 (2014). http://digitalcommons.law.yale.edu/ylsop_papers/12.

Haykel, Bernard. *Revival and Reform in Islam: The Legacy of Muhammad al-Shawkānī*. Cambridge: Cambridge University Press, 2003.

Al-Haytamī, Ibn Ḥajar. *Al-Fatāwā al-ḥadīthiyya*. Cairo: Muṣṭafā al-Bābī al-Ḥalabī, 1970.

Al-Haytamī, Ibn Ḥajar. *Sharḥ al-ʿallāma Shihāb al-Dīn Aḥmad b. Ḥajar al-Haytamī al-Makkī ʿalā mukhtaṣar al-ʿallāma al-faqīh ʿAbd Allāh Bāfaḍl al-Ḥaḍramī*. Bulaq, 1892.

Heinzelmann, Tobias. *Populäre religiöse Literatur und Buchkultur im Osmanischen Reich: Eine Studie zur Nutzung der Werke der Brüder Yazıcıoğlı*. Würzburg: Ergon, 2015.

Held, Pascal. "The Ḥanbalite School and Mysticism in Sixth/Twelfth Century Baghdad." PhD diss., University of Chicago, 2016.

Hershlag, Zvi Y. *Introduction to the Modern Economic History of the Middle East*. Leiden: Brill, 1964.

Heyworth-Dunne, James. *An Introduction to the History of Education in Modern Egypt*. London: Luzac, 1939.

Heyworth-Dunne, James. "Printing and Translations under Muḥammad ʿAlī of Egypt: The Foundation of Modern Arabic." *Journal of the Royal Asiatic Society of Great Britain and Ireland*, n.s., 72, no. 4 (July 1940): 325–49.

Al-Hilālī, Taqī al-Dīn. *Al-Daʿwa ilā Allāh fi aqṭār mukhtalifa*. Casablanca: Dār al-Ṭibāʿa al-Ḥadītha, n.d.

Al-Hindāwī, Muḥammad. *Silsilat majmaʿ maṣāʾib ahl al-bayt*. 4 vols. Beirut: Dār al-Maḥabba al-Bayḍāʾ, 2003.

Hirschler, Konrad. *Medieval Arabic Historiography: Authors as Actors*. London: Routledge, 2006.

Hirschler, Konrad. *The Written Word in the Medieval Arabic Lands: A Social and Cultural History of Reading Practices*. Edinburgh: Edinburgh University Press, 2012.

Ḥishmat, Aḥmad. "Iḥyāʾ al-ādāb al-ʿarabiyya." *Al-Zuhūr* 1, no. 11 (1911): 494–98; no. 12 (1911): 532–38.

Ḥishmat, Aḥmad. "Iḥyāʾ al-lugha al-ʿarabiyya wa-ṭabʿ nawādir muṣannafātihā." *Al-Manār* 13, no. 12 (1911): 937–53.

Hitti, Philip K., Nabih Amin Faris, and Buṭrus ʿAbd al-Malik. *Descriptive Catalog of the Garrett Collection of Arabic Manuscripts in the Princeton University Library*. Princeton, NJ: Princeton University Press, 1938.

Hoffmann, Walther G., Franz Grumbach, and Helmut Hesse. *Das Wachstum der deutschen Wirtschaft seit der Mitte des 19. Jahrhunderts*. Berlin: Springer, 1965.

Hollenberg, David, Christoph Rauch, and Sabine Schmidtke, eds. *The Yemeni Manuscript Tradition*. Leiden: Brill, 2015.

Holtzman, Livnat. "Insult, Fury, and Frustration: The Martyrological Narrative of Ibn Qayyim al-Jawzīyah's *al-Kāfiyah al-Shāfiyah*." *Mamlūk Studies Review* 17 (2013): 155–98.

Holtzman, Livnat. "Islamic Theology." In *Handbook of Medieval Studies: Terms, Methods, Trends*, edited by Albrecht Classen, 1:56–68. Berlin: de Gruyter, 2010.

Homerin, Thomas Emil. "Ibn Taimīya's *al-Ṣūfīyah wa-al-Fuqarā'*." *Arabica* 32, no. 2 (1985): 219–44.

Hoover, Jon. "Ibn Taymiyya as an Avicennan Theologian: A Muslim Approach to God's Self-Sufficiency." *Theological Review* 27, no. 1 (2006): 34–46.

Hourani, Albert. *Arabic Thought in the Liberal Age*. 2nd ed. Cambridge: Cambridge University Press, 1983.

Hudson, Leila. "Reading al-Shaʿrānī: The Sufi Genealogy of Islamic Modernism in Late Ottoman Damascus." *Journal of Islamic Studies* 15, no. 1 (2004): 39–68.

Huhn, Ingeborg. *Der Orientalist Johann Gottfried Wetzstein als preussischer Konsul in Damaskus (1849–1861)*. Berlin: Schwarz, 1989.

Humboldt, Alexander von, and Aimé Bonpland. *Voyage de Humboldt et Bonpland*. 30 vols. Paris: F. Schoell, 1807–35.

Al-Hūrīnī, Naṣr. "Hādhihi fawā'id sharīfa wa-qawāʿid laṭīfa fī maʿrifat iṣṭalaḥāt al-Qāmūs." In Muḥammad b. Yaʿqūb al-Fīrūzābādī, *al-Qāmūs al-muḥīṭ*, corrected by Naṣr al-Hūrīnī and Muḥammad Quṭṭa al-ʿAdawī. Bulaq, 1272/[1855 or 1856].

Al-Hūrīnī, Naṣr. *Ḥāshiyat al-Hūrīnī ʿalā sharḥ al-Yūsī ʿalā risālatihi fī ʿilm al-bayān*. Manuscript. Buraydah: Maktabat al-Malik Saʿūd, ʿIlm al-bayān 3624.

Al-Hūrīnī, Naṣr. *Al-Maṭāliʿ al-Naṣriyya li-l-maṭābiʿ al-maṣriyya fī al-uṣūl al-khaṭṭiyya*. Bulaq, 1275/[1859]. Reprinted 1885 as *Qawāʿid al-imlā'*. Other reprints: Beirut: Mu'assasat al-Risāla, 2001; Cairo: Maktabat al-Sunna, 2005.

Al-Hūrīnī, Naṣr. "Sharḥ al-dībāja." In Muḥammad b. Yaʿqūb al-Fīrūzābādī, *al-Qāmūs al-muḥīṭ*, corrected by Naṣr al-Hūrīnī and Muḥammad Quṭṭa al-ʿAdawī. Bulaq, 1272/[1855 or 1856].

Ḥusayn, Ṭāhā. *Al-Ayyām*. 3 vols. in 1. Cairo: Markaz al-Ahrām, 1992.

Ḥusayn, Ṭāhā. *Fī al-shiʿr al-jāhilī*. Cairo: Maṭbaʿat Dār al-Kutub al-Miṣriyya, 1926.

Al-Ḥusaynī, Aḥmad. *Bahjat al-mushtāq fī bayān ḥukm zakāt amwāl al-awrāq*. Cairo: Maṭbaʿat Kurdistān al-ʿIlmiyya, 1329/[1911].

Al-Ḥusaynī, Aḥmad. *Al-Bayān fī aṣl takwīn al-insān*. Cairo: Maṭbaʿat Kurdistān al-ʿIlmiyya, 1328/[1910].

Al-Ḥusaynī, Aḥmad. *Dalīl al-musāfir*. Bulaq, 1319/[1901 or 1902] (with *al-Qawl al-faṣl* printed in the margins).

Al-Ḥusaynī, Aḥmad. *Al-Durra fī ḥukm al-jarra*. Cairo: Dār al-Kutub al-ʿArabiyya al-Kubrā, 1331/[1913].

Al-Ḥusaynī, Aḥmad. *Iʿlām al-bāḥith bi-qubḥ umm al-khabā'ith*. Cairo: Maṭbaʿat Kurdistān al-ʿIlmiyya, 1327/[1909].

Al-Ḥusaynī, Aḥmad. *Kitāb Dafʿ al-khayālāt fī radd mā jā'a ʿalā al-qawl al-waḍḍāḥ min al-muftarayāt*. Cairo: Dār al-Kutub al-ʿArabiyya al-Kubrā, 1331/[1913].

Al-Ḥusaynī, Aḥmad. *Kitāb Kashf al-sitār ʿan ḥukm ṣalāt al-qābiḍ ʿalā al-mustajmir bi-l-aḥjār.* Cairo: Maṭbaʿat Kurdistān al-ʿIlmiyya, 1326/[1908].

Al-Ḥusaynī, Aḥmad. *Kitāb al-Qawl al-waḍḍāḥ fī anna al-akl min al-uḍḥiyya al-muʿayyana bi-l-jaʿl minhu sunna wa-minhu mubāḥ.* Bulaq, 1322/[1904].

Al-Ḥusaynī, Aḥmad. *Murshid al-anām li-birr Umm al-Imām.* 24 vols. Manuscript. Cairo: Dār al-Kutub al-Miṣriyya, Fiqh Shāfiʿī 1522.

Al-Ḥusaynī, Aḥmad. *Nihāyat al-aḥkām fī bayān mā li-l-niyya min aḥkām.* Bulaq, 1320/[1902 or 1903].

Al-Ḥusaynī, Aḥmad. *Al-Qawl al-faṣl fī qiyām al-farʿ maqām al-aṣl.* Cairo: Maṭbaʿat al-Ādāb, 1315/[1898].

Al-Ḥusaynī, Aḥmad. *Tibyān al-taʿlīm fī ḥukm ghayr al-mabduʾ bi-bism Allāh al-raḥmān al-raḥīm.* Cairo: Maṭbaʿat al-Maymūniyya, 1327/[1909].

Al-Ḥusaynī, Aḥmad. *Tūfat al-raʾī al-sadīd al-aḥmad li-ḍiyāʾ al-taqlīd wa-l-mujtahid.* Cairo: Maṭbaʿat Kurdistān al-ʿIlmiyya, 1326/[1908].

Ibn Abī Ḥātim al-Rāzī. *Ādāb al-Shāfiʿī wa-manāqibuh.* Edited by ʿAbd al-Ghanī ʿAbd al-Khāliq. Cairo: Maktabat al-Khānjī, 1953.

Ibn Abī Ḥātim al-Rāzī. *Kitāb al-Jarḥ wa-l-taʿdīl.* Edited by ʿAbd al-Raḥmān al-Muʿallimī. 4 vols. Hyderabad: Maṭbaʿat Majlis Dāʾirat al-Maʿārif al-ʿUthmāniyya, 1952–53.

Ibn Abī Uṣaybiʿa. *ʿUyūn al-anbāʾ fī ṭabaqāt al-aṭibbāʾ.* Edited by August Müller. Cairo: al-Maṭbaʿa al-Wahbiyya, 1882. 2nd ed., Königsberg: published by the editor, 1884.

Ibn al-ʿAfīf al-Tilmisānī. *Dīwān al-shāb al-ẓarīf.* Bulaq, 1274/[1858].

Ibn ʿAjība. *Al-Futūḥāt al-quddūsiyya fī sharḥ al-muqaddima al-Ājurrūmiyya.* Beirut: Dār al-Kutub al-ʿIlmiyya, 2007.

Ibn al-Akfānī, Hibat Allāh. *Irshād al-qāṣid ilā asnā al-maqāṣid.* In *Two Works on Arabic Bibliography,* edited by Aloys Sprenger. Calcutta: Baptist Mission Press, 1849.

Ibn al-Akfānī, Hibat Allāh. *Irshād al-qāṣid ilā asnā al-maqāṣid.* [Edited by] Maḥmūd Bey Abū al-Naṣr. Cairo: Maṭbaʿat al-Mawsūʿāt, 1900.

Ibn al-Akfānī, Hibat Allāh. *Irshād al-qāṣid ilā asnā al-maqāṣid.* [Edited by] Ṭāhir al-Jazāʾirī. Corrected by Muḥammad Salīm al-Āmidī al-Bukhārī. Beirut: n.p., 1904.

Ibn ʿArabī. *Al-Futūḥāt al-makkiyya.* 4 vols. Bulaq, 1269–74/[1953–57].

Ibn al-ʿArabī, Muḥammad. *ʿĀriḍat al-aḥwadhī fī sharḥ Ṣaḥīḥ al-Tirmidhī.* 13 vols. Cairo: al-Maṭbaʿa al-Miṣriyya and Maṭbaʿat al-Ṣāwī, 1932–34.

Ibn ʿArabshāh al-Isfarāʾīnī, ʿIsām al-Dīn Ibrāhīm b. Muḥammad. *Ḥāshiya ʿalā al-Ḍiyāʾiyya.* Manuscript. Leipzig: University of Leipzig, Refaiya Collection, Vollers 883–09.

Ibn ʿAsākir. *Tabyīn kadhib al-muftarī.* Corrected by Ḥusām al-Dīn al-Qudsī. Damascus: Maṭbaʿat al-Tawfīq, 1347/[1928 or 1929].

Ibn al-Athīr, ʿIzz al-Dīn. *Usd al-ghāba fī maʿrifat al-ṣaḥāba.* Corrected by Muṣṭafā Wahbī. 5 vols. Cairo: al-Maṭbaʿa al-Wahbiyya for Jamʿiyyat al-Maʿārif, 1285–87/[1868–71].

Ibn Bassām, ʿAbd Allāh b. ʿAbd al-Raḥmān. *ʿUlamāʾ Najd khilāl thamāniyat qurūn.* 6 vols. Riyadh: Dār al-ʿĀṣima, 1998.

Ibn Baṭṭa al-ʿUkbarī, Abū ʿAbd Allāh. *Al-Ibāna ʿan sharīʿa al-firqa al-nājiya fī mujānabat al-firaq al-madhmūma.* Edited by Riḍā Muʿṭī. 4 vols. in 9. Riyadh: Dār al-Rāya, 1994.

Ibn al-Daybaʿ al-Shaybānī. *Taysīr al-wuṣūl ilā Jāmiʿ al-uṣūl.* Corrected by Muḥammad Hārūn. 3 vols. Cairo: al-Maṭbaʿa al-Jamāliyya, 1912.

Ibn Fāris. *Al-Ṣāḥibī fī fiqh al-lugha*. Cairo: al-Maktaba al-Salafiyya, 1910.
Ibn al-Furāt [pseud.]. "Iḥrāq dār al-ʿilm bi-Tarābulus al-Shām." *Al-Zahrāʾ* 2, no. 2 (Ṣafar 1344/1925): 110–13.
Ibn Ghannām. *Tārīkh Najd*. Edited by Nāṣir al-Dīn Asad. Damascus: Dār al-Shurūq, 1985.
Ibn Ḥajar al-ʿAsqalānī. *Al-Imtāʿ bi-l-arbaʿīn al-mutabāyina al-samāʿ*. Edited by Abū ʿAbd Allāh Muḥammad Ismāʿīl. Beirut: Dār al-Kutub al-ʿIlmiyya, 1997.
Ibn Ḥamīd, Muḥammad b. ʿAbd Allāh. *Al-Suḥub al-wābila ʿalā ḍarāʾiḥ al-Ḥanābila*. Edited by Bakr b. ʿAbd Allāh Abū Zayd and ʿAbd al-Raḥmān b. Sulaymān ʿUthaymīn. 3 vols. Beirut: Muʾassasat al-Risāla, 1996.
Ibn Ḥazm. *Rasāʾil Ibn Ḥazm*. Edited by Iḥsān ʿAbbās. 4 vols. Beirut: al-Muʾassasa al-ʿArabiyya li-l-Dirasāt wa-l-Nashr, 1983.
Ibn Hibbān al-Bustī. *Rawḍat al-ʿuqalāʾ*. Corrected by Muḥammad Amīn al-Khānjī. Cairo: Maṭbaʿat Kurdistān al-ʿIlmiyya, 1328/[1910].
Ibn Ḥijja al-Ḥamawī. *Khizānat al-adab*. Bulaq, 1273/[1856 or 1857].
Ibn Hishām, ʿAbd al-Malik. *Al-Sīra al-nabawiyya*. Edited by Muṣṭafā al-Saqqā. 2 vols. Cairo: Muṣṭafā al-Bābī al-Ḥalabī, 1955.
Ibn Īyās, Muḥammad b. Aḥmad. *Badāʾiʿ al-zuhūr fī waqāʾiʿ al-duhūr*. Edited by Muḥammad Muṣṭafā. 5 vols. Cairo: al-Hayʾa al-Miṣriyya al-ʿĀmma li-l-Kitāb, 1984.
Ibn Jamāʿa. *Tadhkirat al-sāmiʿ wa-l-mutakallim fī adab al-ʿālim wa-l-mutaʿallim*. Edited by Muḥammad b. Mahdī al-ʿAjmī. Beirut: Dār al-Bashāʾir al-Islāmiyya, 2012.
[Ibn al-Jawzī.] *Akhbār al-nisāʾ*. Incorrectly attributed to Ibn Qayyim al-Jawziyya. Cairo: Maṭbaʿat al-Taqaddum al-ʿIlmiyya, 1901.
Ibn al-Jawzī. *Akhbār al-nisāʾ*. Edited by Barkāt Yūsuf Habbūd. Sidon: al-Maktaba al-ʿAṣriyya, 2000.
Ibn al-Jawzī. *Baḥr al-dumūʿ*. Tanta: Dār al-Ṣaḥāba, 1992.
Ibn al-Jawzī. *Naqd al-ʿilm wa-l-ʿulamāʾ, aw Talbīs Iblīs*. Corrected by Muḥammad Munīr Āghā. Cairo: Maṭbaʿat al-Saʿāda, 1922.
Ibn al-Jīʿān, Yaḥyā. *Kitāb mā bi-iqlīm Miṣr min al-buldān wa-ʿibrat kull baladih*. Manuscript. New Haven, CT: Yale University, Beinecke Library, Landberg 215. Copied Shawwāl 18, 1275/[May 19, 1859].
Ibn al-Jīʿān, Yaḥyā. *Al-Tuḥfa al-saniyya bi-asmāʾ al-bilād al-miṣriyya*. Edited by Bernhard Moritz. Cairo: al-Maṭbaʿa al-Ahliyya, 1898.
Ibn al-Kalbī. *Kitāb al-Aṣnām*. Edited by Aḥmad Zakī. Cairo: al-Maṭbaʿa al-Amīriyya, 1914.
Ibn Kathīr. *Al-Bidāya wa-l-nihāya*. Manuscript. Damascus: Maktabat al-Asad, nos. 14508–16.
Ibn Kathīr. *Al-Bidāya wa-l-nihāya*. 14 vols. Cairo: Maṭbaʿat al-Saʿāda, 1923.
Ibn Kathīr. *Al-Bidāya wa-l-nihāya*. Edited by ʿAlī Shīrī. 14 vols. Beirut: Dār Iḥyāʾ al-Turāth al-ʿArabī, 1988.
Ibn Kathīr. *Al-Bidāya wa-l-nihāya*. Edited by ʿAbd Allāh al-Turkī. 21 vols. Giza: Hajr, 1997–99.
Ibn Khaldūn. *Al-Muqaddima*. Manuscript. Cairo: Dār al-Kutub al-Miṣriyya, Taymūr 355. Copied 1040/[1631].
Ibn Khaldūn. *Al-Muqaddima*. Manuscript. Cairo: Dār al-Kutub al-Miṣriyya, Taymūr 612. Copied 1270/[1854].
Ibn Khaldūn. *Al-Muqaddima*. Manuscript. Istanbul: Süleymaniye, Atıf Efendi, no. 1936.
Ibn Khaldūn. *Al-Muqaddima*. Corrected by Naṣr al-Hūrīnī. Bulaq, 1274/[1857]. Reprint, 1284/[1867].

Ibn Khaldūn. *Al-Muqaddima*. Edited by ʿAbd al-Salām al-Shidādī. 5 vols. Casablanca: Khizānat Ibn Khaldūn, Bayt al-Funūn wa-l-ʿUlūm wa-l-Ādāb, 2005.
Ibn Khaldūn. *The Muqaddimah: An Introduction to History*. Translated by Franz Rosenthal. New York: Pantheon Books, 1958.
Ibn Khaldūn. *Tercüme-yi Mukaddeme-yi İbn Haldûn*. Translated from Arabic to Ottoman Turkish by Meḥmed Ṣāḥib Pīrīzāde. Bulaq, 1275/[1858 or 1859].
Ibn al-Laḥḥām al-Baʿlī, ʿAlāʾ al-Dīn. *Kitāb Tajrīd al-ʿināya fī taḥrīr aḥkām al-nihāya*. Manuscript. Leipzig: University of Leipzig, Refaiya Collection, Vollers 387. Copied Ṣafar 851/[April–May 1447].
Ibn al-Mawṣilī, Muḥammad. *Mukhtaṣar al-Ṣawāʿiq al-mursala ʿalā al-Jahmiyya wa-l-Muʿaṭṭila*. Corrected by Muḥammad ʿAbd al-Razzāq Ḥamza and Ḥāmid al-Fiqī. Mecca: al-Maṭbaʿa al-Salafiyya, 1348/[1929].
Ibn al-Muqaffaʿ. *Al-Adab al-ṣaghīr*. [Edited by] Ṭāhir al-Jazāʾirī. *Al-Muqtabas* 3, no. 1 (1908): 4–18; no. 2 (1908): 117–19. Reprinted in *Rasāʾil al-bulaghāʾ*, edited by Muḥammad Kurd ʿAlī, 17–54. Cairo: Maṭbaʿat al-Ẓāhir, 1326/[1908].
Ibn al-Muqaffaʿ. *Al-Adab al-ṣaghīr*. Edited by Aḥmad Zakī. Alexandria: Jamʿiyyat al-ʿUrwa al-Wuthqā al-Islāmiyya, 1911.
Ibn al-Muqaffaʿ. *Al-Adab al-kabīr*. Edited by Aḥmad Zakī. Alexandria: Jamʿiyyat al-ʿUrwa al-Wuthqā al-Islāmiyya, 1912.
Ibn al-Muqaffaʿ, trans. *Kalīla wa-Dimna*. Bulaq, 1249/[1833].
Ibn al-Muqriʾ, Ismāʿīl b. Abī Bakr. *ʿUnwān al-sharaf al-wāfī fī ʿilm al-fiqh wa-l-ʿarūḍ wa-l-tārīkh wa-l-naḥw wa-l-qawāfī*. Edited by ʿAbd Allāh al-Anṣārī. Beirut: ʿĀlam al-Kutub, 1996.
Ibn al-Nadīm. *Kitāb al-Fihrist*. Edited by Gustav Flügel. 2 vols. Leipzig: F. C. W. Vogel, 1872.
Ibn Nubāta. *Dīwān khuṭab Ibn Nubāta: Wa-yalīhu khuṭab wālidihi Abī Ṭāhir Muḥammad*. [Edited by] Ṭāhir al-Jazāʾirī. Beirut: Maṭbaʿat Jarīdat Bayrūt, 1311/[1894].
Ibn Nubāta. *Majmūʿat khuṭab*. Bombay: n.p., 1865.
Ibn Qarqamās. *Al-Ghayth al-murīʿ*. Manuscript. Leiden: Leiden University, Cod. 2127 (Amin 408).
Ibn Qayyim al-Jawziyya. *Aḥkām ahl al-dhimma*. Edited by Yūsuf al-Bakrī and Shākir al-ʿArūrī. 3 vols. Dammam: Ramādī, 1997.
Ibn Qayyim al-Jawziyya [attrib.]. *Akhbār al-nisāʾ*. Cairo: Maṭbaʿat al-Taqaddum al-ʿIlmiyya, 1901.
Ibn Qayyim al-Jawziyya [attrib.]. *Akhbār al-nisāʾ*. Edited by ʿAbd al-Majīd Ḥalabī. Beirut: Dār al-Maʿrifa, 1997.
Ibn Qayyim al-Jawziyya. *Ighāthat al-lahfān fī ḥukm ṭalāq al-ghaḍbān*. [Edited by] Jamāl al-Dīn al-Qāsimī. Cairo: Maṭbaʿat al-Manār, 1909.
Ibn Qayyim al-Jawziyya. *Al-Kāfiya al-shāfiya fī al-intiṣār li-l-firqa al-nājiya*. Edited by Muḥammad al-ʿArīfī, Nāṣir al-Ḥunaynī, Fahd al-Hudhayl, and ʿAbd Allāh al-Musāʿid. 4 vols. Mecca: Dār ʿĀlam al-Fawāʾid, 2007.
Ibn Qayyim al-Jawziyya. *Al-Ṣawāʿiq al-mursala*. Manuscript. Aleppo: Maktabat al-Awqāf, al-Maktaba al-ʿUthmāniyya, no. 5700.
Ibn Qayyim al-Jawziyya. *Al-Ṣawāʿiq al-mursala*. Manuscript. Baghdad: Maktabat al-Mathaf al-ʿIrāqī, al-Ālūsī, no. 8500.
Ibn Qayyim al-Jawziyya. *Al-Ṣawāʿiq al-mursala ʿalā al-Jahmiyya wa-l-Muʿaṭṭila*. Edited by ʿAlī al-Dakhīl Allāh. 4 vols. Riyadh: Dār al-ʿĀṣima, 1987.

Ibn Qayyim al-Jawziyya. *Ṭarīq al-hijratayn wa-bāb al-saʿādatayn*. 2 vols. Edited by Muḥammad Ajmal al-Iṣlāḥī. Mecca: Dār ʿĀlam al-Fawāʾid, 1429/[2008].

Ibn Qayyim al-Jawziyya. *Al-Ṭuruq al-ḥukmiyya*. Cairo: Maṭbaʿat al-Ādāb wa-l-Muʾayyad for Sharikat Ṭabʿ al-Kutub al-ʿArabiyya, 1899.

Ibn Qutayba. *Adab al-kātib*. Cairo: Maṭbaʿat al-Waṭan, 1882.

Ibn Rushd. *Kitāb Falsafat Muḥammad b. Aḥmad b. Muḥammad b. Aḥmad Ibn Rushd al-Andalusī*. Introduction by Muḥammad Amīn al-Khānjī. Cairo: al-Maṭbaʿa al-Jamāliyya, 1910.

Ibn al-Ṣabūnī, Muḥammad. *Takmilat Ikmāl al-Ikmāl*. Edited by Muṣṭafā Jawwād. Baghdad: al-Majmaʿ al-ʿIlmī al-ʿIrāqī, 1957.

Ibn al-Ṣalāḥ, ʿUthmān Abū ʿAmr. *Muqaddimat Ibn al-Ṣalāḥ*. Edited by Bint al-Shāṭiʾ. Cairo: Maṭbaʿat Dār al-Kutub, 1974.

Ibn Shaddād. *Sīrat Ṣalāḥ al-Dīn al-musammā bi-l-Nawādir al-sulṭāniyya wa-l-maḥāsin al-yūsufiyya*. Cairo: Maṭbaʿat al-Ādāb wa-l-Muʾayyad for Sharikat Ṭabʿ al-Kutub al-ʿArabiyya, 1899.

Ibn Shākir. *Fawāt al-Wafayāt*. Corrected by Naṣr al-Hūrīnī. 2 vols. Bulaq, 1283/[1866].

Ibn Sīdah. *Al-Muḥkam al-muḥīṭ fī al-lugha*. Edited by Muṣṭafā al-Saqqā, Ḥusayn Naṣṣār, Bint al-Shāṭiʾ, ʿAbd al-Sattār Farrāj, Ibrāhīm al-Abyārī, Murād Kāmil, Muḥammad al-Najjār, et al. 12 vols. Cairo: Muṣṭafā al-Bābī al-Ḥalabī, 1958.

Ibn Sīdah. *Al-Mukhaṣṣaṣ*. Corrected by Muḥammad Maḥmūd al-Shinqīṭī al-Turkuzī. 17 vols. in 6. Bulaq, 1316–21/[1898–1903].

Ibn Taymiyya. *Bayān talbīs al-Jahmiyya*. Manuscript. Contained within Ibn ʿUrwa al-Ḥanbalī, *al-Kawākib al-darārī*, vols. 39, 42, 46, and 47. Damascus: Maktabat al-Asad, nos. 567 and 570–72.

Ibn Taymiyya. *Bayān talbīs al-Jahmiyya*. Manuscript. Baghdad: Maktabat al-Awqāf al-ʿĀmma, no. 24217. Copied 1920.

Ibn Taymiyya. *Bayān talbīs al-Jahmiyya*. Edited by Muḥammad b. al-Qāsim. 2 vols. Mecca: Maṭbaʿat al-Ḥukūma, 1971.

Ibn Taymiyya. *Bayān talbīs al-Jahmiyya*. Edited by Yaḥyā al-Hanīdī, Rashīd Muḥammad ʿAlī, Aḥmad Muʿādh Ḥaqqī, Muḥammad ʿAbd al-ʿAzīz al-Lāḥim, Sulaymān al-Ghafīṣ, Muḥammad al-Buraydī, Rāshid al-Ṭayyār, et al. 10 vols. Mecca: Majmaʿ al-Malik Fahd, 2005.

Ibn Taymiyya. *Bughyat al-murtād* [known as *al-Sabʿīniyya*]. In *Kitāb Majmūʿat fatāwā shaykh al-islām Taqī al-Dīn b. Taymiyya al-Ḥarrānī*, 3:[623–758].

Ibn Taymiyya. *Darʾ taʿāruḍ al-ʿaql wa-l-naql*. Edited by Muḥammad Rashshād Sālim. 11 vols. Cairo: Maṭbaʿat Dār al-Kutub, 1971.

Ibn Taymiyya. *Al-Ḥisba fī al-islām*. Cairo: Maṭbaʿat al-Muʾayyad, 1318/[1900 or 1901].

Ibn Taymiyya. *Al-Istighātha* [short version]. In *Majmūʿat al-rasāʾil al-kubrā*, 1:470–75.

Ibn Taymiyya. *Al-Istighātha fī al-radd ʿalā al-Bakrī*. Edited by ʿAbd Allāh al-Suhaylī. Riyadh: Dār al-Waṭan, 1997.

Ibn Taymiyya. *Khulāṣat al-Radd Ibn Taymiyya ʿalā al-Bakrī fī al-istighātha*. Manuscript. Cairo: Dār al-Kutub al-Miṣriyya, Taymūr 281.

Ibn Taymiyya. *Kitāb al-Īmān*. Corrected by Muḥammad Badr al-Dīn al-Naʿsānī. Cairo: Maṭbaʿat al-Saʿāda, 1325/[1907].

Ibn Taymiyya. *Kitāb Majmūʿat fatāwā shaykh al-islām Taqī al-Dīn b. Taymiyya al-Ḥarrānī*. 5 vols. Cairo: Maṭbaʿat Kurdistān al-ʿIlmiyya, 1326–29/[1908–11].

Ibn Taymiyya. *Maʿārij al-wuṣūl ilā maʿrifat anna usūl al-dīn wa-furūʿuhu qad bayyanahā al-Rasūl*. Cairo: Maṭbaʿat al-Muʾayyad, 1318/[1900 or 1901].

Ibn Taymiyya. *Majmūʿ al-fatāwā*. Edited by ʿAbd al-Raḥmān b. Qāsim. 35 vols. Medina: Majmaʿ al-Malik Fahd, 1995.

Ibn Taymiyya. *Majmūʿ rasāʾil*. Corrected by Muḥammad Badr al-Dīn al-Naʿsānī. Cairo: al-Maṭbaʿa al-Ḥusayniyya, 1323/[1905].

Ibn Taymiyya. *Majmūʿat al-fatāwā*. Edited by ʿĀmir al-Jazzār and Anwar al-Bāz. 33 vols. Mansura: Dār al-Wafāʾ, 1997.

Ibn Taymiyya. *Majmūʿat al-rasāʾil al-kubrā*. Corrected by Ḥasan al-Fayyūmī Ibrāhīm. 2 vols. in 1. Cairo: al-Maṭbaʿa al-Sharqiyya, 1323/[1905].

Ibn Taymiyya. *Minhāj al-sunna al-nabawiyya fī naqḍ kalām al-Shīʿa wa-l-Qadariyya*. Published together with *Bayān muwāfaqat ṣarīḥ al-maʿqūl li-ṣaḥīḥ al-manqūl* [a fragment of *Darʾ taʿāruḍ al-ʿaql wa-l-naql*]. Corrected by Ṭāhā b. Maḥmūd al-Qaṭriyya. 4 vols. in 2. Bulaq, 1321–22/[1903–5].

Ibn Taymiyya. *Minhāj al-sunna al-nabawiyya naqḍ kalām al-Shīʿa wa-l-Qadariyya*. Vol. 2. Manuscript. New Haven, CT: Yale University, Beinecke Library, Landberg 2.

Ibn Taymiyya. *Muqaddima fī uṣūl al-tafsīr*. [Edited by] Jamīl al-Shaṭṭī. Damascus: Maṭbaʿat al-Taraqqī, 1936.

Ibn Taymiyya. *Muqaddima fī uṣūl al-tafsīr*. Edited by ʿAdnān Zarzūr. Beirut: Muʾassasat al-Risāla, 1972.

Ibn Taymiyya. *Qāʿida jalīla fī al-tawassul wa-l-wasīla*. [Edited by] Rashīd Riḍā. Cairo: Maṭbaʿat al-Manār, 1327/[1909].

Ibn Taymiyya. *Al-Radd ʿalā al-Bakrī*. Manuscript. Jedda: Jāmiʿat al-Malik ʿAbd al-ʿAzīz, Muḥammad Naṣīf, no. 2886.

Ibn Taymiyya. *Sharḥ al-ʿaqīda al-Iṣfahāniyya* [the shorter commentary]. Manuscript. Istanbul: Süleymaniye, Laleli, no. 2324.

Ibn Taymiyya. *Sharḥ al-ʿaqīda al-Iṣfahāniyya*. Manuscript. Jedda: Jāmiʿat al-Malik ʿAbd al-ʿAzīz, Muḥammad Naṣīf, no. 112.

Ibn Taymiyya. *Sharḥ al-ʿaqīda al-Iṣfahāniyya*. Manuscript. Cairo: Dār al-Kutub al-Miṣriyya, ʿIlm al-kalām Ṭalaʿat 509.

Ibn Taymiyya. *Sharḥ al-ʿaqīda al-Iṣfahāniyya*. In *Kitāb Majmūʿat fatāwā shaykh al-islām Taqī al-Dīn b. Taymiyya al-Ḥarrānī*, 3:[471–622].

Ibn Taymiyya. *Sharḥ al-Iṣbahāniyya* [the longer commentary]. Edited by Muḥammad al-Saʿawī. Riyadh: Maktabat Dār al-Minhāj, 2009.

Ibn Taymiyya. *Talkhīṣ kitāb al-Istighātha al-maʿrūf bi-l-Radd ʿalā al-Bakrī*. Cairo: al-Maṭbaʿa al-Salafiyya, 1346/[1927].

Ibn Taymiyya. *Al-Wāsiṭa bayna al-khalq wa-l-ḥaqq*. Cairo: Maṭbaʿat al-Ādāb, 1318/[1900].

Ibn Ṭiqṭaqā. *Al-Fakhrī fī al-ādāb al-sulṭāniyya*. Cairo: Maṭbaʿat al-Mawsūʿāt for Sharikat Ṭabʿ al-Kutub al-ʿArabiyya, 1317/[1900].

Ibn ʿUrwa al-Ḥanbalī. *Al-Kawākib al-darārī fī tartīb Musnad al-imām Aḥmad ʿalā abwāb al-Bukhārī*. Vol. 85. Manuscript. Cairo: Dār al-Kutub al-Miṣriyya, Tafsīr 47214.

Ibrahim, Ahmad Fekry. *Pragmatism in Islamic Law: A Social and Intellectual History*. Syracuse, NY: Syracuse University Press, 2015.

Al-ʿIdwī al-Ḥamzāwī, Ḥasan. Introduction to Muḥammad b. Ismāʿīl al-Bukhārī, *al-Jāmiʿ al-ṣaḥīḥ*, 1:2–16. Cairo: n.p., 1279/[1863].

Al-ʿIlīsh, Muḥammad. *Fatḥ al-ʿalī al-mālik fī al-fatāwā ʿalā madhhab al-imām Mālik*. 2 vols. Cairo: Muṣṭafā al-Bābī al-Ḥalabī, 1917.

ʿImāra, Muḥammad. *Rifāʿa al-Ṭahṭāwī: Rāʾid al-tanwīr fī al-ʿaṣr al-ḥadīth*. Cairo: Dār al-Shurūq, 2009.

ʿInān, Muḥammad ʿAbd Allāh. "Turāthunā al-ʿarabī al-qadīm: Mā yajibu li-tanẓīm iḥyāʾih." *Al-Risāla*, June 22, 1936, 1007–9.

Irwin, Robert. *Dangerous Knowledge: Orientalism and Its Discontents*. Woodstock, NY: Overlook Press, 2006.

Irwin, Robert. *Night and Horses and the Desert: An Anthology of Classical Arabic Literature*. New York: Overlook Press, 2000.

Al-Iṣbahānī, Abū al-Faraj. *Kitāb al-Aghānī*. 20 vols. Corrected by Naṣr al-Hūrīnī, Ibrāhīm al-Disūqī, [et al.]. Bulaq, 1285/[1868 or 1869].

Al-Iṣfahānī, ʿImād al-Dīn. *Tārīkh dawlat āl Saljūq*. Cairo: Maṭbaʿat al-Mawsūʿāt for Sharikat Ṭabʿ al-Kutub al-ʿArabiyya, 1900.

Al-Iskandarī, Aḥmad, and Muṣṭafā ʿInānī. *Al-Wasīṭ fī al-adab al-ʿarabī wa-tārīkhih*. Cairo: Maṭbaʿat al-Maʿārif, 1919.

Issawi, Charles. *An Economic History of the Middle East and North Africa*. New York: Columbia University Press, 1982.

Al-ʿĪyāshī, ʿAbd Allāh Abū Sālim. *Al-Riḥla al-ʿĪyāshiyya*. Edited by Saʿīd al-Fāḍilī and Sulaymān al-Qurashī. 2 vols. Abu Dhabi: Dār al-Suwaydī, 2006.

Al-Jabartī, ʿAbd al-Raḥmān. *ʿAjāʾib al-āthār*. 3 vols. Beirut: Dār al-Jīl, 1983.

Al-Jāḥiẓ [attrib.]. *Kitāb al-Tāj fī akhlāq al-mulūk = Le livre de la couronne*. Edited by Aḥmad Zakī. Cairo: al-Maṭbaʿa al-Āmiriyya, 1914.

Jamal, ʿAlī b. ʿAbd al-Raḥmān. *Naṣīḥat al-murīd fī ṭarīq ahl al-sulūk wa-l-tajrīd: Wa-yusammā ayḍan al-Yawāqīt al-ḥisān fī taṣrīf maʿānī al-insān*. Edited by ʿĀṣim al-Kayyālī. Beirut: Dār al-Kutub al-ʿIlmiyya, 2005.

Janos, Damian. "Intuition, Intellection, and Mystical Knowledge: Delineating Fakhr al-Dīn al-Rāzī's Cognitive Theories." In *Islam and Rationality: The Impact of al-Ghazālī*, vol. 2, edited by Frank Griffel, 189–228. Leiden: Brill, 2016.

Al-Jaṣṣāṣ, Abū Bakr al-Rāzī. *Aḥkām al-Qurʾān*. [Edited by] Bashīr al-Ghazzī. 3 vols. Istanbul: Maṭbaʿat al-Awqāf al-Islāmiyya, 1335–38/[1917–20].

Al-Jawharī, Ismāʿīl b. Ḥammād. *Tercüme-yi Sıhahu'l-Cevherī*. Translated from Arabic to Ottoman Turkish by Mehmet bin Mustafa el-Vanī. Istanbul: Dar ut-Tıbaat il-Mamure, 1141/[1728].

Al-Jazāʾirī, ʿAbd al-Qādir. *Kitāb al-Mawāqif fī al-taṣawwuf wa-l-waʿẓ wa-l-irshād*. 3 vols. Damascus: Dār al-Yaqẓa al-ʿArabiyya li-l-Taʾlīf wa-l-Tarjama wa-l-Nashr, 1966.

Al-Jazāʾirī, Ṭāhir. *Badīʿ al-talkhīṣ wa-talkhīṣ al-badīʿ*. Damascus: Maṭbaʿat Sūriyā, 1296/[1879].

Al-Jazāʾirī, Ṭāhir. *Fihris muntakhabāt li-nawādir al-kutub*. Manuscript. Cairo: Dār al-Kutub al-Miṣriyya, Fahāris Taymūr 18.

Al-Jazāʾirī, Ṭāhir. *Al-Jawāhir al-kalāmiyya fī al-ʿaqīda al-islāmiyya*. Beirut: al-Maktaba al-Ahliyya, 1320/[1902].

Al-Jazāʾirī, Ṭāhir. *Al-Kunnāsha fī nawādir al-kutub al-makhṭūta*. Edited by Ālāʾ Ṣaqr. Amman: Arwiqa, 2016.

Al-Jazāʾirī, Ṭāhir. *Tadhkirat Ṭāhir al-Jazāʾirī*. Edited by Muḥammad Ramaḍān Yūsuf. 2 vols. Beirut: Dār Ibn Ḥazm, 2012.

Al-Jazāʾirī, Ṭāhir. *Tamhīd al-ʿurūḍ fī fann al-ʿarūḍ*. Damascus: Maṭbaʿat Wilāyat Sūriyā, 1304/[1887].

Al-Jazāʾirī, Ṭāhir. *Tashīl al-majāz ilā fann al-muʿammā wa-l-alghāz*. Damascus: Maṭbaʿat Wilāyat Sūriyā, 1303/[1886].

Al-Jazāʾirī, Ṭāhir. *Tawjīh al-naẓar ilā uṣūl al-athar.* Cairo: al-Maṭbaʿa al-Jamāliyya, 1910.

Al-Jiddāwī, ʿAbd al-Munʿim. *Kuntu qubūriyyan.* Riyadh: Idārat al-Buḥūth al-ʿIlmiyya, 1981.

Al-Jīlānī, ʿAbd al-Qādir. *Futūḥ al-ghayb.* Cairo: Muṣṭafā al-Bābī al-Ḥalabī wa-awlāduh, 1967.

Al-Jindī, Anwar. *Aḥmad Zakī al-mulaqqab bi-shaykh al-ʿurūba: Ḥayātuhu, ārāʾuhu, āthāruh.* Cairo: al-Muʾassasa al-Miṣriyya al-ʿĀmma, 1964.

Al-Jurjānī, ʿAbd al-Qāhir. *Asrār al-balāgha.* [Edited by Muḥammad ʿAbduh and Muḥammad Maḥmūd al-Shinqīṭī al-Turkuzī.] Corrected by Rashīd Riḍā. Cairo: Maṭbaʿat al-Taraqqī, 1320/[1902].

Al-Jurjānī, ʿAbd al-Qāhir. *Asrār al-balāgha.* Edited by Maḥmūd Shākir. Jeddah: Dār al-Madanī, 1991.

Al-Jurjānī, ʿAbd al-Qāhir. *Dalāʾil al-iʿjāz.* [Edited by] Muḥammad ʿAbduh and Muḥammad Maḥmūd al-Shinqīṭī al-Turkuzī. Corrected by Rashīd Riḍā. Cairo: Maṭbaʿat al-Mawsūʿāt, 1321/[1903 or 1904].

Al-Jurjānī, ʿAbd al-Qāhir. *Dalāʾil al-iʿjāz.* Edited by Maḥmūd Shākir. Cairo: Maktabat al-Khānjī, 1984.

Al-Juwaynī, ʿAbd al-Malik. *Al-Kāfiya fī al-jadal.* Edited by Fawqiyya Maḥmūd. Cairo: Dār Iḥyāʾ al-Kutub al-ʿArabiyya, 1979.

Kaḥḥāla, ʿUmar Riḍā. *Muʿjam al-muʾallifīn.* 15 vols. Beirut: Dār Iḥyāʾ al-Turāth al-ʿArabī, 1957.

Karatay, Fehmi Edhem. *Topkapı Sarayı Müzesi Kütüphanesi Arapça Yazmalar Kataloğu.* 4 vols. Istanbul: Topkapı Sarayı Müzesi, 1962–69.

Karatay, Fehmi Edhem. *Topkapı Sarayı Müzesi Kütüphanesi Farsça Yazmalar Kataloğu.* Istanbul: Topkapı Sarayı Müzesi, 1961.

Karatay, Fehmi Edhem. *Topkapı Sarayı Müzesi Kütüphanesi Türkçe Yazmalar Kataloğu.* 2 vols. Istanbul: Topkapı Sarayı Müzesi, 1961.

Al-Karmalī, Anastās Mārī. Review of al-Nuwayrī's *Nihāya* (vol. 1), edited by Aḥmad Zakī. *Majallat Majmaʿ al-lugha al-ʿarabiyya fī Dimashq* 4, no. 5 (1924): 220–26.

Al-Kattānī, ʿAbd al-Ḥayy. *Ibn al-Nadīm wa-kitābuhu al-Fihrist.* Edited by Shawqī Binbīn. Tetouan: Jamʿiyyat al-Aʾimma al-Mālikiyya, 2013.

Al-Kawtharī, Muḥammad Zāhid. "Kalima fī al-iftāʾ" (1936). Reprinted in al-Kawtharī, *al-Ishfāq ʿalā aḥkām al-ṭalāq fī al-radd ʿalā "Niẓām al-ṭalāq" alladhī aṣdarahu al-ustādh Aḥmad Shākir al-qāḍī,* 93–100. Cairo: Maṭbaʿat Majallat al-Islām, n.d.

Al-Kawtharī, Muḥammad Zāhid. "Khuṭūrat al-qawl bi-l-jiha faḍlan ʿan al-qawl bi-l-tajsīm al-ṣarīḥ" (1942). Reprinted in al-Kawtharī, *Maqālāt al-Kawtharī,* 268–75.

Al-Kawtharī, Muḥammad Zāhid. *Maqālāt al-Kawtharī.* Cairo: al-Maktaba al-Tawfīqiyya, n.d.

Al-Kawtharī, Muḥammad Zāhid. *Muqaddimāt al-imām al-Kawtharī.* Damascus: Dār al-Thurayyā, 1997.

Al-Kawtharī, Muḥammad Zāhid. "Namādhij mimmā fī 'Naqḍ al-Dārimī' alladhī ubīḥa nashruh" (1942). Reprinted in al-Kawtharī, *Maqālāt al-Kawtharī,* 262–68.

Al-Kawtharī, Muḥammad Zāhid. *Rasāʾil al-imām Muḥammad Zāhid al-Kawtharī ilā al-ʿallāma Muḥammad Yūsuf al-Binnūrī.* Edited by Saʿūd al-Sarḥān. Amman: Dār al-Fatḥ, 2013.

Al-Kawtharī, Muḥammad Zāhid. *Taʾnīb al-khaṭīb.* Cairo: al-Anwār, 1942. Reprint, Cairo: al-Maktaba al-Azhariyya, 2006.

Kenny, Lorne M. "ʿAlī Mubārak: Nineteenth Century Egyptian Educator and Administrator." *Middle East Journal* 21, no. 1 (1967): 35–51.

Khan, Ahmad. "Islamic Tradition in an Age of Print: Editing, Printing and Publishing the Classical Heritage." In *Reclaiming Islamic Tradition: Modern Interpretations of the Classical Heritage*, edited by Elisabeth Kendall and Ahmad Khan, 52–99. Edinburgh: Edinburgh University Press, 2016.

Khān, Ṣiddīq Ḥasan. *Fatḥ al-ʿallām li-sharḥ Bulūgh al-marām*. Bulaq, 1302/[1885].

Khān, Ṣiddīq Ḥasan. *Ḥuṣūl al-maʾmūl min ʿilm al-uṣūl*. Istanbul: Maṭbaʿat al-Jawāʾib, 1288/[1872].

Khān, Ṣiddīq Ḥasan. *Qaṣd al-sabīl ilā dhamm al-kalām wa-l-taʾwīl*. Edited by Abū ʿAbd al-Raḥmān Maʿshāsha. Beirut: Dār Ibn Ḥazm, 2000.

Khān, Ṣiddīq Ḥasan. *Qurrat al-aʿyān wa-masarrat al-adhhān fī maʾāthir al-malik al-jalīl al-nawāb Muḥammad Ṣiddīq Ḥasan Khān*. Istanbul: Maṭbaʿat al-Jawāʾib, 1297/[1880].

Khān, Ṣiddīq Ḥasan. *Al-Tāj al-mukallal min jawāhir maʾāthir al-ṭirāz al-ākhir wa-l-awwal*. Qatar: Wizārat al-Awqāf wa-l-Shuʾūn al-Islāmiyya, 2007.

Khān, Ṣiddīq Ḥasan, and Aḥmad b. ʿĪsā. *Al-Rasāʾil al-mutabādala bayna al-shaykhayn Ṣiddīq Ḥasan Khān wa-Aḥmad b. ʿĪsā*. Edited by Sulaymān al-Khurāshī. Riyadh: Dār al-Tawḥīd, 2010.

Al-Khaṭīb, Muḥibb al-Dīn. "Faqīd al-ʿarabiyya wa-l-islām: Aḥmad Taymūr Pasha." *Al-Zahrāʾ* 5, nos. 7–8 (Rajab 1349/1930): 556–74.

Al-Khaṭīb, Muḥibb al-Dīn. "Ḥarakat al-nashr wa-l-taʾlīf: Kitāb al-Intiṣār fī al-radd ʿalā Ibn al-Rāwandī." *Al-Zahrāʾ* 2, no. 2 (Ṣafar 1344/1925): 124–26.

Al-Khaṭīb, Muḥibb al-Dīn. "Ḥarakat al-nashr wa-l-taʾlīf: Taṣḥīḥ al-Qāmūs." *Al-Zahrāʾ* 1, no. 6 (Jumādā al-Ākhira 1343/1924): 402–3.

Al-Khayyāṭ, ʿAbd al-Raḥīm. *Kitāb al-Intiṣār wa-l-radd ʿalā al-Rāwandī al-mulḥid*. Edited by Henrik Samuel Nyberg. Cairo: Maṭbaʿat Dār al-Kutub al-Miṣriyya, 1925.

Al-Khuḍayrī, Maḥmūd Muḥammad [M. M. Kh., pseud.]. "Raʾī al-ustādh Margoliouth fī al-shiʿr al-jāhilī." *Al-Zahrāʾ* 4, no. 10 (Dhū al-Ḥijja 1346/1928): 618–30.

Khuwayyī, Abū Yaʿqūb. *Sharḥ al-tanwīr ʿalā Saqt al-zand*. Corrected by Ibrāhīm al-Disūqī. Bulaq for Jamʿiyyat al-Maʿārif, 1286/[1869].

Kilpatrick, Hilary. *Making the Great Book of Songs: Compilation and the Author's Craft in Abū l-Faraj al-Iṣbahānī's "Kitāb al-Aghānī."* London: RoutledgeCurzon, 2003.

Klemm, Verena, ed. *Refaiya 1853: Buchkultur in Damaskus*. Leipzig: Universitätsbibliothek Leipzig, 2013.

Knysh, Alexander. *Ibn ʿArabi in the Later Islamic Tradition: The Making of a Polemical Image in Medieval Islam*. Albany: State University of New York Press, 1999.

Krachkovsky, Ignaty. *Maʿ al-makhṭūṭāṭ*. Translated from Russian by Muḥammad Munīr Mursī. Cairo: Dār al-Nahḍa al-ʿArabiyya, 1969.

Krawulsky, Dorothea. "Masālik al-abṣār fī mamālik al-amṣār li-Ibn Faḍl Allāh al-ʿUmarī (700–749 h./1301–1349 m.): Muḥāwala fī sīra tārīkhiyya li-makhṭūṭātih." *Dirāsāt*, series A, *al-ʿUlūm al-insāniyya* (al-Jāmiʿa al-Urdunniyya) 17, no. 2 (1990): 169–85.

Kruk, Remke. *The Warrior Women of Islam: Female Empowerment in Arabic Popular Literature*. London: I. B. Tauris, 2014.

Al-Kulaynī, Muḥammad b. Yaʿqūb. *Uṣūl al-Kāfī*. Beirut: Dār al-Murtaḍā, 2005.

Al-Kūrānī, Ibrāhīm. *Kitāb al-ʿAyn wa-l-athar fī ʿaqāʾid ahl al-athar*. Manuscript. Cairo: al-Azhar Library, no shelf mark.

Kurd ʿAlī, Muḥammad. "Aṣl al-Muʿtazila." In *al-Qadīm wa-l-ḥadīth*, 148–56. Cairo: al-Maṭbaʿa al-Raḥmāniyya, 1925.
Kurd ʿAlī, Muḥammad. *Khiṭaṭ al-Shām*. 6 vols. Damascus: Maktabat al-Nūrī, 1983.
Kurd ʿAlī, Muḥammad. "Al-Khizāna al-Zakiyya." *Al-Muqtabas* 7, no. 8 (1912): 739–51.
Kurd ʿAlī, Muḥammad. *Kunūz al-ajdād*. Damascus: Maṭbaʿat al-Taraqqī, 1950.
Kurd ʿAlī, Muḥammad. *Al-Mudhakkirāt*. 4 vols. Damascus: Maṭbaʿat al-Taraqqī, 1367/[1948].
Kurd ʿAlī, Muḥammad. "Al-Muʿtazila." *Al-Muqtabas* 3, no. 3 (1908): 240–66.
Al-Kurdī, Muḥammad Amīn. *Kitāb Tanwīr al-qulūb fī muʿāmalat ʿallām al-ghuyūb*. Aleppo: Dār al-Qalam al-ʿArabī, 1991.
Al-Kurdī, Muḥammad b. Sulaymān. *Al-Fawāʾid al-madaniyya fī man yuftā bi-qawlihi min aʾimmat al-Shāfiʿiyya*. Edited by Bassām al-Jabābī. Damascus: Dār Nūr al-Ṣabāḥ, 2011.
Lachmann, Karl. *Kleinere Schriften*. 2 vols. in 1. Berlin: G. Reimer, 1876.
Landberg, Carlo. *Catalogue de manuscrits arabes provenant d'une bibliothèque privée à el-Medîna et appartenant à la maison E. J. Brill*. Leiden: Brill, 1883.
Lane, Edward. *Manners and Customs of the Modern Egyptians*. London: Ward, Lock and Co., 1890.
Al-Laqqānī, Ibrāhīm. *Hidāyat al-murīd li-Jawharat al-tawḥīd*. Edited by Muḥammad al-Khaṭīb. Beirut: Dār al-Kutub al-ʿIlmiyya, 2012.
Al-Laqqānī, Ibrāhīm. *Jawharat al-tawḥīd*. Bulaq, 1241/[1825].
Larsson, Göran. "H. S. Nyberg's Encounter with Egypt and the Muʿtazilī School of Thought." *Philological Encounters* 3, nos. 1–2 (2018): 167–92.
Lauzière, Henri. "The Construction of Salafiyya: Reconsidering Salafism from the Perspective of Conceptual History." *International Journal of Middle East Studies* 42, no. 3 (2010): 369–89.
Lauzière, Henri. *The Making of Salafism: Islamic Reform in the Twentieth Century*. New York: Columbia University Press, 2015.
Lauzière, Henri. "Rejoinder: What We Mean versus What They Meant by 'Salafi': A Reply to Frank Griffel." *Die Welt des Islams* 56, no. 1 (2016): 89–96.
Lawḥ, Muḥammad. *Taqdīs al-ashkhāṣ fī al-fikr al-ṣūfī*. 2 vols. Cairo: Dār Ibn ʿAffān/ Dammam: Dār Ibn al-Qayyim, 2002.
Lewis, Bernard. *The Emergence of Modern Turkey*. 2nd ed. London: Oxford University Press, 1968.
Liebrenz, Boris. "The Library of Aḥmad al-Rabbāṭ: Books and Their Audience in 12th to 13th/18th to 19th Century Syria." In *Marginal Perspectives on Early Modern Ottoman Culture: Missionaries, Travellers, Booksellers*, edited by Ralf Elger und Ute Pietruschka, 17–59. Halle (Saale): Zentrum für Interdisziplinäre Regionalstudien, 2013.
Liebrenz, Boris. "Die Rifāʿīya." In *Das Buch in Mittelalter, Antike und Neuzeit: Sonderbestände der Universitätsbibliothek Leipzig*, edited by Thomas Fuchs, Christoph Mackert, and Reinhold Scholl, 265–79. Wiesbaden: Harrassowitz, 2012.
Maas, Paul. *Textkritik*. Leipzig: G. B. Teubner, 1927.
Madelung, Wilferd. "ʿAbd-al-Jabbār b. Aḥmad." In *Encyclopaedia Iranica*, online edition. Last updated July 14, 2011. http://www.iranicaonline.org/articles/abd-al-jabbar-b-ahmad.
Maden, Şükrü. "Tefsirde Şerh Hâşiye ve Ta'lîka Literatürü." *Tarih Kültür ve Sanat Araştırmaları Dergisi* 3, no. 1 (2014): 183–220.

Madkour, Ibrahim. "Past, Present, and Future." In *The Genius of Arab Civilization: Source of Renaissance*, edited by John S. Badeau and John R. Hayes, 215–18. New York: New York University Press, 1975.

Mahdi, Muhsin. "From the Manuscript Age to the Age of Printed Books." In *The Book in the Islamic World: The Written Word and Communication in the Middle East*, edited by George Atiyeh, 1–15. Albany: State University of New York Press, 1995. Reprinted in *The History of the Book in the Middle East*, edited by Geoffrey Roper, 127–42. London: Routledge, 2016.

Al-Mahdī al-ʿAbbāsī, Muḥammad. *Al-Fatāwā al-Mahdiyya fī al-waqāʾiʿ al-miṣriyya*. 7 vols. Cairo: al-Maṭbaʿa al-Azhariyya, 1301–4/[1883–87].

Al-Majdī, Ṣāliḥ. *Ḥilyat al-zamān bi-manāqib khādim al-waṭan: Sīrat Rifāʿa Rāfiʿ al-Ṭahṭāwī*. Cairo: Maktabat Muṣṭafā al-Bābī al-Ḥalabī, 1958.

Majmūʿ al-mutūn. Bulaq, 1274/[1858].

Majmūʿ mutūn uṣūliyya. [Edited by] Jamāl al-Dīn al-Qāsimī. Damascus: al-Maktaba al-Hāshimiyya, 1324/[1906].

Majmūʿ rasāʾil fī uṣūl al-fiqh. [Edited by] Jamāl al-Dīn al-Qāsimī. Beirut: al-Maṭbaʿa al-Ahliyya, 1324/[1906].

Majmūʿ rasāʾil fī uṣūl al-tafsīr wa-uṣūl al-fiqh. [Edited by] Jamāl al-Dīn al-Qāsimī. Damascus: Maṭbaʿat al-Fayḥāʾ, 1331/[1913].

Al-Maktaba al-Azhariyya: Fihris al-kutub al-mawjūda bi-l-Maktaba al-Azhariyya ilā sanat 1364/1945. Edited by Abū al-Wafāʾ al-Marāghī. 8 vols. Cairo: Maṭbaʿat al-Azhar, 1946–52.

Mālik b. Anas. *Hādhā Muwaṭṭaʾ al-imām Mālik b. Anas b. Mālik b. Abī ʿĀmir al-Aḥaḥī*. Corrected by Muṣṭafā ʿIzz al-Shāfiʿī al-Azharī. Cairo: Maṭbaʿat al-Ḥajar, 1280/[1864].

Malti-Douglas, Fedwa. *Blindness and Autobiography: "Al-Ayyam" of Ṭāhā Ḥusayn*. Princeton, NJ: Princeton University Press, 1988.

Al-Manfalūṭī, Muṣṭafā Luṭfī. *Al-Naẓarāt*. 3 vols. Beirut: Dār al-Kutub al-ʿIlmiyya, 2013.

Al-Manīnī, Aḥmad b. ʿAlī. *Sharḥ al-Yamīnī al-musammā bi-l-Fatḥ al-Wahbī ʿalā Tārīkh Abī Naṣr al-ʿUtbī*. Corrected by Muṣṭafā Wahbī. 2 vols. Cairo: al-Maṭbaʾa al-Wahbiyya for Jamʿiyyat al-Maʿārif, 1286/[1870].

Al-Maqrīzī, Taqī al-Dīn Aḥmad. *Al-Khiṭaṭ = al-Mawāʿiz wa-l-iʿtibār fī dhikr al-khiṭaṭ wa-l-āthār*. Corrected by Muḥammad Quṭṭa al-ʿAdawī. 2 vols. Bulaq, 1270/[1853].

Al-Marʿashlī, Yūsuf. *Nathr al-jawāhir wa-l-durar fī ʿulamāʾ al-qarn al-rābiʿ ashar*. 2 vols. Beirut: Dār al-Maʿrifa, 2006.

Marcel, Jean-Joseph, ed. and trans. *Fables de Loqman surnommé Le Sage: Edition arabe, accompagnée d'une traduction française, et précédée d'une notice sur ce célèbre fabuliste*. Cairo: Imprimerie nationale, 1799.

Margoliouth, David Samuel. "The Origins of Arabic Poetry." *Journal of the Royal Asiatic Society of Great Britain and Ireland*, n.s., 57, no. 3 (1925): 417–49.

Al-Marṣafī, Sayyid b. ʿAlī. *Asrār al-Ḥamāsa*. Vol. 1. Cairo: Maṭbaʿat Abī al-Hūl, 1912.

Al-Marṣafī, Sayyid b. ʿAlī. *Raghbat al-āmil sharḥ al-Kāmil*. 8 vols. Cairo: Maṭbaʿat al-Nahḍa, 1927.

Maʿrūf, Bashshār ʿAwwād. *Fī taḥqīq al-naṣṣ: Anẓār taṭbīqiyya naqdiyya fī manāhij taḥqīq al-makhṭūṭāt al-ʿarabiyya*. Beirut: Dār al-Gharb al-Islāmī, 2009.

Marx, Michael J., and Tobias J. Jocham. "Zu den Datierungen von Koranhandschriften durch die ^{14}C-Methode." *Frankfurter Zeitschrift für islamisch-theologische Studien* 2 (2015): 9–43.

Maṣrī, Maḥmūd. "Al-Maktaba al-waqfiyya fī Ḥalab bayna ʿarāqat al-māḍī wa-taṭalluʿāt al-mustaqbal." Paper presented at the conference "Dūr al-maktabāt wa-l-tawthīq fī al-thaqāfa al-islāmiyya," Aleppo, July 5–6, 2006.

Al-Māturīdī, Abū Manṣūr. *Taʾwīlāt ahl al-sunna*. Edited by Ibrāhīm ʿAwdayn. Cairo: Majlis al-Shuʾūn al-Islāmiyya, 1971.

Al-Māturīdī, Abū Manṣūr. *Taʾwīlāt ahl al-sunna*. Edited by Muḥammad Mustafīd Raḥmān. Dacca: al-Muʾassasa al-Islāmiyya Banghladish, 1982.

Al-Māturīdī, Abū Manṣūr. *Taʾwīlāt ahl al-sunna*. Edited by Fāṭima al-Khaymī. 5 vols. Beirut: Muʾassasat al-Risāla, 2004.

Al-Māturīdī, Abū Manṣūr. *Taʾwīlāt al-Qurʾān*. Edited by Bekir Topaloğlu, Ahmet Vanlıoğlu, Murteza Bedir, Mustafa Yavuz, Ali Haydar Ulusoy, Murat Sülün, Hatice Boynukalın, et al. 18 vols. Istanbul: Dār al-Mīzān, 2005–11.

Al-Maydānī, ʿAbd al-Ghanī al-Ghunaymī. *Al-Lubāb fī sharḥ al-Kitāb*. Edited by Sāʾid Bakdāsh. 6 vols. Beirut: Dār al-Bashāʾir al-Islāmiyya, 2014.

Al-Maydānī, ʿAbd al-Ghanī al-Ghunaymī. *Sharḥ al-ʿaqīda al-Ṭahawiyya: Al-musammā Bayān al-sunna wa-l-jamāʿa li-Abī Jaʿfar al-Ṭaḥāwī al-Ḥanafī*. Edited by Muḥammad Muṭīʿ Ḥāfiẓ and Muḥammad Riyāḍ Māliḥ. Damascus: Dār al-Fikr, 1982.

Al-Māzinī, Ibrāhīm ʿAbd al-Qādir. "Ṭāhā Ḥusayn fī mīzān al-tashkīk: Taḥqīq shakhṣiyyatihi bi-ṭarīqih." *Al-Zahrāʾ* 2, no. 10 (Shawwāl 1344/1926): 612–17.

McCarthy, Justin A. "Nineteenth-Century Egyptian Population." *Middle Eastern Studies* 12, no. 3 (1976): 1–39.

McLuhan, Marshall. *The Gutenberg Galaxy: The Making of Typographic Man*. Toronto: University of Toronto Press, 1962.

Meier, Fritz. "Zum Vorrang des Glaubens und des guten Denkens vor dem Wahrheitseifer bei den Muslimen." *Oriens* 32 (1990): 1–49.

Melvin-Koushki, Matthew. "Persianate Geomancy from Ṭūsī to the Millennium: A Preliminary Survey." In *The Occult Sciences in Premodern Islamic Cultures*, edited by Nader El-Bizri and Eva Orthmann, 151–99. Beirut: Orient-Institut Beirut, 2018.

Messick, Brinkley. "On the Question of Lithography." *Culture and History* 16 (1997): 158–76. Reprinted in *The History of the Book in the Middle East*, edited by Geoffrey Roper, 277–98. London: Routledge, 2016.

Mestyan, Adam. "Ignác Goldziher's Report on the Books Brought from the Orient for the Hungarian Academy of Sciences." *Journal of Semitic Studies* 60, no. 2 (2015): 443–80.

Metcalf, Barbara. *Islamic Revival in British India: Deoband, 1860–1900*. Princeton, NJ: Princeton University Press, 1982.

Michot, Yahya. *Against Smoking: An Ottoman Manifesto*. Oxford: Interface Publications, 2010.

Michot, Yahya. *L'opium et le café: Édition et traduction d'un texte arabe anonyme précédées d'une première exploration de l'opiophagie Ottomane et accompagnées d'une anthologie*. Beirut: Albouraq, 2008.

Midḥat, ʿAlī Ḥaydar. *The Life of Midhat Pasha: A Record of His Services, Political Reforms, Banishment, and Judicial Murder; Derived from Private Documents and Reminiscences . . . with Portraits*. London: John Murray, 1903.

Miskawayh [Ibn Miskawayh]. *Al-Fawz al-aṣghar*. Beirut: n.p., 1319/[1901].

Miskawayh [Ibn Miskawayh]. *Tahdhīb al-akhlāq wa-taṭhīr al-aʿrāq*. Cairo: Maṭbaʿat al-Waṭan, 1298/[1881].

Mitchell, Timothy. *Colonising Egypt*. Cambridge: Cambridge University Press, 1988.
Monroe, James T. "Oral Composition in Pre-Islamic Poetry." *Journal of Arabic Literature* 3 (1972): 1–53.
Morewedge, Parviz. "The Neoplatonic Structure of Some Islamic Mystical Doctrines." In *Neoplatonism and Islamic Thought*, edited by Parviz Morewedge, 51–76. Albany: State University of New York Press, 1992.
Moritz, Bernhard, ed. *Arabic Palaeography: A Collection of Arabic Texts from the First Century of the Hidjra till the Year 1000*. Cairo: Khedival Library, 1905.
Al-Muʿallimī, ʿAbd al-Raḥmān. *Āthār al-shaykh al-ʿallāma ʿAbd al-Raḥmān b. Yaḥyā al-Muʿallimī*. Edited by ʿAlī al-ʿUmrānī, Nabīl b. Naṣṣār al-Sanadī, Muḥammad Ajmal al-Iṣlāḥī, et al. 25 vols. Mecca: Dār ʿĀlam al-Fawāʾid, 2013.
Al-Muʿallimī, ʿAbd al-Raḥmān. *Majmūʿ rasāʾil fī al-taḥqīq wa-taṣḥīḥ al-nuṣūṣ*. Edited by Muḥammad Ajmal al-Iṣlāḥī. Vol. 23 of al-Muʿallimī, *Āthār al-shaykh al-ʿallāma al-Muʿallimī*.
Mubārak, ʿAlī. *ʿAlam al-Dīn*. 4 vols. Alexandria: Maṭbaʿat Jarīdat al-Maḥrūsa, 1886.
Mubārak, ʿAlī. *Al-Khiṭaṭ al-Tawfīqiyya*. 20 vols. in 5. Bulaq, 1304–6/[1887–89].
Mufti, Aamir. *Forget English! Orientalisms and World Literatures*. Cambridge, MA: Harvard University Press, 2016.
Muhanna, Elias. "Encyclopaedism in the Mamluk Period: The Composition of Shihāb al-Dīn al-Nuwayrī's (d. 1333) *Nihāyat al-arab fī funūn al-adab*." PhD diss., Harvard University, 2012.
Muhanna, Elias. *The World in a Book: Al-Nuwayri and the Islamic Encyclopedic Tradition*. Princeton, NJ: Princeton University Press, 2017.
Al-Muḥibbī, Muḥammad Amīn b. Faḍl Allāh. *Khulāṣat al-athar*. 4 vols. Beirut: Dār Ṣādir, 1966.
Muḥyī al-Dīn, Ḥāzim. *Al-Shaykh Ṭāhir al-Jazāʾirī: Rāʾid al-tajdīd al-dīnī fī bilād al-Shām fī al-ʿaṣr al-ḥadīth*. Damascus: Dār al-Qalam, 2001.
Müller, August. "Heinrich Leberecht Fleischer." *Beiträge zur Kunde der indogermanischen Sprachen* 15, nos. 1–2 (1889): 319–37.
Müller, August. "Ueber Ibn Abi Oçeibiʿa und seine Geschichte der Aertze." In *Actes du sixième congrès international des orientalistes, tenu en 1883 à Leide*, 2:259–80. Leiden: Brill, 1885.
Müller, Marcus Joseph. *Theologie und Philosophie von Averroes*. Munich: Königlich Bayerische Akademie der Wissenschaften, 1859.
Al-Munajjid, Ṣalāḥ al-Dīn. "Qawāʿid taḥqīq al-makhṭūṭāt." *Majallat Maʿhad al-makhṭūṭāt al-ʿarabiyya* 1, no. 2 (1955): 317–37.
Al-Munajjid, Ṣalāḥ al-Dīn. *Qawāʿid taḥqīq al-makhṭūṭāt*. 4th ed. Cairo: Dār al-Kitāb al-Jadīd, 1982.
Munīr Āghā al-Dimashqī, Muḥammad. *Namūdhaj min al-aʿmāl al-khayriyya fī idārat al-ibāʿa al-Munīriyya*. Riyadh: Maktabat al-Imām al-Shāfiʿī, 1988.
Al-Murādī, Muḥammad Khalīl. *Silk al-durar fī aʿyān al-qarn al-thānī ʿashar*. 4 vols. Bulaq, 1291–1301/[1874–83].
Al-Muzanī, Ismāʿīl b. Yaḥyā. *Mukhtaṣar al-Muzanī*. Manuscript. Cairo: Dār al-Kutub al-Miṣriyya, Fiqh Shāfiʿī 242.
Al-Nabhānī, Yūsuf. *Shawāhid al-ḥaqq fī al-istighātha bi-sayyid al-khalq*. Cairo: al-Maṭbaʿa al-Maymaniyya, 1323/[1906].

Al-Nābulsī, ʿAbd al-Ghanī. "Īḍāḥ al-maqṣūd fī maʿnā waḥdat al-wujūd." Edited by Rāʾid al-Ṭāʾī and Walīd al-ʿAbīdī. *Majallat al-tarbiyya wa-l-ʿilm* 15, no. 4 (2008): 255–73.

Al-Nābulsī, ʿAbd al-Ghanī. *Kashf al-nūr ʿan aṣḥāb al-qubūr.* Istanbul: Hakikat Kitabevi, 1987.

Nāfiʿ, ʿAbd al-Ḥamīd. *Dhayl Khiṭaṭ al-Maqrīzī.* Cairo: Maktabat al-Dār al-ʿArabiyya li-l-Kitāb, 2006.

Nafi, Basheer M. "Abu al-Thana' al-Alusi: An Alim, Ottoman Mufti, and Exegete of the Qur'an." *International Journal of Middle East Studies* 34, no. 3 (2002): 465–94.

Nafi, Basheer M. "Salafism Revived: Nuʿmān al-Ālūsī and the Trial of the Two Aḥmads." *Die Welt des Islams* 49, no. 1 (2009): 49–97.

Nāmī, Khalīl Yaḥyā. *Al-Baʿtha al-miṣriyya li-taṣwīr al-makhṭūṭāt al-ʿarabiyya fī bilād al-Yaman.* Cairo: Wizārat al-Maʿārif al-ʿUmūmiyya, 1952.

Al-Nasafī, Abū Ḥafṣ ʿUmar. *Al-ʿAqāʾid al-Nasafiyya.* In *Majmūʿ min muhimmāt al-mutūn al-mustaʿmala min ghālib khawāṣṣ al-funūn,* 19–23. Cairo: al-Maṭbaʿa al-ʿIlmiyya, 1313/[1895 or 1896].

Al-Nashshār, al-Sayyid. *Tārīkh al-maktabāt fī Miṣr: Al-ʿAṣr al-mamlūkī.* Beirut: al-Dār al-Miṣriyya al-Lubnāniyya, 1993.

Nasiri-Moghaddam, Nader. "Schefer, Charles-Henri-Auguste." In *Encyclopaedia Iranica,* online edition. Last updated July 15, 2009. http://www.iranicaonline.org/articles/schefer-charles-henri-auguste.

Al-Nawawī, Muḥyī al-Dīn. *Minhaj et Talibin: A Manual of Muhammadan Law according to the School of Shafii.* Translated into English from the French edition of Lodewijk W. C. van den Berg by Edward C. C. Howard. London: W. Thacker, 1914.

Necipoğlu, Gülru. "The Spatial Organization of Knowledge in the Ottoman Palace Library: An Encyclopedic Collection and Its Inventory." In Necipoğlu, Kafadar, and Fleischer, *Treasures of Knowledge,* 1:1–77.

Necipoğlu, Gülru, Cemal Kafadar, and Cornell H. Fleischer, eds. *Treasures of Knowledge: An Inventory of the Ottoman Palace Library (1502/3–1503/4).* 2 vols. Leiden: Brill, 2019.

Nemoy, Leon. *Arabic Manuscripts in the Yale University Library.* New Haven, CT: Yale University Library, 1956.

Nietzsche, Friedrich. "Vom Nutzen und Nachteil der Historie für das Leben." In *Die Geburt der Tragödie, Unzeitgemäße Betrachtungen I–IV, und Nachgelassene Schriften 1870–1873,* edited by Giorgio Colli and Mazzino Montinari, 243–334. Munich: Deutscher Taschenbuch Verlag, 1988.

Noth, Albrecht. "Minderheiten als Vertragspartner im Disput mit dem Islamischen Gesetz: Die 'Nachkommen der Juden von Ḫaibar' und die Ǧizya." In *Studien zur Geschichte und Kultur des Vorderen Orients: Festschrift für Bertold Spuler zum siebzigsten Geburtstag,* edited by Hans Robert Roemer und Albrecht Noth, 289–309. Leiden: Brill, 1981.

Noy, Avigail. "The Emergence of *ʿIlm al-Bayān*: Classical Arabic Literary Theory in the Arabic East in the 7th/13th Century." PhD diss., Harvard University, 2016.

Noy, Avigail. "The Legacy of ʿAbd al-Qāhir al-Jurjānī in the Arabic East before al-Qazwīnī's *Talkhīṣ al-Miftāḥ.*" *Journal of Abbasid Studies* 5, nos. 1–2 (2018): 11–57.

Al-Nuʿmānī, Shiblī. *Riḥlat Shiblī al-Nuʿmānī.* Translated from Urdu by Muḥammad Akram al-Nadwī. Damascus: Dār al-Qalam, 2011.

Nuṣayr, ʿĀyida Ibrāhīm. *Ḥarakat nashr al-kutub fī Miṣr fī al-qarn al-tāsiʿ ʿashar.* [Cairo]: al-Hayʾa al-Miṣriyya al-ʿĀmma li-l-Kitāb, 1994.

Al-Nuwayrī, Shihāb al-Dīn Aḥmad b. ʿAbd al-Wahhāb. *Nihāyat al-arab fī funūn al-adab.* Edited by Aḥmad Zakī Pasha et al. 33 vols. Cairo: al-Muʾassasa al-Miṣriyya al-ʿĀmma li-l-Taʾlīf wa-l-Tarjama wa-l-Ṭibāʿa wa-l-Nashr, 1923–97.

Nyberg, H. S. "Bemerkungen zum 'Buch der Götzenbilder' von Ibn al-Kalbi." In *Δραγμα: Martino P. Nilsson A.D. IV id. iul. MCMXXXIX dedicatum*, 346–66. Lund: Ohlsson, 1939.

O'Fahey, Rex S. *Enigmatic Saint: Ahmad Ibn Idris and the Idrisi Tradition.* Evanston, IL: Northwestern University Press, 1990.

Ong, Walter J. *Orality and Literacy: The Technologizing of the Word.* London: Methuen, 1982.

Owen, Roger. *The Middle East in the World Economy, 1800–1914.* London: Methuen, 1981.

Özgüdenli, Osman G. "Persian Manuscripts i. In Ottoman and Modern Turkish Libraries." In *Encyclopaedia Iranica*, online edition. Last updated July 20, 2005. http://www.iranicaonline.org/articles/persian-manuscripts-1-ottoman.

Parker, David C. *Codex Sinaiticus: The Story of the World's Oldest Bible.* London: British Library, 2010.

Patel, Abdulrazzak. *The Arab* Nahḍah*: The Making of the Intellectual and Humanist Movement.* Edinburgh: Edinburgh: Edinburgh University Press, 2015.

Paton, Andrew Archibald. *A History of the Egyptian Revolution, from the Period of the Mamelukes to the Death of Mohammed Ali.* London: Trübner, 1870.

Paton, Andrew Archibald. *Modern Syrians; or Native Society in Damascus, Aleppo, and the Mountains of the Druses.* London: Longman, Brown, Green and Longmans, 1844.

Pedersen, Johannes. *The Arabic Book.* Translated by Geoffrey French. Princeton, NJ: Princeton University Press, 1984. Originally published as *Den arabiske bog* (Copenhagen: Fischer, 1946).

Pellat, Charles. "Al-Jāḥiẓ." In *ʿAbbasid Belles-Lettres*, edited by Julia Ashtiany et al., 78–95. Cambridge: Cambridge University Press, 2012.

Pertsch, Wilhelm. *Die orientalischen Handschriften der herzoglichen Bibliothek zu Gotha.* 8 vols. Vienna: Kaiserlich-Königliche Hof- und Staatsdruckerei, 1864.

Peters, Rudolph. "Muḥammad al-ʿAbbās al-Mahdī (d. 1897), Grand Mufti of Egypt and His *al-Fatāwā al-Mahdiyya.*" *Islamic Law and Society* 1, no. 1 (1994): 66–82.

Pomerantz, Maurice, and Bilal Orfali. "Maqāmāt Badīʿ al-Zamān al-Hamadhānī: Al-Naṣṣ wa-l-makhṭūṭāt wa-l-tārīkh." *Ostour*, January 2015, 38–55.

Preckel, Claudia. "Islamische Bildungsnetzwerke und Gelehrtenkultur im Indien des 19. Jahrhunderts: Muhammad Ṣiddīq Ḥasan Ḫān (st. 1890) und die Entstehung der Ahl-e ḥadīṯ-Bewegung in Bhopal." PhD diss., Ruhr-Universität Bochum, 2005.

Al-Qāḍī, Wadād. "An Early Fāṭimid Political Document." *Studia Islamica*, no. 48 (1978): 71–108.

Al-Qāḍī Nuʿmān. *Risālat iftitāḥ al-daʿwa.* Edited by Wadād al-Qāḍī. Beirut: Dār al-Thaqāfa, 1970.

Al-Qālī, Abū ʿAlī. *Al-Amālī.* Corrected by Ṭāhā b. Maḥmūd Qaṭriyya. 3 vols. Bulaq, 1324/[1906].

Qāsim, Ḥasan. "Al-Sayyida Zaynab: Wa-hal dufinat fī Miṣr?" *Al-Islām*, December 17, 1932, 14–16.

Al-Qāsimī, Jamāl al-Dīn. *Kitāb Tārīkh al-Jahmiyya wa-l-Muʿtazila*. Cairo: Maṭbaʿat al-Manār, 1331/[1913].

Al-Qāsimī, Jamāl al-Dīn. *Mawʿiẓat al-muʾminīn min Iḥyāʾ ʿulūm al-dīn*. Cairo: al-Maktaba al-Tijāriyya al-Kubrā, 1323/[1905].

Al-Qāsimī, Jamāl al-Dīn. *Tārīkh al-Jahmiyya wa-l-Muʿtazila*. Beirut: Muʾassasat al-Risāla, 1979.

Al-Qāsimī, Ẓāfir. *Jamāl al-Dīn al-Qāsimī wa-ʿaṣruh*. Damascus: Maktabat Aṭlas, 1965.

Al-Qasṭalānī, Shihāb al-Dīn. *Irshād al-sārī ilā sharḥ Ṣaḥīḥ al-Bukhārī*. Published together with Muḥyī al-Dīn al-Nawawī's *Sharḥ Ṣaḥīḥ Muslim*. 10 vols. Bulaq, 1267/[1850].

Qāwuqjī, Muḥammad b. Khalīl. *Hādhihi Istighātha tataḍammanu al-tawassul bi-l-anbiyāʾ al-kirām wa-awliyāʾ Allāh al-ʿiẓām wa-mashāyikh wālidinā*. Shibbin al-Kum: al-Maṭbaʿa al-Naṣriyya, 1323/[1905].

Al-Qazwīnī, Jalāl al-Dīn. *Talkhīṣ al-Miftāḥ*. Published together with al-Taftāzānī's *Mukhtaṣar al-maʿānī*. Calcutta: n.p., 1228/[1813].

Qiṣṣat Sayyidnā Muʿādh. Cairo: Muḥammad Ghazzī al-Nakhkhāl, 1275/[1859]. Cairo: al-Maṭbaʿa al-Kastaliyya, 1277/[1861].

Quatremère, Étienne Marc. "Mémoire sur le goût des livres chez les Orientaux." *Journal Asiatique*, 3rd ser., no. 6 (July 1838): 35–78.

Quṭb, Sayyid. *Ṭifl min al-qariya*. Beirut: Dār al-Shurūq, 1973.

Al-Rāfiʿī, ʿAbd al-Raḥmān. *ʿAṣr Ismāʿīl*. 2 vols. Cairo: Dār al-Maʿārif, 1987.

Al-Rāghib al-Iṣfahānī. *Tafṣīl al-nashʾatayn wa-taḥṣīl al-saʿādatayn*. [Edited by] Ṭāhir al-Jazāʾirī. Beirut: n.p., 1319/[1901 or 1902].

Ragıp Pasha. *Dīwān Rāghib*. Bulaq, 1253/[1837].

Ragıp Pasha. *Safīnat al-Rāghib wa-dafīnat al-maṭālib*. Bulaq, 1255/[1840].

Rahman, Fazlur. *Islam and Modernity: Transformation of an Intellectual Tradition*. Chicago: University of Chicago Press, 1982.

Al-Ramlī, Shams al-Dīn. *Nihāyat al-muḥtāj ilā sharḥ al-Minhāj wa-maʿahu ḥāshiyat al-Shabrāmallisī wa-ḥāshiyat al-Maghribī al-Rashīdī*. 8 vols. Beirut: Dār al-Kutub al-ʿIlmiyya, 2003.

Rapoport, Yossef. "Ibn Taymiyya on Divorce Oaths." In *The Mamluks in Egyptian and Syrian Politics and Society*, edited by Michael Winter and Amalia Levanoni, 191–217. Leiden: Brill, 2004.

Rappe, Sara. *Reading Neoplatonism: Non-discursive Thinking in the Texts of Plotinus, Proclus, and Damascius*. Cambridge: Cambridge University Press, 2000.

Al-Rasāʾil al-mutabādala bayna shaykh al-ʿurūba Aḥmad Zakī Bāshā wa-l-Ab Anastās Mārī al-Karmalī. In *Rasāʾil al-Rāfiʿī* [separate pagination]. N.p.: Dār al-ʿUmriyya, n.d.

Raʾūf, ʿImād ʿAbd al-Salām. *Maṭbaʿat Kurdistān al-ʿilmiyya: Tārīkhuhā wa-maṭbūʿātuhā*. 2013. http://www.alukah.net/library/0/49220/.

Raymond, André. "The Khâlidiyya Library in Jerusalem: 1900–2000." *MELA Notes*, nos. 71–72 (2000–2001): 1–7.

Al-Rāzī, Fakhr al-Dīn. *Asās al-taqdīs*. Cairo: Maṭbaʿat Kurdistān al-ʿIlmiyya, 1328/[1910].

Al-Rāzī, Fakhr al-Dīn. *Mafātīḥ al-ghayb*. 6 vols. Bulaq, 1278/[1862].

Rebhan, Helga, ed. *Die Wunder der Schöpfung: Handschriften der Bayerischen Staatsbibliothek aus dem islamischen Kulturkreis*. Wiesbaden: Harrassowitz, 2010.

Reichmuth, Stefan. "Islamic Reformist Discourse in the Tulip Period (1718–30): Ibrahim Müteferriqa and His Arguments for Printing." In *International Congress on*

Learning and Education in the Ottoman World, Istanbul, 12–15 April 1999, edited by Ali Caksu, 149–61. Istanbul: IRCICA, 2001. Reprinted in *The History of the Book in the Middle East*, edited by Geoffrey Roper, 201–13. London: Routledge, 2016.

Reichmuth, Stefan. *The World of Murtaḍā al-Zabīdī (1732–91): Life, Networks and Writings*. N.p.: Gibb Memorial Trust, 2009.

Reid, Donald M. *The Odyssey of Faraḥ Anṭūn: A Syrian Christian's Quest for Secularism*. Minneapolis: Bibliotheca Islamica, 1975.

Reid, Donald M. *Whose Pharaohs? Archaeology, Museums, and Egyptian National Identity from Napoleon to World War I*. Berkeley: University of California Press, 2002.

Riḍā, Rashīd. *Al-Manār wa-l-Azhar*. Cairo: Maṭbaʿat al-Manār, 1352/[1934].

Riḍā, Rashīd. "Mashrūʿ Iḥyāʾ al-ādāb al-ʿarabiyya." *Al-Manār* 13, no. 12 (1911): 908–12.

Riḍā, Rashīd. "Maʾthara jalīla." *Al-Manār* 1, no. 25 (1895): 481–83.

Riḍā, Rashīd. *Tārīkh al-ustādh al-imām al-shaykh Muḥammad ʿAbduh*. 3 vols. Cairo: Dār al-Manār, 1324–50/[1907–31]. Reprint, Cairo: Dār al-Faḍīla, 2006.

Riḍwān, Abū al-Futūḥ. *Tārīkh maṭbaʿat Būlāq*. Cairo: al-Maṭbaʿa al-Amīriyya, 1953.

Rieu, Charles. *Catalogue of the Persian Manuscripts in the British Museum*. 3 vols. London: British Museum, 1879–83.

Rieu, Charles. *Supplement to the Catalogue of the Arabic Manuscripts in the British Museum*. London: British Museum, 1894.

Al-Rifāʿī, ʿAbd al-Ḥamīd. *Al-Ṣawāʿiq al-mursala ʿalā Tārīkh al-Jahmiyya wa-l-Muʿtazila*. Riyadh: Maktabat al-Rushd, 2007.

Ritter, Hellmut. "Philologika xii: Datierung durch Brüche." *Oriens* 1, no. 2 (1948): 237–47.

Rizvi, Sayyid Muhammad. "Muhibb al-Din al-Khatib: A Portrait of a Salafi Arabist (1886–1969)." MA thesis, Simon Fraser University, 1991.

Robinson, Frances. "Ottomans-Safavids-Mughals: Shared Knowledge and Connective Systems." *Journal of Islamic Studies* 8, no. 2 (1997): 151–84.

Roman, Stephan. *The Development of Islamic Library Collections in Western Europe and North America*. London: Mansell, 1990.

Romanov, Maxim G. "Algorithmic Analysis of Medieval Arabic Biographical Collections." *Speculum* 92, no. S1 (2017): S226–46.

Roper, Geoffrey. "Aḥmad Fāris al-Shidyāq and the Libraries of Europe and the Ottoman Empire." *Libraries and Culture* 33, no. 3 (1998): 233–48.

Roper, Geoffrey. "Fāris al-Shidyāq and the Transition from Scribal to Print Culture in the Middle East." In *The Book in the Islamic World: The Written Word and Communication in the Middle East*, edited by George N. Atiyeh, 209–31. Albany: State University of New York Press, 1995.

Roper, Geoffrey. "The History of the Book in the Muslim World." In *The Oxford Companion to the Book*, edited by Michael F. Suarez and H. R. Woudhuysen, 321–39. Oxford: Oxford University Press, 2010.

Rosenthal, Franz. Introduction to Ibn Khaldūn, *The Muqaddimah: An Introduction to History*, translated by Franz Rosenthal. New York: Pantheon Books, 1958.

Rosenthal, Hans. "'Blurbs' (*Taqrîẓ*) from Fourteenth-Century Egypt." *Oriens* 27–28 (1981): 177–96.

Rūmī. *Masnavī*. Bulaq, 1251/[1836].

Ryad, Umar. "'An Oriental Orientalist': Aḥmad Zakī Pasha (1868–1934), Egyptian Statesman and Philologist in the Colonial Age." *Philological Encounters* 3 (2018): 129–66.

Ryad, Umar. "A Printed Muslim 'Lighthouse' in Cairo: *Al-Manār's* Early Years, Religious Aspiration and Reception (1898–1903)." *Arabica* 56 (2009): 27–60.
Ṣābāt, Khalīl. *Tārīkh al-ṭibāʿa fī al-sharq al-ʿarabī.* Cairo: Dār al-Maʿārif, 1966.
Sabev, Orlin. "Waiting for Godot: The Formation of Ottoman Print Culture." In *Historical Aspects of Printing and Publishing in Languages of the Middle East,* edited by Geoffrey Roper, 101–20. Leiden: Brill, 2014.
Sabra, Adam. "Household Sufism in Sixteenth-Century Egypt: The Rise of al-Sâda al-Bakrîya." In *Le soufisme à l'époque ottoman, XVIe–XVIIIe siècle = Sufism in the Ottoman Era, 16th–18th Century,* edited by Rachida Chih and Catherine Mayeur-Jaouen, 101–18. Cairo: Institut français d'archéologie orientale, 2010.
Sabra, Adam. "Illiterate Sufis and Learned Artisans: The Circle of ʿAbd al-Wahhāb al-Shaʿrānī." In *Le développement du soufisme en Égypte à l'époque mamelouke = The Development of Sufism in Mamluk Egypt,* edited by Richard McGregor and Adam Sabra, 153–68. Cairo: Institut français d'archéologie orientale, 2006.
Ṣabrī, Muṣṭafā. *Qawlī fī al-marʾa wa-muqāranatuhu bi-aqwāl muqallidat al-gharb.* Cairo: al-Maktaba al-Salafiyya, 1354/[1935].
Sachau, Eduard. *Muhammedanisches Recht nach schafiitischer Lehre.* Stuttgart: W. Spemann, 1897.
Saʿdī. *Gulistān.* Bulaq, 1243/[1828].
Al-Ṣafadī. *Nakt al-himyān fī nukat al-ʿumyān.* [Edited by] Aḥmad Zakī. Cairo: al-Maṭbaʿa al-Jamāliyya, 1911.
Saḥnūn. *Al-Mudawwana al-kubrā.* Corrected by Ḥammād al-Fayyūmī al-ʿAjmāwī. 16 vols. in 4. Cairo: Maṭbaʿat al-Saʿāda, 1323/[1905 or 1906].
Sājaqlīzāde, Muḥammad al-Marʿashī. *Tartīb al-ʿulūm.* Edited by Muḥammad al-Sayyid Aḥmad. Beirut: Dār al-Bashāʾir al-Islāmiyya, 1988.
Al-Sakhāwī, Shams al-Dīn. *Al-Ḍawʾ al-lāmiʿ.* 12 vols. in 6. Cairo: Maktabat al-Qudsī, 1934–36.
Al-Sakhāwī, Shams al-Dīn. *Kitāb al-Tibr al-masbūk fī dhayl al-sulūk.* [Edited by] Aḥmad Zakī. Bulaq, 1896.
Al-Sakkākī, Yūsuf b. Abī Bakr. *Miftāḥ al-ʿulūm.* Edited by Nuʿaym Zarzūr. Beirut: Dār al-Kutub al-ʿIlmiyya, 1987.
Salāma, Muḥammad Yusrī. *Muʿjam mā ṭubiʿa min muṣannafāt shaykh al-islām Ibn Taymiyya.* Alexandria: Dār al-Tawḥīd li-l-Turāth, 2010.
Saleh, Walid A. "The Gloss as Intellectual History: The *Ḥāshiyas* on *al-Kashshāf.*" *Oriens* 41 (2013): 217–59.
Saleh, Walid A. "Ibn Taymiyyah and the Rise of Radical Hermeneutics: An Analysis of 'An Introduction to the Foundation of Quranic Exegesis.'" In *Ibn Taymiyya and His Times,* edited by Shahab Ahmed and Yossef Rapoport, 123–62. Oxford: Oxford University Press, 2010.
Saleh, Walid A. "Rereading al-Ṭabarī through al-Māturīdī: New Light on the Third Century Hijrī." *Journal of Qurʾanic Studies* 18, no. 2 (2016): 180–209.
Saliba, George. *Maʿālim al-aṣāla wa-l-ibdāʿ fī al-shurūḥ wa-l-taʿālīq al-ʿilmiyya al-mutaʾakhkhira: Aʿmāl Shams al-Dīn al-Khafrī, 956 h./1550 m. = Late Arabic Scientific Commentaries: Their Role and Their Originality; Works of Shams al-Din al-Khafri, 1550 C.E./956 A.H.* London: Al-Furqan Islamic Heritage Foundation, 2015.
Ṣāliḥiyya, Muḥammad ʿĪsā. *Al-Muʿjam al-shāmil li-l-turāth al-ʿarabī al-maṭbūʿ.* 5 vols. Cairo: Maʿhad al-Makhṭūṭāt al-ʿArabiyya, 1992–95.

Salīm Efendi. *Al-Tuḥfa al-Salīmiyya*. Bulaq, 1256/[1841].

Al-Samʿānī, ʿAbd al-Karīm. *Al-Ansāb*. Facsimile. Leiden: Brill, 1912.

Al-Samʿānī, ʿAbd al-Karīm. *Al-Ansāb*. Edited by ʿAbd al-Raḥmān al-Muʿallimī. 13 vols. Hyderabad: Maṭbaʿat Majlis Dāʾirat al-Maʿārif al-ʿUthmāniyya, 1962–66.

Al-Samʿānī, Manṣūr b. Muḥammad. *Qawāṭiʿ al-adilla*. Edited by Muḥammad al-Shāfiʿī. 2 vols. Beirut: Dār al-Kutub al-ʿIlmiyya, 1997.

Sanad, Muḥammad Ṣalāḥ al-Dīn. "Al-Sayyida Zaynab raḍiya Allāh ʿanhā." *Al-Islām*, December 17, 1932, 17–18.

Al-Ṣanʿānī, Muḥammad b. Ismāʿīl. *Al-Inṣāf fī ḥaqīqat al-awliyāʾ wa-mā lahum min al-karāmāt wa-l-alṭāf.* Edited by ʿAbd al-Razzāq b. ʿAbd al-Muḥsin al-Badr. Medina: al-Jāmiʿa al-Islāmiyya, 2001.

Al-Sanūsī, Yūsuf. *Risāla fī ʿilm al-tawḥīd* [probably his *Umm al-barahīn*]. Bulaq, 1250/[1835].

Sarkīs, Yūsuf Ilyās. *Muʿjam al-maṭbūʿāt al-ʿarabiyya wa-l-muʿarraba*. 2 vols. Cairo: Maṭbaʿat Sarkīs, 1928.

Ṣarrūf, Yaʿqūb. "Al-Taqrīẓ wa-l-intiqād: Fī al-shiʿr al-jāhilī." *Al-Muqtaṭaf* 68, no. 5 (1926): 575–79.

Ṣarrūf, Yaʿqūb. "Al-Taqrīẓ wa-l-intiqād: Al-Juzʾ al-rābiʿ Khiṭaṭ al-Shām." *Al-Muqtaṭaf* 70, no. 4 (1927): 458–60.

Al-Ṣāwī, Aḥmad Ḥusayn. "Muḥammad ʿAbduh and *al-Waqāʾiʿ al-Miṣrīyah*." MA thesis, McGill University, 1954.

Al-Sāwī, ʿUmar. *Al-Baṣāʾir al-naṣīriyya*. [Edited by] Muḥammad ʿAbduh. Corrected by Maḥmūd Muṣṭafā. Bulaq, 1898.

Al-Ṣaymarī, Abū ʿAbd Allāh. *Akhbār Abī Ḥanīfa wa-aṣḥābih*. Edited by Abū al-Wafāʾ al-Afghānī. Hyderabad: Lajnat Iḥyāʾ al-Maʿārif al-Nuʿmāniyya, 1974. Reprint, Beirut: ʿĀlam al-Kutub, 1985.

Sayyid, Ayman Fuʾād. *Dār al-Kutub al-Miṣriyya: Tārīkhuhā wa-taṭawwuruhā*. Beirut: Awrāq Sharqiyya, 1996.

Sayyid, Ayman Fuʾād. "Naṣṣān qadīmān fī iʿārat al-kutub." *Majallat Maʿhad al-makhṭūṭāt al-ʿarabiyya* 4, no. 1 (1377): 125–36.

Sayyid, Aymān Fuʾād, Aḥmad Ḥamdī Imām, Iḥsān ʿAbbās, Maḥmūd ʿAlī al-Madanī, Muḥammad Amīn al-Khānjī, and Maḥmūd Fakhr, eds. *Dirāsāt ʿarabiyya wa-islāmiyya: Muhdāt ilā adīb al-ʿarabiyya al-kabīr Abī Fihr Maḥmūd Muḥammad Shākir bi-munāsabat bulūghihi al-sabʿīn*. Cairo: Maṭbaʿat al-Madanī, 1982.

Al-Sayyid, Riḍwān. *Al-Turāth al-ʿarabī fī al-ḥāḍir: al-Nashr wa-l-qirāʾa wa-l-ṣirāʿ*. Abu Dhabi: Hayʾat Abū Ẓabī li-l-Siyāḥa wa-l-Thaqāfa, Dār al-Kutub al-Waṭaniyya, 2014.

Schaade, Arthur. "Aḥmed Taimûr Paša und die arabische Renaissance." *Orientalistische Literaturzeitung* 33 (1930): 854–59.

Schacht, Joseph. "Aḥmed Pascha Taimūr: Ein Nachruf." *Zeitschrift der Deutschen Morgenländischen Gesellschaft* 84, no. 4 (1930): 255–58.

Schacht, Joseph. *The Origins of Muhammadan Jurisprudence*. Oxford: Clarendon Press, 1950.

Schulze, Reinhard. "The Birth of Tradition and Modernity in 18th and 19th Century Islamic Culture: The Case of Printing." *Culture and History* 16 (1997): 29–72. Reprinted in *The History of the Book in the Middle East*, edited by Geoffrey Roper, 345–88. London: Routledge, 2016.

Schulze, Reinhard. "Mass Culture and Islamic Cultural Production in 19th Century Middle East." In *Mass Culture, Popular Culture, and Social Life in the Middle East*, edited by Georg Stauth and Sami Zubaida, 189–222. Frankfurt am Main: Campus, 1987. Reprinted in *The History of the Book in the Middle East*, edited by Geoffrey Roper, 421–55. London: Routledge, 2016.

Schulze, Reinhard. *A Modern History of the Islamic World*. Translated by Azizeh Azodi. New York: New York University Press, 2000.

Schwartz, Kathryn A. "An Eastern Scholar's Engagement with the European Study of the East: Amin al-Madani and the Sixth Oriental Congress, Leiden, 1883." In *The Muslim Reception of European Orientalism: Reversing the Gaze*, edited by Susannah Heschel and Umar Ryad, 39–60. New York: Routledge, 2019.

Schwartz, Kathryn A. "Meaningful Mediums: A Material and Intellectual History of Manuscript and Print Production in Nineteenth Century Ottoman Cairo." PhD diss., Harvard University, 2015.

Schwartz, Kathryn A. "The Political Economy of Private Printing in Cairo as Told from a Commissioning Deal Turned Sour, 1871." *International Journal of Middle East Studies* 49 (2017): 25–45.

Seetzen, Ulrich Jasper. *Ulrich Jasper Seetzen's Reisen durch Syrien, Palästina, Phönicien, die Transjordan-Länder, Arabia Petraea und Unter-Aegypten*. Edited by Fr. Kruse and K. R. Staatsrath. 4 vols. Berlin: G. Reimer, 1854–59.

Seidensticker, Tilman. "How Arabic Manuscripts Moved to German Libraries." *Manuscript Cultures* 10 (2017): 73–82.

Seyller, John. "The Inspection and Valuation of Manuscripts in the Imperial Mughal Library." *Artibus Asiae* 57, nos. 3–4 (1997): 243–349.

Al-Shāfiʿī, Muḥammad b. Idrīs. *The Epistle on Legal Theory*. Translated by Joseph Lowry. New York: New York University Press, 2015.

Al-Shāfiʿī, Muḥammad b. Idrīs. *Kitāb al-Risāla*. Corrected by Yūsuf al-Jazmāwī. Cairo: al-Maṭbaʿa al-ʿIlmiyya, 1312/[1895].

Al-Shāfiʿī, Muḥammad b. Idrīs. *Kitāb al-Umm*. 7 vols. in 4. Bulaq, 1321–25/[1903–8].

Al-Shāfiʿī, Muḥammad b. Idrīs. *Kitāb al-Umm*. Edited by Rifʿat Fawzī ʿAbd al-Muṭṭalib. 11 vols. Mansura: Dār al-Wafāʾ, 2001.

Al-Shāfiʿī, Muḥammad b. Idrīs. *Al-Risāla*. Edited by Aḥmad Shākir. Cairo: Maṭbaʿat Muṣṭafā al-Bābī al-Ḥalabī, 1940.

Shaham, Ron. "Judicial Divorce at the Wife's Initiative: The Sharīʿa Courts of Egypt, 1920–1955." *Islamic Law and Society* 1, no. 2 (1994): 217–57.

Shākir, Aḥmad. *Jamharat maqālāt Aḥmad Shākir*. 2 vols. Riyadh: Dār al-Riyāḍ, 2005.

Shākir, Aḥmad. *Kalimat al-ḥaqq*. Cairo: Maktabat al-Sunna, n.d.

Shākir, Aḥmad. *Niẓām al-ṭalāq fī al-islām*. Cairo: Maṭbaʿat al-Nahḍa, 1354/[1935 or 1936].

Shākir, Aḥmad. *Taṣḥīḥ al-kutub wa-ṣunʿ al-fahāris al-muʿjama wa-kayfiyyat ḍabṭ al-kitāb wa-sabq al-muslimīn al-Ifranj fī dhālik*. Edited by ʿAbd al-Fattāḥ Abū Ghudda. Aleppo: Maktab al-Maṭbūʿāt al-Islāmiyya, 1993.

Shākir, Aḥmad, Maḥmūd Shākir, and Usāma Shākir. *Min aʿlām al-ʿaṣr*. N.p.: n.p., 2001.

Shākir, Maḥmūd. *Abāṭīl wa-asmār*. Cairo: Maṭbaʿat al-Madanī, 1972.

Shākir, Maḥmūd. *Al-Mutanabbī*. Cairo: Sharikat al-Quds, 1987.

Shākir, Maḥmūd. *Qaḍiyat al-shiʿr al-jāhilī fī kitāb Ibn Sallām*. Cairo: Maṭbaʿat al-Madanī, 1997.

Al-Shallāḥī, Rā'id. "Qaṭf al-ʿanāqīd min tarjamat al-Shinqīṭī al-Talāmīd." In Muḥammad Maḥmūd al-Shanqīṭī al-Turkuzī, *Iḥqāq al-ḥaqq wa-tabri'at al-ʿArab*, edited by Rā'id al-Shallāḥī, 1–93. Kuwait: Gharās, 2005.

Al-Shaʿrānī, ʿAbd al-Wahhāb. *Al-Anwār al-qudsiyya*. Cairo: n.p., 1277/[1860].

Al-Shaʿrānī, ʿAbd al-Wahhāb. *Al-Anwār al-qudsiyya fī maʿrifat qawāʿid al-ṣūfiyya*. Edited by Ṭāhā ʿAbd al-Bāqī Surūr and al-Sayyid Muḥammad ʿĪd al-Shāfiʿī. 2 vols. Beirut: al-Maktaba al-ʿIlmiyya, 1992.

Al-Shaʿrānī, ʿAbd al-Wahhāb. *Al-Jawāqīt wa-l-jawāhir*. Cairo: n.p., 1277/[1860].

Al-Shaʿrānī, ʿAbd al-Wahhāb. *Kitāb Kashf al-ghumma ʿan jamīʿ al-umma*. Corrected by Naṣr al-Hūrīnī. 2 vols. Cairo: al-Maṭbaʿa al-Kastaliyya, 1281/[1864].

Al-Shaʿrānī, ʿAbd al-Wahhāb. *Kitāb al-Mīzān*. Corrected by Ḥasan al-ʿIdwī al-Ḥamzāwī. Cairo: al-Maṭbaʿa al-Kastaliyya, 1279/[1862 or 1863].

Al-Shaʿrānī, ʿAbd al-Wahhāb. *Kitāb al-Mīzān*. Edited by ʿAbd al-Raḥmān ʿUmayra. 3 vols. Beirut: ʿĀlam al-Kutub, 1989.

Al-Shaʿrānī, ʿAbd al-Wahhāb. *Laṭā'if al-minan*. 2 vols. Cairo: al-Maṭbaʿa al-Maymaniyya, 1321/[1903].

Al-Shaʿrānī, ʿAbd al-Wahhāb. *Al-Ṭabaqāt al-kubrā*. Corrected by Ḥammād al-Fayyūmī al-ʿAjmāwī. 2 vols. Cairo: al-Maṭbaʿa al-Sharqiyya, 1299/[1882].

Al-Shaʿrānī, ʿAbd al-Wahhāb. *Al-Ṭabaqāt al-kubrā, al-musammā Lawāqiḥ al-anwār al-qudsiyya fī manāqib al-ʿulamā' wa-l-ṣūfiyya*. Edited by Aḥmad ʿAbd al-Raḥīm al-Sāyiḥ and Tawfīq ʿAlī Wahba. 2 vols. Cairo: Maktabat al-Thaqāfa al-Dīniyya, 2005.

Al-Sharīf al-Raḍī. *Nahj al-balāgha*. [Edited by] Muḥammad ʿAbduh. Beirut: al-Maṭbaʿa al-Adabiyya, 1885.

Shatzmiller, Maya. "An Early Knowledge Economy: The Adoption of Paper, Human Capital and Economic Change in the Medieval Islamic Middle East." CGEH Working Paper Series 64, Centre for Global Economic History, Utrecht University, February 2015.

Al-Shawkānī, Muḥammad b. ʿAlī. *Adab al-ṭalab wa-muntahā al-arab*. Edited by ʿAbd Allāh Sarīḥī. Beirut: Dār Ibn Hazm, 1998.

Al-Shawkānī, Muḥammad b. ʿAlī. *Irshād al-fuḥūl*. Edited by Sāmī Ibn al-ʿArabī. 2 vols. Riyadh: Dār al-Faḍīla, 2000.

Al-Shawkānī, Muḥammad b. ʿAlī. *Itḥāf al-akābir*. Edited by Khalīl al-Sabīʿī. Beirut: Dār Ibn Ḥazm, 1999.

Al-Shawkānī, Muḥammad b. ʿAlī. *Qaṭr al-walī ʿalā ḥadīth al-walī*. Edited by Ibrāhīm Hilāl. Cairo: Dār al-Kutub al-Ḥadītha, 1969.

Shawqī, Aḥmad. *Shawqiyyāt*. 3 vols. Beirut: Dār al-ʿAwda, 1988.

Al-Shaybānī, Muḥammad b. al-Ḥasan. *Kitāb al-Makhārij fī al-ḥiyal = Das Kitāb al-Maḫāriǧ fil-ḥijal des Muḥammad ibn al-Ḥasan aš-Šaibānī*. Edited by Joseph Schacht. Leipzig: J. C. Hinrichs, 1930.

Shaykhzāde, ʿAbd al-Raḥmān b. Muḥammad. *Ḥāshiyat Shaykhzāde ʿalā tafsīr al-Qāḍī al-Bayḍāwī*. Bulaq, 1263/[1847].

Al-Shidyāq, Aḥmad Fāris. *Al-Jāsūs ʿalā al-Qāmūs*. Istanbul: Maṭbaʿat al-Jawā'ib, 1299/[1882].

Al-Shidyāq, Aḥmad Fāris. *Kashf al-mukhabbā fī akhbār Urubbā*. Cairo: Dār al-Kitāb al-Miṣrī, 2012.

Al-Shidyāq, Aḥmad Fāris. *Leg over Leg*. Translated by Humphrey T. Davies. 4 vols. New York: New York University Press, 2014.

Al-Shinqīṭī, Muḥammad Ḥabīb Allāh. *Zād al-muslim fīmā ittafaqa ʿalayhi al-Būkhārī wa-Muslim*. 6 vols. Cairo: Maṭbaʿat Miṣr, 1954–56.

Al-Shinqīṭī al-Turkuzī, Muḥammad Maḥmūd. *Asmāʾ ashhar al-kutub al-ʿarabiyya al-mawjūda bi-khazāʾin makātib Isbāniya*. Edited by ʿAbd al-Raḥmān Balḥāj. Published online, February 28, 2018. https://maurinews.info/investigations/17575/.

Al-Shinqīṭī al-Turkuzī, Muḥammad Maḥmūd. *Al-Ḥamāsa al-saniyya al-kāmila al-maziyya fī al-riḥla al-ʿilmiyya al-Shinqīṭiyya al-Turkuziyya*. Cairo: Maṭbaʿat al-Mawsūʿāt, 1319/[1901 or 1902].

Al-Shirbīnī, Yūsuf b. Muḥammad. *Brains Confounded by the Ode of Abū Shādūf Expounded*. Edited and translated by Humphrey T. Davies. New York: New York University Press, 2016.

Al-Shirbīnī, Yūsuf b. Muḥammad. *Hazz al-quḥūf fī sharḥ qaṣīdat Abī Shādūf*. Bulaq, 1274/[1858].

Al-Shirbīnī, Yūsuf b. Muḥammad. *Ṭarḥ al-madar li-ḥall al-ālāʾ wa-l-durar*. Edited by Muḥammad Yūsuf. Beirut: Dār Ibn Ḥazm, 2003.

Shoshan, Boaz. *Popular Culture in Medieval Cairo*. Cambridge: Cambridge University Press, 2002.

Al-Shūrbajī, Muḥammad Jamāl al-Dīn. *Qāʾima bi-awāʾil al-maṭbūʿāt al-ʿarabiyya al-maḥfūẓa bi-Dār al-Kutub ḥattā sanat 1862*. Cairo: Maṭbaʿat Dār al-Kutub, 1963.

Al-Shurunbulālī, Muḥammad Abū al-Suʿūd. *Fatḥ al-muʿīn ʿalā sharḥ Fatḥ al-Kanz*. 3 vols. Cairo: Maṭbaʿat Jamʿiyyat al-Maʿārif, 1287/[1870].

Al-Sibāʿī, Khālid. *Tārīkh al-Maktaba al-Kattāniyya*. 2 vols. Tangiers: Dār al-Ḥadīth al-Kattāniyya, 2017.

Al-Sijilmāsī al-Lamaṭī, Aḥmad. *Al-Ibrīz min kalām sayyidī ʿAbd al-ʿAzīz al-Dabbāgh*. Cairo: al-Maṭbaʿa al-Maymaniyya, 1316/[1898].

Silvestre de Sacy, Antoine Isaac, ed. *Chrestomathie arabe = al-Anīs al-mufīd li-l-ṭālib al-mustafīd*. 3 vols. Paris: Imprimerie impériale, 1806. 2nd ed., 1826.

Sims-Williams, Ursula. "The Arabic and Persian Collections of the India Office Library." In *Collections in British Libraries on Middle Eastern and Islamic Studies*, edited by Paul Auchterlonie, 47–52. Durham: Centre for Middle Eastern and Islamic Studies, University of Durham, 1982.

Al-Sinānī, ʿAbd al-ʿAzīz, and Jamāl al-Dīn al-Qāsimī. "Taʿāruḍ al-ʿaql wa-l-naql fī al-islām." *Al-Manār* 13, no. 8 (1910): 613–34.

Sing, Manfred. "The Decline of Islam and the Rise of *Inḥiṭāṭ*: The Discrete Charm of Language Games about Decadence in the 19th and 20th Centuries." In *Inḥiṭāṭ—The Decline Paradigm: Its Influence and Persistence in the Writing of Arab Cultural History*, edited by Syrinx von Hees, 11–70. Würzburg: Ergon, 2017.

Snouck Hurgronje, Christiaan. *Mekka in the Latter Part of the 19th Century: Daily Life, Customs and Learning, the Moslims of the East-Indian-Archipelago*. Translated by J. H. Monahan. Leiden: Brill, 2007.

Soskice, Janet Martin. *The Sisters of Sinai: How Two Lady Adventurers Found the Hidden Gospels*. London: Chatto and Windus, 2009.

Spater Mag, Marian. "The Egyptian Library." *Library Quarterly* 16, no. 4 (1946): 341–44.

Spevack, Aaron. *The Archetypal Sunnī Scholar: Law, Theology, and Mysticism in the Synthesis of Al-Bājūrī*. Albany: State University of New York Press, 2014.

Spies, Otto. "Die Bibliotheken des Hidschas." *Zeitschrift der Deutschen Morgenländischen Gesellschaft* 90 (1936): 83–120.

Sprenger, Aloys. *A Catalogue of the Bibliotheca Orientalis Sprengeriana*. Gießen: Wilhelm Keller, 1857.

Sprenger, Aloys. "Catalogues of Oriental Libraries." *Journal of the Asiatic Society of Bengal* 22, no. 6 (1853): 535–40.

Stein, Hans, ed. *Ulrich Jasper Seetzen (1767–1811): Leben und Werk; Die arabischen Länder und die Nahostforschung im napoleonischen Zeitalter; Vorträge des Kolloquiums vom 23. und 24. Sept. 1994 in der Forschungs- und Landesbibliothek Gotha, Schloß Friedenstein*. Gotha: Forschungs- und Landesbibliothek, 1995.

Al-Subkī, Tāj al-Dīn. *Jamʿ al-jawāmiʿ*. Edited by ʿAbd al-Munʿim Ibrāhīm. Beirut: Dār al-Kutub al-ʿIlmiyya, 2002.

Al-Subkī, Taqī al-Dīn. *Al-Sayf al-ṣaqīl fī al-radd ʿalā Ibn Zafīl*. Edited by Muḥammad Zāhid al-Kawtharī. Cairo: al-Maktaba al-Azhariyya, n.d.

Al-Subkī, Tāj al-Dīn. *Sharḥ Mukhtaṣar Ibn Ḥājib*. Edited by ʿAlī Muʿawwaḍ and ʿĀdil ʿAbd al-Mawjūd. 4 vols. Beirut: ʿĀlam al-Kutub, 1999.

Al-Subkī, Tāj al-Dīn. *Ṭabaqāt al-Shāfiʿiyya al-kubrā*. Edited by Maḥmūd Muḥammad al-Ṭanāḥī and ʿAbd al-Fattāḥ Muḥammad al-Ḥulw. 10 vols. Cairo: ʿĪsā al-Bābī al-Ḥalabī, 1964–76.

"Süleymaniye Yazma Eser Kütüphanesi'nde Bulunan Koleksiyonlar ve Kitap Sayıları." Undated PDF document. Istanbul: Süleymaniye Library website. Accessed November 23, 2018. http://www.suleymaniye.yek.gov.tr/Content/UploadFile/Doc/koleksiyonlar.pdf.

Al-Ṣūlī, Muḥammad b. Yaḥyā. *Akhbār Abī Tammām*. Edited by Khalīl ʿAsākir, Muḥammad ʿAzzām, and Naẓīr al-Islām. Introduction by Aḥmad Amīn. Cairo: Maṭbaʿat Lajnat al-Taʾlīf wa-l-Tarjama wa-l-Nashr, 1356/[1937].

Al-Ṣūlī, Muḥammad b. Yaḥyā. *The Life and Times of Abū Tammām*. Translated by Beatrice Gruendler. New York: New York University Press, 2015.

Al-Suyūṭī, Jalāl al-Dīn. *Kitāb al-Itqān fī ʿulūm al-Qurʾān*. Corrected by Naṣr al-Hūrīnī. 2 vols. Cairo: al-Maṭbaʿa al-Kastaliyya, 1279/[1863].

Al-Ṭabarī, Muḥammad b. Jarīr. *Annales quos scripsit Abu Djafar Mohammed Ibn Djarir at-Tabari*. Edited by M. J. de Goeje. 15 vols. Leiden: Brill, 1879–1901.

Al-Ṭabarī, Muḥammad b. Jarīr. *Jāmiʿ al-bayān fī tafsīr al-Qurʾān*. Corrected by Muḥammad al-Zuhrī al-Ghamrāwī. 30 vols. in 10. Cairo: al-Maṭbaʿa al-Maymaniyya, 1321/[1903].

Al-Ṭabarī, Muḥammad b. Jarīr. *Jāmiʿ al-bayān fī tafsīr al-Qurʾān*. Corrected by Naṣr al-ʿĀdilī. 30 vols. Bulaq, 1323–29/[1905–12].

Al-Ṭabarī, Muḥammad b. Jarīr. *Tafsīr al-Ṭabarī = Jāmiʿ al-bayān fī tafsīr al-Qurʾān*. Edited by ʿAbd Allāh al-Turkī. 26 vols. Cairo: Hajar, 2001.

Al-Ṭabarī, Muḥammad b. Jarīr. *Tārīkh al-Ṭabarī*. Manuscript. Berlin: Staatsbibliothek, Sprenger, no. 41.

Al-Ṭabarī, Muḥammad b. Jarīr. *Tārīkh al-Ṭabarī*. Manuscript. Istanbul: Topkapı Palace Library, Ahmet III, no. 2929.

Al-Ṭabbākh, Muḥammad Rāghib. "Dūr al-kutub fī Ḥalab qadīman wa-ḥadīthan." *Majallat al-Majmaʿ al-ʿilmī al-ʿarabī fī Dimashq* 15, nos. 7–8 (1937): 299–310. Reprinted in al-Ṭabbākh, *Maqālāt Muḥammad Rāghib al-Ṭabbākh*, 1:189–214.

Al-Ṭabbākh, Muḥammad Rāghib. *Iʿlām al-nubalāʾ bi-tārīkh Ḥalab al-shahbāʾ*. Edited by Muḥammad Kamāl. 7 vols. Aleppo: Dār al-Qalam al-ʿArabī, 2016.

Al-Ṭabbākh, Muḥammad Rāghib. *Maqālāt al-ʿallāma al-muʾarrikh al-muḥaddith Muḥammad Rāghib al-Ṭabbākh wa-buḥūthuhu fī al-tārīkh wa-l-turāth wa-l-adab wa-l-tarājim wa-muqaddimāt al-kutub allatī ḥaqqaqahā.* Edited by Majd Makkī. 2 vols. Amman: Arwiqa, 2015.

Al-Ṭabbākh, Muḥammad Rāghib. "Al-Sharīf al-Kattānī yazūru Sūriyā." *Al-Iʿtiṣām* (Aleppo) 3, no. 1 (1933). Reprinted in al-Ṭabbākh, *Maqālāt Muḥammad Rāghib al-Ṭabbākh,* 1:326–33.

Ṭāhir, Ḥāmid. *Dār al-ʿUlūm: Rāʾiʿat ʿAlī Mubārak.* Cairo: Dār al-Nashr, n.d.

Al-Ṭahṭāwī, Rifāʿa Rāfiʿ. *Al-Aʿmāl al-kāmila li-Rifāʿa Rāfiʿ al-Ṭahṭāwī.* Edited by Muḥammad ʿImāra. 5 vols. Cairo: Dār al-Shurūq, 2010.

Al-Ṭahṭāwī, Rifāʿa Rāfiʿ. *An Imam in Paris.* London: Sāqī, 2011.

Tājir, Jacques. *Harakat al-tarjama bi-Miṣr khilāl al-qarn al-tāsiʿ ʿashar.* Cairo: Muʾassasat Hindāwī, 2012.

Al-Ṭanāḥī, Maḥmūd. "Bint al-Shāṭiʾ wa-taḥqīq al-turāth." *Majallat al-ʿarabī,* no. 488 (July 1999), online. http://www.3rbi.info/Article.asp?ID=8315. Reprinted in Maḥmūd al-Ṭānāḥī, *Maqālāt al-ʿallāma al-duktūr Maḥmūd Muḥammad al-Ṭanāḥī,* 2:667–76. Beirut: Dār al-Bashāʾir al-Islāmiyya, 2002.

Al-Ṭanāḥī, Maḥmūd. *Fahāris kitāb al-Uṣūl fī al-naḥw li-Abī Bakr b. al-Sarrāj.* Cairo: Maktabat al-Khānjī, 1986.

Al-Ṭanāḥī, Maḥmūd. *Fī al-lugha wa-l-adab: Dirāsāt wa-buḥūth.* 2 vols. Beirut: Dār al-Gharb al-Islāmī, 2002.

Al-Ṭanāḥī, Maḥmūd. *Al-Kitāb al-maṭbūʿ bi-Miṣr fī al-qarn al-tāsiʿ ʿashar.* Cairo: Dār al-Hilāl, 1996.

Al-Ṭānāḥī, Maḥmūd. *Madkhal ilā tārīkh nashr al-turāth al-ʿarabī.* Cairo: Maktabat al-Khānjī, 1984.

Al-Ṭanṭāwī, ʿAlī. *Dhikrayāt.* 8 vols. Jedda: Dār al-Manāra, 1985.

Ṭaşköprüzāde. *Miftāḥ al-saʿāda wa-miṣbāḥ al-siyāda fī mawḍūʿāt al-ʿulūm.* 2 vols. Hyderabad: Maṭbaʿat Dāʾirat al-Maʿārif al-Niẓāmiyya, 1328/[1910].

Al-Tawḥīdī, Abū Ḥayyān. *Al-Baṣāʾir wa-l-dhakhāʾir.* Edited by Wadād al-Qāḍī. 10 vols. Beirut: Dār Ṣādir, 1988.

Taymūr, Aḥmad. *Abū al-ʿAlāʾ al-Maʿarrī: Nasabuhu wa-akhbāruhu, shiʿruhu, muʿtaqaduh.* Cairo: Lajnat Nashr al-Muʾallafāt al-Taymūriyya, 1940.

Taymūr, Aḥmad. *Aʿlām al-fikr al-islāmī fī al-ʿaṣr al-ḥadīth.* Cairo: Dār al-Āfāq al-ʿArabiyya, 2002.

Taymūr, Aḥmad. *Aʿlām al-muhandisīn fī al-islām.* Cairo: Lajnat Nashr al-Muʾallafāt al-Taymūriyya, 1957.

Taymūr, Aḥmad. *Al-Amthāl al-ʿāmmiyya.* Cairo: Lajnat Nashr al-Muʾallafāt al-Taymūriyya, 1956.

Taymūr, Aḥmad. *Al-Āthār al-nabawiyya.* Cairo: Lajnat Nashr al-Muʾallafāt al-Taymūriyya, 1951.

Taymūr, Aḥmad. *Al-Ḥubb wa-l-jamāl ʿinda al-ʿArab.* Cairo: Lajnat Nashr al-Muʾallafāt al-Taymūriyya, 1971.

Taymūr, Aḥmad. *Awhām shuʿarāʾ al-ʿArab fī al-maʿānī.* Cairo: Lajnat Nashr al-Muʾallafāt al-Taymūriyya, 1950.

Taymūr, Aḥmad. *Luʿab al-ʿArab.* Cairo: Lajnat Nashr al-Muʾallafāt al-Taymūriyya, 1948.

Taymūr, Aḥmad. *Al-Mukhtār min al-makhṭūṭāt al-ʿarabiyya fī al-Āsitāna: Risāla min Aḥmad Taymūr ilā Jurjī Zaydān*. Edited by Ṣalāḥ al-Dīn Munajjid. Beirut: Dār al-Kitāb al-Jadīd, 1968.

Taymūr, Aḥmad. *Naẓara tārīkhiyya fī ḥudūth al-madhāhib al-arbaʿa*. Cairo: al-Maṭbaʿa al-Salafiyya, 1351/[1931 or 1932].

Taymūr, Aḥmad. *Qabr al-imām al-Suyūṭī wa-taḥqīq mawḍiʿuh*. Cairo: al-Maṭbaʿa al-Salafiyya, 1346/[1927 or 1928].

Taymūr, Aḥmad. *Risāla lughawiyya ʿan al-rutab wa-l-alqāb al-miṣriyya li-rijāl al-jaysh wa-l-hayʾāt al-ʿilmiyya wa-l-qalamiyya mundhu ʿahd Amīr al-Muʾminīn ʿUmar al-Fārūq*. Cairo: Lajnat Nashr al-Muʾallafāt al-Taymūriyya, 1950.

Taymūr, Aḥmad. *Al-Tadhkira al-Taymūriyya*. Cairo: Dār al-Kitāb al-ʿArabī, 1953.

Taymūr, Aḥmad. *Tarājim aʿyān al-qarn al-thālith ʿashar*. Cairo: Dār al-Āfāq al-ʿArabiyya, 2001.

Taymūr, Aḥmad. *Tārīkh al-ʿalam al-ʿuthmānī*. Cairo: al-Maṭbaʿa al-Salafiyya, 1347/[1928 or 1929].

Taymūr, Aḥmad. *Tārīkh al-usra al-Taymūriyya*. Cairo: Lajnat Nashr al-Muʾallafāt al-Taymūriyya, 1948.

Taymūr, Aḥmad. *Taṣḥīḥ Lisān al-ʿArab*. 2 vols. Cairo: al-Maṭbaʿa al-Jamāliyya, 1334/[1916].

Taymūr, Aḥmad. *Taṣḥīḥ al-Qāmūs*. Cairo: al-Maṭbaʿa al-Salafiyya, 1343/[1924].

Taymūr, Aḥmad. *Al-Taṣwīr ʿinda al-ʿArab*. Cairo: Lajnat Nashr al-Muʾallafāt al-Taymūriyya, 1942.

Taymūr, Aḥmad. *Al-Yazīdiyya wa-manshaʾ niḥlatihim*. Cairo: al-Maṭbaʿa al-Salafiyya, 1347/[1928 or 1929].

Taymūr, Maḥmūd. *Nushūʾ al-qiṣṣa wa-taṭawwuruhā*. Cairo: al-Maktaba al-Salafiyya, 1936.

Tibawi, Abdul Latif. *A Modern History of Syria, Including Lebanon and Palestine*. London: Macmillan, 1969.

Tillier, Mathieu. Review of *La transmission écrite du Coran dans les débuts de l'islam: Le codex Parisino-petropolitanus* by François Déroche. *Journal of Qur'anic Studies* 13, no. 2 (2011): 109–15.

Timpanaro, Sebastiano. *The Genesis of Lachmann's Method*. Edited and translated by Glenn W. Most. Chicago: University of Chicago Press, 2005.

Al-Tirmidhī, Abū ʿĪsā. *Al-Jāmiʿ al-ṣaḥīḥ wa-huwa Sunan al-Tirmidhī*. Edited by Aḥmad Shākir. 3 vols. Cairo: Maṭbaʿat Muṣṭafā al-Bābī al-Ḥalabī, 1937.

Al-Tirmidhī, Abū ʿĪsā. *Ṣaḥīḥ al-imām al-ḥāfiẓ Abī ʿAbd Allāh Muḥammad b. ʿĪsā b. Sūra al-Tirmidhī*. 3 vols. Bulaq, 1292/[1875].

Tomiche, Nada. "Nahḍa." In *Encyclopaedia of Islam*, 2nd ed. Edited by Peri Bearman et al. Leiden: Brill, online edition. http://dx.doi.org/10.1163/1573-3912_islam_SIM_5751.

Al-Ṭūfī, Najm al-Dīn. *Risāla fī al-maṣāliḥ al-mursala*. In *Majmūʿ rasāʾil fī uṣūl al-fiqh*, 38–70. Beirut: al-Maṭbaʿa al-Ahliyya, 1324/[1906]. Also published as "Bāb uṣūl al-fiqh: Adillat al-sharʿ wa-taqdīm al-maṣlaḥa fī al-muʿāmalāt ʿalā al-naṣṣ." *Al-Manār* 9, no. 10 (1906): 721–70.

Tūqādī, Muḥammad al-Sharīf b. Muṣṭafā. *Miftāḥ al-Ṣaḥīḥayn: Miftāḥ Ṣaḥīḥ al-Bukhārī wa-Miftāḥ [Ṣaḥīḥ] Muslim*. Istanbul: Şirket Sahafiye Osmaniye, 1313/[1896].

(Pseudo-)ʿUbaydalī, Yaḥyā b. al-Ḥasan ʿAqīqī. *Al-Sayyida Zaynab wa-akhbār al-Zaynabāt li-l-ʿUbaydalī al-nassāba al-mutawaffā sanat 277 h., amīr al-Madīna wa-ibn amīrihā: Baḥth mustafīḍ wa-athar qayyim wa-tārīkh jalīl*. Edited by Ḥasan Qāsim. Cairo: Idārat al-Ṭibāʿa al-Munīriyya, 1933.

Al-ʿUbaydalī, Yaḥyā b. al-Ḥasan ʿAqīqī. *Tahdhīb al-ansāb wa-nihāyat al-aʿqāb*. Edited by Muḥammad Kāẓim al-Maḥmūdī. Qum: Maktabat Āyat Allāh al-Marʿashī, 1993.

Al-ʿUmarī, Faḍl Allāh. *Masālik al-abṣār fī mamālik al-amṣār*. Manuscript. Istanbul: Süleymaniye, Kara Çelebizade Hüsamettin, no. 296.

Al-ʿUmarī, Faḍl Allāh. *Masālik al-abṣār fī mamālik al-amṣār*. Vol. 1. Edited by Aḥmad Zakī. Cairo: Maṭbaʿat Dār al-Kutub al-Miṣriyya, 1924.

Al-ʿUmarī, Faḍl Allāh. *Masālik al-abṣār fī mamālik al-amṣār*. Edited by ʿAbd Allāḥ b. Yaḥyā al-Sarīḥī. 27 vols. Abu Dhabi: al-Majmaʿ al-Thaqafī, 2001.

Al-ʿUmarī, Faḍl Allāh. *Masālik al-abṣār fī mamālik al-amṣār*. 27 vols. Beirut: Dār al-Kutub al-ʿIlmiyya, 2010.

UNESCO. *World Illiteracy at Mid-Century: A Statistical Study*. [Paris]: UNESCO, 1957.

ʿUways, Sayyid. *Rasāʾil ilā al-imām al-Shāfiʿī: Ẓāhirat irsāl al-rasāʾil ilā ḍarīḥ al-imām al-Shāfiʿī*. Cairo: Dār al-Shāyiʿ, 1978.

Van Dyck, Edward. *Iktifāʾ al-qanūʿ bi-mā huwa maṭbūʿ*. Cairo: Maṭbaʿat al-Hilāl, 1897.

Van Ess, Josef. "Goldziher as a Contemporary of Islamic Reform." In Josef van Ess, *Kleine Schriften*, edited by Hinrich Biesterfeldt, 3:497–511. Leiden: Brill, 2018.

Van Ess, Josef. *Im Halbschatten: Der Orientalist Hellmut Ritter (1892–1971)*. Wiesbaden: Harrassowitz, 2013.

Van Ess, Josef. *Die Träume der Schulweisheit: Leben und Werk des ʿAlī b. Muḥammad al-Ǧurǧānī (gest. 816/1413)*. Wiesbaden: Harrassowitz, 2013.

Verdery, Richard. "The Publications of the Būlāq Press under Muḥammad ʿAlī." *Journal of the American Oriental Society* 91, no. 1 (1971): 129–32.

Versteegh, Kees. *The Arabic Linguistic Tradition*. Vol. 3 of *Landmarks in Linguistic Thought*. London: Routledge, 1997.

Vollers, Karl. *Le neuvième Congres international des Orientalistes tenu à Londres du 5 au 12 septembre 1892*. Bulaq, 1892.

Walbiner, Carsten. "The Christians of *Bilād al-Shām* (Syria): Pioneers of Book-Printing in the Arab World." In *The Beginnings of Printing in the Near and Middle East: Jews, Christians, and Muslims*, edited by Klaus Kreiser, 112–28. Wiesbaden: Harrassowitz, 2001.

Walbiner, Carsten-Michael. "Die Protagonisten des frühen Buchdrucks in der arabischen Welt." In *Das gedruckte Buch im Vorderen Orient*, edited by Ulrich Marzolph, 128–41. Dortmund: Verlag für Orientkunde, 2002.

Walī Allāh al-Dihlawī. *Fuyūḍ al-Ḥaramayn*. Published together with the Urdu translation *Saʿādat kawnayn*. Delhi: Maṭbaʿ al-Aḥmadī, 1916.

Walī Allāh al-Dihlawī. *Ḥujjat Allāh al-bāligha*. Edited by Sayyid Sābiq. 2 vols. Beirut: Dār al-Jīl, 2005.

Al-Wāqidī, Abū ʿAbd Allāh Muḥammad b. ʿUmar [attrib.]. *The Conquest of Syria*. Edited by William Nassau Lees. 2 vols. Calcutta: Bengal Military Orphan Press, 1854–62.

Al-Wāqidī, Abū ʿAbd Allāh Muḥammad b. ʿUmar [attrib.]. *Futūḥ al-Shām*. Corrected by Muḥammad al-Samlūṭī. Cairo: al-Maṭbaʿa al-Kastaliyya, 1282/[1865 or 1866].

Al-Wāqidī, Abū ʿAbd Allāh Muḥammad b. ʿUmar [attrib.]. *Incerti auctoris liber de expugnatione Memphidis et Alexandriae = Kitāb Futūḥ Miṣr wa-l-Iskandariyya*. Edited by Hendrik Arent Hamaker. Leiden: Luchtmans, 1825.

Ward-Perkins, Bryan. *The Fall of Rome and the End of Civilization.* Oxford: Oxford University Press, 2006.
Wehr, Hans, and J. M. Cowan. *A Dictionary of Modern Written Arabic.* 3rd ed. Ithaca, NY: Spoken Language Press, 1976.
Weismann, Itzchak. *Taste of Modernity: Sufism, Salafiyya, and Arabism in Late Ottoman Damascus.* Leiden: Brill, 2001.
Witkam, Jan Just. *De egyptische arts Ibn al-Akfānī (gest. 749/1348) en zijn indeling van de wetenschappen: Editie van het Kitāb Iršād al-Qāṣid ilā Asnā al-Maqāṣid met een inleiding over het leven en werk van de auteur.* Leiden: Ter Lugt Pers, 1989.
Witkam, Jan Just. "Establishing the Stemma: Fact or Fiction?" *Manuscripts of the Middle East* 3 (1988): 88–98.
Witkam, Jan Just. *Inventory of the Oriental Manuscripts of the Library of the University of Leiden.* 28 vols. Leiden: Ter Lugt Press, 2006–16.
Witkam, Jan Just. "The Philologist's Stone: The Continuing Search for the Stemma." *Comparative Oriental Manuscript Studies Newsletter* 6 (July 2013): 34–38.
Wollina, Torsten. "Tracing Ibn Ṭūlūn's Autograph Corpus, with Emphasis on the 19th–20th Centuries." *Journal of Islamic Manuscripts* 9, nos. 2–3 (2018): 308–40.
[Al-Yāzijī, Ibrāhīm.] "Basṭ wa-īḍāḥ." *Al-Ṭabīb* (Beirut), November 15, 1884, 328–37.
Al-Yousfi, Muhammad Lutfi. "Poetic Creativity in the Sixteenth to Eighteenth Centuries." In *Arabic Literature in the Post-Classical Period*, edited by Roger Allen and D. S. Richards, 60–73. Cambridge: Cambridge University Press, 2008.
Al-Zabīdī, Murtaḍā. *Itḥāf al-sāda al-muttaqīn.* 10 vols. Cairo: al-Maṭbaʿa al-Maymaniyya, 1311/[1893 or 1894]. Reprint, Beirut: Muʾassasat Tārīkh al-ʿArabī, 1994.
Al-Zabīdī, Murtaḍā. *Tāj al-ʿarūs.* Edited by ʿAbd al-Sattār Farrāj. 40 vols. Kuwait: Maṭbaʿat Ḥukūmat al-Kuwayt, 1965.
Zakī, Aḥmad. *Dictionnaire biographique des aveugles illustres de l'Orient [par] Safadi: Notice bibliographique et analytique par Ahmed Zéki Pacha.* Cairo: Les Pyramides, 1911.
Zakī, Aḥmad. "Istiftāḥ al-sana al-thāniya." *Al-Islām*, April 29, 1933, 28–30.
Zakī, Aḥmad. *Mashrūʿ ṭabʿ akbar mawsūʿāt ʿarabiyya miṣriyya, aw kitāb Nihāyat al-arab fī funūn al-adab fī 30 juzʾ li-l-Nuwayrī al-miṣrī al-mawlūd bi-l-Nuwayriyya min aʿmāl Banī Suwayf.* Cairo: n.p., 1905.
Zakī, Aḥmad. *Mawsūʿāt al-ʿulūm al-ʿarabiyya wa-baḥth ʿalā Rasāʾil Ikhwān al-Ṣafāʾ = Étude bibliographique sur les encyclopédies arabes.* Bulaq, 1308/[1891].
Zakī, Aḥmad. *Le passé et l'avenir de l'art musulman en Égypte: Mémoire sur la genèse et la floraison de l'art musulman et sur les moyens propres à le faire revivre en Égypte.* Cairo: Imprimerie de l'Institut français d'archéologie orientale, 1913.
Zakī, Aḥmad. *Qāmūs al-jughrāfiyya al-qadīma.* Bulaq, 1317/[1899].
Zakī, Aḥmad. *Al-Safar ilā al-muʾtamar.* Bulaq, 1311/[1894].
Zakī, Aḥmad. *Taqrīr muqaddam ilā maqām fakhāma al-ṣadr al-aʿẓam Ḥusayn Ḥilmī Pasha bi-shaʾn tanẓīm Dār al-Kutub al-ʿUthmāniyya bi-l-Qusṭanṭīniyya.* Istanbul: Maṭbaʿat Aḥmad Iḥsān, 1325/[1907].
Zakī, Aḥmad. *Al-Tarqīm fī al-lugha al-ʿarabiyya.* Bulaq, 1913.
Zaman, Muhammad Qasim. *Modern Islamic Thought in a Radical Age: Religious Authority and Internal Criticism.* New York: Cambridge University Press, 2012.
Al-Zarkashī, Badr al-Dīn. *Luqṭat al-ʿajlān.* Alexandria: Maṭbaʿat Wālidat ʿAbbās al-Awwal, 1908.
Zaydān, Jurjī. *Tārīkh adab al-lugha al-ʿarabiyya.* 4 vols. Cairo: Dār al-Hilāl, 1957.

Zaydān, Yūsuf. *Fihris makhṭūṭāt maktabat Rifāʿa Rāfiʿ al-Ṭahṭāwī.* 3 vols. Cairo: Maʿhad al-Makhṭūṭāt al-ʿArabiyya, 1996.

Al-Zayyāt, Aḥmad Ḥasan. "Awwalu mā ʿaraftu al-Shinqīṭī." *Majallat al-Azhar* 33, no. 4 (1961): 391–95. Reprinted in al-Zayyāt, *Fī ḍawʾ al-risāla*, 247–52. Cairo: Maktabat Nahḍat Miṣr, 1963.

Al-Zayyāt, Aḥmad Ḥasan. "Maḥmūd Ḥasan Zanātī." *Al-Risāla*, December 26, 1949, 1754.

Al-Zayyāt, Aḥmad Ḥasan. "Wafāt al-ustādh Maḥmūd Ḥasan Zanātī." *Al-Risāla*, December 19, 1949, 1749.

Ẓaẓā, Muḥammad Ḥasan. "Bāqa min al-falsafa al-islāmiyya: Al-faylasūf Ibn Miskawayh wa-kitābuhu *Tahdhīb al-akhlāq wa-taṭhīr al-aʿrāq*." *Al-Risāla*, May 9, 1938, 768–70.

Ziadeh, Farhat J. *Lawyers, the Rule of Law and Liberalism in Modern Egypt.* Stanford, CA: Stanford University, Hoover Institution on War, Revolution, and Peace, 1968.

Al-Ziriklī, Khayr al-Dīn. *Al-Aʿlām: Qāmūs tarājim li-ashhar al-rijāl wa-l-nisāʾ min al-ʿarab wa-l-mustaʿribīn wa-l-mustashriqīn.* 3 vols. Cairo: Maṭbaʿat al-ʿArabiyya, 1927–28. 15th ed. 8 vols. Cairo: Dār al-ʿIlm li-l-Malāyīn, 2002.

Zubir, Badri Najib. *Balāghah as an Instrument of Qurʾān Interpretation: The Case of al-Kashshāf.* Kuala Lumpur: IIUM Press, 2008.

Al-Zuḥaylī, Wahba. *Al-Fiqh al-islāmī wa-adillatuh.* 4th ed. 10 vols. Beirut: Dār al-Fikr, 1997.

Zwettler, Michael. *The Oral Tradition of Classical Arabic Poetry: Its Character and Implications.* Columbus: Ohio State University Press, 1978.

Index

Books are indexed under their authors. The Arabic article "al-" is ignored in alphabetization.